International communism and the Communist International

MANCHESTER
UNIVERSITY PRESS

International communism and the Communist International 1919–43

edited by

Tim Rees and Andrew Thorpe

Manchester University Press
Manchester and New York

distributed exclusively in the USA by St. Martin's Press

Published by Manchester University Press
Oxford Road, Manchester M13 9NR, UK
and Room 400, 175 Fifth Avenue, New York, NY 10010, USA

Distributed exclusively in the USA by
St. Martin's Press, Inc., 175 Fifth Avenue, New York,
NY 10010, USA

Distributed exclusively in Canada by
UBC Press, University of British Columbia, 6344 Memorial Road,
Vancouver, BC, Canada V6T 1Z2

British Library Cataloguing-in-Publication Data
A catalogue record for this book is available from the British Library

Library of Congress Cataloging-in-Publication Data

International communism and the Communist International, 1919–1943 /
edited by Tim Rees and Andrew Thorpe.
p. cm.
Includes bibliographical references and index.
ISBN 0-7190-5116-9 (cloth) 0-7190-5546-6 (paperback)
1. Communist International. 2. Communism – History – 20th century.
I. Rees, Tim, 1960– . II. Thorpe, Andew, 1962– .
HX11.I5I54 1999
324.1'75–dc21 98-28361

ISBN 0 7190 5116 9 *hardback*
ISBN 0 7190 5546 6 *paperback*

First published 1998

05 04 03 02 01 00 99 98 10 9 8 7 6 5 4 3 2 1

Typeset in Monotype Photina 10/12 pt
by Servis Filmsetting Ltd, Manchester

Printed in Great Britain by
Biddles Ltd, Guildford and King's Lynn

Contents

Acknowledgements

We have a number of acknowledgements to make. In particular, the British Academy, the Research Committee of the University of Exeter and the Research Fund of the Department of History and Archaeology at Exeter all made vital financial contributions. We are most grateful to Dr Kiril Anderson, Elena Shakhnazarova and the staff of the Russian Centre in Moscow for allowing us to use the archive and making working there so pleasant. Yevgeny Sergeev was a great help to us at the archive and as a research assistant; Andrew Thorpe would also like to thank Dr Peter Cherkassov for his assistance in accessing the archive, and especially Dr Svetlana Toropova for all that she did to help. In connection with the Medlicott Symposium, we would like to thank Dr Neil Riddell for his invaluable assistance throughout; Drs Moira Donald and Jürgen Rojahn, for presenting stimulating papers which unfortunately they were unable to write up for this volume; and all those other colleagues, from Exeter and elsewhere, who contributed so much to the event. We are also grateful to Cynthia Wise who aided us in an hour of technical need. The final thanks must go, however, to Dr Andrei Sokolov of Yaroslavl′ Pedagogical University. It was his trip to Exeter in 1989 which set the whole of our involvement with Russia in motion. Appropriately enough, he came from Moscow, not by air, but by train and boat – a route which had been taken by many British Communists and Comintern agents in the 1920s and 1930s.

List of contributors

Aldo Agosti is Professor of Contemporary History at the University of Turin, Italy. His publications include *La Terza Internazionale: storia documentaria* (3 vols, Rome, 1974–9), *La stagione dei fronti populari* (Bologna, 1989) and *Palmiro Togliatti* (Turin, 1995).

Guillaume Bourgeois is a Lecturer in History at the Centre for the Study of History and Sociology, University of Nanterre, France. He is a member of the editorial board of *Communisme* and his publications include *Les Communistes Français* (Senil, 1985) and *Le Parti Communiste Français dans les années sombres* (Senil, 1986).

Barry Carr is Reader in History at La Trobe University, Australia. His publications include *Marxism and Communism in Twentieth Century Mexico* (Lincoln, NB, 1992) and *The Latin American Left: From the Fall of Allende to Perestroika* (London, 1993).

Carlos Cunha is Assistant Professor of Political Science at Dowling College, Oakdale, New York, USA. His publications include *The Portuguese Communist Party's Strategy for Power, 1921–1986* (New York, 1992) and numerous articles on Portuguese and Bazilian history.

Peter Huber is a Lecturer at the University of Basel, Switzerland. He has published *Stalins Schatten in die Schweiz: Schweizer Kommunisten in Moskau* (Zurich, 1994) as well as a number of articles on the central apparatus of the Comintern.

David Kirby is Professor of Modern History at the School of Slavonic and East European Studies, University of London. Among his publications are *War, Peace and Revolution: International Socialism at the Crossroads* (Aldershot, 1988) and *The Baltic World, 1772–1992* (London, 1995).

Kevin McDermott is Lecturer in History at Sheffield Hallam University, UK. He has published *The Czech Red Unions, 1918–1929: A Study of their Relations with the Communist Party and the Moscow Internationals* (New York, 1988) and, with Jeremy Agnew, *The Comintern: A History of International Communism from Lenin to Stalin* (London, 1996).

Tim Rees is Lecturer in History at the University of Exeter, UK. He has published articles on the history of modern Spain, and has co-authored *Franco's Spain* (London, 1997) and co-edited *Reassessing Revolution in Twentieth Century Europe* (London, 1998).

Yevgeny Sergeev works at the Institute of World History, Moscow, Russian Federation. He researches on the history of the Comintern and on prisoners of war during the First World War.

Wendy Singer is Professor of History at Kenyon College, Ohio, USA. She is the author of *Creating History: Oral Narratives and Resistance in Post-Colonial India* (Oxford, 1997).

S. A. Smith is Professor of History at the University of Essex, UK. Among his publications are *Red Petrograd: Revolution in the Factories, 1917–1918* (Cambridge, 1983) and *Notes of a Red Guard* (Chicago, 1993).

Geoff Swain is Professor of History at the University of the West of England, UK. He has published numerous articles on Comintern and Yugoslav history, as well as *Eastern Europe Since 1945* (London, 1992) and the *Origins of the Russian Civil War* (London, 1995).

Andrew Thorpe is Senior Lecturer in History at the University of Exeter, UK. Among his publications are *The British General Election of 1931* (Oxford, 1991) and *A History of the British Labour Party* (London, 1997).

Artiem Ulunian works at the Institute of World History, Moscow, Russian Federation. He has written extensively on modern Greece and its Communist Party and his publications include *Natsional'no-Osvoboditel'nii Front Gretsii (EAM), 1941–1944* (Moscow, 1991) and *Kommunisticheskaya Partiya Gretsii, 1860–1941* (Moscow, 1992).

Aleksandr Vatlin works at the Institute for Human Rights and Democracy, Moscow, Russian Federation. He has published *Komintern: Pervii Dyesyat Lyet* (Moscow, 1991).

Gerrit Voerman is Director of the Documentation Centre on Dutch Political Parties, University of Groningen, The Netherlands. He has published many articles on the history of the Dutch Communist Party and the political left.

Hugh Wilford is a Lecturer in American Studies at the University of Middlesex, UK. His publications include *The New York Intellectuals: From Vanguard to Institution* (Manchester, 1995).

Sandra Wilson is Senior Lecturer in Asian Studies at Murdoch University, Australia. She has written many articles on modern Japanese history and is the author of a forthcoming book on Japan and the Manchurian Crisis.

List of abbreviations

CB	Caribbean Bureau
CC	Central Committee
CI	Communist International
CYI	Communist Youth International
ECCI	Executive Committee of the Communist International
FEB	Far Eastern Bureau
ICC	International Control Commission
ISB	International Socialist Bureau
ISC	International Socialist Commission
KUNMZ	Communist University of National Minorities of the West
KUTV	Communist University of the Workers of the East
NEP	New Economic Policy
NKVD	People's Commissariat of Internal Affairs
OGPU	Unified State Political Directorate
OMS	Department of International Communication
RC	Russian Centre for the Preservation and Study of Contemporary Historical Documents, Moscow
RILU	Red International of Labour Unions (Profintern)
SS	Linking Service
USSR	Union of Soviet Socialist Republics
WEB	Western European Bureau
WES	Western European Secretariat

Introduction

Tim Rees and Andrew Thorpe

The Communist International (Comintern: also known as the Third International) was founded in March 1919 by the Soviet government in the aftermath of the Russian October Revolution of 1917 and in the midst of a period of massive transformation and upheaval, not just in Russia, but throughout Europe. By the end of 1920, most countries in the world had a Communist party. Such parties were seen as national sections of a world party. As such, they were pledged to participate in and obey the decisions of the central 'party' apparatus. The Comintern remained in being throughout the 1920s and 1930s; despite Stalin's commitment to the principle of 'Socialism in One Country' and apparent abandonment of the idea of world revolution, it was only dissolved in 1943, an action usually interpreted as a sop to the USSR's British and American allies.

The Comintern's history is usually presented in terms of its failure to achieve the goal that was set for it when it was formed. It could be added, of course, that this goal was far from modest: no less, indeed, than world revolution. Even so, the failure to promote a single successful revolution outside Mongolia (itself a rather exceptional case) in the period of its existence must be considered an indication of its lack of effectiveness.

This was not, of course, for want of trying. The First World Congress of the Comintern, in March 1919, was somewhat shambolic, being called hastily and with few genuine delegates from outside Russia. However, Communist parties then began to be formed at a steady rate, so that the Second World Congress (July–August 1920) was much more genuinely representative, with 169 delegates drawn from 41 parties. It was this Congress which adopted the twenty-one conditions for entry to the Comintern, and the organisation's Statutes.

The Third World Congress was held in Moscow in June and July 1921. At the same time, a further international body was established to promote communism. This was the Red International of Labour Unions (RILU), or Profintern, which aimed to spread Communist influence among trade unions. It held five congresses between 1921 and 1930, but fell increasingly into decline in the 1930s before announcing its own demise in 1937. Other international bodies included the Communist Youth International (CYI), which was formed in 1919 and which was dissolved at the same time as the Comintern; the International Peasants' Council, or Krestintern, formed in 1923, but which, after a fairly unsuccessful life, was dissolved in 1933; and the Red Sport International, or Sportintern, which existed from 1921 to 1935, and about which relatively little is known.

By the end of 1921, there were Communist parties in all but four of the European states: Norway (where the party was eventually formed in 1923), Greece (1924), Ireland (1933) and Albania (1941). In Asia, there were by that time Communist parties in China, Korea, the Dutch East Indies, Iran and Turkey (Japan had to wait until 1922, and India until 1928); in North America, they existed in the USA and Canada; and they had also been formed in Australia and New Zealand. Most of Africa was under colonial rule, and so the main emphasis was on getting Communist parties in the metropolitan areas to pursue anti-colonial work: even so, they were formed in 1921 in Egypt and South Africa, while the Algerian Federation of the French Communist Party had been formed the previous year. The one area of the world where Communist parties were still relatively uncommon was Latin America and the Caribbean: by the end of 1921 they existed only in Argentina, Mexico and Uruguay. Although parties were formed in Brazil and Chile in 1922, Guatemala in 1924 and Cuba in 1925, other parts of Central and South America had to wait until after the Sixth World Congress (July–September 1928) showed some interest in the region before they were able to form Communist parties.

Many of these parties operated in difficult circumstances of periodic or, in some cases, permanent illegality. Many of them were small; some were exceptionally so. In 1927, the Comintern claimed a total membership of 1,684,212, but 1,210,954 of these were members of the Soviet party. Of the remaining forty-six parties, only two (Czechoslovakia and Germany) had a membership in excess of 100,000. The parties in France and China both had around 50,000 members. But after these, the next biggest party was the Swedish, with 15,000 members, and the only other party to exceed 10,000 was the American. Just under half the parties had fewer than 1,000 members: those in Palestine and Portugal were quoted as having only seventy each.[1] If anything, most parties suffered from falling memberships between then and the early 1930s (the German party, whose membership rose to around 300,000 in early 1933, being the most obvious exception).[2] By the time of the Seventh (and final) World Congress in July–August 1935, there were seventy-six parties with a total membership of 3,141,000. However, only 785,000 of these were members of parties other than the Soviet one. In addition, fifty of these parties were illegal in their own countries.[3] The leaders and numerous humbler members of many such parties found themselves holed up in Moscow, and many became the victims of the purges in the later 1930s. Stalin went so far as to disband the Polish party altogether in 1938: most of its leaders were executed or sent into forced labour. By that time the Comintern apparatus itself had been thoroughly purged, and former leading figures like Osip Piatnitsky, Bela Kun and Vilgelm Knorin had all been ousted and were later to be shot.

It was no coincidence, perhaps, that Piatnitsky, Kun and Knorin were all purged, for they had been the staunchest resisters, within the Comintern's hierarchy, to the change of 'line' which had taken place during 1934–35 and which had been formally blessed by the new Comintern General Secretary, the Bulgarian Georgi Dimitrov, at the Seventh World Congress. This question of the line is fundamental to an understanding of Communist politics in this period. Broadly speaking, it was determined by the perceived prospects for revolution, and prescribed the attitude which Communists took towards other political organisations, anti-colonial movements, and so forth. During its lifetime, the Comintern changed its line frequently.

At first, the Comintern's line was that of the revolutionary offensive. It was believed that revolution, having taken place in Russia, would soon be followed by Communist conquests of power in Western Europe. For Lenin and his followers, it was axiomatic that the revolution could not survive in 'backward' Russia alone: the Russian Soviet republic could only survive so long as it was buttressed by a Soviet regime in Germany, in particular. For a time it seemed that this might be a real possibility: a fortnight after the First World Congress a Soviet republic was proclaimed in Hungary, and shortly afterwards Bavaria followed. However, these were to prove isolated instances; and in any case the Bavarian republic soon collapsed, to be followed by its Hungarian counterpart in August 1919. Even so, with Russia still in the grips of civil war and hostile foreign intervention, the line remained the same, and was given a new lease of life when the Bolsheviks' victory in the Civil War was followed by the outbreak of war against newly independent Poland. One British Communist later remembered 'the excitement among the delegates' at the Second World Congress, as 'each day we gathered before a huge map of Russia and Poland and marked with red flags the new position of the Red Army as it marched toward Warsaw'.[4] But by the autumn of 1920 the Soviets had been routed, and the plan to spread revolution to the rest of Europe on the bayonets of the Red Army collapsed.

With the ending of immediate prospects of revolution, and the urgent need to rebuild Russia from the social and economic destruction of the Civil War, Lenin's government moved away from war communism and adopted the New Economic Policy (NEP). In the Comintern, similarly, the period of the revolutionary offensive was running out of steam. The failure of an attempted rising in Germany in March 1921 merely underlined the fact. At the Third World Congress in the summer of 1921 Lenin urged greater flexibility and a move towards co-operation with the members, though not the leaders, of 'reformist' working-class organisations like the established trade unions and Socialist parties. In December of the same year, a meeting of the Executive Committee of the Communist International (ECCI) drew up detailed guidelines for the pursuit of this tactic. The united front was predicated on the theory that capitalism had entered a stage of 'temporary stabilisation'. This would, it was assumed, come to an end, but it was, as yet, unclear when this would be. During the period between then and the mid-1920s, Communist parties, on the whole, were more willing than before to co-operate with other organisations, and some successes were achieved in this direction, most notably with the nationalist Guomindang (GMD) in China and the Trades Union Congress (TUC) in Britain. In these cases, the line went a long way to the right, since there was co-operation with the leaders, as well as the members, of these organisations (hence the 'united front from above'). The Comintern appears to have remained interested in the possibilities of revolutionary action, but the defeat of the Bulgarian rising in September 1923, the dismal failure of the 'German October' a month later, the suppression of the Communist rising in Estonia in December 1924, and the outlawing of the Bulgarian Communists following their bombing of Sofia Cathedral in April 1925 all served only to reinforce arguments for the united front.

By the later 1920s, though, the united front line was producing increasingly meagre results for the Comintern. It had always had its critics, not least within the German party, where antipathy towards the Social Democrats was especially strong, but also in many other countries. The collapse of the 1926 General Strike in Britain and the massacre of Shanghai Communists at the behest of the GMD the following year both appeared to show that united front 'allies' were in fact treacherous enemies. Around the same time, Comintern economic analysts began to perceive that the increased rationalisation of industry in the West, coupled with intensifying exploitation of colonies by the metropolitan areas, would lead to a new stage in the class struggle. Increasingly, it seemed, stabilisation was coming to an end. Stalin's role in the shift away from united front tactics remains controversial, but it would be difficult to argue that he alone was responsible for the change: indeed, the rival against whom he is often alleged to have been moving by shifting the line, Comintern chief Nikolai Bukharin, was at least as convinced as Stalin of the need for a change.[5]

The new line, 'class against class', was formally promulgated at the ninth ECCI Plenum in February 1928. It argued that 'temporary stabilisation' was coming to an end: capitalism was now moving back into crisis. In this situation, communism was the only way out of the crisis. Thus it followed that those who argued that there was a 'reformist' way out and that revolution was unnecessary – the Social Democrats – were no longer potential allies, but the key enemy. Worst of all were the 'Left Social Democrats' who used revolutionary phrases but who were really tricking the workers into supporting reformism. The result was as an often bitter struggle against such people. In Germany, the divisions went very deep, and meant a great deal; in some other countries, perhaps, the new tactic took longer for Communists to understand.

Class against class has usually been seen as a disaster. It is true that the membership of most Communist parties did fall at the start of the period, although how far that was due to the economic crisis which gripped the Western world in 1929 and led to a fall in the membership of most working-class organisations is difficult to gauge. It is also not remarked often enough that most parties' membership figures did begin to recover during the early 1930s, when class against class was still in force. The line has even been blamed for dividing a German working class which could otherwise have prevented the rise of Hitler and the Nazis,[6] although few serious historians of Nazism – as opposed to (mainly Trotskyite) observers of Comintern history – would subscribe to such a view today.

With the rise of Hitler, the Labour and Socialist International issued an appeal to the Comintern for unity, but this was met with little enthusiasm in Moscow. Despite the banning of the German Communist Party, Kommunistische Partei Deutschlands (KPD) and the imprisonment of its leader, Ernst Thälmann, there appear to have been hopes that Nazism would prove shortlived, not least because it was expected that the KPD would be well placed to operate underground. Nevertheless, many Communist parties took the chance at least to approach Social Democratic parties with co-operation in mind, although these approaches had few concrete results. By the spring of 1934, however, things were beginning to change. Class against class was still not bringing many results. In certain areas of some Communist parties' work, indeed, it was being effectively subverted, occasionally with the connivance of the Comintern. For example, from January 1932 the ECCI Presidium permitted the British to abandon the idea of separate 'red' unions and go back to working within the 'reformist' unions. In February 1934 French Socialists and Communists united in the streets of Paris against what was feared to be an attempted fascist coup. Then, later in the same month, Dimitrov arrived in Moscow. He had been the head of the Comintern's Western European Bureau (WEB) in Berlin, and had been imprisoned by the Nazis after the Reichstag fire. During his trial he had become a hero for anti-fascists. On arrival in the USSR he had talks with Stalin and various Comintern leaders, and argued for a revision of the line. As McDermott and Agnew put it, 'Stalin must have been impressed', because the Bulgarian was made the Comintern's General Secretary shortly afterwards.[7]

But the shift away from class against class was messy. Key figures in the Comintern hierarchy, as stated above, appear to have resisted moves towards a more conciliatory line. Continuing uncertainties in Soviet foreign policy, and Stalin's own 'wait-and-see' policy, meant that no very clear lead was given from the top. During the remainder of 1934 some individual parties shifted their line somewhat, although the Germans, now in exile, remained adamantly opposed to a change. However, Dimitrov had told the French leader, Maurice Thorez, in May 1934 that 'the walls between the communist and social democratic workers must be broken down', and the almost subterranean shift towards united front policies continued.[8] However, it appears that it was Thorez himself who took the boldest step. Against the advice of his Comintern 'minder' (although possibly with encouragement from higher up the hierarchy), he went to the Radical Party congress that autumn and called for a broad anti-fascist alliance. This was significant indeed, for the Radical Party was not even a party of the working class, but was largely supported by the lower-middle class.

During 1935 the line continued to shift in this direction, and at the Seventh World Congress that summer Dimitrov unveiled the popular front as the Comintern's new line. The idea was that all anti-fascists should unite against the main threat, fascism. The popular front was welcomed in many countries, as offering the Communists unprecedented potential for expansion and prestige. It made most sense in the liberal democracies, and was pursued ardently by the British, French and American parties in particular. In such countries, the popular front made the Communists look like the most sincere opponents of fascism, and membership increased, in some cases dramatically: the French party grew from 86,000 members in 1935 to 328,000 in September 1937. Popular front governments emerged in France, Spain, Chile and, later, Cuba. It can be assumed that even at this stage some resistance to popular frontism remained: for instance, the involvement of a Comintern agent in an attempted Communist coup in Brazil in November 1935 seems not to have been entirely the result of freelancing.[9] As with earlier abortive risings, however, its failure tended still more to emphasise the value of a less combative line.

The popular front has been seen by some as a Communist heyday, yet it was, ultimately, a policy with limited potential. The goal of revolution remained in theory, but had clearly been put onto the back burner for the foreseeable future. Nevertheless, the fact that it remained meant that Communists often refused to participate in popular front governments: they could not go the full way and become reformists. As the French popular front faltered and then in 1938 collapsed, the French Communists found themselves in something of a cul-de-sac. In Spain, the Civil War (1936–39) undoubtedly enhanced the prestige of the Spanish Communists, but the party's behaviour was, in general, anything but revolutionary; and, of course, the war was ultimately lost. By early 1939 the popular front had, to a large extent, gone as far as it could.

The outbreak of a European war in September 1939 led to a further change of line. This affected, particularly, the British and French parties. They had been arguing for a war of defence against fascism, but with the signing of the Nazi–Soviet Non-Aggression Pact that August, this began to look problematic. By October 1939 both parties had changed their line and were arguing that the war was simply an imperialist struggle rather than a crusade against fascism. Clearly, the changed Soviet stance was important here, although it is worth noting that many Communists had had reservations, to say the least, about supporting a war: after all, was this not what Lenin had condemned in 1914?

Although the line changed, however, little of substance came of it. The French party was banned and its leaders were arrested, and the party's conduct after the German invasion of spring 1940 left it in a retrospectively embarrassing position of collaborating, to some extent, with the occupying forces. The British tried to exploit working-class discontent with the war, but did not seriously try to undermine the British war effort, still less promote revolution. During this period the Comintern remained active, but its activity was increasingly focused on the Balkans.[10]

The Comintern's line shifted dramatically following the German invasion of the Soviet Union on 22 June 1941. Now, the defence of socialism as represented by the USSR was the key. This meant that all help had to be given to the USSR, and to its allies, like Britain. Accordingly, the Communist parties in friendly countries were urged to support their governments' war efforts: in Britain, and later the United States, the Communists were ardent advocates of increased war production, on the grounds that such production was helping the Soviet war effort.

The dissolution of the Comintern in May 1943 can be seen, in some ways, as a logical culmination of previous developments. As early as the Seventh World Congress, Dimitrov had told parties that they must stress their own national traditions much more, a policy which led to some curious departures, as with the Americans' slogan that communism was 'twentieth-century Americanism' or their formulation 'Washington–Jefferson–Lincoln–Earl Browder' (Browder was the leader of the Communist Party of the USA (CPUSA)); in France, Thorez had begun defending Catholic schools in the later 1930s, and 'liked to strike a note of patriotic fervour'.[11] Many of the erstwhile functions of the Comintern had, by the later 1930s, been handed over to other agencies of the Soviet state. And the disruption caused to Comintern operations by its enforced evacuation from Moscow to Ufa in late 1941 rendered the organisation still more remote from the people it was meant to be co-ordinating. There can be little doubt, however, that dissolution owed much to Stalin's desire to placate his Western allies, and perhaps in particular to the hope that they would soon open a second front against the Germans in the West.

It cannot be claimed that with the dissolution of the Comintern the Soviet Union's involvement with foreign Communist movements ended. Many earlier Comintern functions had already been absorbed by, for example, the Committee of State Security, Komitet Gosudarstvennoi Bezopasnosti (KGB). The leading figures in the Comintern apparatus, Dimitrov and Dmitri Manuilsky, were co-opted onto the Soviet party's Central Committee, and organisational links with foreign parties remained. Browder's action in 1944 of dissolving the CPUSA as the natural corollary (or so he thought) of the dissolution of the Comintern was soon frowned upon, Moscow using the French Communist Jacques Duclos to condemn 'Browderism' in 1945, after which the party was re-formed. The role of the USSR in co-ordinating the activities of Communist parties in the Eastern European territories that it had conquered by the end of the war is too well known to require elaboration here: so too is their further co-ordination in the Communist Information Bureau (Cominform), which also included the French and Italian parties, in 1947. And, as is now well established, Soviet funding of many Western parties, including the American and the British, resumed later.[12] Having said all that, however, the dissolution of the Comintern was important in that the 'world party' had now come to an end: the organisation set up with such high hopes in 1919 had run its course.

There has not exactly been a dearth of writing on the history of the Comintern over the years. However, until recently the inaccessibility of its central archives in Moscow has meant that much of such writing has lacked empirical credibility. However, the opening of the Moscow archives to Soviet scholars from the later 1980s onwards, and to Western scholars in 1991, as well as the greater freedom of access to the records of the various national Communist parties and their leaders, has led to an enormous growth of interest in this area.

A number of historians have already published work based on these recently opened archives. They include the work of F. I. Firsov, who has published a considerable number of articles in Russian journals and who recently collaborated with Harvey Klehr and John Earl Haynes on *The Secret World of American Communism* (New Haven, 1995), as well as the publications of other Russians, such as Aleksandr Vatlin's *Comintern: The First Ten Years* (Moscow, 1991) and Artiem Ulunian's *The Greek Communist Party* (Moscow, 1992), both published in Russian. Other important works include Aldo Agosti's *Palmiro Togliatti* (Turin, 1995), in Italian, and Peter Huber's *Stalins Schatten in die Schweiz: Schweizer Kommunisten in Moskau* (Zurich, 1994), in German. However, so far there has been little work done by British scholars, or even published in English. One of the few exceptions is the important book by Kevin McDermott and Jeremy Agnew, *The Comintern: A History of International Communism from Lenin to Stalin* (London, 1996). The appearance of a collection of essays edited by Mikhail Narinsky and Jürgen Rojahn, *Centre and Periphery: The History of the Comintern in the Light of New Documents* (Amsterdam, 1996), marked another important step forward in comparative studies of international communism during the Comintern period.

It was on a trip to the Russian city of Yaroslavl′ to investigate the state of history teaching in Russian secondary and higher education in early 1992 that we were first seriously alerted to the possibilities of working in the Comintern archive in Moscow. Following this, we were able to visit it and work there. Increasingly, we became aware that there was great potential for collaborative and comparative work on aspects of Comintern history. Coincidentally, the time was drawing near for the Third Medlicott Symposium in Exeter. This event, endowed by the late W. Norton Medlicott (Professor of History at the University College of the South West, Exeter, between 1946 and 1953), is dedicated to the field of international relations. We decided that the Third Medlicott Symposium, in July 1995, should be devoted to the history of the

Comintern and its relationships with its member parties, and asked a wide range of scholars from many parts of the world to present papers. This book has grown out of that conference.

The brief of each scholar has been to provide new insights into the history of the Comintern and its national sections. Each chapter stands alone, but in its entirety the book adds new and exciting evidence on, and interpretations of, the history of international communism between the wars. The book concentrates on three areas: the central development of the Comintern, the relationship between the Comintern and European parties, and the relationship between the Comintern and parties in Asia and the Americas.

Part I of the book is concerned with the development of the Comintern as an institution. The origins of the organisation are discussed by David Kirby. He provides a careful delineation of the main developments which led from the outbreak of war in 1914 through the Zimmerwald movement to the establishment of the Comintern. Then, in a paper which sets the scene for much of what is to follow in the book, Kevin McDermott demonstrates the value of the recently released Moscow documents to scholars. Finally in this section, attention turns to the organisational nature of the Comintern, with Peter Huber explaining the various changes in the nature and size of the central apparatus.

In Part II, the emphasis is on Europe (initially, at least, the Comintern was a very Eurocentric body). Andrew Thorpe discusses the Comintern and Britain, arguing that the influence of Moscow has been on the whole exaggerated. His analysis is supplemented by the paper of Yevgeny Sergeev, which focuses especially on the issue of 'Trotskyism' in Britain on the eve of the Second World War. Guillaume Bourgeois then analyses some aspects of the relationship between the Comintern and the French Communist Party, Parti Communiste Français (PCF), concentrating particularly on the shadier areas of Moscow's activity in France. Aldo Agosti discusses the vicissitudes of the relationship between the Italian Communist Party, Partito Comunista Italiano (PCI) and the Comintern, demonstrating in particular how the PCI shifted in the Comintern's estimation according to the Italian, Soviet and international situations. Aleksandr Vatlin then turns attention to Germany, showing how closely involved Moscow and its agents were in the various attempts to foment a German revolution, particularly in the early 1920s.

The Comintern was not just interested in the great powers of Europe, however, as a number of papers show. Gerrit Voerman demonstrates how the Communist Party of the Netherlands, Communistische Partij in Nederland (CPN) went from being a bright star in the Communist firmament to a very minor player. Tim Rees then discusses Spain, which had hardly featured in Comintern calculations in the 1920s, but which became the centre of its activity between 1936 and 1939 as the Civil War raged. The less frequently discussed Iberian party, the Communist Party of Portugal, Partido Communista Português (PCP) is analysed by Carlos Cunha. Next, Artiem Ulunian traces the story of relations between the Comintern and the Greek Communist Party,

Kommunistikon Komma Ellados (KKE) and, finally, Geoff Swain discusses Yugoslavia, and offers insights into the continuing activities of the Comintern down to and beyond its dissolution.

Part III of the book turns to the Americas and Asia. In his chapter, Hugh Wilford surveys the historiography of the CPUSA, and argues for a new synthesis which engages critically with the mass of new archival material now available. Barry Carr then looks at the problematic relationship between the Comintern and the Communist movement in Cuba. Next, Steve Smith analyses the relationship between Moscow and the Chinese Communist Party (CCP) in the 1920s, and shows that Moscow's responsibility for the disasters which befell Chinese Communists in the latter half of the 1920s was not as great as has often been alleged. Wendy Singer then takes a critical look at the Comintern's view of peasants through a case study of India. And Sandra Wilson analyses the problems which Communists faced in Japan, and their difficulties in trying to adapt a very alien doctrine to a society with traditions and attitudes which Moscow could scarcely begin to comprehend.

The diversity of arguments put forward in these chapters shows that the availability of new material does not necessarily lead to the closure of debate about the Comintern and its influence. We would continue to stress the need to build upon the work in the chapters in this collection in order to further debates and find new approaches to the study of international communism between the wars. This diversity can be seen by the different conclusions reached by the authors in this volume on key issues, such as the nature of decision-making within the Comintern, the Comintern's relationship to the Soviet leadership (in particular the role of Stalin), and the extent and nature of its control over Communist parties.

No definitive answers to these questions emerge from this book; instead, what the papers show is that we need to break from stereotypes and fixed models to broaden and deepen our understanding of the nature of the Comintern. It was not, despite its own claims, a perfectly operating machine, in which humans were merely cogs. But nor was it an irrelevance. There was, to a greater or lesser extent, and varying over time and circumstances, space for human agency at all levels; but the very existence of the Comintern meant that this agency could never amount to total freedom of action.

Another feature which emerges is the potential that now exists to move beyond what have, hitherto, been the broad central questions of Comintern history. Issues such as gender, anti-colonial struggles, language, ethos and cultural activities (for example, sport, literature and theatre) are of obvious importance. This is not to say that no work has been done in these areas; but there are new opportunities and, in particular, these are areas where the role and impact of the Comintern has not been fully studied. Moreover, it could be argued that these were areas were the Comintern was less of a failure than attention to the purely political would suggest. The Comintern, after all, was concerned to create not just a Communist world, but also a world of communism.

Notes

1 RC 495/3/72, 'Mitgliederzahlen der Sektionen der K.I.', December 1927. These figures differ slightly but not significantly from those announced publicly at the Sixth World Congress and reprinted in J. Braunthal, *History of the International, Volume II: 1914–1943* (London, 1967), pp. 318–19.

2 E. D. Weitz, *Creating German Communism, 1890–1990: From Popular Protests to Socialist State* (Princeton, 1997), p. 246.

3 W. S. Sworakowski, *World Communism: A Handbook, 1918–1965* (Stanford, 1973), p. 89.

4 J. T. Murphy, *New Horizons* (London, 1941), p. 113.

5 N. N. Kozlov and E. D. Weitz, 'Reflections on the origins of the "third period": Bukharin, the Comintern, and the political economy of Weimar Germany', *Journal of Contemporary History*, 24 (1989), 387–410.

6 See, e.g., F. Claudin, *The Communist Movement from Comintern to Cominform* (Harmondsworth, 1975), pp. 161–6.

7 K. McDermott and J. Agnew, *The Comintern: A History of International Communism from Lenin to Stalin* (London, 1996), p. 124.

8 *Ibid.*, p. 125.

9 M. Caballero, *Latin America and the Comintern, 1919–1943* (Cambridge, 1986), pp. 116–20.

10 This becomes clear from a reading of a recent collection of documents for the period before the USSR entered the war: see K. M. Anderson and A. O. Chubaryan (eds), *Komintern i Vtoraia Mirovaia Voina: Chast I, do 22 Iunia 1941* (Moscow, 1994).

11 I. Howe and L. Coser, *The American Communist Party: A Critical History* (Boston, Mass., 1957), p. 339; E. Mortimer, *The Rise of the French Communist Party, 1920–1947* (London, 1984), p. 259; E. H. Carr, *The Comintern and the Spanish Civil War* (London, 1984), p. 83.

12 J. E. Haynes and H. Klehr, '"Moscow gold": confirmed at last?', *Labor History*, 33 (1992), 279–93; F. Beckett, *Enemy Within: The Rise and Fall of the British Communist Party* (London, 1995), p. 147.

Part I

The view from the centre

1

Zimmerwald and the origins of the Third International

David Kirby

Is there anything useful to be said about Zimmerwald? The movement which derived its name from a small village in the Bernese Oberland existed in name for less than five years. On 5 September 1915, thirty-eight delegates left Bern in four charabancs for the hotel Beau Séjour, where they spent the next five days debating why the Second International had failed to act in August 1914, and arguing what should or could be done to resurrect the battered spirit of socialist internationalism and to renew the class struggle. The manifesto agreed to after much wrangling was strong on rhetoric, but offered no practical advice on how the struggle for peace might be pursued. The one positive step taken was the establishment of an International Socialist Commission (ISC) in Bern. It was announced that the Commission was in no way intended to replace the International Socialist Bureau (ISB), and would be dissolved as soon as the latter was in a position to make its voice heard once more. The final outcome of the conference had been a victory for the moderate majority over the revolutionary minority, and although the second conference of the movement, held at Kienthal in April 1916, marked a significant shift leftwards, this failed to satisfy those on the left grouped around Lenin. By the end of the year, Lenin was openly dismissive of Zimmerwald, and was urging the left to organise its own strategy, a position from which he did not deviate during the tumultuous months of 1917.[1]

The ISC was transferred in the summer of 1917 from Bern to Stockholm. After the resignation of Robert Grimm, who was in many ways the inspirer and guiding hand of the movement, control of the ISC passed into the hands of Swedish left-wingers sympathetic to the Bolsheviks. A third Zimmerwald conference was held in Stockholm in September 1917, and the ISC issed a series of information bulletins until the autumn of 1918. The formal demise of the movement took place in Moscow on the evening of 4 March 1919, at the founding congress of the Third (Communist) International (the Comintern). Speaking on behalf of the ISC, Angelica Balabanova warmly endorsed the founding of the

Third International, declaring that Zimmerwald had been established as a provisional organisation to wage a defensive struggle against the war and 'the disgraceful conduct of the social-patriotic majority'. After the decision to found the Third International had been taken and enthusiastically hailed by the assembled delegates, there remained just enough time for greetings to the Ukrainian comrades to be read out, and for the dissident German delegate, 'Comrade Albert', to assure the assembled delegates of his loyalty to the decision taken in spite of his reservations before the session was brought to a close with a perfunctory resolution, unanimously adopted, 'that the Zimmerwald movement be considered disbanded'. An accompanying declaration, signed by Christian Rakovsky, Lenin, Zinoviev, Trotsky and Fritz Platten, claimed that the movement had 'outlived its usefulness': everything that had been revolutionary in Zimmerwald was now passing over to the Communist International.[2]

Having liquidated the movement, the Russian leaders of the new Communist International lost no time in asserting their own credentials. Addressing the eighth congress of the newly-renamed Russian Communist Party (Bolshevik) on 20 March 1919, Grigory Zinoviev could confidently declare: 'You all know, comrades, that the slogan of the Third International . . . was launched five years ago by our party, we are proud to say, at a time when our party stood completely alone in the international arena.'[3]

In the subsequent history and much of the historiography of the Comintern, Zimmerwald was largely relegated to an introductory footnote, a passing phase in the process of transition from the discredited Second to the militant Third International – a transition for which Lenin invariably took the credit (or blame). The Zimmerwald movement is generally seen, and even judged, in the light of what was to follow. In the words of Merle Fainsod, one of the pioneers of scholarly study of the Third International, it drove a wedge into the Second International 'which eventually made a split inevitable', a view echoed by a more recent commentator, who claims that the Zimmerwald conference 'became the springboard for a challenge that would permanently divide the left'.[4] Historians of a Marxist-Leninist persuasion have had no difficulty in endorsing the verdict passed on Zimmerwald at the founding congress of the Communist International: that it had been useful only in so far as it had provided a focal point for truly revolutionary elements.[5]

In a sense, however, seeing Zimmerwald as an impetus towards schism is both to accord it greater importance than it merits, and also to ignore or overlook other significant changes of attitude and activity which were reflected, however imperfectly, in the debates and correspondence of the participants of the movement. In other words, the causes of the break-up of the Second International (though I would much prefer to speak of the explosion of dissent and division which made any return to the pre-war situation impossible) ought more properly to be sought elsewhere, and not in the activities of the Zimmerwald movement as such.

As a potential, if not actual, movement, Zimmerwald was plagued by a number of drawbacks from the start. In the first instance, it was and remained essentially a small, confined circle of dissidents and neutrals. Leading figures of the left, such as Friedrich Adler, Rosa Luxemburg and Karl Liebknecht, although important in the development of radical and revolutionary thinking during the war, played no active part in the movement. In spite of the efforts of Robert Grimm, the energetic secretary of the ISC between 1915 and 1917, and the undoubted spread of interest in and sympathy with the movement, there was never an opportunity for a full-scale debate in which positions could be clearly stated and views properly expressed. It is a moot point how effective such a full-blown conference might have been, but this was the accepted way in which socialists were accustomed to arrive at decisions – very different from the scrappy, often quarrelsome and sometimes bizarre contributions made by participants in the three conferences staged by the movement between 1915 and 1917, the endless wrangling over representation and the intrigues of the Russian and Polish exiles which drove Grimm to exasperation on numerous occasions.[6] Robert Grimm was the one person who might conceivably have provided a firmer sense of purpose and direction to the movement, but he was forced to relinquish the post of secretary after being accused of colluding with the German government in the summer of 1917.[7]

Robert Grimm's fall from grace, at a time when it appeared as if the Zimmerwaldist anti-war message was beginning to attract considerable support, was seized upon with alacrity by socialists in the Allied camp who still supported their governments' war effort, and by their friends elsewhere.[8] His sudden departure from the scene undoubtedly hastened the decline of Zimmerwald, though, in truth, it had begun to fall apart even before the outbreak of revolution in Russia. This has sometimes been attributed to the splitting tactics of the left; but it should also be noted that the growing mood of war-weariness, the public interventions of President Wilson in favour of a negotiated peace settlement, and the increasing activity of the ISB all conspired to provide an opening towards peace, the principal objective of the Zimmerwald majority, in the early months of 1917. As a movement, Zimmerwald was destroyed as much by the chimera of a general peace in 1917 as it was by the machinations of the Leninist left.

Zimmerwald had come into being as a response to the problem much debated by the Second International, but never satisfactorily resolved, i.e. that of war. That 'wars will cease once and for all only when the capitalist economic order is abolished' was regularly proclaimed in the resolutions of the Second International; but the main thrust of the debate was directed towards the prevention of such a frightful occurrence. The amendment added by the left to the 1907 Stuttgart resolution, that 'should war break out anyway', Socialists should strive to take advantage of the ensuing economic and political crisis to arouse the masses and hasten the overthrow of capitalism, was hypothecated upon an event which most Socialists preferred not to contemplate.[9] By the autumn of 1915, however, war had become a ghastly, murderous reality, unlikely to be terminated quickly. The exigencies of war had also dramatically altered the topography of organised labour activity. Thousands of party and trade-union activists were in uniform, working or occupying posts outside their pre-war region. Conditions of work and employment, and the very circumstances of everyday life, changed radically for thousands more. The increased coercive powers of the state, and the enormous structural changes in the economy, with its effects on living standards and conditions, delivered a powerful blow to many of the comfortable assumptions of peacetime social democracy. Writing in 1915, for example, the Austrian trade-union specialist Adolf Braun spoke of the 'quite new mass psychological effects' being caused by the harsh discipline, the burdens imposed and the sacrifices which were having to be made, and the suppression of criticism in wartime conditions. The war had also weakened working-class solidarity, by separating combatants and non-combatants, replacing hourly pay rates by piecework, and by the imposition of constraints on normal activities.[10] Conscription into the ranks and into the factories, the imposition of restrictive regulations and the employment of punitive sanctions against those deemed to be troublemakers, and, most importantly, the constantly changing composition of the labour force created problems for those seeking to defend workers' interests at the shop-floor level. On the other hand, the strains of war generated a huge groundswell of discontent which spilled over in the strikes and demonstrations of 1917–18. Furthermore, the war 'politicised' society in a way hitherto unknown. Even the mildest form of protest could be construed as opposition to the national war effort. As Robert Grimm remarked, even though such actions might be perfectly acceptable in normal times, in war, it was 'revolutionary' for a couple of women to demonstrate against high prices.[11] The strikes which erupted in all the major belligerent countries in 1917–18 grew out of dissatisfaction with working and living conditions, but they quickly acquired a political dimension, as strikers demanded an end to the war and, in the case of Germany and Austria, democratic reforms.

The circumstances of war compelled Socialists of all hues seriously to reconsider many of their previous assumptions and beliefs. Capitalism and imperialism were now seen to have had a far greater influence on working-class life and political attitudes than had hitherto been suspected. A sudden 'community of interest' between workers and capitalists had come into being, argued Max Adler, whilst, for Herman Gorter, the passive nationalism of a working class dependent on capitalism for its livelihood had been bolstered by a reformist leadership which had accepted colonial policies and acquiesced in imperialist designs. For many on the right, the interventionism of the state represented a major new development, offering new opportunities for the organised proletariat to control their conditions of work and life.[12] The severing of international links and the preoccupation of the reformist Socialists with national issues and interests may also have effected an important shift of emphasis, as John Horne has argued, with the reformist Socialists in Britain and France at least brought by the experience of war to embrace fully the liberal democratic preventive approach towards war as the prerequisite for proceeding towards social and socialist progress.[13] Internationalism in the broadest sense revived in 1917 because it seemed to offer the best hope of ending the war, and the programme of sanctions, arbitration and democratic control which had been adopted by the pre-1914 Second International to combat the threat of war became a cornerstone of the 'New Diplomacy'.[14] But socialist internationalism predicated on the primacy of the class struggle and uncompromising refusal to collaborate with bourgeois government was irrevocably split by the war. Intransigent supporters of the war effort and others, castigated by the left as 'social patriots', were unlikely to be easily forgiven by those who wished to rescue the honour of the International. Those of the anti-war centre, labelled by Lenin as 'social pacifists', in turn faced the problem of how to convert the growing war-weariness of the masses into positive political support, a task made that much harder by the emergence of a new alternative of workers' power through the soviets. Finally, the foundation of a Third International cut the ground from beneath the feet of those in the centre who were unwilling to return to the fold of an unreconstructed Second International, but who had no desire to cut themselves off entirely from the mainstream of the European labour movement.[15]

The rapidity with which the Third International was erected and the ignominious winding-up of the ISC has tended to obscure the significance of Zimmerwald as the first serious, critical look at the failings of the international socialist movement. Notwithstanding the confusion and lack of agreement over the way forward amongst the delegates assembled in the Swiss village in September 1915, their deliberations do set them apart from an even more confused ruck of socialists of the centre, who were still trying to come to terms with the war. Significantly, the meeting opened with the reading of a letter from the imprisoned Karl Liebknecht, which specified the two main tasks of the delegates: order in the ranks of those who were determined to remain faithful to the principles of international socialism, and a remorseless settling of accounts with the traitors of the Socialist parties of the belligerent countries who had betrayed these principles. The majority of the assembled delegates were probably more enthusiastic about the symbolism of Liebknecht's anti-war stance than about his message, it is true, and there was an obvious division between those who wished to maintain unity as long as possible, and who believed that the masses could be won over more effectively by remaining within the party, and those who placed clarity before unity.[16] But there were also very real differences between the general tone and tenor of the discussions at Zimmerwald and at other international socialist gatherings. The conferences of the so-called northern neutrals in Copenhagen (January 1915), of the socialists of the Allied countries in London (February 1915) and of the socialists of the Central Powers in Vienna (April 1915) were silent on the issue of the 'civil truce' concluded between organised labour and governments, had little to say about the class struggle, and would certainly not have been the recipients of

Karl Liebknecht's inflammatory appeal for civil war, not civil peace. There was also a perceptible difference in the positions and attitudes of leaders of moderate opposition 'minorities' such as Hugo Haase, Jean Longuet and Ramsay MacDonald and those endorsed by the Zimmerwaldists.[17]

As I have already suggested, there is an inherent problem in any attempt to assess the impact of Zimmerwald, in that those who were actively involved in the movement remained few in number, and were perhaps more noteworthy as individuals, rather than as representatives of a major party or tendency. Zimmerwald was to acquire a broader notoriety in 1917–18, in much the same way as did the Russian Revolution, as a symbol of the desire for peace. The 'pacifist' tendencies of the movement were seized upon from the beginning by Lenin, and there can be little doubt that the primary aim of the majority of those who rallied to the movement was the ending of the war. It would, however, be erroneous to assume that 'social pacificism' was merely the soft centre of a hardcore reformism, which had seemingly triumphed in most of the major socialist parties of Europe outside the Russian empire.[18] The experience of wartime conditions no longer permitted the diverse strands within the labour movement to agree to differ within the relatively harmless ambit of the conference hall or the party press. In common with other citizens, party activists had their lives radically altered by the conflict. Some were drafted on to government-sponsored committees and commissions, or even into ministerial office. Far more found themselves in the trenches, and those who remained behind in the mines and factories had to work and operate under quite different circumstances to those of peacetime. Those who claimed or endeavoured to speak on behalf of the working class constantly had to reconcile the irreconcilable and to contend with unpalatable truths. Friedrich Ebert confessed to the Reichstag in April 1916 that 'it has not been easy for us social democrats to defend the prevailing system as well as the defence of our country', a situation which became far worse as the hunger and misery mounted.[19] But at the other extreme of the political spectrum, militants who preached revolutionary action could also encounter indifference and even downright hostility from workers with families, or who were earning good wages. Beneath the mood of resentment and war-weariness, which could persuade large numbers to strike, demonstrate, even to make revolution, there was also a strong undercurrent of disillusionment with the organised labour movement. In the end, it might be argued, this was far more significant for the already divided labour movement than were the fears of being swept aside or swamped by the radicalised, untutored masses which so exercised moderates, or the spontaneity of the masses upon which the left pinned their hopes.[20]

The war greatly intensified the degree of conflict between the moderates and radicals (though we should note that a number of individuals passed from one camp to another as a result of the war). The splits within the labour movement cannot be blamed solely upon the activities of the revolutionary left, for the right was more than happy to take the opportunity either to marginalise or to exclude their opponents.[21] That there was often a deep unwillingness to break with the party by many on the left has less to do with a secret affinity with or attachment to reformism (as the minions of Comintern never ceased to proclaim) than with a desire to capture the party from the grasp of those who were widely regarded as compromised and beyond the pale. It may be that rather too much emphasis has been placed upon external developments, such as the founding of the Communist International and the activities of its agents, and not enough attention paid to what might be described as the battle for the working class. In focusing for so long on the activities of the left and the echoes of revolution, historians of the labour movement have tended to overlook the fact that the much-reviled reformists still retained the support of a substantial number of workers. For many 'majority' Socialists, the war did present new possibilities and opportunities; that these were not fully realised, or turned out to be illusory, should not be allowed to obscure the more purposeful, even dynamic aspects of majority reformism.[22]

The support that the 'majority' Socialists continued to enjoy after 1918 deserves closer scrutiny; but there was undeniably a significant shift leftwards, especially in the immediate post-war years, and it is this with which we are primarily concerned here. One of the more striking features about left-wing discourse before and during the war is the gradual shift away from notions of organised, purposeful class militancy towards greater faith in mass action. The prime exponent of the 'new tactic' of mass action was Anton Pannekoek, whose writings were probably more influential than is often realised. In 1912, he had clashed with Kautsky over revolutionary tactics and mass action. In his study of social democracy and the war, published in 1915, he attacked the reformism of the established parties, and predicted that revolutionary socialists would be obliged to operate as small groups, trying to win over the masses from the old parties. Socialism no longer rested in the hands of the parties with their talented speakers, cosy politicians, noble humanitarianism, well-paid, self-satisfied reformist party workers; it lay in the hands of the 'dark masses of the wretched and oppressed'.[23] The social and political convulsions of wartime and the weakening of established patterns of party organisation and procedure tended, if anything, to strengthen belief in the efficacy of mass action. For Karl Liebknecht, the capacity for action of a party was not measured by the number of its members, but by its relationship with the masses. It was not programmes and manifestos, or 'mechanical discipline and dead organisational forms, but the energy, will and decisive initiative of the masses themselves' which would make the party a truly revolutionary force.[24] Rejection of a reformist, bureaucratised party and trade-union leadership *and* of the 'revolutionary passivity' of orthodox Marxism, on the one hand, and enthusiasm for spontaneous mass action on the other were distinguishing characteristics of the revolutionary left in Europe in the second decade of the twentieth century. There were significant differences of emphasis, and areas of disagreement, especially over the importance of parliamentary activity, or the role of the party, and a distinction should also be made between the more obviously 'political' revolutionary strand, represented, for example, by the Spartakists and Internationalists in Germany and revolutionary syndicalism. But what is important is that the war experience seemed merely to many on the left to intensify the gulf between a sterile reformist leadership (and a self-satisfied labour aristocracy) and a radicalised proletariat, often outside the formal union organisation, working in large concentrations, probably semi- or unskilled, which by its actions seemed to reveal a truly revolutionary élan.

Having made these preliminary observations, I should now like to return to the question posed as the beginning of this chapter. Is there any purpose in rescuing the corpse of Zimmerwald from the grave to which it was consigned by the founders of the Communist International after they had neatly extracted the vital fluids of Leninism ? Was there, in fact, a Zimmerwaldist alternative to the eventual permanent outcome of attempts to reforge a more militant International ?

During the first eighteen months of its existence, the ISC, under Robert Grimm's leadership, had avoided being sucked into the turbulent waters of Russian revolutionary politics, and had sought to act as a central source of support and information for all strands of opposition to the civil truce, pro-war policies of the reformist Socialist parties. This changed dramatically in 1917. The February Revolution suddenly opened up a huge debate on the war. The appeal of the Petrograd soviet, addressed to the peoples of the entire world, to 'take into their own hands the decision of the question of war and peace' and the subsequent call for an international socialist conference, had an enormous impact, reinforced by a wave of strikes in all the major belligerent countries and mutinies in the French armed forces.[25] The soviet peace initiative launched in the spring of 1917 contained clear echoes of the Zimmerwaldist programme. According to Nikolai Sukhanov, one of the members of the commission established by the soviet to prepare the conference, the Menshevik internationalists managed to secure agreement that the conference should not be treated as a kind of talking-shop, incapable of militant and decisive action. Only those parties and groups which had broken with the policy of national unity and opposed their governments were to be invited.[26] The proposals of the commission, which were laid before the Executive Committee of the soviet on 31 May, made endorsement of the position enunciated in the soviet appeal of 27 March a condition for participation in the conference. This was, however, abandoned by the Executive Committee, much to the disgust of the internationalists. Instead of making the liquidation of the policy of national unity a *condition* for participation, the soviet invitation now made it the principal *task* of the conference. Even this proved too much for the Allied Socialist ministers still in Russia, for whom Stockholm was at best an opportunity to accuse the German majority socialists of complicity in their government's war effort.

It was, however, a blow, and perhaps a decisive one, to the efforts of the internationalists in Russia and elsewhere to establish unequivocally the principles of a popular peace movement. The soviet initiative had been widely hailed as Zimmerwaldist in spirit.[27] It even had support on the right wing of the Bolshevik party, where Lenin was alone in wishing to break entirely with the Zimmerwald movement.[28] But the public backtracking of the soviet executive in the face of protests by the Allied minister Socialists, and the commitment of the provisional government, in which representatives of the soviet now sat, to launching a summer offensive drastically lowered the stock of the Russians as argonauts of peace. The ISC distanced itself from the soviet initiative, claiming that it would simply open the door to the social patriots; there was a real danger of a shift away from revolutionary mass action to sanctioning minister socialism – something to which Grimm had also alluded in his speech at the Menshevik internationalist congress at the end of May.[29] The composition of the ISC changed with the resignation of Robert Grimm, and the three Swedes – Zeth Höglund, Ture Nerman and Carl Carleson – and Angelica Balabanova, the new secretary, were closely associated with the Zimmerwald left and openly sympathetic towards the Bolsheviks. They were, however, inclined to support Zinoviev's tactic of trying to capture the movement, rather than break with it entirely, as Lenin advocated, and they also objected to attempts by Aleksandra Kollontai and Karl Radek to proclaim a boycott of the soviet-sponsored conference, on the grounds that this could only be decided by the third Zimmerwald conference. The invitation to a third Zimmerwald conference, issued by the ISC on 18 July, provoked a counterblast two days later by the Bolsheviks and their allies in the Zimmerwald left. Their appeal urged revolutionary socialist organisations and workers to send delegates to Stockholm 'to confer with representatives of the committed internationalist organisations on the furtherance of the struggle for peace, and in view of the split in the Zimmerwald union brought about by the vacillating and hesitating elements, to confer on the coming together of the revolutionary social democratic elements'.[30]

This appeal, in all likelihood inspired by Lenin's exhortations, failed to attract support.[31] Lenin's own choice of suitable parties for such a meeting was virtually restricted to a few minor groups with which he had had dealings. The German Spartakists were, for example, missing from the draft list he drew up at the end of August. In Lenin's eyes, the initiative had clearly passed to the Bolsheviks, 'the only party of internationalists in the world having as many as seventeen newspapers, etc.'.[32] Unlike Zinoviev, who still believed that the left could capture the Zimmerwald movement, or Radek, who pinned his hopes on a resurgence of revolutionary proletarian internationalism from below, Lenin was now looking to his party to take the initiative.[33] 'Not until the proletarian revolution has triumphed in at least one country, or until the war has come to an end, may we hope for a speedy and successful movement towards the convoking of a *great* conference of revolutionary internationalist parties of various countries; nor for their consent to a formal adoption of a new programme.'[34] And although Lenin did not discount the potential capacity of the war-weary masses of Europe for making revolution, he did not discern any organised party comparable to the Bolsheviks with the will, energy and leadership necessary to provide the inspiration and guidance for such a revolution. Lenin's 'International of action' in the autumn of 1917 was located primarily in Russia itself, where the crisis was rapidly maturing.

Lenin's ideas on the seizure and exercise of power were often misunderstood, even by his allies. Support for the idea of a revolutionary democratic government in Russia, elaborated in early September by moderate Bolsheviks and Menshevik internationalists, was hailed in Stockholm as a triumph for Zimmerwald and Lenin, whose *On Compromises* was seen as laying the foundation for this unity.[35] However, Lenin quickly abandoned the idea of peaceful struggle between the parties in the soviets, and from his hiding-place in Finland urged the Bolshevik Central Committee to prepare for a seizure of power.[36] Persuading his colleagues on the Central Committee of the necessity of this action took up most of Lenin's time during October, and he had little to say on developments elsewhere in Europe. He was scornfully dismissive of the third Zimmerwald conference, describing it as a gathering of people not even in agreement on the main issues, and, as such, incapable of really acting together. In his frenetic one-man campaign to push his party into a seizure of power in Russia, he claimed confidently that the world was on the brink of revolution, but there is little or no mention in his writings of who was to provide the necessary leadership elsewhere in Europe that he insisted the Bolsheviks could and should provide in Russia.[37] The moral high ground in the international revolutionary workers' movement, in Lenin's eyes, had, by the autumn of 1917, been firmly occupied by his party.

In the event, the seizure of power for which Lenin fought so tenaciously, against the better judgement of many of his senior party colleagues, completely overshadowed the activities of the Zimmerwaldists in Stockholm and elsewhere. But although the Russian Revolution continued to act as a beacon of light for the left, it did not inspire immediate emulation. The struggle for peace remained the overriding priority. The appeal issued jointly by the ISC and the Bolshevik delegation in Stockholm on 8 November 1917 called on workers to support the Russian Revolution not by words, but by deeds. They were urged to demonstrate and strike, and to build workers' and soldiers' soviets; but the main purpose of this activity was to force governments to make peace. The manifesto agreed upon at the third Zimmerwald conference gave more concrete expression to this by calling for a united international mass strike for a socialist peace. There was no indication in the manifesto of how this was to be organised, however.[38]

According to the American historian Robert Wheeler, this call to action was taken up in Germany, where 'there is no question that the January [1918] strikes had an international dimension'.[39] The German Independant Social Democratic Party, Unabhängige Sozialdemokratische Partei Deutschlands (USPD) attempted to direct and co-ordinate the strike, but the aims were far from revolutionary. There is less evidence of a direct link between the

Zimmerwaldist call for a mass struggle for peace in the other instances of strike action in 1918, in France and Britain, for example. On the other hand, there is plenty to suggest that for those disenchanted with the failure of the Second International to present a forceful socialist case for peace in 1917–19, Zimmerwald acquired a significant symbolic value, even after the movement was officially declared buried in Moscow. As late as February 1921, the Swiss Socialist Party, in a circular addressed to all parties belonging to neither the Second nor the Third International, could declare that the conference about to be held in Vienna represented a logical step along the route laid down at Zimmerwald and Kienthal.[40] Wheeler makes the point that no one made any reference to the founding congress of the Communist International at the USPD party congress in Berlin on 2–6 March 1919. The congress was critical of the decision of the USDP leadership to be represented at the Bern conference, and the loudest applause was reserved for Klara Zetkin's call for the continuation of the work of Zimmerwald.[41] The two parties which had been founder members of the Zimmerwald movement, the Italian and the Swiss, voted in congress in 1919 to join the Third International. But a membership referendum overturned the decision of the Swiss Socialist Party conference, and a significant section of the Italian Socialist Party, Partito Socialista Italiano (PSI) actively backed subsequent Swiss and German efforts to convene a gathering of revolutionary internationalists to negotiate with the Communist International. In September 1919, the *Reichskonferenz* of the USPD reported that the party leadership had taken the initiative to establish contacts with other parties 'on the basis of Zimmerwald and Kienthal' to forge a new International that would be free of the taint of patriotic socialism and of the dogmas of Bolshevism, democratic yet *aktionsfähig* in the event of a crisis. The resolution ultimately reached at the party's Leipzig congress at the end of the year took this a stage further, though there was by now a much stronger sentiment in favour of joining Comintern if it proved impossible to construct a new, revolutionary International.[42]

The programme of action adopted by the USPD Leipzig congress, which spoke of the creation of a dictatorship of the proletariat and soviet democracy, offered some kind of basis upon which a new International could be forged, and during the early months of 1920 there was a flurry of discussions amongst themselves, and correspondence with the Executive Committee of the Communist International (ECCI) by the non-aligned European socialist parties. In these manoeuvrings, the ECCI made few concessions, and by the time the non-aligned parties finally formed themselves into a union at Vienna, the disintegration of the centre-left had already begun. To see the malevolent hand of Comintern and its agents as the instrument behind this process would be to ignore the many fissures and cracks which already existed in the labour movements of Europe. But by its very existence, Comintern posed a problem for those who had broken with the Second International camp, but had doubts about submitting unconditionally to Moscow's terms, for it was already an

International in being, and could claim as its basis, not simply a programme of action, but a successful socialist revolution. Against this, all appeals to the spirit of Zimmerwald and the necessity of creating a truly revolutionary International would inevitably sound rather feeble.

The fact that a significant proportion of the non-aligned parties of 1919 were drawn into the Communist International in 1920–21 does not, however, demonstrate any kind of organisational or ideological superiority of that body, for quite large numbers were also to depart over the next few years. Whilst it is difficult to agree with André Donneur's argument that, had the union of centrist parties been effected in the spring of 1920, 'the contours of the schisms which ravaged the parties during the autumn and winter of 1920 would have been very different', there is nevertheless some substance in his conclusion that the splits in the centrist parties were to some extent artificial, as is proved by the return to the ranks of the social democratic parties from 1921 onwards.[43] In a very real sense, what happened in 1919–21 was a collision of two very different radical traditions, one essentially conspiratorial and insurrectionist, the other with a deep belief in the revolutionary spontaneity of the masses – decentralist, distrustful of the leadership principle, strong on rhetoric, less so on planning and action. To attempt to trace the impact of that collision through party and union fractures is not always very helpful, not least because it puts a very 'institutional' structural gloss upon a rather different sort of conflict. Thus it is that I would argue for Zimmerwald to be considered less for what it achieved or did not achieve as an organised movement, but for what it epitomised. It was very much a wartime phenomenon, but the issue of peace had stood high on the agenda of the Second International before 1914, and was to remain a priority for the left in Europe long after the signing of the peace treaty. Zimmerwald was firmly set in the 'curative' tradition of the left, that 'capitalism means war, socialism peace'.[44] Its affiliated groups were diverse, often divided and frequently at odds with one another, much in the spirit of the old pre-war Second International; but many recognised the value of such diversity. Some of the most serious quarrels took place within the Zimmerwald left. Radek and Zinoviev, for example, two of the most prominent figures of the Communist International, found themselves at odds with Lenin in 1917.[45] The Scandinavians found themselves attacked by Lenin for their pacificism, the Poles for their stance on the national question. The Zimmerwald movement was important in that it provided a very handy platform for Lenin, though his role in it has in all probability been greatly exaggerated by subsequent events and the efforts of countless historians. Had Lenin fallen out of his sealed train, had the Bolsheviks *not* seized power in Russia, then, I would suggest, the moral militancy of the Zimmerwald movement would have provided powerful sustenance to those on the left in post-war Europe who sought to break with reformism, and to re-establish the principles of uncompromising class struggle. The movement as such foundered in 1917; but its legacy passed to those who remained outside the two main camps of communism and social democracy, the constant critics on the margins who came together in the 1930s as the International Bureau for Revolutionary Socialist Unity. The claims made at the Comintern founding congress in Moscow to inheritance of the mantle of Zimmerwald merely served the necessary purpose, of giving some European legitimacy to what was essentially a Russian affair – the seizure of power, and the hasty creation of a Third International to justify and defend that action. There is a world of difference between the adamant tones of the twenty-one conditions, with their insistence on agitation in the armed forces, and the Zimmerwaldian concepts of revolutionary internationalism in which the struggle for peace predominated, between the emphasis upon the directive role of the central committee and the stress upon mass action. Far from being the inheritors of the Zimmerwaldist tradition, the founders of the Communist International were its hijackers.

Notes

1 See Lenin to V. A. and S. N. Karpinsky, 8 January 1917, and his letter of 17 February 1917 to Aleksandra Kollontai, in E. Hill and D. Mudie (eds), *The Letters of Lenin* (London, 1937), p p. 405–7, 410–12. For evidence of conflict between the ISC and the left in the winter of 1916–17, see the documents in H. Lademacher (ed.), *Die Zimmerwalder Bewegung* (The Hague, 1967), I, pp. 649–62, 682–4. It should, however, be said that Lenin's dismissal of the Zimmerwald movement as a broken reed was not shared by many of his party colleagues, who wished to take over and steer the movement in a leftward direction. See D. Kirby, *War, Peace and Revolution: International Socialism at the Crossroads 1914–1918* (Aldershot, 1986), pp. 189–92.

2 J. Riddell (ed.), *Founding the Communist International: Proceedings and Documents of the First Congress, March 1919* (New York, 1987), pp. 171–3, 181–3. For a slightly different version of events, see A. Balabanoff, *My Life as a Rebel* (New York, 1938), pp. 215–16.

3 'Die kommunistische Internationale. Berichte des Gen. Sinowjew auf dem 8. Kongress der KPR, 20.3.1919', *Die Internationale*, 5/6 (1919), 26.

4 M. Fainsod, *International Socialism and the World War* (Cambridge, Mass., 1935, reprinted New York, 1966), p. 61. R. Craig Nation, *War on War: Lenin, the Zimmerwald Left, and the Origins of Communist Internationalism* (Durham and London, 1989). A similar conclusion was reached by Hildemarie Meynell in her unpublished Oxford B.Litt. thesis of 1956, although she dates the inevitability of the split in the Second International from the failure of the Zimmerwaldists and the Russo-Dutch-Scandinavian Committee to realise a socialist peace conference in Stockholm in 1917. H. Meynell, 'The Second International 1914–1923' (unpublished Oxford B.Litt. thesis, 1956), pp. 69, 137. See also J. Humbert-Droz, *L'Origine de l'Internationale communiste* (Neuchâtel, 1968), p. 246.

5 Examples of the Marxist-Leninist interpretation include: Ia. G. Temkin and B. M. Tupolev, *Ot vtorogo k tret'emu internatsionalu* (Moscow, 1978), and A. Reisberg, *Lenin und die Zimmerwalder Bewegung* (Berlin, 1966).

6 See, for instance, Pavel Akselrod's letter of 18 October 1915, complaining about an article published by Radek in *Berner Tagwacht*, and warning Grimm that Zimmerwald must either break its connections with Lenin and his collegues, or face

the consequences of compromising and ruining the whole enterprise. H. Lademacher (ed.), *Die Zimmerwalder Bewegung* (The Hague, 1967), II, pp. 174–6. For further correspondence, see *ibid.*, pp. 217–19, 236–7, 250–4.

7 On the so-called Hoffmann affair, see O. H. Gankin and H. H. Fisher, *The Bolsheviks and the World War* (Stanford, Calif., 1940, reprint, 1968), pp. 613–29.

8 On the activities of Albert Thomas, the French socialist minister who was in Petrograd when the Hoffmann-Grimm affair blew up, and of the pro-Allied Swedish socialist leader Hjalmar Branting, see Kirby, *International Socialism*, pp. 121–7.

9 For the Stuttgart and Copenhagen resolutions, see Riddell, *Proceedings*, pp. 33–5, 69–70. See also: G. Haupt, *Socialism and the Great War* (Oxford, 1972), pp. 20–9.

10 A. Braun, 'Kriegspsychologie und Gewerkschaften', *Der Kampf*, September 1915, 305–16. There is a perceptive study of the wartime experiences of the Viennese working class by Reinhard Sieder in R. Wall and J. Winter, *The Upheaval of War: Family, Work and Welfare in Europe, 1914–1918* (Cambridge, 1988), pp. 109–38.

11 *Protokoll über die Vorhandlungen des Parteitages des SP der Schweiz von 20 und 21 November 1915* (Lucerne, 1916), p. 104.

12 M. Adler, 'Zur Ideologie der Weltkrieg', *Der Kampf* (March 1915), pp. 115–29. H. Gorter, *Het imperialisme, de wereldoorlog en de sociaal-demokratie* (Amsterdam, 1915), pp. 52–65. On the relationship of socialism and the state, see the articles by K. Renner, 'Probleme des Marxismus', *Der Kampf*, April–October 1916.

13 J. Horne, *Labour at War: France and Britain 1914–1918* (Oxford, 1991), pp. 314–5.

14 On the evolution of the Second International's 'preventive' strategy on war, see M. Grass, *Friedensaktivität und Neutralität* (Bonn-Bad Godesberg, 1975), pp. 13–23. See also A. Mayer, *Political Origins of the New Diplomacy 1917–1918* (New Haven, 1959).

15 This tended to obscure the possible incompatibility between Communist internationalism as proclaimed by Moscow and international relationships entered into by Moscow, a question posed by the right-wing French socialist Solomon Grumbach, *17e congrès national tenu à Strasbourg les 25–29 février 1920* (Paris, 1920), pp. 387–90, and the basis of Pietro Melograni's book, *Lenin and the Myth of World Revolution* (Atlantic Highlands, NJ, 1989).

16 The position of the Zimmerwaldist majority was well expressed by Alphonse Merrheim at the Zimmerwald conference: 'A revolutionary movement can *only* arise out of the struggle for peace. You, comrade Lenin, are concerned with the desire to lay the foundation of a new International, not with the demand for peace. . . . We do not want to emphasize what divides us, but what unites us.' Cited in J. Riddell (ed.), *Lenin's Struggle for a Revolutionary International: Documents, 1907–1916* (New York, 1984), p. 312. On the Zimmerwald conference, see Nation, *War on War*, pp. 85–91; Kirby, *International Socialism*, pp. 78–81.

17 'Civil truce' is a translation of the German term *Burgfriede*, which the Social Democratic Party Reichstag group symbolically concluded in voting unanimously for war credits on 4 August 1914. The French used the term 'Union sacrée'. There are full details of the 1915 conferences in Humbert-Droz, *L'Origine* and Grass, *Friedensaktivität*, passim.

18 As Lenin, at least, seems to have believed; see his speeches to the Third All-Russian Congress of Soviets in January 1918: V. I. Lenin, *Collected Works* (Moscow, 1964), XXVI, pp. 471–2, 473–4, and his earlier comments on the Stockholm conference of the Zimmerwald movement, *ibid.*, pp. 220–2.

19 F. Ebert, *Schriften, Aufzeichnungen, Reden* (Dresden, 1926), I, p. 317. For evidence of pressure on party leaders from the grassroots, see, for example, the interventions of Hennig and Reusshaus at a Social Democratic Party of Germany, Sozialdemokratische Partei Deutschlands (SPD) leadership meeting in April 1917. *Protokoll der Sitzung des erweiterten Parteiausschusses der SPD, 18–19.4.1917* (Berlin, 1917), pp. 8–10.

20 On the fluctuating moods of workers, see, for example, the memoirs of a Spartacist militant, K. Retzlaw, *Spartakus: Aufstieg und Niedergang* (Frankfurt-am-Main, 1972). The mood of workers in France is considered in an article by M. Gallo, 'Quelques aspects de la mentalité et du comportement ouvriers dans les usines de guerre, 1914–1918', *Mouvement Social*, 56 (1966), 3–33. Horne, *Labour at War*, pp. 296–301, makes some perceptive points about the changed perspectives of the working class brought about by the war.

21 Thus, the official newspaper of the German trade unions stoutly defended the policy of the *Burgfriede*, and demanded that short shrift be given to *Spaltungspropagandisten* who threatened that policy. *Correspondenzblatt*, 3 (1916),19; 17 (1916), 177.

22 On labour reformism in France and Britain, see Horne, *Labour at War*, esp. pp. 261–301.

23 A. Pannekoek, 'De sociaaldemokratie en de oorlog', *De nieuwe tijd* (1915), 137–51. Pannekoek's 1912 article is reproduced in D. A. Smart (ed.), *Pannekoek and Gorter's Marxism* (London, 1978), pp. 50–73.

24 K. Liebknecht, *Gesammelte Reden und Schriften*, VIII (Berlin, 1966), pp. 546–53. Liebknecht was speaking at the second meeting of the Internationale group on 19 March 1916. In *Spartakusbriefe*, Liebknecht spoke of recapturing the party from below, by mass rebellion, rather than splitting it. *Spartakusbriefe* (Berlin, 1958), pp. 132–3.

25 The text of the appeal, made on 14/27 March 1917, is in R. Browder and A. F. Kerensky (eds), *The Russian Provisional Government 1917* (Stanford, 1961), II, pp. 1077–8. On subsequent events, see J. Stillig, *Die russische Februarrevolution 1917 und die sozialistische Friedenspolitik* (Cologne-Vienna, 1977). Kirby, *International Socialism*, pp. 95–187.

26 N. N. Sukhanov, *Zapiski o revoliutsii* (Berlin, 1922), IV, pp. 85–6. A. N. Shliapnikov (ed.), 'Fevral'skaia revoliutsiia i evropeiski sotsialisti' *Krasnyi Arkhiv*, 15 (1926), 79–80. Breaking the civil truce was one of the conditions endorsed by the second Zimmerwald conference in Kienthal, 1916.

27 See for example the comment of *Izvestiia* on the appeal, 18–31 March 1917, in Browder and Kerensky, *Provisional Government*, II, pp. 1079–81, and Ture Nerman's comments on the invitation drafted by the Soviet commission in the Swedish left-wing newspaper *Politiken*, 5 June 1917, under the heading 'Ryska arbetarrådet på Zimmerwalds linje'.

28 *Sed'maia (aprel'skaia) vserossiiskaia konferentsiia RSDRP(b): Protokoly* (Moscow, 1958), pp. 228–34, 253–5.

29 *Politiken*, 14 July 1917. Grimm's speech is reproduced in Gankin and Fisher, *The Bolsheviks*, pp. 609–13.

30 *Politiken*, 26 July 1917.

31 Lenin had written on 11 June to Karl Radek in Stockholm, urging him to go ahead and organise a conference of left-wing internationalists. Lenin, *Collected Works*, XLIII, p. 362. In August, Lev Kamenev tried unsuccessfully to persuade the

Bolshevik Central Committee that the left should attend the Soviet–Dutch–Scandinavian Stockholm conference to prevent it becoming an instrument of the imperialists. This earned him a fierce rebuke from Lenin.

32 'To the Bureau of the Central Committee (Abroad)', 30 August 1917: Lenin, *Collected Works*, XXXV, p. 321. 'On Zimmerwald', written in the first half of September 1917, *ibid.*, XXV, p. 303.

33 K.Radek, 'Zimmerwald auf dem Scheideweg',*Arbeiterpolitik*, 18 August 1917.

34 'Revision of the party programme', written in mid-October 1917, Lenin, *Collected Works*, XXVI, p. 174.

35 See, for example, the report of the decision of the Petrograd Soviet on 14 September to back Kamenev's resolution for the formation of a revolutionary democratic government in *Politiken*, 15 September 1917, and the report on the democratic conference in the *ISK Nachrichtendienst*, 26 (25 October 1917), which concluded that Lenin's article 'On Compromise', published in *Rabochii Put'* on 19 September was a clear indication that the threat of counter-revolution in Russia had brought all the parties of the left together. Lenin's final paragraph, which cast doubt on whether the path to peaceful development was still open, seems to have been overlooked.

36 For a discussion of Lenin's 'moderate' phase in September and his sudden switch, see A. Rabinowitch, *The Bolsheviks Come to Power* (New York, 1976), pp. 168–72, 178–82. There are some shrewd observations on Lenin and the international wartime situation in: R. Service, *Lenin: A Political Life* (London, 1991), II, pp. 239–47.

37 'The tasks of our party in the International', written in October 1917: Lenin, *Collected Works*, XXVI, pp. 220–2. 'The crisis has matured', *ibid.*, pp. 74–85.

38 The appeal and the manifesto are printed in A. Balabanoff, *Die Zimmerwalder Bewegung 1914–1919* (Leipzig, 1928), pp. 97–100, 111–12. See also Kirby, *International Socialism*, pp. 195–6 and Nation, *War on War*, pp. 199–203.

39 Quotation from Robert Wheeler's contribution to a symposium edited by C. Bertrand, *Revolutionary Situations in Europe, 1917–1922* (Toronto, 1977), p. 42. For fuller detail, see R. Wheeler, *USPD und Internationale* (Frankfurt-am-Main, 1975), pp. 36–8.

40 Cited in A. Donneur, *Histoire de l'union des partis socialistes pour l'action internationale (1920–1923)* (Geneva, 1967), p. 66. There may have been more than a trace of parochial pride in this declaration, however.

41 Wheeler, *USPD*, pp. 55–6, 61, 76.

42 *Ibid.*, p. 80ff. D. Morgan, *The Socialist Left and the German Revolution* (Cornell, 1975), p. 303, for the resolution. See also A. Lindeman, *The 'Red Years': European Socialism vs. Bolshevism, 1919–1921* (Berkeley, 1974).

43 Donneur, *Histoire*, p. 56.

44 This phrase was employed in the resolution on 'the war danger', drafted by the Socialist Workers' Party of Germany and approved at the conference of 'left-wing' parties and groups in Berlin, 5–6 May 1932. ILP Papers, item 68, British Library of Economic and Political Science.

45 See, for example, M. Hedlin, 'Zinoviev's revolutionary tactics in 1917', *Slavic Review*, 2 (1975), 19–43, and Ia. G. Temkin, *Lenin i mezhdunarodnaya sotsial-demokratiya* (Moscow, 1968), pp. 565–91.

2

The history of the Comintern in light of new documents

Kevin McDermott

In 1966 Milorad Drachkovitch and Branko Lazitch bemoaned the fact that the bulk of source material on the Communist International remained secret, submerged like 'an iceberg'.[1] With the advent of Gorbachev's *glasnost'* and particularly since the collapse of the Soviet Union in 1991, sizeable chunks of that iceberg have begun to melt. As a consequence, the historiographical and documentary base for the study of the Comintern has enlarged dramatically. Since the late 1980s Russian and Western analysts have produced a prodigious amount of new work on the Communist International and its member 'sections'. Much of this research draws on the vast holdings of the Comintern Archive in the Russian Centre for the Preservation and Study of Contemporary Historical Documents, *Rossiiskii tsentr khraneniia i izucheniia dokumentov noveishei istorii* (RC), formerly the Central Party Archive, in Moscow.[2] Two main questions are addressed in this chapter. First, how has this unprecedented access to hitherto confidential material enriched our understanding of the Comintern? Second, what are the dangers, if any, of relying on the Comintern Archive as the prime source for the history of the international Communist movement in the inter-war period?

Before tackling these issues, it may be useful to outline what I consider to be the major controversies in Comintern history. There is, of course, no overall consensus on this matter, but it is possible to isolate several themes that have attracted scholars for many decades. First, continuities and discontinuities between the Leninist and Stalinist regimes in the Comintern: was the latter the logical outcome of the former? Second, relations between the central Comintern authorities in Moscow and the national Communist parties: was the highly centralist Bolshevik model universalised or did parties retain a measure of autonomy? Third, the relationship between the Comintern and official Soviet foreign policy: was the Communist International merely an instrument of the Soviet state? And, finally, the crucial issue of the attitudes adopted by Communists towards the social democrats: how were they to win over a majority of the organised working class for revolutionary perspectives in an essentially non-revolutionary era?

Each of these broad themes conceals a multitude of more detailed and problematic questions, but the crucial one is the whole issue of power relations in the Comintern. It seems to me that there were at least three hierarchical layers of influence in the international Communist movement: the Soviet leadership's 'control' over the Executive Committee of the Communist International (ECCI) in Moscow; the ECCI's 'control' over the national party leaderships; and the latter's 'control' over the party rank and file. Was this a one-way relationship, with all the orders emanating from the central authorities, as most historians have assumed, or was there scope for interaction between the various proactive and reactive elements? Another moot point is whether Communist parties faithfully carried out the directives coming from Moscow. As Alexander Dallin noted more than twenty years ago in relation to Soviet domestic affairs: 'in general, the concern among Western scholars with decision-making may well have contributed to a neglect of the extent to which a policy can be subverted in the process of its implementation.'[3]

In this unresolved debate between history 'from above' and 'from below', it is very important not to underestimate Soviet dominance of the Comintern. Foreign Communists *did* succumb to the dictates of the Stalinists, and *did* loyally trumpet the glories of the USSR. However, it is equally important, in my opinion, to recognise that the inter-war Communist experience should not be reduced to the crude equation 'Communist Party = Comintern = agent of Moscow'. In this sense, recent research which places Communist activity firmly in its national, as well as international, context, and which analyses the interaction between centre and periphery is a vital corrective to earlier 'top-down' studies.

Many key issues in Comintern history are now subject to closer scrutiny and reinterpretation as a result of the 'grand opening' of primary sources. The first example is Comintern congresses and the meetings of the Executive Committee. Each of the seven world congresses and thirteen ECCI plena between 1919 and 1935 has its own separate inventory (*opis*) in the Archive, and these contain much fuller stenographic reports than the published versions.[4] Greater access to archival material has therefore allowed us to compare and contrast the two, and identify gaps, omissions and distortions, which one would assume were more prevalent in the Stalinist period. We are now able to probe the positions taken by Comintern and foreign Communist leaders behind closed doors on various tactical and strategic questions, to analyse their disagreements and arguments, some of which were vehement. To this extent, the façade of monolithic unity portrayed in public by the Bolshevik guardians of the Comintern can be challenged.

A fine example of dissent to be found in the Archive is William Gallacher's speech at a meeting of the ECCI Political Secretariat in Moscow in November 1927. He railed against the Comintern's demand that the Communist Party of

Great Britain (CPGB) should refuse to support Labour candidates in parliamentary elections (late 1927 marked the beginning of the 'class against class' tactics). Gallacher fulminated: 'The Party decided on their parliamentary policy . . . and then from the International comes a proposal for re-consideration. It is entirely out of the question . . . I tell you, the Politburo [of the CPGB] will not consider the matter as it is. It cannot.'[5] Initial doubts were also expressed by Harry Pollitt and John Campbell, but ultimately to no avail.[6] The Comintern leaders got their way and the British party, like all others, was compelled to pursue the ruinous policies of the 'Third Period'.

A second pivotal theme for re-examination is the means through which the Moscow centre was able to enforce its will on the national sections. On many occasions 'imposition' was unnecessary. Member parties willingly accepted the correctness of the 'Moscow line'. But when difficulties arose there were various control mechanisms, ranging from ECCI agents, who were despatched, either on a short- or long-term basis, to oversee the activities of specific parties, to the detention of recalcitrant foreign Communists in Moscow, to outright expulsion for 'deviationism'.[7] Stalin was especially adept at this last method. His tendency to favour *otsechenie*, the 'chopping-off' of troublesome comrades, is well documented.[8]

Another common means of influencing developments abroad was the funding of foreign parties – 'Moscow Gold', as it is known. I definitely do not wish to sensationalise this issue. Certain recent publications have, arguably, overstated the financial dependence of Communist parties on the Comintern and depicted foreign Communists as simply spies for the Soviet state.[9] However, it cannot be doubted that payments from Moscow were a lifeline for many impecunious national sections. A good example of the figures involved concerns the CPGB. On 3 January 1922, a meeting of the Comintern's Budget Commission noted that £24,000 had been allocated to the CPGB, presumably for the year 1921. Moreover, Francis Beckett in his book on the British party says that £55,000 (the equivalent of £1,000,000 today) was provided by the Bolsheviks to set up the organisation in 1920. Other parties subsidised by the Comintern in 1921 included the German, French, Czechoslovak, Italian, American and many others. The total amount of funds transferred to foreign Communists in that year represented 10 per cent of the entire Comintern annual budget.[10] It appears that Moscow continued to send financial inducements abroad on this scale until at least the early 1930s, when it is possible that a certain restraint was imposed.[11]

The structure of the Comintern's central administrative organs is another key area, which until now has remained relatively underexplored. Greater access to archival sources has allowed scholars to reassess the periodic reorganisations of the Comintern apparatus in the 1920s and 1930s and to reconstruct the composition and functions of the leading ECCI departments.[12] The latest research suggests that the organisational changes, even the major 'anti-bureaucratic' upheaval of autumn 1935, strengthened the centralisation of power and facilitated Stalin's direct control over the Communist International's governing institutions. Although it appears that Russian functionaries in the various ECCI departments may not have enjoyed numerical dominance, there can be no doubt that Bolsheviks increasingly held top positions in the key bodies. More controversially, recent studies demand a reconsideration of the impact of middle-ranking departmental cadres in the apparatus. Extrapolating from Peter Huber's painstaking research, it could be argued that the delegation of work by the Comintern leadership to departmental officials fostered a sort of power-shift in which effective decision-*implementation*, as opposed to decision-*making*, rested with behind-the-scenes bureaucrats. Does this mean that we should shift our focus away from the Dimitrovs and Manuilskys towards lower-level departmental heads? Were these people the real power-brokers in the Comintern?

A fourth theme of critical importance is that of Stalin's role in the Comintern. The standard interpretation is that he was consumed with the task of building 'socialism in one country' and regarded the Communist International with disdain – the 'corner shop' (*lavochka*) is how he reportedly referred to Lenin's 'world army of the revolution'. It is often argued that he cynically manipulated hundreds of thousands of loyal foreign Communists, treating the Comintern as a mere instrument of Soviet state interests. Indeed, there is much evidence from the 1930s and 1940s to support this view. But the Russian archives have yielded a valuable source even on this perennial conundrum. Stalin's private letters to Molotov had languished in the Central Party Archive since 1969. Their publication by Yale University Press in 1995 has permitted a more nuanced understanding of the 'boss's' complex relationship with the international Communist movement. Here we see a Stalin seriously engaging with the prospect of revolutionary transformations in both the East and West, particularly in the period 1926–29. The British General Strike and the turbulent developments in China seemed to offer distinct possibilities of revolutionary upheaval. In October 1929 Stalin threw his habitual caution to the winds. He impressed upon Molotov the need to organise a military uprising in Manchuria, which would 'establish a revolutionary government (massacre the landowners, bring in the peasants, create soviets in the cities and towns, and so on)'.[13] Nothing came of the 'plan', but the letters do suggest that we may need to reassess the rather one-sided image of Stalin as 'betrayer' of the world revolution.

Finally, a major theme open to re-evaluation is that of the Great Terror, about which the Stalin letters are silent. We now have a clearer, though far from full, picture of the process of the assault on the Comintern, about its victims, why certain foreign parties and individuals were targeted, how many were arrested and shot (though all figures remain highly tentative). But there are still major 'blank spots': we need to construct in much greater detail the nature of the links between Comintern functionaries and the People's Commissariat of Internal Affairs, Narodny Komissariat Vnutrennikh Del (NKVD). What role did

Comintern leaders play in the terror? Should the Great Purges continue to be viewed as essentially an expression of the 'mad Georgian's' power lust? Or should we cast our net further afield in looking for explanations?[14]

The most important source for getting to grips with these intriguing questions is probably the diary of the Bulgarian Georgi Dimitrov, General Secretary of the Comintern from 1934 to 1943. He kept this diary, religiously it seems, from 1934 to his death in 1949. The originals are in the possession of his adopted son in Sofia, but a copy also exists in the Moscow archives.[15] These diaries, the authenticity of which no one seems to doubt, really are a treasure-trove. We can tell this just from the few short extracts that appeared in Soviet journals during the *glasnost′* era. They provide a keen insight into Stalin's ambivalent attitude towards the 'turn' in Comintern policy in 1934 from 'social fascism' to the popular front, and they also give us a fascinating picture of his mental landscape at the time of the Great Terror. Hence, in February 1937 he told a doubtless terrified Dimitrov: 'All of you there in the Comintern are working in the hands of the enemy.' Nine months later, in November 1937, the 'boss' made his point crystal clear: 'We must chase out the Trotskyites, shoot them, destroy them. They are worldwide provocateurs, the most vile agents of fascism.'[16]

In the same month, Stalin delivers the following remarkable incitement to terror at a private reception in honour of the twentieth anniversary of the Revolution:

> anyone [he warned] who attempts to destroy the unity of the socialist state, who aspires to detach from it ind[ividual] parts and nationalities is an enemy, a sworn enemy of the state; of the peoples of the USSR. And we shall destroy any such enemy, even if he is an old Bolshevik, we shall destroy his whole kith and kin. Anyone who encroaches on the unity of the socialist state in action or in thought, yes, even in thought, will be mercilessly destroyed. To the final destruction of all enemies . . .! (Cries of approval: To the Great Stalin!)

Dimitrov promised to 'do everything in my power' to ensure the Comintern took the 'Great Leader's' thoughts into account.[17] He kept his word. It has been calculated by the Russian expert Fridrikh Firsov that more than two hundred Comintern functionaries were repressed in the years 1936–38, many of whom were shot.[18] As is well known, countless foreign Communist émigrés resident in the USSR, from the leaders right down to the rank and file, were also arrested, deported to the Gulag or shot. The entire Polish party was disbanded on Stalin's orders on suspicion of being infiltrated by fascist and Trotskyist agents. Dimitrov and other Comintern dignitaries did endeavour to save a number of colleagues and friends, but were generally unsuccessful. It is interesting, by the way, that Harry Pollitt, General Secretary of the CPGB, was also suspected of maintaining contacts with 'enemies of the people'. His defence in private of Rose Cohen and her Russian husband, Petrovsky, both of whom disappeared into the whirlwind, raised more than a few eyebrows in Moscow. Archival records show, apparently, that in 1937–38 the Russians considered removing Pollitt as General Secretary. Furthermore, it has been reported that the NKVD planned a trial at which Pollitt was to be the prime defendant, accused of recruiting Comintern militants to the British Intelligence Service. Fortunately for Pollitt, the trial for some reason never took place.[19]

The image of the Comintern during the Great Terror is thus contradictory. On the one hand, it suffered dreadfully – whole departments of the Executive Committee were decimated, leading activists were arrested, and hundreds of thousands of loyal foreign Communists were sucked into the maelstrom. On the other, there is evidence of gross complicity and duplicity, denunciations and informing, the slavish trumpeting of invective against the 'Trotskyite-Bukharinite scum'. The flames of repression were fanned from within. Documents exist which seem to confirm that Comintern leaders actually requested the purging of certain compromised organs in the Moscow apparatus. One such is the letter sent by Dimitrov and Manuilsky to the Central Committee of the Soviet party in October 1937, in which they called for the liquidation and urgent reorganisation of the Department of International Communication, Otdel Mezhdunarodnoi Sviazi (OMS), the mysterious body responsible for the Comintern's clandestine activity.[20] The job was indeed undertaken by Stalin's NKVD henchman in the ECCI, Mikhail Moskvin (Trilisser). The once proud 'world party of the revolution' was unable or unwilling to resist the gradual imposition of Stalin's personal dictatorship, and, more to the point, connived at its own destruction. It has been persuasively argued that by the mid-1930s the Comintern had become a mere adjunct of the Soviet state, used by Stalin as a prop for his domestic and foreign policy priorities.

Many historians have used the Moscow archives to corroborate this 'orthodox' reading of the Comintern as an instrument of the Stalinist state. This is unquestionably a powerful argument. But in my opinion exclusive reliance on material from the Comintern Archive raises several problems. For a start, since 1992 there has been a worrying retrenchment in terms of access to archival holdings. Some vital *opisy*, such as Dimitrov's, Manuilsky's and Piatnitsky's secretariats (nos 73–7, 10 and 19), have been reclassified and no one knows when they will be reopened. In addition, one suspects that masses of documents relating to the Communist International are kept in other top secret Russian archives. Collections such as Stalin's personal archive and the protocols of the Russian Politburo are still kept firmly under Yeltsin's lock and key in the Kremlin, in the so-called Presidential Archive. The Committee of State Security, Komitet Gosudarstvennoi Bezopasnosti (KGB) Archive, as far as I know, is only just beginning to be made available. The one relevant institution where real progress seems to have been made is the Foreign Ministry Archive. A wealth of information must exist there about the links between the People's Commissariat of Foreign Affairs (Narkomindel) and the Comintern, which should go some way to answering the pivotal question of the Communist International's subservience to the diplomatic requirements of the Soviet state.

Regardless of the problems of accessibility, there are also important methodological pitfalls which have to be borne in mind. Firstly, there is the suspicion that the former Soviet archives may not contain the really juicy information that historians are looking for. As Chris Ward has noted in his text *Stalin's Russia*, in a world where table-talk, the telephone and unminuted conversations dominated politics we can assume that many, perhaps most, key directives were never written down in the first place and never found their way into any archive.[21] There are, then, inherent limitations.

Next is the perennial problem of authenticity and accuracy of archival documents. Can we be sure, for instance, that the speeches of delegates at Comintern congresses and ECCI plena were rendered accurately in the records? It is quite possible that the stenographic reports of certain speeches were later altered to delete compromising passages or phrases.[22] But overt censorship (and self-censorship) is just one hazard. These reports were delivered in many languages and were presumably transcribed by translators/interpreters, whose skills must have been sorely put to the test. Speeches and memoranda were routinely translated into several languages, which, admittedly, can make the job of the researcher somewhat easier. But in the process of translation nuances and subtleties of expression could be missed. Even Russian documents occasionally exist in different versions in different *fondy*, allowing scope for misrepresentation and confusion. It may be objected that all historians have to exercise caution regardless of the origins and nature of their sources. This is true, but extra diligence is required, I think, in the archives of the former Soviet Union.

Just as significant is the old temptation of looking for archival material that backs up preconceived assumptions about Stalin's and the Comintern's dominance over the national Communist parties. Historians, dare I say it, tend to find what they want to find. But the crucial point is that the very nature of the Comintern Archive may distort our understanding of the international Communist movement. What I mean is, the bulk of the archival deposits in Moscow reflects the central workings of the Comintern and its various departments. There are countless files on the Executive Committee, its Presidium, its Secretariat, the numerous commissions that were set up, and so on. By concentrating on the central organisational and control mechanisms of the Comintern, there may be a danger of losing sight of a fundamental issue, namely, how exactly were Comintern directives carried out by the national sections, often thousands of miles from Moscow? Being immersed in the wonders of the central archives does not mean that we should forget the wider world of Communist activity in national and local communities. Stalinist discipline, conformity and ideological dogmatism should not, of course, be underestimated. Far from it. But it is essential in my opinion to strike a reasonable balance between Muscovite control from above and scope for adaptation from below, severely limited though this was for most of the 1930s.

The Comintern Archive is thus an indispensable source, but in the final analysis it is one among many. It must be supplemented by other sources, including the voluminous secondary literature, much of which does not rely on Russian archival material.[23] It could even be suggested that our overall conception of Comintern history has *not* been radically altered by freer access to the archives. In most cases, I would say, archival discoveries have tended to confirm existing interpretations, rather than cut startling fresh ground. Undoubtedly, though, whole new vistas are opening up for future researchers. The Archive has large holdings on diverse themes which have until now been underexplored in both Western and Russian historiography. These include the cultural policies of the Communist movement, the role of women in the Comintern, the activities of the so-called 'front organisations', such as the Red International of Labour Unions (Profintern), the Communist Youth International, the Peasant International (Krestintern), the Red Sports International (Sportintern) and a host of associations and bureaux sponsored by the Comintern for specific purposes. But as far as I can judge no new general theories or models of the international Communist movement have emerged. Recently, a certain convergence of view between Russian and Western scholars can be detected, which posits an essentially negative evaluation of the Comintern, seeing the roots of its Stalinist degeneration in its undemocratic Leninist origins. With Marxism-Leninism now totally discredited, I suspect this view will continue to be the orthodoxy for the foreseeable future.

Notes

1 M. Drachkovitch and B. Lazitch, 'The Communist International', in M. M. Drachkovitch (ed.), *The Revolutionary Internationals, 1864–1943* (Stanford, 1966), pp. 196–7.

2 For a discussion of Soviet literature from the *glasnost'* era, see K. McDermott, 'Rethinking the Comintern: Soviet historiography, 1987–1991', *Labour History Review*, 52:3 (1992), 37–58. The most recent general survey of the Comintern is K. McDermott and J. Agnew, *The Comintern: A History of International Communism from Lenin to Stalin* (London, 1996).

3 A. Dallin, 'Domestic factors influencing Soviet foreign policy', in M. Confino and S. Shamir (eds), *The U.S.S.R and the Middle East* (Jerusalem, 1973), p. 38.

4 See the very useful guide to the Russian Centre for the Preservation and Study of Contemporary Historical Documents, *Kratkii putevoditel': Fondy i kollektsii, sobrannye Tsentral'nym partiinym arkhivom* (Moscow, 1993).

5 Russian Centre for the Preservation and Study of Contemporary Historical Documents (RC) 495/3/43, 173–4.

6 See the National Museum of Labour History, Manchester, Archive of the Communist Party of Great Britain (NMLH-CPGB), Klugmann Papers, CP/IND/KLUG/04/01.

7 The activities of one well-travelled ECCI emissary are graphically described in the memoirs of J. Humbert-Droz, *De Lénine à Staline: dix ans au service de l'Internationale communiste, 1921–1931* (Neuchâtel, 1971). For a detailed discussion of Moscow's relations with the Swiss party, based on archival material, see B. Studer, *Un Parti*

sous influence: le parti communiste suisse, une section du Komintern 1931 à 1939 (Lausanne, 1994).

8 See F. I. Firsov, 'Stalin i Komintern', *Voprosy istorii*, 8 (1989), 10. On Stalin's direct intervention in the affairs of the German party and in the crucial ECCI Presidium session of December 1928, see A. Iu. Vatlin and Iu. T. Tutochkin (eds), *'Pravyi uklon' v KPG i stalinizatsiia Kominterna: Stenogramma zasedaniia Presidiuma IKKI po germanskomu voprosu 19 dekabria 1928 g.* (Moscow, 1996).

9 See H. Klehr, J. E. Haynes and F. I. Firsov (eds), *The Secret World of American Communism* (New Haven and London, 1995).

10 On the funding issue, see RC 495/18/136; F. Beckett, *Enemy Within: The Rise and Fall of the British Communist Party* (London, 1995), p. 12; F. Firsov, 'Lenin's concept of a world Communist party and the development of the Comintern', (unpublished manuscript), 8–12. [Published in German under the title, 'Lenins Konzeption einer kommunistischen Weltpartei und die Entwicklung der Komintern', in Th. Bergmann, W. Hedeler, M. Kessler and G. Schäfer (eds), *Theorie und Praxis in historischer Perspektive* (Mainz, 1994), pp. 245–57]; D. Volkogonov, *Lenin: Life and Legacy* (London, 1995), pp. 50, 391–403.

11 Harry Pollitt's speech to the CPGB Politbureau on 14 January 1932 suggests that the coffers in Moscow were beginning to dry up. See NMLH-CPGB, microfilm, original reel 4.

12 See, for instance, F. I. Firsov, 'Komintern: mekhanizm funktsionirovaniia', *Novaia i noveishaia istoriia*, 2 (1991), 32–47; B. Studer, 'La réorganisation du Comité exécutif de l'IC en octobre 1935', *International Newsletter of Historical Studies on Comintern, Communism and Stalinism*, 1:3/4 (1993/94), 25–30; P. Huber, 'L'appareil du Komintern 1926–1935: premier aperçu', *Communisme*, 40–1 (1995), 9–35; P. Huber, 'The central apparatus of the Comintern: new statistical evidence', in K. McDermott and J. Morison (eds), *Politics and Society Under the Bolsheviks: Selected Papers from the Fifth World Congress for Central and East European Studies* (forthcoming, 1998); G. Adibekov and E. Shakhnazarova, 'Reconstructions of the Comintern organisational structure', in M. Narinsky and J. Rojahn (eds), *Centre and Periphery: The History of the Comintern in the Light of New Documents* (Amsterdam, 1996), pp. 65–73; G. M. Adibekov, E. I. Shakhazarova and K. K. Shirinia, *Organizatsionnaia struktura Kominterna, 1919–1943* (Moscow, 1997).

13 L. T. Lih, O. V. Naumov and O. V. Khlevniuk (eds), *Stalin's Letters to Molotov, 1925–1936* (New Haven and London, 1995), p. 182.

14 A recent detailed work on the terror in the Comintern is P. Huber, 'The Cadre Department, the OMS and the "Dimitrov" and "Manuilsky" secretariats during the phase of the *Terror*', in Narinsky and Rojahn (eds), *Centre and Periphery*, pp. 122–52. See also F. I. Firsov, 'Stalin i Komintern', *Voprosy istorii*, 9 (1989), 14–16; F. I. Firsov, 'Chistka apparata Kominterna', (unpublished manuscript), 1–38; P. Huber and B. H. Bayerlein, 'Première esquisse des structures répressives du Komintern. Le cas des communistes suisses à Moscou', *Communisme*, 32–4 (1993), 147–76; B. A. Starkov, 'The trial that was not held', *Europe-Asia Studies*, 46:8 (1994), 1297–315; M. Pantéleiev, 'Les "purges" staliniennes au sein du Komintern en 1937–1938: quelques repères sociologiques', *Matériaux pour l'histoire de notre temps*, 34 (1994), 24–5; M. Panteleiev, 'La terreur stalinienne au Komintern en 1937–1938: les chiffres et les causes', *Communisme*, 40–1 (1995), 37–52. The original Russian version of this article was later published as M. Panteleev, 'Repressii v Kominterne

(1937–1938 gg.), *Otechestvennaia istoriya*, 6 (1996), 161–8; K. McDermott, 'Stalinist terror in the Comintern: new perspectives', *Journal of Contemporary History*, 30:1 (1995), 111–30.

15 Dimitrov's diaries are due to be published in English in three volumes by Yale University Press.

16 Cited in Firsov, 'Chistka apparata Kominterna', 30, 36.

17 Cited in A. G. Latyshev, 'Riadom so Stalinym', *Sovershenno sekretno*, 12 (1990), 19.

18 Firsov, 'Chistka apparata Kominterna', 36. Another Russian scholar maintains that 113 ECCI operatives were arrested, although this figure does not include all categories of Comintern functionaries. See Panteleiev, 'La terreur stalinienne au Komintern', 38.

19 A. Vaksberg, *Hôtel Lux: Les Partis frères au service de l'Internationale communiste* (Paris, 1993), pp. 228–32; see also the biographical sketches drawn up on Pollitt and other British party leaders by the ECCI Cadres Department in RC 495/74/41.

20 'Riad sektsii Kominterna. . . .okazalis' tselikom v rukakh vraga', *Istoricheskii arkhiv*, 1 (1993), 220–1.

21 C. Ward, *Stalin's Russia* (London, 1993), p. 143.

22 Such practices were undoubtedly rife during the Cominform era. See G. Procacci (ed.), *The Cominform: Minutes of the Three Conferences 1947/1948/1949* (Milan, 1994), pp. xi–xii.

23 There is a fine corpus of work on the American, German and, to a lesser extent, British parties, spanning both political and social historical perspectives.

3

Structure of the Moscow apparatus of the Comintern and decision-making

Peter Huber

The Executive Committee of the Communist International (ECCI) was the highest organ of the Comintern between congresses. In this role it chose leading organs. The Comintern made no secret of who staffed them. For their part, the Presidium, the Organisation-Bureau (Orgbureau, 1924–26) and the Secretariat or the Political Secretariat delegated certain powers concerning the employing of staff to commissions, whose area of responsibility is only now coming to light.[1]

Personnel decisions

During the phase in which the apparatus was being built up (1924–26) the Orgbureau determined how many people the departments could employ. It was left to the departmental heads to apply for competent staff from the member parties. The frequent appeals from Moscow to help strengthen the apparatus show that the parties were not very keen to relinquish cadre to the centre.[2] The Orgbureau had to keep on telling heads of department to fill the gaps in the apparatus and to submit the names to prove that they had done so.[3] Even in the early stages, the Orgbureau and the ECCI Secretariat fell back on the rather well-known method of setting up commissions to deal with problems, which, however, instead of lightening the top functionaries' agenda, merely made it fuller. Traces of a Commission to Improve the Communist International Apparatus in autumn 1925 and an Apparatus Commission in spring 1926 are an indication of reduced bodies – consisting of members of the Orgbureau and the Secretariat – to dismiss, confirm or refuse to employ new staff. Under the point 'Publishing Department (French Section)' the Apparatus Commission, consisting of O. A. Piatnitsky, O. Geschke and M. Heimo stated: 'Comrades Kaminski, Levinson, Revo, Rusakova to be dismissed and (female) Comrade Drogotshiner to be put at the disposal of the PCF [French Communist Party, Parti Communiste Français]. Comrade Weiner to be made Secretary of the French Section. (Female) Comrade Gaillard to be made French shorthand-writer and technical secretary of the French-speaking Regional Secretariat.'[4] In its next session the high-ranking commission, without giving any reason, refused the application of ECCI Secretary and Orgbureau member, Jules Humbert-Droz, to employ his wife in the Regional Secretariat that he headed.[5]

Between 1926 and 1933 the Secretariat (known after 1927 as the Politsecretariat) was assisted by two commissions for dealing with staffing questions. As of March 1926 the Little Commission (also known as the Select Commission) devoted itself to 'questions of a strictly confidential nature'. Its work included: 'Confirming the employment and dismissal of responsible political staff in the ECCI apparatus; resolutions concerning any expenditure by the apparatus and the publishing office exceeding 5,000 roubles.'[6]

The Standing Commission also decided staffing questions and consisted partly of the same people as the Little Commssion. The duties of the two commissions were so similar that in the archives the classification of their minutes is confused. As part of the political 'purging' of the ECCI apparatus in autumn 1929, the Standing Commission set up a commission consisting of Comrades W. Ulbricht, Piatnitsky, B. A. Vassiliev, Mirov (Cells Bureau), Heimo and Abramov, of the Comintern's secretive Department of International Communication, Otdel Mezhdunarodnoi Sviazi (OMS).[7] At the beginning of the 1930s, at the latest, worries about the political reliability of the ECCI staff became a central issue. Comrade Zirotinsky, deputy head of the OMS and head of the 'Confidential Instructors Sub-Department', told the Little Commission to be on the watch for 'penetration of the ECCI apparatus by foreign and even hostile elements'. Until 1931 the Little Commission (or the Standing Commission) and the Politcommission, which had been dealing with administrative matters on behalf of the Politsecretariat since autumn 1929, had the exclusive authority to employ new staff. In 1931 these bodies were still dividing up the responsibilities amongst themselves as follows: 'The Politcommission will appoint politically responsible staff (heads of the Regional Secretariats and Departments and their deputies, editors and responsible editorial secretaries for the periodicals, and instructors). The Standing Commission will appoint referents, heads of technical departments, Regional Secretariat and Department secretaries, translators and people gaining work experience.'[8]

Not all the requests put forward by heads of department (M. E. Kreps) and by an ECCI Secretary (O. Kuusinen) received the necessary support, however. For instance, their proposal,'to employ (female) Com. Girich as editorial secretary for the periodical *Under the Banner of Marxism* and to find her somewhere to live' was refused on the grounds of her unsuitability.[9] In autumn 1931, under a new ruling, two more bodies suddenly appeared, which in summer 1932 combined to form the Cadre Department: the Organisation Department's Cadre Section and the Sub-Department of Confidential Labour Service. They were closely linked to the Russian Communist Party and the secret police – the United State Political Directorate, Obyedinyonnoye Gosudarstvennoye Politicheskoye Upravleniye (OGPU), later the People's Commissariat of Internal Affairs,

Narodny Komissariat Vnutrennikh Del (NKVD) – and it was their job to look closely into the past lives of applicants suggested by the Politcommission or the Little Commission. Such links with the OGPU can be seen in the correspondence in the cadre file of the Swiss, Berta Zimmermann, who had applied to work for the OMS. Zirotinsky asked OGPU's Special Department for 'an investigation' of her record.[10] The staff plan for 1932 reveals an eight-strong Special Department, which joined the Organisation Department's Cadre Section to form the Cadre Department. The Cadre Department, set up on the Russian pattern, put an end to the existing staffing policy, split as it was between the Little Commission, the Standing Commission and the Politcommission. The files of the Little Commission dwindle away in 1933 and those of the Standing Commission in February 1934. After this simplification the Politcommission decided all requests for personnel, which the heads of the departments and the regional secretariats laid before them after approval by the Cadre Department; the Administrative Department was responsible for employing technicians.[11]

The Seventh World Congress and the restructuring of the entire Moscow apparatus, which started in autumn 1935, put personnel decisions into the hands of the ten-strong ECCI Secretariat, which, before making any resolutions, had the Cadre Department investigate biographical data and certificates of political good conduct. After this preliminary investigation the ECCI Secretary, who wanted to employ someone new in his regional department, proposed his candidate at the next ECCI Secretariat session. As a rule the ECCI Secretaries acceded to his request.[12] The combined ECCI Secretaries had only to confirm the apparatus's *political* staff (assistant secretaries, referents, heads of department and their deputies); General Secretary Georgi Dimitrov dealt with technical staff 'at the application of Comrade Moskvin, who is in charge of the general supervision of the whole apparatus'. The same procedure was used for apportioning leave.[13]

It is not surprising that the ECCI Secretariat undertook politically motivated dismissals, particularly in the years of the Great Terror, 1936–38. Currently, the available sources make it impossible to decide whether it initiated dismissals by arousing suspicion, or whether, on the contrary, it only reacted to party exclusions by the ECCI party organisation or to NKVD arrests. It seems, though, that in the 'triangular game' between the ECCI Secretaries, the party organisation and the NKVD, all combinations were possible. The ECCI minutes offer evidence of all variations. On the whole, the ECCI Secretaries reacted with a dismissal once the party organisation had started proceedings or had concluded matters by exclusion from the party. For its part, the party organisation often used exclusion to ratify actions already concluded by the NKVD.[14]

The apparatus in figures

Even nowadays it is difficult to find figures concerning the Moscow apparatus. The reason for this is not just the proverbial affectation of mysteriousness surrounding the Comintern apparatus from its earliest days, but also the leading Comintern bodies' lack of interest in statistics, which persisted till the beginning of the 1930s. When, in 1931, the Little Commission requested Cirul', head of the newly formed Cadre Section in the Organisation Department, to submit figures to the apparatus on the basis of the personal dossiers, he indignantly reported being faced with 'chaos': 'If anyone thinks the staff's personal dossiers are filed tidily and according to year, he is mistaken. The dossiers piled up in the cellar are often soaked through and rotting away, not just the ones going back to 1920 but even the latest ones from 1930.'[15] Things did not get better until 1932 when the Cadre Department set about systematising information on the staff. As these files are largely closed to research, we are dependent on individual documents which have found their way into files that are now open.[16]

The figures in the following section on the Moscow apparatus must be approached with caution. Certain departments (e.g. OMS) or sections of them (the Administrative Department's commandatura) do not always appear in the annual staff plans; some of the Publishing Department's employees were not integrated into the ECCI budget. The expression 'ECCI apparatus' is hazy, its limits undefined. The annual budget presented by the Comintern's Administrative Department included the apparatus of the Communist Youth International (CYI) but not that of the Profintern, the Peasants' International, the Sport International, and so on. And then, of course, there was always the last doubtful factor of the 'technical', as opposed to the 'political', staff, who were often not included in the figures. Table 3.1 gives an impression of the apparatus as it was in 1926. Russian employees accounted for only 45.4 per cent of the total, which was to change only slightly up till 1933. Indeed, in the three politically central departments (Organisation, Agitprop, Information) Russians accounted for only 36 per cent. The two departments with the most staff are clearly the Administrative Department (including the commandatura) and the Publishing Department (including press and translation), two typical 'service undertakings', with a high percentage of 'technical' staff. The members of the Administrative Department's staff are not listed according to nationality, but it seems likely that in 1926 they were mostly Russian.[17] As to non-Russians in the apparatus, Germans were clearly in the lead, followed by French, British and Swiss. Unfortunately, the 1926 questionnaire does not list 'Jewish' as a nationality, in contrast to a 1933 set of statistics listing Jews as the next most numerous nationality to Russians as shown in table 3.2.

From 1928 onwards the regional secretariats played an increasingly important role. Originally conceived as auxiliary organs for the ECCI Secretaries and Presidium, their staff was increased from year to year at the expense of the political departments. Symptomatic of this refocusing around the Politcommission and the regional secretariats was the liquidation of the Information Department in October 1929. In May 1932 the Standing

Table 3.1 *The staff of the ECCI departments, 1926*

	Russian	*German*	*French*	*British*	*Swiss*	*Hungarian*	*American*	*Polish*	*Other*	*Total*
Organisation Department	5	3	1		2	1	1		3	16
Agitprop Department	11				4		2		1	18
Information Department	6	5		1	3	3	2	1	6	27
Publishing Department	26	12	11	7	1		4	1	1	63
East Department	19			1			1		11	32
Women's Department	3	2			1					6
Co-operatives Department	6	2								8
Administrative Department	n/a	n/a	n/a	n/a	n/a	n/a	n/a	n/a		97
OMS	n/a	n/a	n/a	n/a	n/a	n/a	n/a	n/a		33
Secretariat of CYI	14	9	1						5	29
Secretariat of ECCI	8	5				2			2	17
Total										346
%	45.4	17.6	6.0	4.2	4.2	3.7	3.2	2.3	13.4	100

Source: RC 495/46/7, 'Material on the report on the results of the reorganisation of the work of the ECCI and its apparatus', n.d. (Summer 1926); RC 495/19/398a, 'Report on the ECCI staff and apparatus', n.d. (1926).

Table 3.2 *Apparatus staff according to nationality, 1933*

	%
Russian	47.3
Jewish	13.4
German	9.1
Latvian	5.7
French	3.6
English	3.2
Hungarian	2.7
Polish	2.7
Other	12.3

Source: RC 495/7/25, Cirul′, report on ECCI employees, 28 March 1933 (based on questionnaires completed by 528 staff).

Commission approved a staffing plan, shown in table 3.3, agreed by the Administrative Department in co-operation with the heads of the departments and the regional secretariats.

Thus, together with the 21 employees at the OMS in 1931, in 1932 the Moscow apparatus of the ECCI and the CYI employed some 500 people. In 1931 the Administrative Department's financial section was paying 447 people every month – not counting the OMS – which is not far off our calculations. In 1933 Cirul′, deputy head of the Cadre Department, wrote in a report of as many as 666 employees, about only 526 of whom the Cadre Department had a proper dossier. Indeed, in a letter to Piatnitsky, Cernomordik and Cirul′ estimate that the apparatus had 800 employees, since neither the publishing staff nor the employees of the Hotel Lux appear in the ECCI budget.[18]

As of 1933 we find more and more mention in the leading bodies of 'reducing the apparatus'; numerous internal scenarios worked out to put an end to the 'extensive parallelism in the work between the Departments and the Regional Secretariats'. This call for re-dimensioning was followed by deeds: 1933 saw the dissolution of the Agitprop Department and the Organisation Department.[19] The reorganisation which took place in autumn 1935 – the dissolution of the regional secretariats and the strengthening of the 10 ECCI secretariats – cost an unknown number of employees their jobs. The new staff plan (excluding CYI, OMS and commandatura) allowed for only 336 people, although it is not possible to assess to what extent the deconstruction of the central apparatus was countered by an expansion of institutions which did not formally belong to the ECCI. It is probable that here, too, the practice already mentioned of 'exporting' posts from the ECCI budget and thrusting them upon related institutions was again brought into play. For instance, in 1935 the Publishing Department employed 65 people, of whom 'eight are to be paid

Table 3.3 *The staff of the departments and the regional secretariats, 1932*

Presidium of ECCI	10
Secretariat of Politcommission	13
Bureau of Secretariat (with archives)	29
Regional secretariats:	
Central European	14
Roman	12
Anglo-American	12
Latin-American	8
East	19
Polish-Baltic	8
Balkan	9
Scandinavian	6
Organisation Department	13
Agitprop Department	12
Publishing Department	16
Translation Department	71
Women's Department	7
Co-operatives Department	9
Department for Work in Rural Areas	3
Administrative Department (with garage)	90
OMS	??
Special Department	8
Library/newspaper expedition	14
Practicians	20
International Control Commission	3
Editorial staff *Communist International*	7
Protection of fraternal parties	5
Apparatus of CYI	55
Total	473

Source: RC 495/7/21, Standing Commission minutes and appendix, 8 May 1932.

from the ECCI budget and the rest from the publishing house's income'. However, the actual publishing house, the Publishing Co-operative of Foreign Workers in the Soviet Union (PCFWSU) employed no fewer than 185 people in spring 1937.[20]

A last ECCI staff plan from spring 1941 (including the commandatura) shows only a minimum staff reduction compared with the reduced staff plan of autumn 1935 (see table 3.4). The Cadre Department still had a staff of 48; on the other hand, the secretariats, their apparatus and the party representatives plummeted from 94 to 54 – an expression of the political defeats suffered in the meantime by the Comintern (and the Soviet Union).

Table 3.4 *ECCI staff in March 1941*

Secretaries	9
Apparatus of Secretariat	35
Central archives	12
Representatives of parties	10
International Control Commision	7
Cadre Department	48
Department for Press and Agitation	39
Translation Section	50
Department for Propaganda	23
Editorial staff of *Communist International*	4
Administrative Department	191
Total	428

Source: RC 495/18/1330, 'ECCI Staff for 1941', 18 March 1941.

Overlapping leading organs (1919–35)

Sessions of the ECCI members and Presidium were held rarely, and were mainly concerned with a general political survey of the situation; up till 1926 the Secretariat and the Orgbureau were in charge of leadership. In 1925 a discussion was started in the ECCI Secretariat concerning diversification of the main organs of leadership. As so often, the Secretariat set up a commission, consisting 'of Comrades Piatnitsky, Kuusinen and Heimo, in order to consider, with staff from the various departments, the various questions concerning faults and difficulties in their work and how matters can be improved'.[21] As we have seen, the discussions resulted in the concentration of the regional secretariats according to geographical / cultural considerations and in the splitting up of the leading levels concerned with day-to-day political leadership. As of 1926 the Secretariat created – partly from its own ranks and always with the approval of the Presidium – numerous additional leading organs, whose staff and responsibilities both overlapped. This urge to organise may have originated in the painful realisation that the revolutionary breakthrough in the West had failed. Subconsciously, the belief that revolution could be 'magicked' into coming about by specialisation within the leadership apparatus and by discipline may also have played a role. It is possible that the confirmed realisation in the Communist parties and the ECCI apparatus of Western society's 'temporary stabilisation', and their belief that revolution could be brought about, misled the ECCI's top organs to think that only a 'perfected' leadership apparatus could influence the flow of history in the direction of world revolution. There was also a highly political element, the fight against 'Trotskyism' in the Communist Party of the Soviet Union (CPSU), which led to the Comintern cadre's belief that only subordination and the assumption of Soviet experience was the way forward for the Communist International. Only future research based on intensive study of the files will reveal why, in 1925 and 1926, the leading organs decided on a reorganisation which was to lead to a 'session inflation' in the years to come. We have listed below the various leading organs which constantly got in each other's way, especially between 1926 and 1935:

Orgbureau (1921–26): In 1925 it was given the following responsibilities: 'Besides the most important questions affecting the CPs the Orgbureau is to discuss the most important organisational questions affecting the ECCI apparatus. The three functional departments (Org[anisation], Inform[ation], Agitprop [Agitation and Propaganda]) are to put in a report every three months and submit a working plan for the next three months.'[22]

ECCI Secretariat (1919–26): This was the executive organ of the ECCI, the Presidium and the Orgbureau and had the following responsibilities:

(a) Preparing the questions to be put to the 'decision-making organs' of the ECCI (ECCI Presidium).
(b) Carrying out the resolutions passed by these organs.
(c) Permanent supervision to check that the resolutions were put into effect by both the ECCI apparatus and the individual sections.
(d) Leading the ECCI apparatus in accordance with the resolutions passed by the Presidium and the Orgbureau.[23]

Politsecretariat (1926–35)

Politcommission of the Politsecretariat (1929–35)

Minor Commission (1926–35): Founded in accordance with a resolution passed by the Presidium in December 1926: 'The Political Secretariat is to select from among its members a Minor Commission to concern itself with underground activities and important administrative matters.'[24]

Standing Commission (1926–34): Dealt with 'absolutely confidential' questions on behalf of the Presidium, the Orgbureau and the ECCI Secretariat.

Bureau of the Secretariat, Chancellery Office (1924–41): Headed by Heimo (1925–31), Gerisch (1932–37), Krushkov (1938), Sergeev (1937, 1939–41). Responsible for minutes, dispatch and archives. In 1932 it had a staff of twenty-eight and still retained eleven in 1935 (without dispatch and archives), while in 1941 it had thirty-five (without archives).

In spring 1934 – more than a year before the general reorganisation of the ECCI apparatus after the Seventh World Congress – the Standing Commission dissolved itself. Its responsibilities were taken over by the already existing Minor

Commission and the Politsecretariat's Politcommission. This was a first step towards doing away with the 'duplication' so often complained of.

Strengthened ECCI secretariats (1935–41)

The reorganisation which took place in autumn 1935 centred around getting rid of the regional secretariats, increasing the staff of the ten ECCI secretariats and stressing the importance of the Cadre Department, which also supervised and, if necessary, changed party leaderships. This new division of responsibilities represented a considerable break in Comintern tradition, which, by and large, was based on the 1926 restructuring. The resolution for the changes and the sketching out of the new apparatus were published in the mid-1990s.[25]

What follows is a provisional list of staff who worked for varying lengths of time in one of the ten ECCI secretariats between 1935 and 1941; the list does *not* include the permanent party representatives attached to the secretariats. Heads of secretariats are underlined.

G. Dimitrov (General Secretary): K. I. Cirkov (1938), G. Dirr, A. K. Golcev (1935), Eklund (1939), V. S. Kruskov (1938–39), J. Krymov (1935), J. Rosner (1938–40), T. Mandoljan (1936), P. A. Mif (1935), B. N. Ponomarev (1936–42), Prochorova (1938), A. P. Sergeev (1935–36), B. Smeral (1939–41), A. I. Stern (1938–?), P. T. Tatarenko (1938–42), B. A. Vassiliev (1935), E. Walter (1935–38).

P. Togliatti (responsible for Central European countries 1935–37): Bakar Abu (1936), E. Kerber (1936–37), A. P. Kraievsky (1936–37), H. Nuding ('Degen', 1935), E. Rupprecht (1935), J. Schwab (1935), G. B. Smoliansky (1935–36), R. Urban (1936), H. Wehner ('Funk', 1937).

D. S. Manuilsky (responsible for Roman countries 1935–41): Bertoni (1938–39), O. Brandao (1938–?), S. S. Dzierzynskaja (1938–42), L. Monnerau ('Garnier', 1937), L. Genin, E. Gerö (1935–42), E. V. Golubeva (1939–?), V. M. Kachan (1935), M. J. Koker (1935–37), Lukina (1939–?), S. Minev ('Stepanov', 1935–42), J. Z. Mirov (1935–?), A. M. Polumienko (1938–?), A. L. Rasumova ('Cigerovic', 1935–38), T. P. Sidkova, C. Servet (1935–37).

A. Marty (responsible for Anglo-American countries 1935–41): A. Berei (1935), Bertoni (1937–38), Bloomfield (1936–38), Brown (1935), S. Kapelovic (1935), B. Francis (1937), J. Krymov (1935), Mayorski (1935), R. Michel (1936–?), I. G. Mingulin (1935–37), Naumann (1935–41), M. Raylock (1935–37), N. Ross (1939–41), B. I. Schick (1937–41), Siksoi (1935), Varbot (1935), R.S. Vitol (1936).

W. Pieck (responsible for Balkan countries 1935–41): I. B. Bogdanov (1938–41), K. V. Bojkov (1939), G. M. Dimitrov ('Grosdanov'), S. D. Dimitrov ('Marek',

1937–41), Fabrian (1935), M. Gorecki (1935), V. V. Gromov (1935–41), H. Horwitz ('Walecki', 1935–37), Lasman (1939), S.M. Miller 1935–36), M. I. Moravskaja (1935–37), 'Petrovsky' (K. Horvatin?, 1935–36), Spiridonov (1936–37), 'Walter' (J. Broz, 'Tito', 1935), 'Klassner' (P. Wandel, 1937–41).

O. Kuusinen (responsible for the Far and Middle East 1935–39): K. M. Abakumov (1938–39), Alekseev (1935), Balakina (1935–39), 'Fred' (1935–36), B. S. Frejer (1937), Kim-Sian (1937), S. M. Miller (1935–37), A. S. Parsadanova (1939), B. A. Rabinovic (1938–39), Samochin (1935), Sorky (1935), N. I. Svezov (1938), Tchoi Shenu (1935–37), J. I. Wolk (1935–37).

W. Florin (responsible for Scandinavia 1935–41): L. Brann (1935–37), R. Gyptner ('Magnus', 1937–41), G. Keller (1937–41), R. B. Magnuson (1938–41), H. Meyer ('Most', 1935–37), M. Moritz (1935–36), G. J. Sonberg (1935).

Wang Ming (responsible for Latin America 1935–39): O. Brandao (1936–38), K. I. Cirkov (1939), E. Haaf (1935–?), J. Gómez (1935–36), N. Karlina (1939), Kobylanski (1936), V. N. Kucumov (1935–36), 'Marucci' (D. Maggione, 1935–37), Meskovskaya (1935–36), S. S. Pestkovski ('Banderas', 1937), Stakanov (1939).

D. Ibarruri/J. Díaz (responsible for Spain and Latin America 1939–41): I. Levi Rodriguez-Falcon ('Tobosso', 1940–41), E. Simorra Gutierrez (1939–40), K. Levi-Rodriguez (1939–40), E. Castro Delgado (1940), Bertoni (1940), M. Sendin López (1939–43), E. Gonzales (1943).

M. A. Trilisser ('Moskvin'; responsible for Polish-Baltic countries 1935–38): G. S. Alikhanov (1935–36), A. D. Dobrovolskaja (1935–37), M. P. Filimonov (1936–38), C. Fortrefflich ('A. Fiszer', 1935–37), M. Heimo (1935–36), E. I. Solomov ('Glebov', 1937).

K. Gottwald (responsible for Central European and Polish-Baltic countries 1938–41): Ilatovskaja (1939–40), V. Kopesky (1938–39), St Mayor ('Gondek', 1939–41), V. Siroky (1938–40), Stark (1939–41), H. Strom (1939–?), E. Svoboda (1939–41).

Did the 1935 reconstruction bring the fraternal parties more autonomy and in any way relax the monolithic structure inside the party? At the moment, the only indication of this is two letters written by Dimitrov to Stalin in October 1934, months before the reorganisation. Dimitrov complained about the slowness of the Moscow apparatus and put the case for staff reductions combined with the transference abroad to the fraternal parties of some responsibilities.[26] However, the dissolution of the West European Bureau (WEB) in Berlin, explicitly mentioned in the reorganisation resolution, only ratified something which was a result of Hitler's coming to power. The Communist Party leaderships no longer dared to protest against Moscow's resolutions, so that an advance checkpoint like the WEB had lost its function. For instance, the unconditional support for the hunting down of 'Trotskyists' in the Soviet Union and abroad proves that, after years of political abjuration rituals, the leadership apparatus was no longer capable of even the slightest independence.

The reconstruction of 1935 assigned to the party representatives new functions. Each Communist Party had to send to Moscow a permanent representative who was appointed to one of the ECCI Secretaries. They belonged now to the ECCI staff and enjoyed its services (catering, free trips and so on); they no longer had to deal with the enquiries of emigrants in trouble. The newly elected ECCI Secretaries needed them as a connecting link to the fraternal parties.[27]

Many small parties, like the Swiss, sent their first permanent representative to Moscow in autumn 1935. As the ECCI Secretaries had to confirm every new party representative, the minutes from 1935 to 1941 allow us to get a list of party representatives in the central apparatus of the Comintern (see table 3.5). It does not appear that the brusque reconstruction of autumn 1935, particularly the dissolution of the regional secretariats, had anything to do with political differences of opinion or rivalry between apparatus sections. Even though in the train of the restructuring some leading personalities (Piatnitsky, Knorin, Kun, Abramov) left and were later liquidated, on the whole the reasons for the reconstruction were probably purely practical. As far as we can see at present, during the internal discussions preceding the restructuring no factors emerge which would indicate differing political concepts.

The OMS Courier Service: purged and taken over by the NKVD

Trilisser was the only ECCI Secretary to fall victim to the Terror; his Secretariat was dissolved (1938) and its special responsibilities (OMS) and cadre problems were taken over by Dimitrov.[28] In the guide book to the Russian Centre there is no reference to a 'Secretariat Trilisser' file.[29] During the 1935 reorganisation one of the responsibilities assigned to Trilisser was the Secret Department. In all likelihood this was the OMS, which, starting in autumn 1935, was purged and, in 1936, received the new title Linking Service, Sluzby Svjazi, (SS). From then on it was Trilisser who, during sessions of the ECCI Secretaries, introduced SS staffing and organisational changes. The long-time head, Jakov Abramov, was demoted and, in July 1936, removed from the ECCI apparatus, the ECCI minutes recording that 'Com. Abramov has shown no willingness to carry out the duties assigned to him by the ECCI Secretariat as Deputy Head of the Linking Service', and that the Secretariat resolved to free him from his duties in the Linking Service of the ECCI Secretariat and to put him at the disposal of the CC of the CPSU.[30]

The cadre file of the Swiss, Berta Zimmermann, who from 1933 to 1937 headed the OMS Courier Service and its successor, the SS Central Office in

Table 3.5 *Party representatives in the Comintern central apparatus, 1935–41*

Name	*Party*	*Dates as representatives*
Adomas	Lithuania	1940
Airoldi, J.	France	1939
Aleksa, Z. ('Angaretis')	Lithuania	1935–37
Antikainen,T.	Finland	1941
Arnot, R. P.	England	1936–38
Arrachard, R.	France	1935
Belevsky, J. S.	Poland	1937
Bianco, V.	Italy	1940–41
Boeck, H.	Belgium	1935
Bogdanov, I. B.	Bulgaria	1938
Bortnowski, B. ('Bronkowski')	Poland	1935–36
Campbell, J. R.	England	1938–39
Castro Delgado, E.	Spain	1939–40
Charles, Th. ('Williams')	Canada	1936
Chen Shaoyü ('Wang Ming')	China	1935–37
Ciufoli ('Battista')	Italy	1935–38
Codovilla, V.	Argentina	1935–36, 1938–41
Cogniot, G.	France	1936–37
Copic, V. ('Senko')	Yugoslavia	1935
Darcy, S. ('Randolf')	USA	1935–37
Decaux, J.	France	1937–38
Dengel, P.	Germany	1937–38
Dennis, Eugene ('Ryan')	USA	1937–38
De Paula Oliveira, F. ('Queiros')	Portugal	1935
Dshon-Li	China	1937–38
Escobedo, A.	Cuba	1936–37
Evangelista, Cr.	Philippines	1939
Ewen, T.	Canada	1938–39
Fan-Lin	China ?	1937
Ferdi, B.	Turkey	1935–37
Filipovici, E. ('Tschoban')	Rumania	1935–37
Fischer, E. ('Wieden')	Austria	1935–38
Fürnberg, F.	Austria	1938–40
Galoen, J.	Norway	1936–37
Gerö, E.	Hungary	1936, 1939–40
Gonzales Alberdi, P. ('Bernard')	Argentina	1937–38
Grossmann, K.	Austria	1935
Grzetic, I. ('Fleischer')	Yugoslavia	1935–37
Hernández, J.	Spain	1940–41
Ho Chi Minh ('Chayen')	Indochina	1935–36
Hruska, C. ('Tom'),	Czechoslovakia	1935–39
Iskrov, P. ('Christov')	Bulgaria	1935–36 (with Kolarov)
Jezierska, R.	Poland	1937 (secretary)
Kempe, G.	Sweden	1937
Kerrigan, P.	England	1935
Kolarov, V.	Bulgaria	1935–37 1939–41 (with Iskrov)

Table 3.5 (*cont.*)

Name	*Party*	*Dates as representatives*
Kon-Sin	China	1935 (with Wang Ming)
Kopecky, V.	Czechoslovakia	1940–41
Koplenig, J.	Austria	1941
Krumins, J.	Latvia	1935–37
Kun, B.	Hungary	1935
Lacerda, F. ('Ledo')	Brazil	1935–41
Lafertte, E.	Chile	1938
Lager, F.	Sweden	1937–38
Lie, O.	Norway	1935
London, A. ('Blake')	Australia	1937–38
Mäkinen, J. ('Stein')	Finland	1935–37
Mamedov, I. A.	Greece	1935
Marrat, I.	Turkey	1937–41
Mayer, K.	Switzerland	1935–38
Mehring, R.A.	Estonia	1935–37
Meison, S.	Australia	1936–37
Mertens, S.A. ('Skulski')	Poland	1936
Morgan, N.	Canada	1937
Morris, L. ('Porter')	Canada	1935
Munch-Petersen, A.	Denmark	1936–37
Nordboe, L.	Norway	1937–38
Nosaka, S. ('Okano')	Japan	1935–36, 1938–40
Pieck, W.	Germany	1935 (with Schubert)
Pipenstock	Germany	1939 (secretary)
Rakosi, M.	Hungary	1941
Ramsi	Syria	1935–36
Salim Habud	Syria	1936–37
Schalker, C.	Holland	1937–38
Schubert, H. ('Richter')	Germany	1935 (with Pieck)
Springhall, D. F. ('Gibbons')	England	1939–40
Stefanov, B. ('Draganov')	Rumania	1937–41
Struik, A.	Holland	1936
Szanto, B.	Hungary	1937–39
Tchen-Lin	China	1938–39
Toohey, P.	USA	1938–39
Torres, A.	Argentina	1937
Tuominen, A.	Finland	1935
Tutti, M.	Italy	1938–40
Ulbricht, W.	Germany	1938–41
Vidiella, R.	Catalonia	1940
Vilar, C. ('Pérez')	Cuba	1937–38
Wiatrek, H. ('Weber')	Germany	1936–37
Wretling, A.	Sweden	1935–36
Yamamoto, K. ('Tanaka')	Japan	1936–37
Zarev, I.I.	Bulgaria	1939–40 (secretary)
Zvedre, O.	Latvia	1936–37 (secretary)

Table 3.6 *Heads and deputies of the OMS (SS), 1921–43*

	Head	*Deputy*
Piatnitsky, O. A. (1882–1938)	1921	
Vompe, P. (1890–1925)	1922–25	1922
Grolman, M. G.	1925 for some months	
Abramovic, A. E. ('Albrecht', 1888–?)	1926	
Abramov, A. L. (1895–1938)	1926–35	November 1935–July 1936
Flieg, L. (1893–1939)		1932
Rylski, A.		1934–October 1935
Sorkin, G. Z.		July 1936–41
Melnikov, Boris N. (?–1938)	November 1935–May 1937	
Anvelt, Ya. Ya. (1884–1937)	June–December 1937	
Sucharev, K. P. (1899–?)	1939–41	1938
Morozov, I. A.	1942–43	

Moscow, is very informative about the purges in the Moscow apparatus and its take-over by the NKVD. From spring 1935 onwards the signature of Zimmermann's immediate superior, Abramov, is missing from authorisations to make special payments. Since 1921, together with Piatnitsky, he had been building up the OMS apparatus in the West, and was considered the greatest expert on the network connecting the parties with the Comintern Central Office in Moscow. This key post attained significant importance at the time of the show trials.[31] However, suspicion of having independent channels of contact to former and potential opponents in the West also fell on other members of the staff. From 1936 onwards the Russian B. N. Melnikov signed on behalf of the OMS.

The reorganisation of the OMS – now SS – carried out in 1936 also affected the forms which Comintern staff had to hand in when applying for an extension of their residence permits. The SS forms had ten questions. Nine of these had to be filled in by the relevant member of the Cadre Department or the Secret Department; but the seventh was to 'be filled in by the SS'. As far as we know this is the first recorded mention of a 'Secret Department' and it poses some questions. Was it a newly created position in the Comintern Central Office, to supplement the Cadre Department's work of registration and link it to the NKVD?[32] A document from the the cadre dossier of the Dutchman Wim Rutgers proves that there was at this time a 'secret section' for gathering information about staff members in Soviet firms – and in the Comintern Cadre Department, too. A report from Ya. M. Zysman also indicates the existence of a secret post within the SS or the Comintern for keeping an eye on the staff. In 1936 Zysman checked out OMS/SS staff member S. Bamatter and admitted: 'Müller and I rather think that there is a certain connection between the collapse of our ciphering and Bamatter. But so far we have no definite evidence that would pin it on him. The case must be carefully examined. There is a questionnaire about Bamatter in the Special Department.'[33] Perhaps these three posts mentioned (Secret Department, Secret Section, Special Department) prove the existence of the Special Department long suspected by the Danish historian Niels E. Rosenfeldt, which, proceeding from the Soviet party, managed to worm its way into the OMS/SS and the entire Comintern Central Office in Moscow.[34]

In March 1937 Zimmermann got a hint of what was to happen to her in the next two months. An SS courier, who in summer 1936 had taken secret letters from Moscow to Madrid, wrote a report in March 1937 stating that Zimmermann was present in the SS Central Office on the top floor of the Comintern building when a Comrade 'Walter' gave him a secret letter to take to Madrid in summer 1936.[35] In the meantime, both the sender, 'Walter', and the recipient in Madrid had fallen into disfavour, which automatically threw suspicion on the courier, 'Rogers', and the witness, Zimmermann. Berta Zimmermann had to write a short 'declaration'.[36] Zysman passed it on to L. M. Poliacek, an NKVD officer. While Zysman and – as we shall see – the SS deputy Sorkin kept an eye on the Comintern's SS section, cadre leader Alikhanov sent Poliacek material about the staff in other, less sensitive Comintern departments. Poliacek turns out to be the key figure who had all the threads in his hands. He belonged to that area where, in 1937, the NKVD and the Comintern intersected. We lose all trace of him after spring 1938.[37]

To throw light on the accusations sent in against SS staff, a commission was set up under the President of the International Control Commision (ICC), Jan Anvelt. Sorkin, who was present at the ICC sessions, kept Poliacek informed about the interrogations. In the investigation of SS staff Sorkin played the same role as Zysman; both acted as links to Poliacek, the NKVD's man.[38] A few days after Sorkin's report to Poliacek, Fritz Platten, Zimmermann's husband, told the party committee at his place of work 'that early this morning the NKVD searched my flat and arrested my wife'. It is not possible to discover whether this NKVD intervention pre-empted a resolution by Anvelt's commission. However, it is certain that, because of the reports Zysman and Sorkin sent to Poliacek, the NKVD knew exactly where matters stood in the investigation against Zimmermann. Following the preliminary spadework of Zysman, Sorkin and Anvelt, the NKVD decided just when the arrest would be carried out.[39]

The Zimmermann cadre files give us an initial impression of the functioning – and the end – of the OMS. The OMS had a cadre leader of its own, a German, Gustav Golke, who was arrested in spring 1937.[40] No other ECCI department suffered so much in the purges as did the OMS/SS. The personnel list of the SS apparatus of 1940 shows that the staff had been renewed and 'russified'. A new generation of young Russians – many of them with experience in NKVD work – had replaced the 'old' generation with experience in the Western labour movement. Veterans like Zysman and P. Ch. Mezis, who had entered the OMS in the 1920s, were exceptions.

Table 3.7 *Members of the restructured Liaison Service (S.S) in 1940* [41]

Name	*Date of Birth*	*Stated Nationality*	*Joined CPSU*	*Joined SS*	*Comments*
Blinov, K. I.	1901	Russian	1932	1938	Instructor
Voroncov, A. F.	1914	Russian	Non-party	1940	
Kogan, A. I.	1908	Jewish	1930	1939	
Sector 1					
Kac, Z. G.	1913	Jewish	1932	1938	Instructor
Korsun, I. M.	1912	Russian	1939	1938	Instructor
Blinov, A. S.	1906	Russian	1932	September 1937	Instructor
Bojkov, I. I	1910	Russian	Komsomol 1931	1937	Instructor
El'bert, S. E	1908	Ukrainian	1939	1934	Secretary
Sector 2					
Gel'fand, M. A	1909		1939	1940	Head of sector 2
Sector 3					
Zysman, Ya. M.	1886		1917	December 1936	Head of sector 3
Kazakov, G. M.	1904	Russian	1924	June 1937	Instructor
Book-keeping					
Basmakov, M. Z	1892	Russian	1917	August 1938.	
Mezis, P. Ch	1887	Latvian		November 1920	
Nikonenko, A. N.	1895	Russian	1924	1930	
Meskov, G. P.	1898	Russian	1939	July 1939	
Sector 'S'					
Nikolaev, A. K.	1900	Russian	1920	1938	Head of sector
Dimitrova, E. M.	1902	Bulgarian	1926	1938	
Sazonov, V. I.	1911	Russian	1931	1938	
Aronova, M. A.	1911	Ukrainian	Komsomol 1926	1940	
Sector 4					
Baranov, I. A.	1912	Russian	1939	1940	Head of sector
Potemkin, I. V.	1900		1938	November 1938	
Vugrecov, I. P.	1899	Russian	non-party	August 1938	
Medvedev, T. M.	1892	Russian	1918	July 1936	

Table 3.7 (*cont.*)

Name	*Date of Birth*	*Stated Nationality*	*Joined CPSU*	*Joined SS*	*Comments*
Kazinik, I. I.	1909	Belorussian	Komsomol 1925	1939	
Krjuk, N. I.	1915	Ukrainian	Komsomol 1930	November 1938	
Sector 5					
Pavlov, D. K	1895	Russian	1919	June 1937	Head of sector
Voroncov, I. N.	1908	Russian	1932	July 1938	
Maslov, A. A.	1911	Russian	Komsomol 1933	July 1937	
Sector 6					
Samoilov, A. A.	1889	Russian	1920	1927	Head of sector
Guseva, A. E.	1899	Russian	1920	November 1938	
Muraveva, E. D.	1910	Russian	1940	July 1938	
Sector 7					
Orlov, M. A.	1910	Russian	1932	August 1938	Head of sector
Egorov, V. A.	1910	Russian	1932	July 1938	
Sysoev, M. M.	1909	Russian	1931	July 1938	
Vorobev, A. V.	1910	Russian	1938	1940	
Petrov, G. D.	1910	Russian	non-party	1940	
Peicev, I. P.	1901	Bulgarian	CP Bulgaria 1920	1930	
Masanov, V. F.	1898	Russian	non-party	1932	
Kostin, M. G.	1906	Russian	1931	1940	
Rudiaga, I. A.	1912	Ukrainian	Komsomol 1931	November 1936	
Sector 8					
Cechlov, K. V.	1911	Russian	1939	October 1938	Head of sector
Elizarov, F. M.	1907	Russian	1931	1938	
Nedosivina, E. P	1905	Russian	1927	August 1938	
Sector 9					
Bukatin, E. A.	1907	Russian	Komsomol 1925	1932	Head of sector
Zimin, A. V.	1907	Russian	1937	1939	Engineer
Savickaia, V. M.	1909	Russian	1940	1934	Engineer

Table 3.7 (*cont.*)

Name	*Date of Birth*	*Stated Nationality*	*Joined CPSU*	*Joined SS*	*Comments*
Majorova, E. K.	1906	Russian	1928	October 1938	Engineer
Sector 10					
Capurin, P. K	1909	Russian	1932	1940	Head of sector
Sustrov, I. St.	1904	Russian	1926	1940	
Dubinin, V. S.	1915	Russian	Komsomol 1936	November 1939	
Out of Moscow					
Podchaliusin, Ja. N	1913	Russian	1938	June 1938	
Masukov, L. V.	1910	Russian	Komsomol 1932	November 1938	
Cirkov, K. I.	1904	Russian	1925	1940	
Frumnin, G. A.	1904	Russian	1925	1940	
Choznev, S.	1913	Kazakh	Komsomol 1934	December 1937	
Slynev, V. V.	1907	Russian	1930	1939	
Georgiev, S. A.	1902	Bulgarian	1925	1930	

On looking at the purges in the ranks of former OMS staff, we can identify some people who were pressing ahead with the process. The ICC president, Anvelt, presided over several commissions and, in searching for prosecution points, depended on an ICC spokesman, the Estonian P. Timm. Zysman and Sorkin collected material for the prosecution. They passed this on to the NKVD liason officer Poliacek, whereupon the NKVD intervened as it saw fit. From 1936 onwards a central role was played by the long-time NKVD cadre M.A. Trilisser ('Moskvin'). Zealous and worried SS staff sent their denunciations to Moskvin and to Manuilsky, who was actually investigating the other ECCI departments.[42] Moskvin and Manuilsky had been representing the CPSU in the ECCI Presidium since 1935. While the third man – Stalin – kept in the background and never appeared on any of the investigating commissions, they, together with Anvelt and Alikhanov from the Cadre Department, led the concrete investigations. With the exception of Manuilsky, they all died violent deaths a few months later. Indeed, Anvelt died while being interrogated by Poliacek.

This terror dynamic, which swallowed up its own perpetrators, was the subject of observation years before the Comintern archives were opened. Robert Conquest, in particular, using Western sources of memoir literature and the Soviet press, managed to follow the thinning in the ranks of the NKVD.[43] Comintern files and documents for the military procurator provide further information. The swift conclusion of many careers in this branch, the ease with which persecutor became victim, can be reconstructed using examples from both central and peripheral areas of the apparatus for repression. The end of the protagonists of terror, who had an absolutely free hand in choosing their victims in 1937, came in 1938–39 when the CPSU leadership began trying to rid itself of the agents of repression who were acting too independently and to prevent their excesses. This desire for normalisation after the blood-letting of 1937 became obvious at the Central Committee Plenum held in January 1938, which condemned the 'practice of acting in a formal and soullessly bureaucratic way when confronted with the fate of Party members'. Indeed, the eighteenth Party Conference, held in spring 1939, announced the victorious conclusion of the purges and spoke out against the excesses for which officials had been responsible in recent years.[44]

In those days, people like Poliacek were treated as scapegoats. By pointing the finger at certain NKVD officials, the party turned the former perpetrators into the new 'victims'. In so doing it supported the widely-held belief that Stalin had not known about the terror. The people who had been arrested and condemned were quick to seize upon this interpretation, rather than have to accept that their petitions to Stalin had always been hopeless.[45]

A reservoir of strength for the Red Army, 1939–45

Almost without exception the new structures given to its Moscow apparatus by the Secretariat in 1935 remained in force till the beginning of the Second World War. In 1938 Gottwald took over from Togliatti (who was sent to Spain) the responsibilities for the Central European countries and from Trilisser (who was arrested) the responsibilities for the Polish-Baltic countries. André Marty, chief of the Interbrigades in Spain, passed the Anglo-American countries over to Kuusinen until 1939. In 1939 Dolores Ibarruri and José Díaz were co-opted onto the Secretariat, which closed the gap caused by Trilisser's arrest and the return home of Wang Ming (till then responsible for Latin America). The ECCI staff found itself involved in far greater turbulence. The ECCI Secretaries assented to either ICC interrogation or arrest by the NKVD by giving their blessing to lists with staff names struck off. Thus, in the minutes for 31 July 1937, we can read: 'Confirmation of the striking off of the following names from the staff list of the apparatus of the ECCI Secretariat: Remmele, Kraevsky, Alikhanov, Dobrovolskaja, Ortega, Cernomordik, Cernin, Bronkovsky, Valesky, Gerisch, Mehring, E. Müller, Eberlein, Smoliansky, Wolk.'[46]

By March 1941 there had been further changes in the apparatus. The secretariats of Wang Ming, Trilisser and Kuusinen had disappeared. Kuusinen had been named head of the puppet government of Terioki during the Finno-Soviet war in December 1939 and was now president of the Finno-Karelian Republic.[47] Compared to 1935, the ECCI staff was slightly smaller, with the exception of the Administrative Department, which shot up from 97 (1926) to 191 (see table 3.8).

Table 3.8 *ECCI apparatus, March 1941*

Members of the Secretariat: Dimitrov, Manuilsky, Togliatti, Florin, Pieck, Marty, Diaz, Ibarruri, Gottwald	9
Apparatus of the Secretariat: a total of 35, subdivided into:	
Office: Sergeev, Belke, Genina, Udalova	4
Auxiliaries	16
Polit assistants	15
Central Archives: Bevs	12
Party Representatives:	10
Control Commission: Gennari, Cchackaia, Smeral, Dengel	4
Staff: Scheinmann, Lukanov, Bucharova	3
Cadre Department: a total of 48, subdivided into:	
Office: Guljaev, Belov, Vilkov	8
Central European countries: Head: Försterling	7
Roman countries: Head: Blagoieva	4
Balkan countries: Head: Vladimirov	3
Anglo-American countries: Head: Volkov	1
South American countries: Head: Badalian	2
Scandinavian countries: Head: Mol'tke	2
Eastern countries: Head: unknown	4
Colonial countries: Head: Kozlov	1
Personnel: Head: Ivanova	2
Staff archives: Head: Silova	6
Youth Cadre: Head: Rebrov	6
Interbrigade archives: Head: D'Onofrio ('E. Fimmen')	2
Press and Agitation: a total of 39, subdivided into:	
Leadership: Geminder, Sverma, Doidzasvili, Werner, Dellin	5
Telegraph Agency: Head: Glaubauf	12
Information Section: Nogradi ('Kellermann')	13
Photo Service: Head: Apelt, F. ('Becker')	4
Radio Section: Head: Wehner ('Funk')	5
Translation Service: a total of 50, subdivided into:	
Office: Head: Krylova	10
Russian Section: Head: Kupisko	10
German Section: Head: Günther	13
English Section: Head: Gavurina	5
French Section: Head: Krenhaus	7
Spanish Section: Head: Rosen	5
Propaganda Department: a total of 23, subdivided into:	
Office: Head: Lovcuk	5
Publishing Section: Head: Appelt, R.	4
Text Books: Head V. Cervenkov ('Vladimirov')	3
Library: Head: Rebane	11
Editors of *Communist International*:	
Fischer ('Wieden'), Schilling, Lode, Winter	4
Administrative Department: a total of 191, subdivided into:	
Office: Head. Pisarenko	7

Table 3.8 (*cont.*)

Administration: Head: Koniuskov	9
Accounts: Head: Miasnikov	9
Culture: Head: Trifanov	3
Removals/Building: Head: Falin	2
Catering: Head: Kazennov	5
Commandant's Office: Security guards	84
Technicians	72
Total:	429

Source: RC 495/18/1330, 'ECCI Staff for 1941', 18 March 1941

Immediately obvious from Table 3.8 is the volume of the Administrative Department, which alone accounts for 45 per cent of the apparatus. Although the European parties were destroyed or driven underground by prohibition, Moscow kept up an apparatus only slightly smaller than in the euphoric years of the popular front – in Moscow the years of the Terror. Obviously the Soviet leadership wanted to keep all its options open and regarded the Moscow apparatus and the illegal foreign cadre linked with it as a welcome reservoir of strength which could still be useful to the Soviet Union. After the invasion by the German Army and the evacuation to Kujbisev and Ufa in the late autumn of 1942, the Red Army was able to make use of the remnants of the Comintern apparatus either to get news through to the West or to work as propaganda officers on the home front.[48]

Notes

1 On research to date, cf. F. Svatek, 'Gli organi dirigenti dell'Internazionale comunista: loro sviluppo e composizione (1919–43)', *Movimento operaio e socialista*, 1–3 (1977); J. Degras, *The Communist International 1919–1943*, 3 vols (London, 1956–71); V. Kahan, 'The Communist International 1919–1943: the personnel of its highest bodies', *International Review of Social History*, 21 (1976), 151–85.

2 Cf. call for action from Togliatti in *Protokoll der Erweiterten Exekutive der Komintern, Moskau 22. November bis 16. Dezember 1926* (Hamburg, 1927), pp. 842–3.

3 RC 495/26/9, Orgbureau minutes, 9 October 1924. Cf. RC 495/274/236, complaint from E. Woog ('Stirner'), head of the Information Department in letter to the Secretariat, 3 October 1924.

4 RC 495/46/7, minutes, 23 March 1926. Revo is the pseudonym of the Austrian Otto Machl (1898–1973); Rusakova was still working in the Translation Department in 1931; Mireille Gaillard was working for Inprecorr in Berlin in 1932.

5 RC 495/46/7, minutes, n.d. [March 1926]; for biographical details of Jenny and Jules Humbert-Droz, see P. Huber, *Stalins Schatten in die Schweiz: Schweizer Kommunisten in Moskau: Gefangene und Verteidiger der Komintern* (Zurich, 1994), pp. 301–2.

6 RC 495/46/7 'Resolution by the Secretariat concerning the tasks and working

methods of the Secretariat's Little Commission', undated [1926]; 'Statutes for the ECCI, its organs and apparatus', 30 March 1926.

7 RC 495/7/11, minutes, 24 August 1929. On the result, see F. Firsov, 'Die Säuberungen im Apparat der Komintern', in H. Weber and D. Staritz (eds), *Kommunisten verfolgen Kommunisten: Stalinistischer Terror und Säuberungen in den kommunistischen Parteien Europas seit den dreissigerJahren* (Berlin, 1993), pp. 37–51.

8 RC 495/7/16, Standing Commission minutes, 3 January 1931; RC 495/7/15, letter from Sirotinskij, 24 September 1930.

9 RC 495/7/19, Standing Commission minutes.

10 RC 495/20/764, letters from Zirotinsky, 20 August 1931, 8 September 1931; resolution on employment in the apparatus, 7 October 1931.

11 RC 495/7/25, 'Suggestions concerning apparatus staff', Standing Commission minutes, 28 March 1933. See, for instance, RC 495/4/349, Politcommission, 11 May 1935.

12 RC 495/18/115517, minutes, January 1937, with added 'character sketch' of Solomov; RC 495/18/1073, 'On the procedure to be followed for admission into the ECCI apparatus', 8 February 1936. Here we must mention, as an exception to the rule, K. Gottwald's objection to the employment of the Englishman Ben Francis: see RC 495/18/1224, appendix to minutes, 11 September 1937.

13 RC 495/18/1083, minutes, 11 April 1936; RC 495/18/1073, 'On the procedure . . .'.

14 RC 495/18/1213, Secretariat minutes, 31 July 1937; RC 495/18/1227, 'List', 23 October 1937, signed Kotel'nikov.

15 RC 495/25/205 report 'To the Little Commission', 21 October 1931.

16 Piatnitsky Secretariat (495/19), Commission for Reorganising the Apparatus (495/46), Organisation Department (495/20), Secretariat (495/18).

17 The large number of Russian names in the Administrative Department appearing in the 1932 staff plan clearly indicates Russian dominance: see RC 495/7/21 'ECCI budget for 1932'.

18 RC 495/18/981, letter, 2 March 1933; RC 495/25/205, report Cirul', 'To the Little Commission', 21 October 1931; RC 495/7/25, report Cirul', 'ECCI Employees', 28 March 1933.

19 See P. Huber, 'Abteilungen und Ländersekretariate um 1933', *The International Newsletter of Historical Studies on Comintern, Communism and Stalinism*, 2: 5 (1995), 69–73; RC 495/18/981, letter from Cirul' and Cernomordik, 2 March 1933.

20 RC 495/18/1081, undated list; RC 495/4/353, Politcommission minutes, 3 July 1935. Figures on the reconstruction from RC 495/18/1020 and 1073.

21 RC 495/46/3, minutes 'Informationsberatung', 5 November 1925.

22 RC 495/46/5, 'Memorandum on the Reorganization', n.d.

23 RC 495/46/10, 'Regulations for the ECCI', n.d.

24 RC 495/46/9, resolution, 12 December 1926.

25 P. Huber, 'L'appareil du Comintern 1935: premier aperçu', *Communisme*, 40/41 (1995), 9–35; cf. B. Studer, *Un parti sous influence* (Lausanne, 1994), p. 161.

26 RC 495/73/1, Dimitrov to Stalin, 6 October 1934.

27 RC 495/20/761, 'Bestimmungen über die Tätigkeit der Parteivertreter beim EKKI', 8 March 1936.

28 RC 495/18/1261, minutes, 4 December 1938.

29 RC (ed.), *Kratkii putevoditel'*, Isdatel'stvo Blagovest, (Moscow, 1993).

30 RC 495/18/1100, minutes, 14 July 1936; RC 495/1871031, minutes, 27 November 1935.
31 RC, K. A. Zimmermann, Abramov to Administration, 9 January 1935.
32 RC, K. A. Zimmermann, 'Questionnaire', 21 November 1936.
33 RC, K. A. Bamatter, 'Personal description', quoted in certificate, signed Zysman, 26 February 1939; RC, K. A. Rutgers Andrianov to Cadre Dept., 3 November 1938.
34 N. E. Rosenfeldt, *Stalin's Secret Chancellery and the Comintern: Evidence about the Organisational Patterns* (Copenhagen, 1991).
35 RC, K. A. Zimmermann Report from Rogers, 27 March 1937.
36 *Ibid.*, 'Declaration by Comrade Berta', 4 April 1937.
37 KGB Archives, dossier Zimmermann, reasons for rehabilitation, 2 June 1956.
38 RC, K. A. Zimmermann, Sorkin to Poliacek, 29 May 1937.
39 RC, K. A. Platten, Platten to Party committee, 4 June 1937. Platten (1883–1942) was arrested in Moscow in 1938 and later executed (KGB Archives, Platten dossier).
40 RC 495/18/1225.
41 Excludes 8 people working in the Administrative Section.
42 RC, K. A. Zimmermann, Stucevsky to ECCI Party commission, 23 June 1937.
43 R. Conquest, *Inside Stalin's Secret Police: NKVD Politics, 1936–1939* (London, 1985).
44 Resolution of the eighteenth Soviet Party Conference, Moscow 1939, p. 48. 'Über die Fehler der Parteiorganisationen beim Ausschluss von Kommunisten aus der Partei. Über das formalistisch-bürokratische Verhalten zu den Berufungen von aus der KPdSU(B) Ausgeschlossenen, und über die Massnahmen zur Beseitigung dieser Mängel', *Die Kommunistische Internationale*, 3:4 (1938), 366–74.
45 See the eye-witness account of a former prisoner in H. Damerius, *Unter falscher Anschuldigung: 18 Jahre in Taiga und Steppe* (Berlin and Weimar, 1990), pp. 58–9, 105, 347.
46 RC 495/18/1213, minutes, 31 July 1937.
47 RC 495/18/1285, minutes, 29 June 1939.
48 There has been little research so far into the role of the Comintern in the Second World War, but some indications can be found in memoirs like those of P. Robotti, *La Prova* (Bari, 1965), pp. 302–65; W. Leonhard, *Die Revolution entlässt ihre Kinder* (Cologne, 1987), pp. 157–245; R. Von Mayenburg, *Hotel Lux: Das Absteigequartier der Weltrevolution* (München/Zürich, 1978); G. Ceretti, *A l'ombre des deux T. 40 ans avec Palmiro Togliatti et Maurice Thorez* (Paris, 1973); E. Castro Delgado, *J'ai perdu la foi à Moscou* (Paris, 1950); J. Hernández, *La Grande Trahison* (Paris, 1953). A first study has recently been published by N. S. Lebedeva and M. M. Narinski, *Komintern i vtoraia mirovaia voina* (Moscow, 1994).

Part II

The parties and the Comintern: Europe

4

The Communist International and the British Communist Party

Andrew Thorpe

It was inevitable that the Communist International, as an organisation seeking to promote world revolution, would take particular notice of Britain. The latter was, after all, the world's leading imperial power. It was still one of the world's leading industrial nations. It had one of the most powerful labour movements: by 1919 the trade unions were stronger than ever before, and the Labour Party, until recently little more than an appendage of the Liberals, had declared its socialist intent in 1918 and emerged as a fully independent organisation. And the British had managed to cut off their king's head more than two and a half centuries before Tsar Nicholas II became the victim of the Bolsheviks' regicidal tendencies.

It was, therefore, with high hopes that the Communist Party of Great Britain (CPGB) was formed in the summer of 1920. Yet the party was to remain the despair of Comintern headquarters. A British revolution did not come, nor did it even look like a remote possibility. Industrial militancy between 1918 and 1922 ended, ultimately, in a series of resounding defeats for vanguard unions like the miners and the engineers. The General Strike of 1926, which had been eagerly awaited in Moscow, passed off largely peaceably and ended in ignominious defeat for the unions. The Conservative Party, either alone or in coalition, remained in office for the whole period between 1919 and 1943 except for two short-lived minority Labour governments in 1924 and 1929–31. The CPGB's membership, which started at around 4,000, was as low as 2,555 by 1930, and did not exceed 12,000 before 1937. Even in July 1939 it was only 17,756. There were only five Communist MPs in the whole of the period. Times like mid-1924, when the Comintern felt that the party's efforts were 'very good indeed', with 'considerable satisfaction [being] expressed' were rare, to say the least.[1] More typical were the private comments of Georgi Dimitrov (subsequently Comintern General Secretary) in 1932, that '[o]ur British movement is a pain. It will not grow, neither will it die. [CPGB General Secretary] Harry Pollitt and his crowd are as snobbish and as incapable as revolutionary mass work as they are English.'[2] The criticisms were so strong and so frequent that by the later 1930s Pollitt was forced to vent his feelings of irritation by reverting to a kind of defensive patriotism, writing to a colleague in Moscow that there was 'no need to feel ashamed' of the CPGB, and ending tartly '[f]orgive me for being British'.[3]

By that time, Pollitt appears to have formed a generally negative opinion of the impact of the Comintern on the development of the CPGB and this is a view which has been taken by most historians who have studied the relationship.[4] However, the opening of archives in Britain and Russia, and the growing historiography on the Comintern and its constituent parties based on such records, allow us to attempt a more nuanced portrayal of the relationship.

This chapter seeks, therefore, to reconsider the extent to which the Comintern in Moscow influenced the development of the far left in Britain in the period 1919–43. As I have shown elsewhere, the weapons in Comintern's armoury for controlling the CPGB were by no means insignificant, but they were neither so easily nor consistently deployed, nor as effective, as many historians have assumed.[5] Contrary to what might have been expected, neither the Moscow archives nor the records retained by the party in Britain sustain the image of a monolithic party subservient to Moscow's every whim. What follows is necessarily brief, but it does suggest, on the basis of research on those papers, that Comintern's influence over the development of British Communist politics has been exaggerated by most observers.

Formation

The Comintern was founded in March 1919; its British section followed within sixteen months. The first Unity Convention of 31 July–1 August 1920 saw the coming together of the British Socialist Party (BSP), the Communist Unity Group of the Socialist Labour Party (SLP) and various smaller and local bodies into the CPGB. A further Unity Convention in January 1921 finally brought in various left-wing members of the Independent Labour Party (ILP), plus the small but not insignificant Communist Party (British Section of the Third International) (CP(BSTI)) – formerly the Women's, and then the Workers' Socialist Federation (WSF).

The question of Comintern involvement in all this has aroused considerable attention. Some have argued that, but for Moscow's involvement (and especially money), the party might never have been formed.[6] However, this has to be seen sceptically. Desire for socialist unity, internationalism and positive enthusiasm for Bolshevik Russia were all more important than the machinations of Russian emissaries. Without such factors, no amount of Russian cash could have swung the British far left.

The enthusiasm for 'socialist unity' in Britain was no invention of the Comintern. As long ago as the 1890s, it had been favoured by many on the left.[7] It is true that the prospects of complete unity were dashed by the formation (and survival) of the Labour Party. However, the urge to unify as many socialists as possible in a party not dominated by the trade unions remained significant, and led to the formation of the British Socialist Party (BSP) in 1912 by an alliance between the Social Democratic Party and the left wing of the ILP. Even after this, the BSP continued to hope for further moves towards unity; its re-affiliation to the Labour Party in 1916 can be seen less as a sign of weakness (although that was a factor) than as a positive move to attract more socialists to its ranks. Calls for closer co-operation with the ILP were common in the BSP press from that year onwards.[8] Far-left parties supported each others' candidates at the 1918 general election.[9] Unity was on the agenda before Comintern was formed, and would almost certainly have come to some kind of fruition even without the latter's intervention.

Internationalism was axiomatic for the far left. British socialists had been genuinely distressed that the Second International had failed to prevent war in 1914, and, particularly once the chauvinist 'super-patriot' H. M. Hyndman and his cronies had been ousted from the BSP in 1916, that party campaigned for a revival of all-embracing internationalism as the best way to end the war. For a time BSPers hoped that they would be able to do this through the Labour Party, but the latter's determined refusal to talk to German socialists while the war proceeded, and its participation in the Lloyd George Coalition which was committed to the unconditional surrender of the Central Powers, made this harder and harder to sustain. And, despite all the best efforts of the far left, Labour remained committed to a revival of the Second International with the socialists of France and other Allied powers, rather than a 'real' international. Small wonder, then, that there was little sympathy for the conference at Berne in early 1919 to revive the old International.[10] When the Communist International was formed, the BSP supported affiliation to it overwhelmingly, not because of Russian money, but because the great majority of its members now had no faith in the idea of a weakly controlled organisation on the old lines.[11] This desire for a new start on the international front simply mirrored the desire for a fresh beginning at home through the achievement of much greater unity among far-left groups.

Admiration for the Russian Bolsheviks also played a significant part in pushing their British comrades towards forming a Communist party. But this admiration preceded the formation of the Comintern, and would have continued regardless of it. Between 1917 and 1920, pro-Russian activities increasingly bound the British far left together, starting with the Leeds convention of June 1917 and the campaign to set up workers' and soldiers' councils which followed it, and culminating in the big 'Hands Off Russia' campaign against Allied intervention which peaked in 1920. British far-left enthusiasm for the Bolsheviks could be seen in, for example, the fact that the first edition of Trotsky's *History of the Russian Revolution*, published by the BSP, sold out within three months, despite its high price.[12] It may be true that none of Lenin's works was available in English *before* the Bolshevik Revolution, but efforts were soon being made to rectify this situation. *The Call*, the BSP's weekly paper, published an article by Lenin in July 1918, and another the following month; soon afterwards the party published his 'Lessons of the Russian Revolution' as a pamphlet, although distribution was hindered by a police raid.[13] In September 1919 his *The State and Revolution* was published, and a pamphlet, 'Towards Soviets', followed in January 1920.[14] Two months later, *The Call* was advertising a 'Splendid Cabinet Portrait' of Lenin, 'beautifully mounted', at 9*d*. (or 7 shillings per dozen).[15] Lenin's *The Proletarian Revolution and the Renegade Kautsky* and Zinoviev's short book, *Lenin: His Life and Work* were published in April and June 1920 respectively.[16] The point of all this is that it shows, first, that despite the early lack of knowledge about Lenin in Britain, he was extremely popular on the far left, and that, second, the party was well prepared for Lenin's most significant intervention, namely *Left-Wing Communism: An Infantile Disorder*, from which extracts were published in July 1920, just ahead of the first Unity Convention.[17]

Leading British Communists cannot fail to have been influenced by their meetings with Lenin (and other Russians) at this time, or by his polemical attacks on those Britons, like Sylvia Pankhurst and William Gallacher, who were dubious about going into a BSP-dominated Communist Party.[18] It is also clear, of course, that the Comintern, though still a pretty ramshackle organisation, did have large sums of money to disburse, and that these were resources which various people on the British left were keen to access. On the whole, though, it seems that the Comintern did not dictate the formation of a British party. It did not need to do so; something like it would have appeared in any case. At most, it helped the dominant groups to select who should, and should not, be in the party.

Certainly, the Comintern did use its influence to ensure that the new party was committed to affiliation to the Labour Party and working through Parliament. Both of these points were deeply contested within the groups which formed the new party, and it seems reasonable to argue that the Comintern's influence was significant here. However, even without such intervention, the CPGB would probably have moved in this direction. The largest group feeding into the CPGB, the BSP, was affiliated to the Labour Party at the time and had never been committed to an abstentionist policy where Parliament and local government were concerned.[19] The SLP, seen by writers like Challinor as the more promising vehicle for revolution in Britain, split over the question of joining the new party, with only the minority Communist Unity Group under Thomas Bell, J. T. Murphy and Arthur MacManus eventually coming in. Yet the alternative offered by the SLP majority was predicated on industrial unionism, which in turn required a strong industrial labour movement; and, with the onset of a deep recession at almost exactly the same time that the CP was formed, this became less and less realistic. Indeed, the SLP was soon in a state of headlong collapse.[20] Thus, while the Comintern was keen to push its own particular conception of the nature of a British Communist Party, it seems reasonable to argue that, regardless, there was a great deal of native support for the formation of the party on the basis on which it was eventually established.

Organisation

Party organisation is another area where the heavy hand of the Comintern has been detected by many authors. Certainly, the Comintern, following Lenin, was closely concerned with this issue. The broad argument which has emerged is that while the Comintern was rather haphazard in its early years, it became increasingly bureaucratised as the Soviet regime became established and prospects for revolution diminished; and that this bureaucratisation was reflected in the CPGB.

A particular source of support for this argument has been discerned in the work of the CPGB's 'Bolshevisation Commission'. It comprised Pollitt, Rajani Palme Dutt and Harry Inkpin, and worked from March to September 1922. Its aim was to provide tighter operating systems within the CPGB. This commission tried to shift the party away from the old-style organisation of the BSP, in particular, towards the Bolshevik model: hence new emphasis was placed on democratic centralism, factory groups, and so on. Hinton and Hyman have argued, in fact, that the influence of Comintern was positively deleterious here because, given the conditions of Britain in the 1920s, the CPGB was never going to become the mass party which was the logical outcome of Bolshevisation. The process, started by the Comintern, simply led to an overburdening of members at a time when the far left should really have been concentrating on building up 'a substantial cadre of revolutionaries'.[21] In fact, however, it can be argued that the CPGB here ran ahead of the Communist International. Far from being imposed by Moscow, the Commission appears to have been native-based, and certainly its members clashed seriously and repeatedly with Michael Borodin, the Comintern representative in Britain at the time.[22]

More broadly, it would be foolish to try to argue that the influence of the Comintern over the way the party organised itself was insignificant. At the very least, the terminology of party organisation – Central Committee, Politbureau, factory cell, and so on – was imported wholesale from Moscow. From the early days of the party's existence, and particularly after the development of a larger and more sophisticated Comintern bureaucracy in 1924, Moscow's advice rained in on the CPGB leadership. It is clear from reading that advice that the party took a great many organisational leads from the Communist International. The latter was keen to push the party towards greater activity in a wide range of areas, including factory cell work, work with women, youth work, anti-colonial work and anti-militarist work. And, of course, the Comintern always took a very keen interest in the party press, repeatedly pushing, in particular, for the establishment of a daily newspaper, which finally appeared in January 1930.[23]

However, a number of qualifications need to be made. First, it is clear that the party leadership could often resist the Comintern in many of these areas. Until the end of the 1920s, for example, the party stalwartly and successfully refused to consider seriously the question of a daily paper. It refused, despite strong prompting, to put front organisations like the International Class War Prisoners Aid on an individual membership basis.[24] Nor did Comintern advice always, or even often, run against the grain of thinking within the CPGB's own leadership. For example, Pollitt warmly welcomed the suggestion, made in December 1931, that the party should establish Scotland, London, South Wales and Lancashire as 'concentration districts', since it allowed the party to prioritise its efforts and resources at a time when it was spreading itself too thinly.[25] Further, if the Comintern's advice had been generally resented, it would be hard to explain why the party was so keen to receive Comintern instructors: the CPGB leadership can be found calling for the return of Borodin in February 1924, and of Max Petrovsky after he was withdrawn from close involvement with the CPGB in late 1928, for example.[26]

It is difficult to sustain the argument that, without Comintern influence, the party would have been able to focus its efforts better. Regardless of the Communist International, ex-SLPers and most ex-BSPers were convinced of the desirability of factory work, many ex-BSPers were sure of the need for parliamentary action, ex-WSFers had no doubt about the need to develop work with women, and many individuals, of whom the Dutt brothers and Shapurji Saklatvala are only the best-known examples, were passionately committed to anti-colonial work.

It might be argued that 'Moscow Gold' allowed the party to develop an over-elaborate superstructure. We do know, certainly, that considerable sums of money were sent into Britain, certainly until the early 1930s, from Moscow to support the CPGB. Yet the money was not always spent in ways the Comintern saw as being desirable (as, for example, with the outright purchase of the King Street headquarters in 1920 for £7,500); and, in addition, the Comintern was never (at least after the first year) so free with its money that the party was not forced to prioritise somewhat, so that in some areas its expenditure was little more than that necessary to convince Moscow that something was being done.[27] At most, the Comintern could target its money at various pressure points to force the party's hand, which seems to have been the case with the setting up of the *Daily Worker*. But even here, to argue that no British Communists wanted to establish a daily newspaper at that point would be utterly misleading. Moreover, it has been suggested that regular Comintern funding of the British party ended in 1932.[28]

Finally, it is misleading to compare the pre-Communist groups with the CPGB in respect of organisation. That this point has been hitherto totally ignored in the literature says a great deal about the narrow vision of many historians of British communism. All British parties had been bureaucratising steadily since the mid-nineteenth century, and the big extensions of the franchise which took place in 1918 and 1928 speeded the process still further. The CPGB was not the only party which, in a new era of mass democracy, was emphasising organisation over ideology. During the 1920s the Labour Party – and the Trades Union Congress (TUC) – became more professional and bureaucratised, to the extent that the Comintern, with some justification, believed that the formerly 'federal' Labour Party was becoming just like a continental social democratic party by the later 1920s.[29] Nor was this only true of the left; the Conservative Party was also reorganised to a very considerable extent between the wars, so that by 1930 its headquarters 'had become an entrenched bureaucratic force in the party'.[30] In the face of this centralisation and bureaucratisation, it can be argued, a Communist party organised on the – very weak – lines of the old socialist groups would have fared even worse at the hands of Labour and union officialdom.[31] Those parties which fared worst of all between the wars, when compared to their pre-war performance, were the Liberals and the ILP, neither of which managed significantly to adapt and modernise their organisation in the period.

In short, while the impact of the Comintern on the organisation of the CPGB cannot be ignored, there were sound British reasons for the fact that it was less open and more bureaucratic than its socialist predecessors, and it is misleading to blame the Comintern alone for the way the CPGB developed.

The party 'line'

A further area where the Comintern's heavy hand has been detected is in the party 'line'. The various lines taken have been described earlier in this volume (see Introduction); and they are very convenient 'boxes' into which to fit interpretations of Communist history in the period of the Comintern's existence. However, the idea that a flick of a lever in the Kremlin led to immediate and complete changes in the way Communists the world over saw that world owes more to the myths and legends of the totalitarian school than it does to the more complex reality. In the period of revolutionary offensive (to 1921), for example, the CPGB was, with the Comintern's encouragement, seeking affiliation to the Labour Party and, far from unleashing armed insurrections, fighting parliamentary by-elections. After the General Strike of 1926, in the midst of the 'united front' period, the CPGB has been seen as swinging a long way to the left in its trade-union work.[32] During 'class against class', the CPGB continued – indeed was encouraged by Moscow – to use the slogan of the 'united front', but this time 'from below', while early attempts to form Communist trade unions were, with one partial and complex exception (the United Mineworkers of Scotland), so unsuccessful that the party was soon seeking to work through the reformist unions again, long before the enunciation of the popular front at the Seventh World Congress of 1935.[33]

Given the erratic, and in some ways weak, nature of Comintern control, there was usually quite a bit of slack in the 'line', which could be used by imaginative and enterprising leaders like Pollitt to pursue a policy more in tune with their own perception of their organisations' needs. All Communist parties had some room for manoeuvre, and this was especially the case with the CPGB, given that its – by the early 1930s rather unusual – legal status gave British Communists more potential for autonomy than many of their foreign comrades. In addition, the lower down the party organisation one went, the more scope for autonomy there was.[34] In other words, while the lines did exist, and could not be *openly* flouted, there was usually scope for tacit negotiation within them. It was, after all, one thing to promulgate the line in theory, but another thing to apply it in practice. Fishman's argument, that '[i]t may indeed be more appropriate to describe the Third Period as a Curve or a Bend which veered between the centre and the extreme left according to varying circumstances' can in some ways be applied to the concept of 'the line' more generally.[35]

If the lines themselves were less rigid than has sometimes been alleged, it also appears that British Communists' approaches to politics varied to such an extent that the idea of party members simply following 'orders from Moscow' is untenable. At every turn of the line, there was dissent, and this did not disappear once the line had been changed. During the formation of the party there were strong disagreements on parliamentary action and the question of affiliation to the Labour Party. Such divisions had characterised the pre-1917 British far left, and it would have been surprising had they disappeared immediately after the CPGB was formed.

In a sense, the Comintern's shift to united front tactics in December 1921 was no massive change for the CPGB, since the latter was already pursuing affiliation to the Labour Party; yet, even so, over a fifth of the votes at the party's policy conference of March 1922 were cast against the united front.[36]

Most observers have taken the view that the leftward shift to class against class in 1928–29 was an imposition from Moscow. In fact, however, it excited strong support from, *inter alia*, leading figures like Palme Dutt, Murphy and Pollitt; younger members like William Rust; one of the party's leading woman members, Helen Crawfurd; and from the party's only MP at the time, Saklatvala. Some regions, most notably London and Tyneside, were also strongly in favour of the change.[37] Even among advocates of class against class, however, there were disagreements. Murphy wanted the formation of a new party, the National Workers' Political Federation, to act as a halfway house collecting the political levy from trade-unionists who no longer supported the Labour Party.[38] In London, there was no significant right-wing resistance to the new line, but class against class came under attack from the left, with ultra-leftists demanding that trade-unionists should be called upon to stop paying the political levy to the Labour Party.[39] Such views were not confined to the capital.[40] The idea that the pro-united front leadership was widely representative of the wider party, and that therefore class against class was an alien imposition on a party largely free of sectarianism, is not one which close study of the documents can sustain; in some ways, it was the CPGB leadership, and not the Comintern, which was out of line with the party as a whole.

The shift away from class against class also aroused division, rather than a slavish and monolithic adherence to Moscow's wishes.[41] Even after the change to the popular front line had been made in 1935, with the imprimatur of the Seventh Comintern Congress, some Communists remained unreconstructed 'third perioders'; interestingly, even Pollitt had to tread a wary path when talking to the London district of the party in 1938, stressing that the popular front was 'not a retreat from Socialism'.[42]

And, similarly, many welcomed the more sectarian line which many have supposed was 'imposed' by Comintern shortly after the outbreak of the Second World War. Superficially, it appears otherwise: the party had agreed to Pollitt's line of a 'war on two fronts' against Nazi Germany and the British government, and this was overturned when D. F. Springhall returned from Moscow with the message that the Comintern leadership regarded the war as an imperialist struggle with which Communists should have nothing to do, and that hence the CPGB should withdraw its support for the British war effort. In fact, however, there was considerable support for a new line within the party, as Pollitt's enthusiasm for a war of national defence against fascism seemed to many to go against the whole basis of Communism.[43] Second, the extent to which the line did really change in fact (as opposed to in theory) is highly debatable.[44]

Leadership

A further charge usually made is that the Comintern selected and de-selected leaders of the party at will. Such a suggestion will come as little surprise to historians of other Communist parties of the period: men like Ernst Thälmann in Germany, Maurice Thorez in France, Earl Browder in the United States and Wang Ming in China have all been seen as, essentially, tools of Moscow, replacing earlier, more troublesome leaders as the ruthless Stalinisation of the Comintern proceeded.[45] For Britain, the parallel development is usually seen as having taken place in 1929, when a 'new Stalinist leadership' came to power, with 'Pollitt, under the guidance of Dutt, [as] the Comintern's man in charge'.[46]

It would be facile to argue that the Comintern was not deeply concerned with the question of party leadership. But it would be just as foolish to posit a situation in which Moscow was constantly intervening to change leaders. Certainly, the Comintern, or perhaps more accurately individuals and groups within the Comintern apparatus, did have favourites within the CPGB. At certain points during the 1920s various people were encouraged to believe that they had the 'ear' of senior figures in Moscow.[47] The encouragement of critics of the existing party leadership in order to keep the latter 'up to the mark' was a tactic the Comintern learnt early and never forgot.[48]

The picture of a Comintern eager to make the change in 1929 is, however, somewhat misleading. The Communist International had tried hard to work with the old leadership; it is important to remember that the big change did not come until more than a year after the ninth Executive Committee of the Communist International (ECCI) Plenum (February 1928) which had, in effect, ushered in 'class against class'. The problem was that the old leadership continued to interpret the line with a united front bias, against the wishes, not only of the Comintern, but of a very substantial section of the CPGB membership, and, arguably, against the realities of the British political situation.[49] Certain members of the old leadership also managed to discredit themselves. The party secretary, Albert Inkpin, was relieved of control over the party's finances in 1928 after a particularly embarrassing scandal over money-laundering had come to light in the capitalist press and threatened reprisals against, not just the party, but the USSR itself.[50] But the fact that he was eventually succeeded as General Secretary in early 1929 by Campbell, another 'right-winger', suggests no great keenness on the part of Comintern to carry through a massive change in the leadership if one could be avoided.[51]

Further, Pollitt was not the only British Communist to be well thought of in Moscow by the later 1920s. By then, Murphy was a long-standing Comintern favourite, and appears to have been at least a strong possibility to take over the party leadership. Murphy had met Lenin in a staged meeting in 1920.[52] During the period 1926–28 he was resident in Moscow as the party's representative on the ECCI. It seems likely that the rather truculent and arrogant Murphy found his head being turned by flattery and promises; he was clearly popular with Moscow, being put up to attack the British leadership's handling of the General Strike in autumn 1926, moving the expulsion of Trotsky from the Comintern in September 1927, and joining with Petrovsky to attack his comrades' views on the colonial question at the Sixth World Congress in 1928.[53] E. H. Carr goes so far as to imply that Murphy's position in the party was largely due to the patronage of the Comintern.[54] Murphy was an early advocate of a shift from the united front strategy, and was increasingly seen as Moscow's man by many of his leading comrades in Britain.[55]

It says a lot, then, that he ultimately lost out to Pollitt in the fight to become General Secretary, despite the latter's past right deviations (he had wanted, for example, to change the CPGB's name to the Workers' Party in 1924, and had initially harboured very strong reservations about abandoning the united front).[56] Pollitt was probably more able, certainly more likeable, and undoubtedly more popular within the party than Murphy. In other words, the Comintern did not simply back the person who was most likely to be slavish towards it: it looked for someone who seemed to be, basically, loyal, but who also had ability and who would be able to command the respect of the broad party membership. It was to put up with quite a lot from Pollitt over the years to come, but was prepared to do so before October 1939 on the grounds that he was without peer among Communists for his combination of ability and popular appeal.

Similarly, the very idea of a Dutt–Pollitt axis, so long a mainstay of the literature, is now coming into serious doubt. We know that the two men worked closely together on the Bolshevisation Commission of 1922, and that Dutt and his Comintern agent wife, Salme, corresponded frequently with Pollitt while they were living in Brussels between 1924 and 1936. Yet recent work on Pollitt has gone a long way towards proving that he was not the mere cipher described by Pelling and others, but a shrewd and effective political operator in his own right.[57] When the minutes of the Central Committee meeting in October 1939, which culminated in Pollitt's resignation over the change to the 'imperialist war' line, were published in 1990, they tended to reinforce this impression: at one point Pollitt tells Dutt pointedly that 'I was in this movement practically before you were born'; at another, he says bluntly '[i]f you want to have a political conviction, Dutt, you have to learn how to present a case in a different manner to what you did this morning [*sic*]'.[58] Pollitt's papers provide further evidence that their relationship was not as close as has been thought. By anyone's standards, 1930 was a crucial year for class against class and the new leadership. If there was anything in the notion of a Dutt–Pollitt axis, then one would have expected extensive contact and correspondence between the two men, with Pollitt, in particular, pestering his 'mentor' Dutt for advice and guidance. Yet Dutt remained in Brussels, and there seems to have been little communication at all. In August Dutt wrote to Pollitt, 'Hooray for your letter. Of course we were convinced that you were angry with us and had cast us off. . . . [I]t was the first picture of the position that we have had for months.'[59] It is true that Pollitt and the Central Committee received lots of mail from Brussels, but it was not seen as holy writ in any sense, and seems often to have been completely ignored.[60] Yet if the Dutt–Pollitt axis is largely an invention of historians, then it follows that they could not have been installed by Moscow as a joint leadership in 1929.

There is a further blow to the idea that Pollitt was installed by a dictatorial Moscow to tame the party. As Fishman has suggested, his position at first was far from secure, and others were making the running. What she describes as the 'Young Turks' seem to have formed the real driving force in the leadership.[61] Significant figures in this group included Rust, Robin Page Arnot, Walter Tapsell and the London organiser, R. W. Robson. They were supported by Gallacher, now busily re-establishing his left-wing credentials after 'dangerous' flirtations with 'rightism' in 1927–29.[62] By contrast, one of Pollitt's closest personal allies, the disgraced 'right-winger' Campbell, was summoned to Moscow by the Comintern as deputy to Alex Hermon, the CPGB's 'Young Turk' representative there.

What then happened was an interesting revelation of how a canny leader could work against the Comintern's favourites. During the first four months of 1930 Pollitt gave the Young Turks enough rope with which to hang themselves. He took the credit for the fact of the *Daily Worker*'s appearance that January, while allowing Rust, its editor, to be the focus of widespread discontent both in Britain and Moscow about its format, style and content.[63] Robson came in for criticism as a result of the London district's lacklustre showing in the unemployment campaign that March.[64] Arnot blotted his copybook by failing to prepare a resolution for the Central Committee.[65] Gallacher was hauled over the coals for raising the perspective of a new national miners' union too soon.[66] And Tapsell was exposed to attack by his handling of the party's campaign during the West Yorkshire woollen textile lockout of spring 1930, culminating in complaints that he had got out of a meeting by complaining of illness and had then been seen the same night going to the cinema.[67] All this was faithfully passed on to Moscow by Pollitt, as required by the Comintern, whose officials were left to draw their own, negative, conclusions. Meanwhile, Hermon's incompetence was such that Campbell was soon being regarded by the Moscow apparatus as the *de facto* British representative there.[68] The failure of the Young Turks' line of approach to trade-union work merely reinforced these unfortunate impressions, going against the Comintern's 'Leninist inheritance' which 'emphasised results'.[69] The result was that, by mid-1930, Pollitt and, to a lesser extent, Campbell had done enough to emerge as the key figures in the party leadership. They were to remain such, and further embed their positions, until the partial withdrawal of Comintern goodwill in the later 1930s was capped by their behaviour in opposing the 'imperialist war' line in 1939.[70] The key point is that real leadership had to be *achieved* by Pollitt: it was not, and could not have been, simply awarded to him by Moscow. Thus, while it would be true to say that, ultimately, leaders needed Comintern support, it was also the case that a leadership producing results was preferred to one that was not, and that the more cunning a leader was, the better chance they had of remaining *in situ*. In short, the relationship was, once again, more complex than trite formulations about 'imposition' and 'orders from Moscow' will allow.

The experience of Campbell in 1929–30, however, is suggestive of one area where Moscow clearly did make a difference. It could be used as a repository for awkward characters. While there, working for the Comintern or the Profintern, they would be encouraged to see the merits of the correct line. This exile befell not only Campbell, but also Andrew Rothstein and the South Wales miners' leader, Arthur Horner. It seems to have worked in the case of Rothstein, but Horner came back just as much his own man as he had gone, and was soon back in conflict with the 'line'.[71]

Language and ethos

The Comintern does appear to have had a strong influence on the language and ethos of the British far left. It should be stressed at this point that, contrary to popular myth, Marxism was not unknown or unimportant in Britain before 1914, and there was a significant, if rather weak, Marxist tradition from the 1880s onwards. Early Labour intellectuals showed an interest in Marxism: for example, Ramsay MacDonald had felt the need to polemicise against Marx, while the 'revisionism' debate had been watched with some interest. But Leninism was less well known, and its language was quite alien to the Britain of the 1920s.

To a certain extent, though, one can be sure that, Comintern or not, there would have been a degree of imitation and adaptation of Leninist, and perhaps later Stalinist, slogans. After all, it was unlikely that British Communists would have wanted to pass up the chance to use the language which had apparently led their Russian comrades to success. As seen above, publication of Lenin's works began very soon after the Bolshevik Revolution. One leading article in the BSP's paper even enjoined its readers to 'learn to speak Russian', meaning not the Russian language, but the Russian way of doing things.[72]

There can be equally little doubt, however, that Comintern intensified this trend very greatly indeed. In large things and small, the language of Comintern became, to a great extent, the language of British communism. Phrases like 'the dictatorship of the proletariat' became *de rigeur*. When it is remembered that German was the language of the Communist International, it will not come as a surprise to note that so, too, did terms like 'sharpening', 'differentiation', 'concretisation', and the like, all of them reasonable, perhaps, in German, but all of them fairly horrible in English.

That this is not a trivial point can be seen in the fact that, even at the highest levels of the party, there were periodic grumbles about having to speak in 'German-English' or 'Russian-English', and a perception that such language was off-putting to workers who might otherwise have been attracted.[73] On the other hand, however, given that the CPGB was never likely to become a true mass party, this jargon became a valuable means of self-identity for resolute and dedicated Communists, a language of their own which set them apart and made them special.[74] To be 'sectarian' is, after all, double-edged: if sects rarely grow very large, they are, perhaps, less likely than looser groupings to disappear altogether. The language of British communism was not so much transformed by the Comintern as pushed very hard in a particular direction it might well have taken anyway.

There was a similar blend of native and Comintern influence to be found in the developing ethos of British communism. For example, Communist self-discipline was increasingly stressed. This elided easily (conceptually if not always actually so) into a kind of puritanism, paralleling developments within the Soviet Union. Recently published reminiscences of the children of Communists bear this out very strongly.[75] This is not to say, of course, that all lived up to the image: far from it. One son of Communists feels that '[a] lot of CP [members], especially the men, would use the excuse that they were saving the world to . . . philander and stuff like that'.[76] However, such philandering was frowned on when it came to the attention of the party's leaders. George Hardy of the Communist-led National Minority Movement was exiled to Moscow and then China in 1926 when he left his wife for the party's confidential typist, who was expecting his child. The party's acting secretary, Robert Stewart, was incandescent with rage, commenting that 'without wishing him undue harm I trust that I will not require to be intimately associated with his type' because his 'opinion of Hardy's conduct [was] better not written'.[77]

In short, one should not assume that the puritanism of the party was totally imported. Communist puritanism grew easily out of chapel puritanism: and, as one or two writers have begun to notice, there were significant links between protestantism and communism in Britain.[78] There did develop 'a strong inhibition against drink', but this was not really imported: people like Stewart, Gallacher and Murphy, had been committed teetotallers long before the Comintern had even been thought of.[79] In short, Communist self-discipline was just as much an organic growth out of the British labourist ethos as it was an import from the East.[80]

Epilogue and conclusion

By the later 1930s, Pollitt was becoming increasingly irked by the Comintern.[81] But Dimitrov was stressing the need for parties to emphasise their national traditions, and it seemed that a new, freer future for the party might shortly be on offer. In anticipation of this, a new party constitution was drafted in readiness for the CPGB's Sixteenth Congress in October 1939. The place of the Comintern within the draft was significant. The first mention of the Communist International came on the last page of nine. This in itself was an important change: so too was the content of the passage, which stated merely that the party was 'affiliated to' the Communist International (a weakening of the old formula that the CPGB was merely a branch of the world Communist Party) and that resolutions and decisions of Comintern congresses (no mention was made of other Comintern bodies) would be 'considered' by the Party Congress or the Central Committee.[82]

Of course, the Sixteenth Congress did not take place in October 1939 because of the outbreak of war and the change of line and leadership. In a sense, it could be argued that the changes which took place that autumn were a mockery of ideas of a more independent party. However, these changes (and those which took place in June 1941 to restore Pollitt and move the line towards full support for the British war effort in alliance with the USSR) were more or less the last gasps of Comintern intervention.[83]

The dissolution of the Comintern in 1943 was generally welcomed in British Communist circles.[84] But, on the other hand, the party leadership seems to have been irked that the CPGB was not included in the Communist Information Bureau (Cominform) when the latter was established in 1947.[85] And most leaders of the inter-war generation remained committed to the Soviet Union to the end. Pollitt, who died in 1960, was never to take down the portrait of Stalin from his wall; Dutt's last article for his journal *Labour Monthly* in 1974 was to emphasise 'the accelerating advance in the relative strength and constructive role of socialism represented by the Soviet Union'; and Rothstein was to become the Number One member of the hardline Communist Party of Britain when it was formed in 1991.[86]

By 1943, the CPGB was well established as part of the British political scene, and in trade unions and the workplace. While it would never again reach the 60,000 members claimed in that year, its membership was to remain generally above 30,000 until the 1970s, and did not fall below the level of its pre-war peak until 1983, at a time when the Soviet system was under fierce attack and the CPGB itself faced severe competition from a plethora of alternative and, in many ways, more attractive far-left groupings. It was not a large Communist Party compared to some, either between the wars or after 1945, but it did achieve a greater influence and significance in Britain than the statistics alone would suggest.

The issue of whether the Comintern was to blame for the failure of 'the British revolution' is not worth serious discussion. As Crick has recently argued for the CPGB's forerunner, 'one cannot criticise [it] for what it could not seriously hope to have achieved'.[87] There was never a serious prospect of a British revolution in the period, and to test British communism against the benchmark of the failure to establish a Soviet Britain is utterly unrealistic. In fact, the party did have some achievements to its credit, though these were by no means as great as official party historians like Klugmann and Branson would claim. In addition, the existence of a well-organised far-left body did at least help to keep reformist leaders up to the mark: fears of the revolutionary left helped keep Labour's leaders from going too far to the right,[88] and it might be argued that the rightward march of the Labour Party leadership since the mid-1980s might well have been a good deal more difficult had there been a more potent far left around able to exercise the 'gravitational pull' that had once been exercised by the CPGB.[89]

Two central assumptions have informed this article. The first is that the CPGB was not an alien imposition, constantly pulled this way and that by the Comintern. The second is that the party was, to a large extent, the master of its own fate. It has suited most historians simply to condemn the Communist International as a pest, a hazard, a positive danger to the far left in Britain. It is clear, certainly, that having to answer to Moscow did make life difficult for the party at various times, and that its close involvement with the USSR under Stalin did implicate it in some of the less palatable aspects of twentieth-century history. Yet, at the same time, the Comintern did help the party to stay together, and at least did not hinder it too much, most of the time, in providing its own solutions to the problems it faced. While the Comintern could, and sometimes did, intervene to change particular situations, it did not change, and could not have changed, the course of British history. Those who look for the reasons why Britain did not become a better – or worse – place than it did will have to find other reasons than the intervention of Soviet-based bureaucrats in the affairs of the British left.

Notes

1 RC 495/100/150, Robert Stewart [in Moscow] to CP Central Committee, 25 August 1924.
2 J. Valtin, *Out of the Night* (London, 1988 [1941]), pp. 285, 680.
3 RC 495/100/1040, Pollitt to Campbell, 30 March 1939.
4 Older views (from varying perspectives) are reflected in H. Pelling, *The British Communist Party: A Historical Profile* (London, 1958); H. Dewar, *Communist Politics in Britain: The CPGB from its Origins to the Second World War* (London, 1976); N. Branson, *History of the Communist Party of Great Britain, 1927–1941* (London, 1985); L. J. Macfarlane, *The British Communist Party: Its Origins and Development until 1929* (London, 1966); and R. Martin, *Communism and the British Trade Unions, 1924–1933: A Study of the National Minority Movement* (Oxford, 1969). Among the more important recent works, see esp. N. Fishman, *The British Communist Party and the Trade Unions, 1933–1945* (London, 1995); K. Morgan, *Against Fascism and War: Ruptures and Continuities in British Communist Politics, 1935–1941* (Manchester, 1989), and *Harry Pollitt* (Manchester, 1993); and J. Callaghan, *Rajani Palme Dutt: A Study in British Stalinism* (London, 1993).
5 A. Thorpe, 'Comintern "control" of the Communist Party of Great Britain, 1920–1943', *English Historical Review*, 113, (1998), 637–62.
6 See esp. W. Kendall, *The Revolutionary Movement in Britain, 1900–1921: The Origins of British Communism* (London, 1969), esp. pp. xii, 301–2; also R. Challinor, *The Origins of British Bolshevism* (London, 1977), p. 241.
7 D. Howell, *British Workers and the Independent Labour Party, 1888–1906* (Manchester, 1983), pp. 390–5; L. Barrow and I. Bullock, *Democratic Ideas and the British Labour Movement, 1880–1914* (Cambridge, 1996), pp. 39, 75, 83, 85, 140; M. Crick, *The History of the Social Democratic Federation* (Keele, 1994), pp. 83–91, 222–36; K. Laybourn, 'The Failure of Socialist Unity in Britain, *c*.1893–1914', *Transactions of the Royal Historical Society*, sixth series, 4 (1994), 153–75.
8 *The Call*, 4 May 1916; 27 June 1916.
9 See e.g. *Ibib.*, 12 December 1918.
10 *Ibid.*, 13 February 1919.
11 *Ibid.*, 24 April and 9 October 1919.
12 *Ibid.*, 17 April and 24 July 1917. It sold at two shillings (10p).
13 *Ibid.*, 18 July, 15 August, 24 October 1918.
14 *Ibid.*, 18 September 1919, 15 January 1920.
15 *Ibid.*, 4 March 1920.
16 *Ibid.*, 8 April, 17 June 1920.
17 *Ibid.*, 29 July 1920.
18 See, e.g., J. T. Murphy, *New Horizons* (London, 1941), pp. 123–31; T. Bell, *Pioneering Days* (London, 1941), pp. 212–26; W. Gallacher, *Revolt on the Clyde: An Autobiography* (London, 1949 edn [1936]), pp. 248–53.
19 Crick, *Social Democratic Federation*, p. 292.
20 Challinor, *Origins of British Bolshevism*, pp. 274–5.
21 J. Hinton and R. Hyman, *Trade Unions and Revolution: The Industrial Politics of the Early British Communist Party* (London, 1975), pp. 71–4.
22 Callaghan, *Rajani Palme Dutt*, pp. 50–1; Morgan, *Harry Pollitt*, pp. 26, 31–2.
23 See, *inter alia*, RC 495/72/2, Anglo-American-Colonial group minutes, 13 April

1922, report by Bell; RC 495/100/98, 'Report on the internal situation', 17 March 1923; RC 495/100/299, ECCI closed letter to CPGB Central Committee, 8 May 1926; RC 495/100/419, Politbureau minutes, 19 April 1927; RC 495/100/28, Anglo-American Secretariat minutes, 10 August 1927; RC 495/100/554, ECCI Presidium, 'closed letter' to CPGB Central Committee, 27 February 1929.

24 RC 495/100/233, Politbureau minutes, 25 August 1925; RC 495/100/231, Central Executive Committee minutes, 3–4 October 1925.

25 RC 495/100/728, ECCI organisation department to CPGB Central Committee, 27 December 1931.

26 RC 495/100/159, Politbureau minutes, 31 February 1924; RC 495/100/485, Bell to ECCI Political Secretariat, n.d. [late 1928]; RC 495/100/619, Pollitt to Politbureau, 7 February 1929; RC 495/100/620, Rothstein to Politbureau, 8 February 1929.

27 See Thorpe, 'Comintern "control" ', 648–50.

28 National Museum of Labour History (NMLH), Manchester, Communist Party microfilms, reel 15, Politbureau, 14 January 1932; K. McDermott and J. Agnew, *The Comintern: A History of International Communism from Lenin to Stalin* (London, 1996), p. 56.

29 S. Berger, *The British Labour Party and the German Social Democrats, 1900–1931: A Comparative Study* (Oxford, 1994), *passim*; A. Thorpe, *A History of the British Labour Party* (London, 1997), pp. 62–4.

30 J. Ramsden, *The Age of Balfour and Baldwin, 1902–1940* (London, 1978), p. 231.

31 Crick, *Social Democratic Federation*, pp. 298.

32 Fishman, *British Communist Party*, pp. 31, 36.

33 *Ibid.*, pp. 48–82.

34 For more on these points, see Thorpe, 'Comintern "control" ', *passim*.

35 Fishman, *British Communist Party*, p. 35.

36 RC 495/72/2, Anglo-American-Colonial section minutes, 10 April 1922; NMLH, CP/CENT/CONG/01/04, papers of fourth CPGB Congress, St Pancras, 18–19 March 1922.

37 For Pollitt, Murphy, Crawfurd and Saklatvala, see RC 495/100/493, Central Executive Committee minutes, 7–9 January 1928; for Dutt, see Callaghan, *Rajani Palme Dutt*, pp. 115–21; for a discussion of Saklatvala, see M. Squires, *Shapurji Saklatvala* (London, 1990), pp. 52–4, 99–103; for Rust, see RC 495/100/555a, Rust, 'The coming congress of the Communist Party of Great Britain', n.d. [but January 1929]; for Tyneside and London, see NMLH, CP/IND/DUTT/28/09, M. Ferguson (Tyneside district organiser) to Politbureau, 13 July 1929, and London district party committee, resolution, 'Closed letter of the ECCI', 20 July 1929.

38 RC 495/100/494, Central Executive Committee minutes, 30 June–2 July 1928.

39 RC 495/100/497, Politbureau minutes, 3 April 1928.

40 RC 495/3/63, Gallacher reported in ECCI Political Secretariat minutes, 20 April 1928.

41 NMLH, CP/CENT/CONG/03/05, Dutt, 'Comments on draft resolutions II, received 26 January 1935', n.d.; CP/IND/DUTT/01/11, Salme Dutt to Dutt, 8 July 1935; Fishman, *British Communist Party*, pp. 75–6; Callaghan, *Rajani Palme Dutt*, p. 151.

42 NMLH, CP/LON/CONG/0/04, report of annual congress of London district of CPGB, June 1938.

43 D. Hyde, *I Believed: The Autobiography of a Former British Communist* (London, 1950),

pp. 68–9; M. Macewen, *The Greening of a Red* (London, 1991); Attfield and Williams, *1939: The Communist Party and the War* (London, 1984), pp. 54–8, 99–109.

44 Fishman, *British Communist Party*, pp. 256–7; Morgan, *Against Fascism and War*, pp. 108–9.

45 F. Borkenau, *World Communism: A History of the Communist International* (Ann Arbor, Mich., 1962); R. N. Tannahill, 'Leadership as a determinant of diversity in Western European Communism', *Studies in Comparative Communism*, 9, (1976), 346–68, at 351–2; R. T. Phillips, *China since 1911* (London, 1996), p. 107. While such views have been revised in some cases (see, e.g., Morgan, *Harry Pollitt* and J. G. Ryan, *Earl Browder: The Failure of American Communism* (Tuscaloosa, Ala., 1997)), they remain current in others: see, e.g., E. D. Weitz, *Creating German Communism, 1890–1990: From Popular Protests to Socialist State* (Princeton, NJ, 1997), p. 183. This probably suggests that there is either a need to rehabilitate Thälmann (in particular), or, and perhaps more likely, that there were significant differences between these people which means that they cannot simply be lumped together as 'Moscow's men'.

46 Pelling, *British Communist Party*, p. 52.

47 See, e.g., RC 495/100/27, Bell to Lenin, 14 August 1921; RC 495/100/98, Rothstein to Radek, 23 June 1923; RC 495/100/520, Murphy to Bukharin, 26 January 1928.

48 See Thorpe, 'Comintern "control" ', 653–5, for more on this.

49 This was an argument favoured by Comintern officials: see O. Piatnitsky, *World Communists in Action* (London, 1930), p. 8.

50 RC 495/100/497, special Politbureau minutes, 22 June 1928; RC 495/100/520, Murphy to Politbureau, 25 June 1928, describing the event as the 'most serious' in the party's history.

51 RC 495/100/617, Campbell to Bell [in Moscow], 22 January 1929.

52 Murphy, *New Horizons*, pp. 123–31; D. N. Jacobs, *Borodin: Stalin's Man in China* (Cambridge, Mass., 1981), p. 82.

53 RC 495/100/346, Central Executive Committee minutes, 14 October 1926; Murphy, *New Horizons*, p. 277; I. Deutscher, *The Prophet Unarmed: Trotsky, 1921–1929* (Oxford, 1959), p. 359; RC 495/100/520, Murphy to bureau of British delegation to Sixth World Congress, 20 August 1928; Macfarlane, *British Communist Party*, p. 206.

54 E. H. Carr, *Foundations of a Planned Economy*, vol. 3 (London, 1976), p. 378; and *The Twilight of Comintern, 1930–1935* (London, 1982), p. 217.

55 RC 495/100/411, Gallacher's comments in ECCI Presidium minutes, 22 November 1927.

56 RC 495/100/231, Central Executive Committee minutes, 3–4 October 1925; RC 495/100/493, Pollitt reported in Central Executive Committee minutes, 7–9 January 1928.

57 See especially Fishman, *British Communist Party*, and Morgan, *Harry Pollitt*.

58 F. King and G. Matthews (eds), *About Turn: The British Communist Party and the Second World War* (London, 1990), pp. 199, 210.

59 NMLH, CP/IND/POLL/3/3, Dutt to Pollitt, 1 August 1930.

60 See, e.g., RC 495/100/688, Dutt to CPGB Central Committee, 6 January 1930; NMLH, CP/IND/POLL/3/3, Dutt to CPGB Central Committee, 12 November 1930.

61 Fishman, *British Communist Party*, pp. 33–43.

62 RC 495/72/27, Anglo-American Secretariat minutes, 19 November 1927; RC 495/100/411, ECCI Presidium minutes, 22 November 1927; RC 495/100/497, Politbureau minutes, 27 and 29 June 1928.
63 See, e.g., RC 495/100/673, Politbureau minutes, 30 January 1930; RC 495/100/673, special Politbureau minutes, 17 February 1930; RC 495/100/685, Tapsell to CPGB Secretariat, 29 April 1930; RC 495/100/663, Campbell [in Moscow] to CPGB Secretariat, 30 April 1930.
64 RC 495/100/693, CPGB control commission, 'Report on March 6th', n.d. [but *c.*March 1930].
65 RC 495/100/673, Politbureau minutes, 20 March 1930.
66 RC 495/100/673, Politbureau minutes, 27 March 1930. He was also criticised over the 6 March campaign: see RC 495/100/693, CPGB control commission, 'Report on March 6th', n.d. [but *c.*March 1930].
67 RC 495/100/673, Politbureau minutes, 24 April 1930; RC 495/100/678, 'Comrade Gallacher's report concerning comrade Tapsell', n.d. [but *c.*April 1930].
68 See Thorpe, 'Comintern "control" ', 645.
69 Fishman, *British Communist Party*, p. 42.
70 See *Times Literary Supplement*, 5 May 1966, for Dutt's assertion that the Comintern took soundings in 1937 about replacing Pollitt.
71 For Rothstein and Horner, see Thorpe, 'Comintern "control" '.
72 *The Call*, 14 February 1918.
73 RC 495/100/617, Campbell to Bell [in Moscow], 14 March 1929; RC 495/100/231, Central Executive Committee minutes, 3–4 October 1925.
74 R. Samuel, 'Class politics: the lost world of British communism, part three', *New Left Review*, 165 (1987), 52–91, at 82.
75 P. Cohen, 'Red Roots: From Lenin to Lennon', in *idem* (ed.), *Children of the Revolution: Communist Childhood in Cold War Britain* (London, 1997), pp. 21–9, at p. 29; N. Temple, 'Squaring the Circle', in *ibid.*, pp. 89–101, at p. 94.
76 A. Sayle, 'Non-Stop Party', in *ibid.*, pp. 43–51, at p. 51.
77 RC 495/100/357, Stewart to Murphy, 19 October 1926.
78 H. Francis, 'Community and chapel', in Cohen (ed.), *Children of the Revolution*, pp. 123–36, at pp. 125–6; see also R. Samuel, 'British marxist historians, 1880–1980: part one', *New Left Review*, 120 (1980) 21–96, at 49–55.
79 R. Samuel, 'The lost world of British communism', *New Left Review*, 154 (1985), 3–53, at 11; Beckett, *Enemy Within*, p. 10, 15.
80 There is not space to go into this fully here, but cf. the nature of the CPGB as revealed here with that of the Labour Party described in H. M. Drucker, *Doctrine and Ethos in the Labour Party* (London, 1979).
81 See Thorpe, 'Comintern "control" ', 661.
82 NMLH, CP/CENT/CONG/04/12, 'Draft constitution of the Communist party of Great Britain', n.d. [but *c.*August 1939].
83 M. Johnstone, 'The CPGB, the Comintern and the war, 1939–1941: filling in the blank spots', *Science and Society*, 61 (1997), 27–45.
84 NMLH, CP/CENT/CIRC/01/03, CPGB circular, 'The Communist Party and the Comintern', 26 May 1943.
85 N. Branson, *History of the Communist Party of Great Britain, 1941–1951* (London, 1997), p. 157.
86 B. Pollitt, 'Voyage around my father', in Cohen (ed.), *Children of the Revolution*, pp.

102–22, at p. 113; Callaghan, *Rajani Palme Dutt*, p. 286; Beckett, *Enemy Within*, p. 228.

87 Crick, *Social Democratic Federation*, p. 291.

88 For more on this, see A. Thorpe, '"The only effective bulwark against reaction and revolution": Labour and the frustration of the extreme left', in A. Thorpe (ed.), *The Failure of Political Extremism in Inter-War Britain* (Exeter, 1989), pp. 11–28; A. Thorpe, 'Arthur Henderson and the British political crisis of 1931', *Historical Journal*, 31 (1988), 117–39, at 123.

89 R. Samuel, 'Staying power: the lost world of British Communism, part two', *New Left Review*, 156 (1986), 63–113, at 110.

5

The Communist International and a 'Trotskyite menace' to the British Communist movement on the eve of World War II

Yevgeny Sergeev

Introduction

The history of the activities of Trotskyite organisations in Britain in the 1930s is one which should be of considerable scholarly interest, especially so when we consider the place of the so-called 'Left Opposition' in the political spectrum of Europe in that period. The Spanish Civil War, the establishment of the popular front government in France, the struggle against fascism and against the war danger in many European countries (including Britain), were all marked by a degree of Trotskyite participation and influence. At the same time, the Comintern in the 1930s fluctuated between the Stalinist purges and the policies of the united and popular fronts. A fierce struggle ensued, with bitter accusations by the Kremlin leadership against Leon Trotsky and his fervent adherents throughout the world.

There are three main reasons for my revisiting the problem of British Trotskyism. First, some new sources have recently become available to academics in the Russian Federal Archives. Second, although some work has been done in the area, there is still a degree of underestimation of the importance of this particular issue among historians.[1] And, finally and more generally, there remain significant differences among scholars as to how to interpret Comintern history in general.[2]

This chapter examines the question of whether there was a real menace to the Comintern from Trotskyite organisations in Britain on the eve of the Second World War. First, I will discuss the composition of Trotskyite groups in Britain in the later 1930s, then review some of the work of these groups. Finally, I will present a brief outline of the measures against Trotskyism insisted upon by Comintern headquarters in its directives to the Communist Party of Great Britain (CPGB).

The sources for this chapter include the records of the clandestine Foreign Department of the Soviet People's Commissariat of Internal Affairs, Narodny

Kommissariat Vnutrennikh Del (NKVD). The head of this structure after the purges of 1937–38 was V. Dekanazov, who served subsequently as Ambassador to Germany until 22 June 1941, and was then one of the closest followers of Lavrentii Beria, being executed after the latter's downfall in 1953. During 1939, Dekanazov submitted two top secret information dispatches, prepared by his agents in Britain, to two of the leading figures in the Executive Committee of the Communist International (ECCI) – the Comintern's General Secretary, Georgii Dimitrov, and one of its leading secretaries, Otto Kuusinen. These reports, are dated 22 April and 21 August 1939, and are now stored in the Russian Centre for the Preservation and Study of Contemporary Historical Documents (the former Central Party Archives) in Moscow. They offer fresh insights into the Soviet authorities' perceptions of Trotskyism in Britain, and of the activities of the CPGB in countering it. The archives contain the typewritten copies of the agents' reports, plus handwritten notes from Dekanazov himself; and they seem to have been forwarded to Stalin, in accordance with the routine procedures of the NKVD. [3]

The inner composition of Trotskyite groups in Britain

It is well known that early in the 1930s there arose groups and parties of the Left Communist Opposition in a number of European countries, as well as in North and South America. Leon Trotsky corresponded with these bodies intensively, met their representatives, gave them his recommendations, and generally persuaded and inspired his followers. In mid-1932, about a dozen members of the CPGB, who disagreed with the party's 'January Resolution' (which marked a return to working through the 'reformist' trade unions and hence a shift away from extreme leftism) left the party and formed the British Section of the Left Opposition, better known as the Balham Group.[4]

Meanwhile, after 1932, when it disaffiliated from the Labour Party, the Independent Labour Party (ILP) increasingly became one of the main centres of Trotskyism in Britain. In 1933, the Paris conference of Trotskyites established the International Bureau for Socialist Unity, with its headquarters in London, and Fenner Brockway, the ILP's secretary, became secretary of the new organisation as well.[5]

Over the years that followed, Trotskyite groups in general, and the British Trotskyites in particular were riven by splits, factional controversies, squabbles, mutual accusations and ideological discord. To try to resolve the situation, the adherents of the Left Communist Opposition, with the support of Trotsky himself, summoned the Constituent Congress of the Fourth International on 3 September 1938. Twenty-one representatives from eleven countries, including Britain, participated.[6] In the confused international situation of 1938–39, this event led to the Soviet secret service paying even greater attention to the Trotskyites' activities. More generally, Moscow's interest in the internal political life of Britain was increasing because, as Dimitrov put it: 'England plays a tremendous role in international politics. Its position decisively affects a number of bourgeois democratic countries and the whole international situation. All the present events emphatically put forward the question of the role of the British working class both on a national and an international scale.'[7] Therefore, one of the things contained in the secret dispatches of NKVD agents is an outline of Trotskyite organisations in Britain in connection with the broader British political situation.

The openly Trotskyite organisations, however, were not the centre of attention so far as Moscow was concerned. Most attention was devoted to the ILP. This body annoyed Moscow most of all. The dispatches indicate some concrete reasons for the Kremlin's ire: 'the ILP holds a definite position in the country'; 'there are lots of its supporters among the workers'; 'it has four MPs'; 'it issues a well-known periodical, *New Leader*'; 'it is getting in touch with overseas parties', such as the Workers' Party of Marxist Unity, Partido Obrero de Unificación Marxista (POUM) in Spain and the Socialist Party of Workers and Peasants in France, and so on. In addition, the ILP was seen as seeking reaffiliation to the Labour Party, and constantly initiated the establishment of different mass public leagues and associations of a pacifist orientation, such as the Socialist Anti-War Front and the Non-Conscription League.

At the same time that they regarded the ILP as the most dangerous – because disguised – Trotskyite organisation, NKVD agents also expressed their indignation at the passivity of the Communist Party's membership in 'revealing and neutralising' the attempts of the Trotskyites to widen their influence among the workers and on the British public at large. In the dispatch of 21 August 1939, NKVD agents complained that 'the daily routine of the CPGB membership, beginning with the Central Committee and ending with the rank and file, contradicts correct slogans and resolutions adopted at Party congresses'. The CPGB 'did not think it necessary to expose the genuine Trotskyist face of the ILP leaders together with their real intentions before the Labourists and to highlight a mortal menace which exists for the Labour party, should the Trotskyites affiliate to it'. So far as we can judge, the possible success of an ILP application for affiliation, compared with the total failure of the Communist Party's attempts to achieve the same end, aroused a sharp negative reaction from Stalin and the Comintern leadership.

Another body of British Trotskyites which fell under the view of the NKVD was the National Council of Labour Colleges (NCLC). This educational and propaganda organisation was supported, according to the dispatches, 'by a definite number of trade unions and Labourists'. The NCLC set up schools, classes, lectures and seminars for workers. Lecturers included Raymond Postgate and George Padmore; they, and others, were identified by the NKVD as Trotskyites. In the opinion of the NKVD agents, the regular appearances of these Trotskyites at public lectures, together with their anti-Soviet tirades in the NCLC periodical *Plebs*, enabled them 'to penetrate more successfully into the ranks of the British working class, to corrupt and stupefy it'. Thus the participation of some

Communist activists, like Marjorie Pollitt and Robin Page Arnot, in the NCLC seemed a genuine blasphemy to the orthodox minds of the Comintern. Comintern officials, in fact, rapidly demanded an immediate termination to such participation, and total censure for CPGB members who failed to heed the prohibition.

Paradoxically, the more outspokenly and avowedly Trotskyite groups were of far less concern to the NKVD. Such bodies included the Marxist Group (headed by C. L. R. James) and the Marxist League (under Harry Wicks and Hugo Dewar), which united late in 1938 as the Revolutionary Socialist League (RSL); D. Harber's Militant Group, which, along with a part of a group headed by Reg Groves, later joined with the RSL to form the United Revolutionary Socialist League; and several lesser bodies headed by people like Padmore and Postgate.

These groups were essentially small, even insignificant, as a threat to the mainstream labour movement or the Communist Party. As such, the amount of concern expressed by the NKVD agents might seem excessive, even paranoid. Of course, such paranoia was a feature of Communist politics in the later 1930s and could be the explanation for the NKVD's interest. However, further analysis shows that the reasons for the Kremlin's deep concern regarding the activities of the Trotskyite movement in Britain lay on a different plane – that of foreign policy.

Phantom and real menaces for the Kremlin from British Trotskyites

Secret agents were concerned with a number of areas of Trotskyite activity in Britain. One area of concern was that 'the Communists were incapable of distinguishing Trotskyist propaganda at meetings and conferences and of opposing it effectively'. Another point which drew slashing criticism from the agents was 'the lack of theoretical development inside the CPGB': here, adverse comment was made on the lukewarm attitude of the party membership towards the propagation and exposition of the notorious catechism of Stalinism, the *History of the Communist Party of the Soviet Union (Short Course)*, which had just been published.

The authors of the dispatches castigated the CPGB leadership for its lack of 'proper activities and vigilance' against Trotskyism. As evidence of the lassitude of the leadership in this area, concrete examples of contacts between Communists and individuals identified as Trotskyites were quoted: such contacts, it was said, took place via the ILP, the NCLC and the RSL, and in particular through collaboration in various suspect organisations such as the Left Book Club and the Non-Conscription League. The dispatch of 21 August was particularly critical in this respect:

> According to information from the CPGB Central Committee, the Trotskyists have recently flooded the national book market with their writings, leaflets and

> brochures. They publish six – seven monthly and one weekly periodicals [*sic*] while at the same time controlling the Labourist paper 'Forward' in Glasgow. By contrast, the Communists confine themselves to issuing a few volumes of Lenin's works and were late to initiate distribution of the *Short Course*.

And, more generally, the dispatches contained a series of reproaches addressed to the CPGB. These might be called standard ones which were made to all European Communist parties, and they were habitually employed by the Comintern to motivate repressions and purges in Communist parties during the period.

However, the above-mentioned 'menaces' to the Communist movement in Great Britain were phantom and sham. There must have been something else behind the blind accusations made against the British Communists. To my mind, this factor was the possible reaction of the CPGB rank and file, and of British public opinion at large, to the foreign policy of the Stalinist leadership of the USSR.This suggestion is proved by a noteworthy phrase in the dispatches to the effect that 'some comrades may feel confused and be at a loss if the capitalist mass media starts to comment in this or that way on the conclusion of a treaty between the Soviet Union and Germany after the Munich betrayal'. Thus, Stalin seems to have made a deliberate choice in favour of Hitler as early as the spring of 1939, that is, half a year before the final act of signing the notorious pact with the Nazi dictator. This, in turn, seems to me to refute the idea that the Nazi–Soviet Pact of August 1939 was agreed to by the Soviet leadership solely because of the breakdown of negotiations with the Western democracies.

The NKVD agents' reports show that, on the eve of the Second World War, Stalin and his clique were doing their best to attain three main aims. First, they intended to take over trade unions in Western Europe (in the case of British unions, the then Comintern leader, Bukharin, had asserted at an ECCI Presidium meeting as long ago as 1927 that in the event of war the unions would 'certainly not support us but may be of some use as ballast around the legs of the government'[8]). Second, they planned to utilise popular front structures as a reserve means of insurance against 'imperialist encirclement'. Finally, they tried to minimise the political damage done to their image as anti-fascist fighters as a result of their secret and later open co-operation with Berlin.

In all this, the battle against Trotskyism in Britain was a key element in the strategy, for the Trotskyite movement was potentially a major obstacle to the brainwashing of the workers and the left in Britain by the Comintern. We can also see that the open public declarations of Communist leaders regarding the need for the unity of anti-fascist forces was just a propagandistic smokescreen, behind which the Soviet government could pursue its aim of an agreement with Germany. It is no accident, therefore, that the most celebrated biographer of Trotsky, Isaac Deutscher, described an episode dating to the very eve of the war. This was when the French Ambassador to Germany, Robert Coulondre, visited Hitler in Berlin. While listening to the latter's seemingly interminable boasting about the advantages gained by Berlin as a result of the Molotov–Ribbentrop Pact, Coulondre remarked gingerly: 'You are thinking of yourself as victor . . . but have you given thought to another possibility – that the victor may be Trotsky?' In reply, Hitler was alleged to have leapt up and shouted that the menace of Trotsky's possible victory 'was one more reason why France and Britain should not go to war against the Third Reich'.[9]

It was for this same reason that the Stalinist leadership was seeking to prevent the Trotskyite opposition from gaining any kind of ideological influence over the population of Great Britain. This eagerness to suppress the extension of such influence clearly explains the Kremlin's open discontent with CPGB passivity regarding the ILP, NCLC, Non-Conscription League and so on, and with its perceivedly lacklustre efforts in spreading Communist periodicals and literature through the country.

In short, the negative reaction of Stalin was not caused by the Trotskyites' tactics of 'entryism' (that is, the attempt to penetrate both Communist and Labour organisations with a view to setting up Trotskyite fractions within them).[10] It stemmed, instead, from the fear that the Trotskyites would use their position to criticise both the internal situation within, and the foreign policy of, the first socialist state.

The Kremlin's remedies

The possibility of a loss of face for Stalin and the Comintern in the international working-class movement in the last months before the Second World War compelled the Soviet leadership to demand that the British Communists stir up a bitter struggle against the followers of Leon Trotsky. The party membership was told to carry out a series of tasks to this end. First, they should carry out an intensive propaganda campaign through District Party Committees (especially in London and Scotland) among workers, youngsters, women and sympathisers in order to expose the Trotskyites' clandestine work. Second, they should pay close attention to the ideological treatment of the non-white ex-colonial population, concentrated in areas such as London, Liverpool, Cardiff and Tyneside. Third, they were told to publish facts and figures relating to the Moscow trials and events in Spain, China and so on, in order to reveal the pernicious anti-Soviet and anti-Comintern nature of the Trotskyites' calls for working-class unity. Fourth, they were ordered to give the utmost priority to the proselytisation of the ideas contained in the *Short Course* and to do their utmost to popularise J. R. Campbell's book, *Soviet Policy and Its Critics* (1939), so as to counter the Trotskyites' arguments. Finally, the British leadership was ordered to execute a thoroughgoing purge of its party membership.

All of these remedies were proposed by the Kremlin for two reasons: to provide a propagandistic cover for Stalin's manoeuvres in international affairs, on the one hand, and to preserve a certain degree of influence over British workers and the broader public through the Comintern channels in Britain, on the other.

Conclusion

The study of newly accessible archival sources – the dispatches of clandestine agents of the NKVD's Foreign Department in Britain – enable me to conclude that Left Communist Opposition activists, whether affiliated to the Fourth International or not, constituted a genuine menace, not to British communism, but to Stalin's plans and manoeuvres to reorientate Soviet policy towards collaboration with Germany. These efforts aimed to enlarge the range of instruments in the hands of the Soviet leadership, which used them ruthlessly to influence public opinion in the Western democracies, while preparing a notorious pact with Germany behind the scenes.

It became, therefore, extremely important for Stalin to remove all the obstacles in the way of imperial domination. Leon Trotsky and his supporters constituted one of these barriers, and not an easy one to overcome. Hence, there was an urgent necessity for Moscow to neutralise the Trotskyites in the citadel of world capitalism, Great Britain.

Finally, it is clear that all the manoeuvring of Comintern leaders at this time was due to the fact, not that they were concerned to build a brilliant Communist future for Britain, but that they were seeking to make adequate preparations for a new round of wars and revolutions.

Notes

1 On the subject of British Trotskyism in the 1930s, see especially B. Reid, *Ultra-Leftism in Britain* (London, 1969); R. Groves, *The Balham Group: How British Trotskyism Began* (London, 1974); R. J. Alexander, *The Lovestoneites and the International Communist Opposition of the 1930s* (London, 1981); J. Callaghan, *British Trotskyism: Theory and Practice* (Oxford, 1984) and *The Far Left in British politics* (Oxford, 1987); S. Bornstein and A. Richardson, *The War and International: A History of the Trotskyite Movement in Britain, 1937–1949* (London, 1986); N. Branson, *History of the Communist Party of Great Britain, 1927–1941* (London, 1985); J. Jupp, *The Radical Left in Britain, 1931–1941* (London, 1982); K. Morgan, *Against Fascism and War: Ruptures and Continuities in British Communist Politics, 1935–1941* (Manchester, 1989); and B. Pimlott, *Labour and the Left in the 1930s* (London, 1977).

2 See K. McDermott and J. Agnew, *The Comintern: A History of International Communism from Lenin to Stalin* (London, 1996).

3 RC 495/74/42; 495/100/1036. Except where stated, all quotations which follow come from these two documents.

4 Groves, *The Balham Group*, pp. 8–9; Branson, *History of the Communist Party of Great Britain*, pp. 240–9.

5 Alexander, *Lovestoneites*, p. 290.
6 D. Volkogonov, *Trotskii: Politicheskii Portryet* (Moscow, 2 vols, 1994), II, p. 226.
7 G. Dimitrov, 'The working class against fascism', *Communist International* (July 1936), 52.
8 A. Vatlin, *Trotskii i Komintern* (Moscow, 1991), p. 15.
9 I. Deutscher, *The Prophet Outcast: Trotsky, 1929–1940* (London, 1963), p. 515.
10 Reid, *Ultra-Leftism in Britain*, p. 17; Callaghan, *British Trotskyism*, p. 163.

6

French communism and the Communist International[1]

Guillaume Bourgeois

It is a truism to say that the very recent and, unfortunately, still partial, opening of the Soviet archives in Russia means the start of a new era for research about French communism. While introducing an international conference about the archives, held in April 1995 at Nanterre University, the great French specialist Annie Kriegel noted: 'We no longer work under menace, with passion or fearing polemics. More than paleontologists looking at few remains, we are now physiologists, capable of examining a whole skeleton.'[2]

The first result of this opening of the archives has been the unification of the various and separate fields in which French academics worked until recently. Up to that time, scholars might have worked on the social nature and roots of French communism; or on the national and international strategies of French Communists; or on the modelling so favoured by political scientists and sociologists. But they rarely integrated the three approaches. However, this threefold division is now obsolete and, given the existing strength and richness of the historiography of French communism, it can be seen that the impact of these voluminous new documents is very important.

Before saying a little more about the debate which started in France concerning these questions, which was first historiographical, but which rapidly became political as well (because in France everything rapidly becomes political), this chapter presents a brief summary of various episodes in the history of the French Communist Party, Parti Communiste Français (PCF) about which we now know a little more; it gives some examples of research concerning the party apparatus which seem particularly revealing; and, finally, it demonstrates how the large field of international relations, mixed with intelligence and political affairs, generated a quite explosive potion, which forces a reassessment of many other areas of historical knowledge, some of them quite distant from Communist Party history. Looking back at the history of the PCF, and its relations with the Communist International, presents France with some problems with its own image or, more precisely, with the image of its past.

From the origins of the PCF to the eve of World War II

In their book about the PCF[3] Professors Courtois and Lazar emphasised that only a limited amount of research has been done so far in the Russian archives about the party's very early years, and so we know only a little more than we did about the party's birth. However, an important source for this subject is now accessible, namely Marcel Cachin's notebooks. Marcel Cachin was the founding father of the PCF, and the link between the old French socialist tradition, represented by leaders like Jules Guesde, and the new Bolshevik project.

The Marcel Cachin notebooks show very precisely, day by day, how the two French Socialist delegates who visited Moscow in order to negotiate about a possible affiliation to the Comintern – Louis-Oscar Frossard and himself – moved from a position of open hostility to Bolshevism to a complete state of fascination. This demonstrates how correct Annie Kriegel was in stressing the importance of the short historical conjuncture of Soviet victories in 1920 in the rallying of French Socialists to communism. But it also underlines the extent to which belief, in an almost religious sense, played a decisive role. As the great trade-unionist, Alphonse Merrheim, who was present in Zimmerwald, commented on this rallying:

> When people ask me my impression about Lenin, I am used to saying: 'He is a Guesdist, but a hundred times more sectarian than the Guesdists all together, which makes quite a lot. At the same time, Lenin is ten times more intelligent than Guesde, and he has got this other and strong advantage of having travelled everywhere throughout the world and that he speaks or understands nearly every language.'

A second area to explore is the degree of political autonomy that parties had, as opposed to the idea of complete submission to Stalin through the Communist International. I have tried to find several contradictory examples of this for the French case, in the 1930s.

Let us take the year 1934. The decisive turn ordering an end to the aggressive politics of the PCF towards social democracy came from Moscow on 25 June in the shape of a menacing telegram to the French Politburo. But there is a contradictory example from later in the same year when the General Secretary of the PCF, Maurice Thorez, seems to have played a decisive role in the elaboration of the concept of the popular front policy. After he was severely criticised by Togliatti for his initiatives in this direction, Thorez defended his views in front of the Executive Committee of the Communist International (ECCI) on 9 December 1934. Manuilsky, on hearing Thorez's arguments, said that he was very interested in his statement and then reported to Stalin. This was the beginning of a big shift, which culminated in the formal adoption of the popular front strategy at the Comintern's Seventh World Congress in the summer of 1935.

This is very interesting, because it turns pre-existing views of these events on their head. In the first case, the PCF was supposed to have accepted a united front under pressure from below within France, especially after the Paris riots of 6 February and the quest for unity marked by the coming together of Socialist and Communist demonstrators on 12 February. In the second, it has been assumed that the popular front was the general response of Comintern headquarters to the growing co-operation of Communists in various countries with the Socialists. Yet in fact it was a response to a specifically French initiative. At the same time, circumstances had to be right for someone like Thorez to have such a significant impact. It would be misleading to assume that he could do as he liked when he liked. On two occasions, on 21 May 1936 and again on 20 March 1938, explicit telegrams from Moscow show the Comintern clearly forbidding the PCF from participating in Leon Blum's popular front government; and this order was obeyed.

If this suggests submission on the part of the French party, then we have to ask by what kind of means Stalin could control the PCF so well. The answer is that he could do so through a certain type of organisation, unique in the whole of world history – the Comintern. A few biographical cases from the French experience will help to underline the extent and nature of Comintern control.

The Communist International and the French cadres question

Louis Torcatis is well known in French Catalunya: there are dozens of streets bearing his name in towns as well as villages. Why? Because during the 1930s he was, at the same time, a famous rugby player, an excellent schoolmaster, and a notorious Communist; and, eventually, he became a Resistance hero after being shot by the Vichy police in May 1944.

We already knew that Torcatis had strong disagreements with the Communist Party in 1938 and that he left shortly afterwards. But we never had full details of how the whole thing happened, or of the nature of his conflict with the Central Committee. When in Moscow, I had the opportunity to consult various files covering the PCF. It transpires that the details were all there, from 1938 onwards, and included a few words about the non-proletarian behaviour of Torcatis. Each member of the local leadership had been awarded a mark, and Torcatis's was the worst! In a report he wrote in the Soviet capital sometime later, the leading Comintern official André Marty, who was born in Perpignan, explained the correctness of the decision to purge such elements, the main reason being that Torcatis's brother-in-law was a Trotskyist.

The case of Torcatis shows quite clearly the extent of Comintern's control over Communist parties. Even a question of secondary importance such as this finds an answer in Moscow: autobiographies of party activists, for example Torcatis', submitted to the Comintern Cadre Commission were used as evidence to purge party members. Going through the organisational committee papers in Moscow, I even noticed that, on some occasions, there was enough material to write the main outline of a social history of small towns, or even of big villages, in France during the period between the two world wars.

Another example, once again in Southern France, comes from Toulouse, where a deep crisis shook the party leadership in 1929. The city's leading Communist was expelled for being an 'opportunist'. The roots of this 'opportunism' were, for sixty-five years, a source of great interest for historians. Did it happen within a frame of deep regionalism? Was this man considered a contemptuous intellectual (he was himself a professor of history)? Did it start with a political rivalry, opposing aggressive fractions in various cells of the region?

There were elements to confirm each of the theories. All the witnesses who were questioned by us, as historians, had something to say about it, and we believed them. But in fact, the very few who knew the truth took it with them to the grave. And this truth is, in fact, very surprising. The so-called affair was contrived, and the expulsion, believed by thousands of local militants to be genuine, was in fact a protective smokescreen. The recently disclosed French police papers show that an investigation was being undertaken concerning military espionage in Toulouse, and the Soviet archives show that this investigation could easily have implicated this leader, since he was deeply involved.

Detailed knowledge based on newly available archives, in short, suggests a very different picture of the affair from that initially painted. Accordingly, the biography of this leader looks quite different in this light. In this case, and that of Torcatis, two of numberless Communist deceptions are exposed by new documents.

What is true for such major characters in the micro-history of the PCF could also be said about some of the leading characters of French communism. Jacques Duclos, for instance, who was for nearly forty-five years second in command of the PCF under three different general secretaries, is a good case in point. We now know a lot more about the career of Duclos thanks to Professor Mikhaïl Narinsky, deputy director of the Institute of World History in Moscow. After Duclos's involvment, in 1932, in an incredible affair (once again related to military espionage), he left France for two years in order to clean the slate and gain a fresh start. He was at the same time viewed unfavourably in Moscow for having transgressed the basic conspiratorial rules. This led him to a very paradoxical situation. Then, because he did not comply fully with the general turn of Comintern policy in September 1939 regarding the definition of the war as imperialist in nature (for reasons very different from those of the British party General Secretary, Harry Pollitt), Duclos was sentenced to death by Stalin. However, this sentence was never carried out and he survived as a leading figure in the PCF until the 1960s.

This 'punishment syndrome' appears to have been a core element of regular relations between the Comintern and its national sections. I will focus on two further cases to show it more precisely: those of Jean Jérôme and Jacques Denis, both of whom were very important in the PCF after the Second World War.

Jean Jérôme was for nearly forty years the manager of the PCF's finances, and was well known for being an *éminence grise* for the General Secretary. Jacques Denis was the head of the International Department of the French party. The situation with regard to these two men was enigmatic. Although their names were put down in black and white in official Communist reports, they were known by their pseudonyms, based on the conspiratorial pattern of the double Christian name. They had no public human face: not a single press agency had a picture of them until the mid-1980s.

The Russian archives tell us a lot more about these two men and give the key to their dramatic rise inside the organisation to the highest levels of the PCF. From the autobiography Jean Jérôme wrote for the Comintern Cadres Commission in 1938, we know that in the mid-1930s he had been in charge of the penetration of the oppositional fraction of the PCF, Que Faire?, which had amongst its leaders a member of the French Politburo, André Ferrat. Another leader of this fraction was a Polish Comintern delegate in France, who was a member of the French Central Committee and who had been in charge the propaganda commission. Through this Comintern delegate, known as 'Constant' (his real name being George Kagan), Que faire? was in touch with the Polish party leadership and its members inside the Moscow apparatus, including people like George Purmann.

Jean Jérôme, whose real name was Michael Feintuch and who was a stateless Jewish Pole, explains in his autobiography how underground work allowed the Comintern apparatus to unmask this large 'Trotskyist' provocation in various countries, and especially in Poland. What he did not yet know was that the denunciation he made became one of the reasons for the complete liquidation of the Polish Communist Party and for the extermination of its cadres in 1938–39.

The case of Jacques Denis may be a similar example of this strange connection between causes (spilling blood) and effects (advancement which led to the top of the national apparatus). I say 'it may' because we know from a People's Commisariat of Internal Affairs, Narodny Komissariat Vnutrennikh Del (NKVD) file disclosed by Arkadi Vaksberg[4] that amongst the three people who seem to have killed Willi Münzenberg in France, just after the defeat of the French army in 1940, was a man called Spiewak, the true name of Jacques Denis. It just so happens that Jacques Denis was in South West France, in a political refugee camp, at the same time as Münzenberg. It also happens that Jacques Denis escaped from the camp, as did Münzenberg and, later on, went to the Lyons area. The body of Willi Münzenberg was found hanged in a forest close by.

One could write a crime novel about the cases of Jérôme and Denis. As historians, we cannot say very much more than what our sources show. But, on the other hand, the documentary reality accessible to historians of communism tells a story which goes far beyond what was, until a very recent date, seen as fiction, if not pure anti-Communist rubbish. However, a further question remains open, and that is: how far did the kinds of issue raised above affect, not just a small world of 'believers', but also French political life more broadly? This is a particularly important question for France, where a native version of communism has been a major political phenomenon for more than seventy years. The final part of this chapter addresses this issue briefly.

Communism as a plot?

Why was Communism in France so important, for so long? A large number of very interesting works have been written on this subject, in particular on the chances for its success, especially under the strong influence of André Siegfried's pioneering work on French politics. Such questions as religious traditions, economic factors and even the singularity of France's geography have been taken into account. If these theses were stimulating in their time, how can they cope with the following suggestion: the PCF happened to survive thanks to a deep relation with the major trade-union federation, the General Confederation of Workers, Confédération Générale du Travail (CGT). The party gained control of the CGT through a pure Bolshevik process of infiltration of a mass movement, and maintained its dominance thanks to a rigid bureaucratism devoid of any concessions to democracy.[5] This basic reality shaped the party's personality as mainly '*ouvriériste*', which could be translated as 'working-class fundamentalist'.[6]

This very singular character of communism, which is specific to the PCF, can disconcert many commentators of contemporary history who see Communist policies as being like the proceedings of any other party. Can the opening of the Russian archives promote in any way the role of some poeple as agents and the general vision of the history of communism as a plot? An important dimension must be taken into account here: that of national sensibility. A well-known French historian, specialising in Victorian Britain, very recently asserted that researchers on the Comintern Archive were in danger of being likened to commentators on *The Protocols of the Elders of Zion*. This might be understandable if the author was a Stalinist hardliner, but he is indeed a very good Catholic! Why such over-sensitivity? Probably because, as I said earlier, France finds it more and more difficult to look back to that part of its past which is related to the Soviet Union.

Looking at the field of international relations between the two countries, the first significant works produced using the Soviet foreign affairs archives show precisely how the leaders of the main French political party between the two wars, the middle-class *Parti radical*, were the target of a very strong disinformation campaign in favour of Franco-Soviet co-operation and, later, for a Franco-Soviet alliance. Evidence in support of this view includes, for example, visits by Edouard Herriot, chairman of the *Parti radical*, to the Ukraine in 1933, where he saw a number of entirely artificial, but prosperous-looking villages, while the whole country was, in reality, starving. And the offensive towards the *Parti radical* was not only propagandistic in form: it seems more and more likely that Soviet intelligence agents did penetrate the entourage of several Radical personalities and especially that of Pierre Cot, for a time Minister of Aviation.[7] In November 1940, when Pierre Cot was in New York, escaping from the German occupation of France, he contacted Earl Browder, General Secretary of the American Communist Party, and declared that he was 'ready to perform any kind of mission'. We know this from the telegram Browder sent to Pavel Fitine, chief of the external services of NKVD. By the time he died in the 1970s, Cot was well known to be a fellow-traveller of the PCF. Can he be regarded, therefore, as having been an agent, as Professor Courtois believes? Or was he just a hopeless boasting fool as Professor Berstein, specialist on the history of the *Parti radical*, asserts? The strong controversy on this issue has included polemical papers in the main French historical journals.

There is an extra emotional element involved here: Pierre Cot's major assistant in the late 1930s was Jean Moulin, who later became a chief of the French Resistance under Charles de Gaulle and died in 1943 after having been arrested by Gestapo officer Klaus Barbie. A 1945 Committee of State Security, Komitet Gosudarstvennoi Bezopasnosti (KGB) interrogation report quotes Jean Moulin as being one of the informers of Soviet intelligence's chief resident, Henri Robinson, during the late 1930s.[8] Many said this document was a forgery, but in fact it is not. A purely external criticism of the Russian sources is of very little value. The Russian archives have been open since 1991, and so no plot was involved in their being made available to researchers. It is true that not all the papers may be present; some, doubtless, have been removed or discarded, as is the case with all collections of primary sources. But the papers which remain in the archive are one hundred per cent authentic. Who could have falsified a hundred million pages? And with what aim?

Submission, autonomy, agents, conspiracy – these are some of the key-words which will be used and discussed for a long time in relation to international communism between the wars. Quite surprisingly, the last of these – conspiracy – now seems to be that which is the most difficult for researchers to accept. It may be a sign of how our eyes and mentalities can deform or re-order the essential nature of a former project. After all, from Babeuf's *Conjuration des Egaux* to the last variation of Leninist parties, communism was never designed by its inventors as something other than a plot. Looking through the Comintern archives, we can see that the major part of Communist activity was described as one of so-called 'conspiratorial work'. One can still believe that the conspiracy was that of proletarians from all countries. But one can also say that it was mainly led by one man, head of one socialist state, in one country.

This plurality of opinions may be a result of the multiplicity of sources which it is now our job to synthesise. Ending her last article in *Communisme*, Annie Kriegel made this significant remark:

> I recently had the opportunity to compare police files kept in Lille and the dossiers of the Comintern about the same events, surrounding the spring 1931 textile workers strike in northern France. One could believe, after a first reading, that these materials are not describing the same thing. But indeed they are: what the first knows and says, the second does not know and does not say. And *vice versa*. For the historian, it is a determining established fact.

Notes

1 When the Third Medlicott Symposium took place in July 1995, we already knew that Annie Kriegel was fighting against her dreadful illness. She died five weeks after the Exeter conference. Having been one of her closest collaborators over the last fifteen years, I feel indeed more cruelly the disappearance of this great mind. I affectionately dedicate this chapter to her memory.

2 University of Paris X-Nanterre, 10–11 April 1995, international conference organised by the Centre d'Études d'Histoire et de Sociologie du Communisme, *Les archives du système soviétique, premières approches*. Annie Kriegel's paper was called 'Au seuil d'un nouveau cycle d'étude du phénomène communiste'.

3 S. Courtois and M. Lazar, *Histoire du parti communiste français* (Paris, 1995).

4 A.Vaksberg, *Hotel Lux* (Paris, 1993).

5 On 19 June 1946, Benoît Frachon, main Communist leader of the CGT, explained to Mikhaïl Suslov the internal balance of the union leadership: 'On the one hand, there are six Communists as members of the CGT's Bureau, and, on the other hand, six Socialists. The thirteenth member is Pierre Lebrun, officially a *radical-socialiste*, in fact a member of the PCF.' The conversation between the actors was published in *Communisme*, 35–7 (1994), 31–42.

6 A. Kriegel and G. Bourgeois, *Les Communistes français dans leur premier demi-siècle (1920–1970)* (Paris, 1985), especially chapter 6.

7 T. Wolton, *Le Grand Recrutement* (Paris, 1993).

8 G. Bourgeois, 'Vie et mort de Henri Robinson', *Communisme*, 40–1 (1995), 85–116.

7

The Comintern and the Italian Communist Party in light of new documents, 1921–40

Aldo Agosti

Among the non-ruling Communist parties, the Italian Communist Party, Partito Comunista Italiano (PCI) has been for over forty years the strongest in terms of members, number of voters and political influence, as well as the most lively intellectually and the richest in international initiative. The anomaly represented by the development of the PCI after 1944 has caused rivers of ink to flow from the pens of sociologists and political scientists, foreign as well as Italian. However, even its history in the period (1921–43), during which it was, as the other Communist parties, a section of the Comintern, shows some very interesting specific features, which have for many years attracted the attention of historians and given rise to a profusion of studies, often of great scholarly value. This was allowed, among other factors, by the fact that a particularly wide and varied series of sources became available at a relatively early stage.

The problem of sources is of special importance for a party like the PCI, which was forced into clandestinity after 1926. Although the fact that the party's decision-making centres were mobile has inevitably meant that records have become dispersed in public and private archives, the particularly liberal Italian legislation regarding the use of state archives has allowed the filling of many blanks. Moreover, it must be stressed that the PCI was the only Communist Party to open its archives (for the period up to the Second World War) to scholars of all countries and of all schools of thought, and this happened as early as the beginning of the 1960s.

The purchase by the Gramsci Institute in Rome of much of the PCI archives kept in Moscow has allowed the history of the Communist International's relations with its Italian section to be studied in depth, and on the basis of a much richer documentation than that generally available for other Communist parties. Paolo Spriano, author of the monumental five-volume *Storia del PCI*, the first volume of which was published in 1967, was even criticised for having focused too exclusively on this aspect, and for having left the party's deep roots in Italian society in the background.[1] In reality, although it is true that the social history of the PCI is only partly explored,[2] the opening of the Comintern archives has thrown light, were it still needed, on how strongly the party depended on the Communist International. This first and still incomplete disclosure has made available a further mass of documents, many of remarkable interest, through which this relation can be seen in a new light.

The birth of the PCI, sanctioned by the Leghorn Congress of January 1921, was characterised by a paradox, which was bound to leave its mark on the relations between the Comintern and its Italian section. Indeed, the PCI was the last of the Communist parties founded following a plan corresponding to the strategic hypothesis of the 'approaching revolution'; that is, the last to be founded separating the vanguard of the organised proletariat from the morass of reformism and 'centrism', so as to guide the proletariat towards installing a Soviet regime. At the same time, it was the Italian situation, marked earlier than in other countries by an impetuous revival of reactionary violence against the workers' movement, which showed that hypothesis to be an anachronism.

The PCI took its first steps during a political era already dominated by the spread of fascism, and characterised by crisis and a decline in all proletarian organisations, without exceptions. Although the entire party executive (with the only partial exception of Antonio Gramsci) showed itself at the beginning to be even less astute than the Comintern strategists in their evaluation of fascism, this close interdependence between the birth and establishment of the Communist movement, on the one hand, and the affirmation of the Fascist dictatorship, on the other, left an indelible mark in the genetic inheritance of Italian Communists: the problem of analysing fascism and of the fight against it dominated their horizons without interruption and conditioned their relations with the Communist International in a determinant way.

The rigid and doctrinaire ideology of Amado Bordiga, who was nominated Party Secretary at Leghorn, was in a sense functional to the necessarily defensive phase, amounting to a state of siege, in which the PCI developed. It was well suited to the intransigent mood of a party which had developed in sharp contrast to socialist tradition, and which tended to boast of discipline and organisational efficiency as its marks of distinction. On the other hand, a party of this type experienced serious difficulty in applying the new Comintern directives, which prescribed the conquest of a majority of the working class as the premise of revolutionary action and the united front with the Socialists as preferred tactics. Although the PCI payed lip-service to the discipline of the Communist International, it did not in fact make any serious attempt to apply the tactics of the united front in Italy.

The contrast with the Communist International became more serious when, after a further Socialist split in October 1922, the Moscow Executive brought up the problem of a reunification with the PSI; only a small 'right-wing' minority led by Angelo Tasca and Antonio Graziadei was in favour of this prospect. In early 1923, the party leadership resigned amid controversy, just before the Fascists, who had now been in power for a few months, began their severe repression of the PCI. This was a difficult moment for the new party: with many of its leaders in gaol and with dramatic organisational problems, it had to defend its line against the Communist International, which apparently intended to push the policy of fusion with the Socialists, relying on Tasca's 'right-wing' minority.

The Comintern leadership fought a fierce political battle against Bordiga right from the beginning of 1922; but it did everything in its power not to burn its bridges with a leader for whom it felt great admiration. In June 1923, immediately after the end of the third Plenum of the Executive Committee of the Communist International (ECCI) which had imposed a new composition of the PCI's Political Bureau, including in it Tasca's minority, Comintern President Grigorii Zinoviev wrote an extremely significant letter to Bordiga, who had been arrested in February and was still in prison. After hinting at the possibility of the Vatican's agreement to an exchange of prisoners with the Russian bishop, Ceplitsk (the same means which were to be attempted to free Gramsci in 1928), he continued:

> And now to the Italian questions. You will have heard from the comrades of the decisions taken here. I am very afraid you will not agree with these decisions. But, dear friend, here, too, we are counting on your help. The Comintern situation in this question is certainly not an easy one. We all love you (you personally and your closest friends) as true fighters, as comrades close to us in spirit. It is not easy to reproach you. But you have made some serious errors . . . If you, comrade Bordiga, from prison oppose our decisions, you will put us in a desperate situation. It is not possible to enter into polemic with a friend when he is in prison, but nor is it possible to keep quiet. You must understand this and help us. [3]

It is well known that Bordiga did not go back on his position, and his relations with the Communist International deteriorated even further. It was Gramsci who first realised that the situation was no longer tenable. He was aware that the party could survive only if it remained loyal to the Comintern, and he began to try to build a new leadership which would be able to head off the 'right-wing' group, but which would also be able to keep its distance from Bordiga – which now appeared an inevitable step. Within a few months, Gramsci was able to bring some important party leaders over to his position. Immediately after the elections in April 1924, in which the Communists scored a relatively encouraging result, the crisis caused by the murder of the Socialist leader Giacomo Matteotti left room for the PCI to take the political initiative, which it did with more flexibility and a better sense of manoeuvre than in the past. Though results in terms of collaboration with other components of the anti-Fascist opposition were not immediate, the PCI's organisational success was remarkable: membership had dropped below 9,000 in 1923, but numbers increased to reach 18,000 in 1924 and 25,000 in 1925. The character of the party underwent a profound transformation. The application of the Comintern directives concerning Bolshevisation was grafted onto the renewal process which the leadership under Gramsci had already begun, proving possible to translate it into forms which strengthened and extended the party's roots in society.

The increase in membership mostly comprised new recruits, although some of it came from militants who had returned to the fight after the severe repression of 1923. The nature of the party changed, and this struck a serious blow to Bordiga's position. The shift to the left of the Fifth Comintern Congress (June–July 1924), which seemed to mirror some of Bordiga's positions (for example the slogan 'worker's government' was abandoned), did not question the relationship of trust which had grown up between the ECCI and the party leadership under Gramsci. The constitution of the Bordiga left into a fraction sharpened the tones of the internal struggle, which went on with no holds barred and with administrative methods only barely within the statutes of the party. The Comintern supported Gramsci without hesitation. The highest peak of tension with Bordiga was reached at the sixth ECCI Plenum (February–March 1926), when he spoke in plenary session, probably the last true opposition speech to be heard in an assembly of the Communist International. Then, Bordiga had a serious altercation with Stalin: when the former asked if Stalin thought that the development of the Russian situation was linked with the one of world revolution, the latter found no reply to this unheard-of sacrilege other than to say 'May God forgive you for having asked such a question'.[4] The idea of the Italian leader returning to the ranks of Comintern did not completely die even then, however; initially it was hoped to use Bordiga in the international apparatus, and this idea was finally abandoned only some months later, more because of the PCI's reluctance than because of Moscow's opposition.

On the other hand, not even the new leadership under Gramsci had a trouble-free relationship with the Communist International, whose support had been determinant in its taking control of the PCI in spring 1924. There were serious differences of opinion concerning the tactics to be adopted after the assassination of Matteotti, and in particular over the Communist dissociation from the boycott of Parliament which the other anti-Fascist opposition parties had begun. Later, as is well known and documented, in a letter to the Soviet Party in October 1926, signed by Gramsci, the party's Political Bureau expressed its perplexity concerning the will of the majority to crush the unified opposition. Palmiro Togliatti, who at that time represented the party in Moscow, made a more realistic evaluation of the inevitability of that conflict, and had no doubt about the need for the Italian party to side with the majority. So, following Bukharin's advice, he decided not to deliver the letter to its addressee. This caused a rupture in his friendly political relationship with Gramsci, but could not avoid a shadow of diffidence toward Italian Communists.

Nor were political questions the only ones subject to dispute. In the extremely difficult conditions in which the PCI was operating, in a precarious semi-legal state, the Comintern's logistical and organisational help became increasingly determinant. In April 1924 Moscow's decision to cut the budget drastically clearly caused some perturbation among Italian Communists, so much so that Umberto Terracini, the PCI representative at ECCI, felt himself obliged to deny the report of 'Christophe' (Jules Humbert-Droz) to the effect that the budget reduction had had a negative influence on the morale of the leaders. To this end, he quoted a passage from a recent letter from Italy, in which Togliatti said:

> We fully understand the political value of the reduction of funding which Comintern has decided. This reduction, which is the same for all European Parties, is a way of pushing these Parties to live in closer relations with the masses, not only as an expression of ideas, but also as organisational machinery . . . The political work will not be less but more . . . if from day to day we have to resolve the problem of not losing contact with the masses in order to continue to exist and to operate.[5]

In reality, despite these praiseworthy intentions, the PCI increasingly depended on help from the Comintern. The Special Laws of November 1926 forced it into total clandestinity, and it could scarcely count any longer on any form of self-financing in Italy. It is true that it still had considerable grass-roots supports among the masses of emigrant workers, especially in France, who provided the party with solidarity, money, logistical support, accommodation addresses and, above all, cadres ready to go back to Italy, even illegally. But all this would not have been anywhere near enough without the financial support of the Communist International.

For a party operating in these conditions, the sense of belonging to the 'world army of the revolution' was a very strong factor of identity and cohesion, and also a source of faith in the future. The 'cast-iron link' with the Communist International and with the Soviet Union became another part of the Italian Communists'genetic inheritance.

Of the increasing number of small clandestine parties gravitating around the Communist International, the Italian party kept its special status for some time, and continued to enjoy extra attention. To some extent, this was because it was the section of that country where an unheard of form of reaction was being put to the test. But also the role Togliatti earned for himself in the inner circle of the Comintern executive, during the period that Bukharin was its head, must be evaluated in all its importance. For some years his position was one of unstable equilibrium between the central organs of the Communist International and his post as head of the PCI, and he undoubtedly helped to ensure that Moscow did not lose sight of his party's problems.

On the political plane the long-term disagreement between the Communist International and the PCI seemed at last to be resolved. The Lyon PCI Congress (January 1926) had laid down a line which emphasised the 'popular' character of the Italian revolution, and did not rule out the party fighting for intermediate democratic ends, like a Constituent Assembly. This line was further clarified by the group around Togliatti, who became party Secretary after

Gramsci was imprisoned. Though it met a certain opposition from the Youth Federation (Luigi Longo, Pietro Secchia), it was substantially in agreement with the more flexible attitude which the Comintern had held under Bukharin's leadership.

After the Sixth Comintern Congress (July–September 1928), Bukharin fell into disgrace, and Togliatti unequivocally distanced himself from the former's position of the early months of 1929. However, he did not succeed in stopping the entire PCI's line, as it had developed from 1926 onwards, from being subjected to heavy criticism, which called into question the leadership itself. The clash with Manuilsky in the Italian Commission of the tenth Plenum was eloquent: 'Ercoli' (Togliatti's Comintern pesudonym) did not hide his dissent, in particular concerning the opinion which likened Italian social democracy to social fascism; but he declared that the will of the Comintern was law. He had clearly decided to bow down to a political line which, at least initially, he accepted with reluctance, choosing as ground for his activities one where he could at least partly 'control' the effects of the Comintern line, and moderate in part its application.

From that moment onwards, the PCI's relations with the Communist International again became very tense – but they were no longer relations of political confrontation and discussion, though within a definite uncontested hierarchy, as they had continued to be until 1928. The PCI line was continually questioned not for its strategic foundations, but for how it was applied, and it underwent heavy, even ungenerous attacks, sometimes from both sides at once. After having criticised the Italian party from the left and having put strong pressure on it to make an about-turn in its policies in 1929, the Comintern intervened the following year to put a brake on them and to correct their effects. The most frequent accusation against the PCI became that of 'Carbonarism', that is the tendency to conspiratorial sectarianism and estrangement from the real problems of the masses. But it only had to go a fraction too far in correcting that defect – for instance seconding trade unions' demands without adding the right political watch-words – for the PCI leadership to be accused of 'yielding opportunistically', and of 'economistic deviation'. From the correspondence between the party representatives in Moscow and the Foreign Centre in Paris, and even more clearly from the minutes of the Italian commissions of the Comintern's Roman Secretariat, it can be seen that there was a situation of permanent uneasiness, aggravated by a difficulty in communication which probably was not only due to objective conditions. From this standpoint, the exchange between Togliatti and B. A. Vassiliev of the Comintern Secretariat during a meeting of the Roman Secretariat in August 1932, is particularly significant:

> ERCOLI: Allow me to say a couple of words about our relations with the C.I. We are not satisfied with our relations with the C.I. [VASSILIEV: Nor are we]. It is probably mainly our fault, of course, I mean, up to now it hasn't been our fault, but I am sure you can help it to become our fault.[6]

The ironic intention was clear in Ercoli's words, since he went on to accuse the Comintern leadership of having systematically ignored the documentation which the PCI sent to Moscow, and of not having ever replied to the requests for advice which the Italians had made, apart from severely criticising all their weaknesses in organisational or conspiratorial work. Vassiliev's reply ('I sent word at least three times that if the comrades of the PCI felt it was necessary to come before the Plenum to discuss vital questions, they should say so') revealed an attitude of detached condescension, rather like the relationship between a powerful landlord and his vassal in an outlying province. Ercoli was clearly not satisfied with this, and instead, in the name of the Political Bureau, proposed that the Comintern send to the PCI 'a representative or an instructor who could follow our work step by step'. He added:

> We believe that in this way you could give us more help, an effective help to resolve our problems. When we come here to discuss things, once a year, Vassiliev says each time that he knows nothing on the PCI, he complains about the lack of information, he criticizes and attacks everything. But afterwards, nothing changes. We believe that our links with the CI need to be improved.[7]

It must be stressed that since 1924–26, when Jules Humbert-Droz had, with some regularity, followed the activity of the 'Centrale' (Head Office) of the PCI, there had not been a Comintern representative permanently detached to its direction: clearly, at first it was thought that Togliatti, thanks to his dual function as party leader and member of the inner circle of the Comintern (the Presidium, the Executive and even the Secretariat) could ensure an adequate link. But, at least from 1929 onwards, the trust which the inner circle of Comintern leadership felt towards 'comrade Ercoli' was sadly diminished. We do not know why the decision to send a permanent Comintern representative to Paris was not taken, although, as we have seen, the Italian section reached the point of asking for it; probably the PCI was not considered important enough at this stage to be assigned a 'tutor'.

Things changed with Togliatti's return to Moscow at the end of August 1934, with the task of preparing the report to the Seventh World Congress on the fight against the risk of war. Ercoli became again a high-ranking Comintern officer and, shortly after the Congress, he was nominated a member of the Secretariat, and became the deputy (*Stellvertreter*) of Georgi Dimitrov. But this did not lead to any great improvement in relations between the Comintern and its Italian section: indeed, in some ways, they became more complicated. Togliatti's dual role created problems. As Giorgio Amendola, a young cadre working in Paris in those years has written,

> Togliatti did not fail to tell Ruggero Grieco [who acted as party leader in his absence] his opinion on the developments of the situation, to suggest political positions and to advise action to be taken. But when Grieco made the effort to put into practice the advice he received, Togliatti did not fail to criticise the ways in which

> his suggestions had been taken and translated into political action. Togliatti's criticism, often harsh and sometimes even contemptuous, deeply disturbed Grieco, who was already worried, and made him insecure in his work. What is more, that criticism could not but fuel perplexity and discussions among the inner circle, which undermined the authority of the comrade in charge of the party's activity.

As proof that the trouble lay in the foundations, and that the mechanism inherent in the structure of relationships between centre and outlying parts obeyed a cast-iron and unchangeable rationale, Ercoli himself became one of the severest critics of his party. He frequently criticised the way in which the PCI applied the united front line with the Socialists in 1934, and then again in 1935, and he called the Foreign Centre back to a stricter observance of the 'doctrine of the main enemy' and of the defence of the USSR.

The most controversial question was that of action within the mass fascist organisations. After the first undoubted successes, at least in terms of proselytising, the *svolta* (turn-about) implemented in 1930 had undergone a serious crisis, which coincided with the phase in which fascism completed and perfected its organisation as a reactionary mass regime. Although it did not question the general strategic prospects on which the *svolta* was based, the PCI did carefully analyse the new situation in the country. The most mature expression of this analysis were the Lectures on Fascism (Lezioni sul fascismo) given by Togliatti in Moscow in January 1935 to the Italian Communist cadres. The PCI was becoming aware of the need to penetrate the mass organisations of fascism, to exploit every legal space to undermine from within the consensus on which the regime was built. As for the Comintern, its position oscillated between forcing the Italian party in this direction and then putting on an abrupt brake. In any case, the PCI was accused of delays and shortcomings of every sort. It is interesting to quote Manuilsky's conclusion at the proceedings of the Italian Commission which met in December 1935:

> I would like here to raise a question about which you must reflect very carefully, because it may at first sight seem bizarre: the question of the united front. At this time, the problem of the united front in Italy must not be raised in terms of the united front with the Socialists, nor with the Anarchists: let comrade Gallo [Longo] do that abroad. I would like you to say that it is Gallo who is head of the monopolists of the united front abroad. The problem of the united front in Italy is that of the united front with the fascists.[9]

The ironic reference to Longo is significant. In the second half of 1935, the Foreign Centre in Paris, in particular with Grieco – and Longo – showed a certain optimism over the possibility of united action among the emigrant parties. They seemed to be moving towards openly tackling the problem of 'succession' to fascism, hypothesising the formation of a popular strongly anti-fascist government after its fall. In Moscow, on the other hand, Togliatti, loyal to Manuilsky's indications, was reluctant to mortgage the future with commitments of too limiting a nature to the forces of emigration ('the Paris types'), and stressed instead a slow erosion of the regime through the withdrawal of the 'fascist masses', recommending 'giving an anti-capitalist rather than an anti-fascist character to our agitation'.[10]

This divergence of views was linked to the fact that relations between PCI and the Comintern again increased in importance for Moscow because of the evolution of the international situation. War broke out in Ethiopia, and the PCI was no longer just a small persecuted party, but gradually took on the function of an important pawn on the international chess-board from the standpoint of the overall strategy of the Comintern in the fight for peace and also from that of Soviet foreign policy, whose aim was to isolate the 'main enemy', Hitler's Germany. The intensive correspondence with the Foreign Centre in Paris between the end 1935 and the early months of 1936 shows an Ercoli taking great care to call his party back to the responsibilities which derived from this position.

Subjected to this pressure, the PCI began to show signs of disorientation. In August 1936, it launched a manifesto, 'To save Italy, Reconciliation of the Italian People', which was both an attempt to come into line with the insistent requests from Moscow and from Togliatti, tending to put the questions of social agitation before those of a politico-institutional nature, and also at the same time a somewhat ungainly imitation of the patriotic tones which had characterised the French Communists' election campaign. The manifesto went as far as to make the demands of the Fascist programme of 1919 its own, which caused considerable concern among Communist militants, above all those who were in prison or in exile, and reservations among the other anti-Fascist parties.

Togliatti, who had created the basic political line of the manifesto, if not its actual wording, shortly afterwards distanced himself from it: the watchword of 'reconciliation' was no longer opportune at a moment where civil war in Spain induced Soviet foreign policy to back anti-fascism. The episode reveals the difficulties in relations between Comintern and its Italian section. These difficulties were not always smoothed over, and, indeed, were sometimes aggravated by the fact that one of the highest officers of the Secretariat was the recognised leader of the PCI.

With Togliatti's departure for Spain, the role of the party's representative at the ECCI was taken over by trusted cadres, who had, however, far less political authority. And, with the victory of fascism in Ethiopia, Italy was again less important for the Comintern. It was not simply by chance that meetings of Italian Commissions became much less frequent, and that Manuilsky's Secretariat was entrusted with the Commissions' responsibilities. In any case, it seems fairly clear that the PCI was still looked on by Moscow with a mixture of arrogance and suspicion: arrogance, because the results of its attempts to undermine the Fascist regime from within were very modest, and, indeed, its organised presence in Italy tended to lessen rather than to grow; suspicion, because an emigrant, clandestine party appeared especially permeable to the attacks of 'agents provocateurs'. As is known, in the Comintern of the second half of the 1930s, the distinction between fascist provocation and Trotskyist provocation was increasingly narrow, tending to disappear entirely.

The PCI accepted the verdicts of the sensational public trials against ex-Bolshevik leaders without reserve, and Togliatti excelled himself by making an implacable denunciation of the 'crimes of the Trotskyist bandits'. A large number of the PCI's rank-and-file militants were killed during the Stalinist Great Terror. The accusations aimed at the PCI of insufficient vigilance against Trotskyism were intensified from 1937 onwards, and caused mistrust and disarray in the leadership in exile. In varying forms, accusations, often veiled, were levelled at many top-level cadres: from Grieco to Dozza, from Montagnana to Sereni. Although Togliatti had probably some initial responsibility for creating this atmosphere, he subsequently intervened to put a brake on the effects of the resulting crisis. On a short mission to Paris in 1938 he apparently succeeded in calming the waters, and helped to assuage the harsh polemics, in some cases of a personal nature, between the exiled party leaders, but until the beginning of the war, and even afterwards, the PCI had no authoritative leadership, and was thus particularly subject to Comintern pressure.

Having returned to Moscow from Spain in May 1939, Ercoli was increasingly busy with the Italian party, partly because he was seriously worried by its situation, partly because, as will be shown, his role in the Comintern was probably under discussion. Writing to Dimitrov in July 1939, Ercoli stressed 'his deep desire for an "Italianisation" of his next job'.[11] Clearly, there were numerous reasons why Togliatti should again make the full weight of his function as 'supervisor' of the PCI leadership felt: despite the good results recorded in the field of unity of action with the émigré anti-Fascist forces, and particularly with the Italian Socialists, the PCI had not gained any ground in the estimation of the Communist International leadership – at the Eighteenth Congress of the Soviet Communist Party, in March 1939, Manuilsky had again stressed its 'great weakness'. Casually overturning the accusations levelled at it in 1938, he now accused it of masking its 'opportunistic passiveness' behind empty defeatist watchwords.

In late July 1939 the Comintern sent Togliatti to Paris: the decision was probably taken for much more important reasons than the need to put order back into the PCI. With the prospect of a war, which by now was considered imminent, he had to take on the leadership of a 'reserve' command centre of the Comintern outside the USSR. We now know that on 4 September, when the war had just started, Dimitrov, clearly still unaware that 'Alfredo' – as Togliatti was in the main called after his mission in Spain – had meanwhile been arrested, sent to Paris the following telegram:

> It is necessary to send Alfredo, Clément [Eugen Fried] and Luis [Vittoria Codovilla] to a neutral country to organise there the commercial centre of our firm. This centre must be immediately linked with the central office of our firm, establish ties

> with its branches, develop the greatest commercial activity, so to prevent our competitors from profiting by the current situation against the interests of our trade. [12]

Whatever the reason was, when it was announced that the Nazi–Soviet pact of non-aggression had been signed, Togliatti was in Paris. As far as it is known, neither his nor the PCI's attitude differed from the line followed by the Comintern: the pact was presented as a clever Soviet move thwarting the plans laid by Western democracies to divert Hitler's expansion against the USSR, and at the same time it was considered not incompatible with an improvement of the USSR's relations with Britain and France. Nor was the denunciation of Hitler's fascism as the main factor causing the war attenuated in this phase. Apparently, two days after the pact, Togliatti said to Celeste Negarville, a young cadre in the Foreign Centre, that, if war broke out, the French party should 'take a similar attitude to that of Clemenceau before he entered the government during the 1914–1918 War: harsh criticism of any weakness shown by the government in conducting the war'.[13]

However, on 1 September 1939, 'Alfredo' was arrested by the French police, and spent six months in prison, being freed in circumstances which seem to imply a decisive intervention of the Soviet Secret Services in French justice.[14] Thus, the PCI found itself having to cope with the tempest without its leader. The Comintern archives throw some rays of light on the very harsh polemic which engaged the leadership in the early days of September, after the Comintern had obliged the Communist parties to take a rigorously equidistant position from the two 'imperialist' blocks. A report of December 1939, probably drawn up by 'Tuti' (Rigoletto Martini), the PCI representative in Moscow, reveals that the strongest reservations about the new direction were those of 'Nicoletti' (Giuseppe Di Vittorio):

> Nicoletti, who like all of us at the end of August had approved the pact without reservation, and enthusiastically welcomed the Soviet advance into Byelorussia and Western Ukraine, by the end of September maintained that, after having obtained these great results, it would have been in the USSR's interests to make a sudden about-turn in its policies and attack Germany. At bottom, Nicoletti thought that the pact of non aggression could not be anything else, on the USSR's part, than a short-term manoeuvre, and that soon the USSR would have returned to the policy of an Anglo-Franco-Soviet pact and to the 'democratic' countries' fight against fascism. From all this he reached the conclusion that we should not abandon our old political positions on this question: popular front, joint action.[15]

On the contrary, according to the same report, 'Garlandi' (Ruggero Grieco) supported the position – defined as being wrong and equally dangerous – that held that the main enemy was Anglo-French imperialism: a position which was all the more criticisable since it was judged to be clearly related to the party's position of 1936–37 on national reconciliation. Dozza, Sereni and Ciufoli, too, apparently made a series of observations which went 'in the direction of weakening the fight against our own imperialism'. The report concludes with a reference to the positions of 'certain old comrades' now deported to Ventotene, who can clearly be identified as Umberto Terracini and Camilla Ravera:

> These comrades do not come out into the open but, as in the past, they insist on knowing whether this new about-turn has caused internal crises in the various Communist parties. They insist on having news about the situation in the Soviet party. . . . These old comrades' position worries us greatly, because each month a certain number of deportees are freed from this island, go back home and are considered as Communist leaders. We will do what we can to send the most recent material and with the material a letter giving these comrades a serious political warning. Some of them have been out of the party's active political life for a dozen years, but their diffident and semi-trotskyist attitude towards the CI and above all towards the Soviet party cannot be tolerated for long.[15]

In reality, Terracini and Ravera kept their reservations, and the Communist Collective of Ventotene internees, after a long polemic, in January 1943 went so far as to decree their expulsion, a measure which Togliatti, from Moscow, judged inopportune, for the repercussions it might have had on the militants' morale, among whom, especially, Terracini was very popular. On 10 February 1943, from Ufa (to where the Comintern headquarters had been moved), while expressing an acid judgement on Ravera, he wrote to Vincenzo Bianco, the party representative in Moscow:

> Terracini is a force. He lacks a consistent ideological basis, but he is an excellent agitator and a careful organiser, full of initiative. Moreover, all our cadres who have spent some time in prison, i.e. some thousands, know him as a leader and are in some way attached to him. If possible, we have to prevent Terracini from leaving prison in the future as the leader of an opposition group fighting the party. [14]

Actually, Togliatti himself seems to have got into some difficulties. After his return from Spain, for some reason, his position in the ECCI Secretariat had already been weakened, and it did not improve much after his arrest in Paris, although Dimitrov did all that he could to ensure his liberation. But somebody clearly was trying to undermine his authority. In September 1940 the Cadres Section sent to the ECCI a report on his activity which stressed all the most controversial moments of his career – among other things, Ercoli was accused of having boycotted all attempts at obtaining Gramsci's liberation through some kind of exchange.[18] According to the memoirs of his former secretary, Nina Bocenina, some time in 1941 Togliatti was even arrested for one day, and his office searched by the People's Commisariat of Internal Affairs, Narodny Komissariat Vnutrennich Del (NKVD).[19]

Despite these misadventures, Ercoli did not stop being busy with the PCI, which became the main object of his daily work. In August 1940, two months after his return to the USSR, he presented a report to the Presidium accusing the leadership which had been in control of the party in Paris during the early months of the war of 'having completely failed in its tasks'. A subsequent Presidium resolution, dated 10 August, hard-heartedly listed all the errors committed: the party had taken up positions 'with enormous delay' on the problems of the war, with a manifesto containing 'serious political errors' (the use of the expression 'Hitler's aggression against Poland' was considered such); it had given watchwords not suited to the concrete situation in Italy ('transformation of the imperialist war into a civil war'); it had dropped all links with Italy and with the working class, for a long time neglecting the problem of creating a clandestine organisation in the country; it had lowered the level of vigilance, adapting itself 'to the conditions of life of a democratic country like France'. 'All this', the resolution concluded, 'has caused the beginning of a process of decomposition of the leading group, and, finally, its capitualation and failure before the practical tasks of the struggle against imperialist war.'[20]

Thus, the decision to dissolve the Central Committee, already taken two years earlier, was confirmed; shortly before, a coded telegram signed by Togliatti had informed Paris that also 'the old members of the PCI Directorate, with the exception of Gallo [Longo], were freed from their obligations'.[21] The responsibility of leading the PCI was entrusted to Togliatti only, aided by two minor officers. The varying fortunes of the PCI in its relations with Moscow had thus reached perhaps their lowest point, and few could have foreseen that in only five years that political group of exiles, with feeble and precarious links in the country, would become the strongest Communist Party in the West.

Notes

1 P. Spriano, *Storia del Partito comunista italiano*, 5 vols (Turin, 1967–75)
2 See, for example, the stimulating essay by P. Corsini in G. F. Porta, *Avversi al regime: Una famiglia comunista negli anni del fascismo* (Rome, 1992); G. De Luna, *Donne in oggetto. L'antifascismo nella società italiana 1922–1939* (Turin, 1995).
3 RC 495/19/55.
4 'Verbale della riunione del 22 febbraio 1926 della delegazione italiana al Comitato esecutivo dell'Internazionale comunista con Stalin', *Annali della Fondazione Giangiacomo Feltrinelli* 8 (1966), 269.
5 RC 495/19/55.
6 RC 495/32/115.
7 *Ibid.*
8 G.Amendola, *Storia del Partito comunista italiano 1921–1943* (Rome, 1978), pp. 255–256.
9 RC 495/32/182.
10 See the letters of Togliatti to PCI Secretariat, to Grieco and to Dozza of October and November 1935, now in P. Togliatti, *Opere*, vol. 4, 1 (Rome, 1979), pp. 23–35.
11 RC 495/74/251
12 RC 495/184/4.
13 See the whole page of Negarville's diary, quoted by P. Spriano, *Storia del Partito comunista italiano*, vol. 3 (Turin, 1970), p. 315.
14 This can be inferred from Togliatti's personal file, in RC 495/221/1, which confirms

what was already ventilated in G. Cerreti, *Con Togliatti e con Thorez. Quarant'anni di lotte politiche* (Milan, 1973). For further details, see A. Agosti, *Togliatti* (Turin, 1996), pp. 252–7.

15 RC 495/10a/186 'Rapport du PCI italien', 9 December 1939.

16 *Ibid.*

17 RC 527/1.

18 The report is in the personal file, in RC 495/221/1. The accusation is said to come from Gramsci's wife and sister-in-law, but there is no evidence whatsoever that it is true. As far as we know, Togliatti did his best in 1928 and again later to press the Comintern for Gramsci's liberation. See P. Spriano, *Gramsci in carcere e il Partito* (Rome, 1977), and also *L'ultima ricerca di Paolo Spriano: Documenti, L'Unità* (Rome, 1988).

19 Sergio Bertelli (ed.), *La segretaria di Togliatti: Memorie di Nina Bocenina*, (Florence, 1993), pp. 20–3.

20 RC 495/2/275.

21 RC 495/184/8.

8

The testing-ground of world revolution: Germany in the 1920s

Aleksandr Vatlin

For the founders of the Communist International, Germany was more than just the cradle of the theory of proletarian revolution: it was the most favourable environment for the translation of that theory into practice. Advanced industry and a powerful working-class movement, combined with an incomplete transformation to bourgeois-democratic forms, meant that it appeared to be promising territory for a leap forward to socialism. This was a position accepted in one way or another by most Socialists from the start of the twentieth century. The outbreak of war in 1914 led to a temporary sense of national unity in Germany, relegating the class contradictions of German society to the background. However, the failure of the push for swift victory and the full militarisation of the nation's economy brought the idea of a revolutionary solution of the crisis back on to the agenda. Such a revolution seemed almost inevitable after the Bolsheviks had seized power in Russia. The Bolsheviks made no secret of their ambitions to extend their victory to the West, and primarily to Germany, which was only separated from the Russian expanses by a narrow front line.

The impact of the Russian Revolution alone was not enough, however: a wave of meetings of solidarity with Soviet Russia, strikes in January 1918, and occasional fraternisations between German and Russian troops on the Eastern Front did not set off a revolutionary outbreak in Germany. The Bolsheviks under Lenin had to reconcile themselves to this fact, and even went as far as signing the 'shameful' Treaty of Brest-Litovsk with the Kaiser's government to end the war between the two countries. This treaty actually reinforced the strategic and domestic positions of the existing German regime.

The Brest Treaty was the first to lay bare the conflict between the ideological postulates and the foreign policy interests of the newly born power, a conflict which was to be part of Soviet politics throughout the years of its history. That conflict was always especially marked in relation to Germany.

In the early years of the Soviet regime the primacy of concrete national interests over world revolutionary utopias was far from evident. The Bolshevik dictatorship in Russia, considered by its creators to be the first spark of a world conflagration, made no sense without the transfer of revolution to the advanced countries of Europe. Lenin stressed time and again that, following a socialist revolution in the West, Russia would be forced to move back to the periphery of world progress. It is doubtful, however, whether the Bolsheviks would have stepped down and assumed the role simply of the Communist masters of the world's outlying peripheries. They could only see themselves in the thick of events, in the leadership of a proletarian revolution, although a revolution whose headquarters were likely to shift, sooner or later, from Moscow to Berlin.

The military defeat and collapse of the German empire brought a new tide of expectations in the Soviet Communist leadership. These expectations soon gave way to disappointment, but only in so far, as Lenin put it, as 'Germany was evidently living through February rather than October'. The Bolsheviks' appeal of January 1919 for the immediate creation of a Third International – purged of opportunism – was nothing more than a covert abandonment of the Marxist postulate which asserted the inevitability of a world proletarian revolution as a natural historical process.

The concept of the Third International was fundamentally different from those of its two predecessors: it pushed to the forefront a subjective factor and the use of a lever of social transformations. In other words, the emphasis was shifted from the thesis of revolution as a midwife of history to the thesis of the party as a midwife of revolution. It was evidently a transfer of Russian ideological extremism originating from the 'Narodnaya Volya' (Free People) movement, rather than a mere mechanical transfer of the Russian experience into the 'world framework'. The label 'Made in Russia' would stick to the Comintern throughout its activity, providing a good opportunity for its opponents to seek the 'Kremlin's designs' across the world. The Comintern's basic postulate asserted that the 'old world' was doomed. It was this proposition that came to be part and parcel of the Communist Party of the Soviet Union (CPSU), and which remained so up to Gorbachev's time.

But let us return to the time when Moscow's hand in the political affairs of European states was quite evident. The diplomatic blockade of Soviet Russia and the ongoing Russian Civil War meant that extending the revolution had to take second place, for a time, to survival. However, the clandestine methods learnt by revolutionaries in Tsarist Russia, now backed by the resources of state power, stood the Bolsheviks in good stead. Whereas at the start of the century the first copies of Lenin's *Iskra* were secretly delivered from Germany to Russia, in less than twenty years Comintern leaflets undertook the journey in the opposite direction, and could now do so under the cover of being diplomatic mail.

No one could match Karl Radek in the application of Bolshevik methods on the international scene. Even in a German prison, as Carr pointed out, he could exert a significant influence.[1] In late 1919 the Western European Bureau

(WEB) of the Comintern was formed in Berlin. This was the first attempt to create a centre to control forthcoming combat operations right on the spot. The Communists delegated to the Bureau had to overcome many difficulties to get from Russia to the West; and, when they arrived, they were greatly disappointed by the weakness of the leftist factions in the Western European working-class movements. They were, on the whole, generals without an army – functionaries without parties, who had failed to get through the tough fabric of trade unions and social democracy and reach the broad proletariat.

The speedy creation of a broad popular base required a sound financial policy – a fact of which the Bolshevik leaders were well aware. There is no doubt that Comintern channels were used to pump significant funds to various countries. In August 1991, the Comintern's archives were opened to researchers other than CPSU functionaries; and this made it feasible to look closely into the Communist International's book-keeping operations. From this study emerged the importance of 'Comrade Thomas' (Yakov Reich), who was based in Berlin, as a conduit of funds to the German revolutionary movement.[2]

Thomas reported in summer 1920, at the height of the Russo-Polish War, that the main task of the WEB and the German Communist Party, Kommunistische Partei Deutschlands (KPD) was to disrupt arms supplies from the Allied nations to Poland. However, the coin had a reverse side, too: German Communists were preparing to welcome the Red Army on their soil, were actively learning Russian, and were even designing welcoming banners. It was also an open secret that the Bolshevik leaders in the summer of 1920 were not thinking about the restoration of the Russian frontiers of 1913, but were keen to encourage a revolution in Germany and do away with the 'sanitary cordon' of the newly formed Polish state. The plans for internationalising the civil war were frustrated, ultimately, by 'non-class' nationalism, which refuted the Marxist view that proletarians had no fatherland. Comintern theoreticians simply failed to understand this phenomenon, and thirteen years later were watching again helplessly as Nazism grew rapidly in Germany.

The end of the civil war in Russia led to a change in the Comintern's methods. In its first year, the Communist International had been essentially a circle of enthusiasts disseminating, in Lenin's words, the ideas of 'world Bolshevism': now it became a significant instrument controlling the activity of like-minded people abroad. The growth of its staff tackling the problems of world revolution was increasingly paralleled by the diminution of hopes that the latter would be forthcoming. The increasingly obvious gap between the slogans and realities was made even clearer by the forced retreats of the Bolsheviks in domestic policy, most notably the abandonment of war communism and the introduction of the New Economic Policy (NEP).

Conscious of this gap between promise and performance, Lenin tried to put revolution back at the centre of the stage. Opening the Tenth Congress of the CPSU in March 1921, he stated that 'the Communist International . . . has become part and parcel of the working-class movement in all the major advanced countries of Europe – more than that, it has become the chief factor of international politics'.[3] This obviously called for concrete confirmation from the leaders of the Comintern, and an attempt to provide it was not slow in coming. The Comintern emissaries, Bela Kun and A. Guralsky, who had been in Germany since February 1921, urged the KPD to launch an armed revolt, without concealing that its main aim was to help the Russian Revolution. The KPD leader, Paul Levi, opposed such a step, and was expelled from the party as a result. Despite such opposition, actions were started in the Mansfeld region, but were rapidly and bloodily suppressed by Reichswehr troops and the police.

The defeat of March 1921 was the first of Comintern's 'German lessons'. The first inferences to be taken from this were noteworthy, for they would be typical for subsequent 'lessons'. First and foremost, the German leadership was accused of indecisiveness and right-wing opportunist hesitations; this was followed by a radical reshuffle of the leadership, while the Comintern leadership in Moscow remained totally above criticism. For all that, the latter had to borrow some of the conclusions reached by their defeated opponents. The emergence at the Third Comintern Congress (June–July 1921) of a slogan 'Closer to the Masses' was inseparable from the March defeat and criticism of Levi and Klara Zetkin, which was approved by Lenin and Trotsky.

The beginning of an extensive struggle for a popular base in the European working-class movement signified the sharpening of the conflict with the social democrats. The tactics of a united front, as proposed by Radek, aimed at the ultimate dumping of the social democrats, and the acute arguments at the first Executive Committee of the Communist International (ECCI) Plenum in February 1922 boiled down to only one thing – whether co-operation with other workers' parties would be for merely propagandist purposes, or whether it would be a real political alliance.

In the short but instructive history of the single working-class front, both its German roots and its German dominating idea were quite natural. The unstable democratic foundations of the Weimar Republic provided an objective community of interests among forces anxious to protect it from rightist attacks. The failure of the Kapp Putsch of March 1920 had already shown the potential power of a united front action. Although the Communists remained committed to the view that the Weimar democracy could only be a precursor of the dictatorship of the proletariat, this could not really be an obstacle when it was deemed necessary to throw disagreements with the social democrats overboard for a while. A decade later, when a more dangerous political gambler was striving for power in Germany, the united front slogan was no longer accepted by the workers as a guide to action; apart from the amassed potential of mutual hatred in the working-class movement, a certain part was also played in this respect by the complete dependency of the KPD on Moscow 'directives'. This was a dependency which began to take shape in the early years of the Comintern's history.

Symbolically, the conference of the three Internationals which aimed to find ways of overcoming the split was held in the Reichstag building in Berlin

(2–5 April 1922). But the only chance to reunite the working-class movement between the wars was lost because the conference focused its attention on the situation in the Soviet Union, rather than on the movement's own burning problems.[4] With the European situation now stabilising after the post-war crisis, the Fourth Comintern Congress (November–December 1922) saw a clear mood of frustration and pessimism.

Therefore, Comintern strategists now paid greater attention to any manifestations of instability and social conflicts, and in this respect Germany remained the most interesting target. The burden of reparations and the traditions of authoritarian government added to hurt national feelings and government reshuffles, and all this, taken together, provided a favourable environment for political upheaval. The occupation of the Ruhr area by French and Belgian troops at the start of 1923 was interpreted in Moscow as an objectively revolutionary situation. The leaders of the CPSU and the Comintern considered that, after long months of expectation, the time of decision had come, and the KPD fully shared these sentiments. Any strike by German workers was treated in the Soviet press as a precursor of the forthcoming revolution. Radek was sent to Germany to analyse the situation on the spot.

The recently opened Comintern archives, as well as the presidential archives in the Kremlin (which became available to scholars for a short time in the early 1990s), make it possible to assess the real scale of the Communist International's efforts to lay the groundwork for a Russian-style 'October' in Germany in 1923. Going through these documents, one cannot but be surprised at how far these Berlin-bound directives were from the real state of affairs, and at how great were the efforts to change this state of affairs into a 'world revolution'. The planned publication, by a group of Russian and German scholars, of documents on a German 'October' will put an end to all arguments about the correlation of centralised and democratic principles in the Communists' activities in those years. The plans for a German revolution were discussed and adopted in the Soviet Politburo, while the German Communists were assigned the role of providing information and fulfilling the decisions adopted. Comintern acted as the driving gear between Moscow and Berlin.

The Cuno government resigned on 12 August 1923. On hearing of this while on holiday in the Caucasus, Comintern President Grigorii Zinoviev gave the signal to start preparations 'in the near future for an uprising and a decisive battle'. All Russian Politburo members were urgently recalled from their holidays, and at their meeting on 23 August adopted a definite plan for preparing a revolution in Germany. These included Russian military mobilisation, economic aid to German workers, and the revision of the Comintern's policy in Germany. An ad hoc Politburo commission was set up to exercise permanent control over developments in that country.

The formation of commissions and the holding of conferences on a German revolution which as yet only existed in the minds of Communist functionaries reflected how far the process of bureaucratic deterioration of Communist structures had gone. Resolutions which were passed lagged behind German developments. When a five-party conference to discuss the situation finally convened in Moscow after a month's delay, it became bogged down in minor points and utopian details. It was decided, for example, that the Ruhr coal mines should be destroyed by a proletarian government in order to stop them falling into French hands, despite Radek's more sober observation that 'the workers will drive us away from their mines with sticks when we come to explode them'.

The Russian Politburo followed events in Germany and the five-party conference with anxiety. A great deal was at stake, and a good chance could not be missed yet again. 'The destiny of the Comintern is inseparable from the destiny of a German revolution', stated Zinoviev on 1 October, and three days later he told the conferees of the Politburo's directives to start an armed uprising under the leadership of the KPD on 9 November. The German Communists were promised financial and military support, Radek and Georgi Pyatakov were sent to Berlin, and the group of Politburo representatives going to Berlin included (in great secrecy) the Soviet Ambassador to Germany, Nikolai Krestinsky.

But the German revolution did not materialise. At the last moment, the putsch was called off, although too late to prevent the Communists in Hamburg from starting a rising which ended only in bloodshed and defeat. The infant, the birth of which had been expected at any minute, remained only in its parents' dreams. Historians used to link the Bolsheviks' disappointment at the aborted revolution with the sharpening of the inner-party struggle at the top of the CPSU. Anticipating recriminations against himself, and having enlisted the support of Stalin and Kamenev, Zinoviev launched an ideological offensive with regard to the 'lessons of the German October' at the moment when Trotsky's close associates, Radek and Pyatakov, were still in Berlin.

Less attention was paid by historians to the negative impact exerted by the debates on the lessons of the German October, and on the methods practised by the Comintern at large. The German leaders, Heinrich Brandler and August Thalheimer, became scapegoats due to the efforts of Zinoviev. They were blamed for exceedingly optimistic assessments of the KPD's readiness for action, and accused of cowardice at the crucial moment. So any manifestation of political realism running counter to Moscow's political directives was labelled as rightist opportunism.

Brandler himself, when describing the rebellion of the Hamburg Communists in a letter to Zetkin on 27 October 1923, gave a realistic picture of developments, writing that 'the workers sympathised with the fighters but stood aloof, their hands in their pockets. It seems to us that this is indicative of the fact that things in the whole of Germany would have been somewhat the same as they were in Hamburg' had a nationwide insurrection been launched. Such arguments were not to the liking of the CPSU leaders who, as Zetkin wrote to her associates on 6 November, had to face the 'exposure of illusions'.

The cadre reshuffle in the KPD, undertaken by Zinoviev to avoid personal responsibility, removed from the party leadership those figures who had not broken completely with the views of a united working-class movement on the eve of the First World War. The bridges were being burnt, and Comintern was withdrawing into itself, nourishing the sparse ranks of its supporters with leftist phrases, with hopes for the forthcoming upheavals of the capitalist system and financial support from Moscow. With things as they were, submission to directives from above became absolute, while the complex political realities of Weimar were interpreted to fit the ready-made answers of a world revolution – it was all 'Bolshevisation', according to Heinz Neumann, one of those who emerged to replace the ousted right-wing leaders of the KPD.

After 1923 the German question remained high on the Comintern's agenda, but now in terms of improving matters in the KPD rather than focusing on Germany's prospects at large. Using ultra-left rhetoric, the party's new leaders, Ruth Fischer and Arkady Maslow, tried to loosen organisational dependence on Moscow. However, the Comintern immediately struck back. Dmitri Manuilsky, who had taken over from Radek as the Comintern's German expert, stayed in Germany for almost a year, tailoring a 'proletarian nucleus' in the KPD under Ernst Thälmann. After the party's Frankfurt Congress (April 1924), Fischer was only narrowly saved from the fate of her predecessors, Brandler and Thalheimer – exile to the 'honour' of one of the back-street offices of the Comintern in Moscow.

Germany's stabilisation, and the weakening of the KPD, meant that the attention of the Comintern's leaders now turned towards the East in seeking revolutionary opportunities, with the Chinese revolution of 1924–27 pushing Europe into the background. Moscow urged the Communist parties to demonstrate solidarity with colonial nations, while being hesitant to adjust these parties' tactics to new conditions of political struggle in their own countries. Thus, Nikolai Bukharin, who in 1926 became, effectively, the leader of the Comintern, criticised as too audacious the proposals of KPD leaders like Zetkin and Ernst Meyer for workers' control over production and the nationalisation of the key branches of German industry. Denouncing these proposals at the seventh ECCI Plenum (November–December 1926), Bukharin could only put forward meaningless arguments, such as 'our slogan is nationalisation in the conditions of the proletarian dictatorship', that 'the slogan of workers' control must be advanced in the context of the socialisation of industry', and so on.

In trying to cut themselves off from the new realities of social and economic life by the use of verbal radicalism, and by treating attempts to adapt to such realities as a variety of opportunism, the Comintern's leaders were, in effect, telling the Communist parties to keep quiet. The parties should wait for a more favourable political situation, and do what the Comintern told them in the meantime. The KPD and Lenin's former associate, Willi Münzenberg, for example, did a lot of successful anti-colonial work in this period. Having lost all its colonies after the First World War, Germany became the ideal location for the headquarters of the League Against Imperialism.

The situation within the KPD remained negative in the mid-1920s. Any ideological innovations, or simple attempts to call things by their proper names, aroused sharp opposition from left-wing elements who saw the influence of social-reformism all around the KPD. Moreover, the leading nucleus under Thälmann remembered the experiences of their predecessors, and preferred to deviate a hundred steps to the left rather than half a step to the right. The leaders of the CPSU and the Comintern made frequent cadre reshuffles in the KPD, trying to determine the optimal mix between 'leftists' and 'rightists' in the KPD Central Committee. The results, though, were instability within the party itself, and frequent accusations by the KPD's political opponents that it was under the control of Moscow, lacking in national character, and so on.

One of the reasons behind the Comintern's retreat in Germany in the second half of the 1920s was an inadequate analysis of Germany's geopolitical potential. Lenin's theory of imperialism laid emphasis on the quantitative indicators of aggressiveness (military production, armies, colonies), which clearly could not place post-Versailles Germany among the world's principal predators. In 1926, Bukharin had to limit himself to declaring that 'German imperialism, if viewed statistically, is an absolutely specific imperialism: from the point of view of dynamics it is on the way towards genuine imperialism.' Similar ideas were expounded in the book, *The Revival of German Imperialism* (1928), by Richard Sorge, at that time a Comintern official and later a legendary Soviet intelligence agent.

Another reason for Germany's relegation to the background in the strategic ideas of the Bukharin Comintern lay in the country's obvious pro-Western foreign policy, which suggested that the Germans were now permanently reconciled with the Treaty of Versailles. This suited neither Soviet foreign policy nor Comintern tactics, both of which had a stake in confrontation between Germany and the West – suffice it to recall the 1922 Soviet–German Treaty of Rapallo and the Communists' collaboration with 'National Bolsheviks' during the occupation of the Ruhr (when Radek had made favourable gestures towards the political right and claimed that the KPD was the true upholder of Germany's national cause). As Bukharin reminisced at the seventh ECCI Plenum, in 1923 it had seemed that the following situation could have emerged:

> An alliance – a military alliance – between bourgeois Germany and Soviet Russia, a common struggle against French imperialism. After the victory, there could be naturally a turning point in strategy and a common struggle of armed and organised forces of the Russian and German proletariat against the German bourgeoisie.[5]

Though at the end of the 1920s the Comintern did not venture to speculate on a 'national liberation war of Germany against Versailles', the pro-Western orientation of the Weimar Republic's governments in that period created an illusion that the danger of revenge was a settled issue, an illusion that played a fatal role on the eve of the Second World War. This is, however, a rare case: such illusions were equally shared by politicians in Moscow, Paris and London.

New tactics were proposed by the European Communist parties in the autumn of 1927 and adopted by the ninth ECCI Plenum (February 1928). Unlike the united front, this new 'class against class' strategy was not tailored using the German yardstick. Class against class put an end to co-operation with other workers' parties and demanded a decisive break with traditions of bourgeois parliamentarism. It was primarily the British and French parties that had to reorganise themselves: their problems, indeed, were (unlike the Germans') individual items on the agenda of the ninth Plenum. For the KPD, the Comintern's leftward turn meant another campaign against right-wing opportunism. This simply meant greater disunity within the party. The tension that resulted led to confusion among supporters of the party and joy for their opponents. The labels imported from the USSR did not help, either: any Communist Party was sure to have both 'Trotskyites' and 'Zinovievites', and later on 'Bukharinites', too.

The tension of inner-party clashes in the second half of the 1920s undermined the democratic potential of the working-class movement: there was also a significant degradation of the Communist elite, for no manifestations of political and ideological independence could be tolerated. The consequences were not hard to see. Vissarion Lominadze, a spokesman for the CPSU and the Comintern at the Eleventh Congress of the KPD (Essen, March 1927), sent a report to Moscow on 17 March 1927 about Thälmann's oratory. The report leaves no doubt that Moscow knew the real state of affairs, but had just reconciled itself to a lesser evil:

> He was reading the congress report for more than three hours, in one and the same tone, often looking into his papers, piling up one heavy phrase with 'academic words' onto another, made a few annoying errors (corrected afterwards in the shorthand report), often repeated himself, etc. The audience soon got tired and were not listening with the same attention from the middle of the report onwards.[6]

Paradoxically, the KPD got its second wind in the late 1920s, but as a result, not of Moscow's directives, but of a panic on the New York stock exchange. The economic crisis undermined Weimar and its fragile social balance, and thrust radical forces back to the forefront. An apocalyptic view of the state of capitalism, plus the narrow frameworks of Comintern doctrine, prevented the KPD from drafting an anti-crisis programme that could unite broad sections of the population. In these crisis years, the KPD received votes only from those who did not see any alternative within the framework of 'the chaos of the market and private property'.

A broader popular base was gained by the KPD's anti-Fascist programme, for many had been attracted by the Communists' decisiveness and readiness for extra-parliamentary action. Albeit inconsistently, the KPD adhered to 'counterrevolutionary' ideas, defending the Weimar Republic and opposing the Nazis. It would not be correct, perhaps, to say that a split in the working-class movement predetermined the victory of Nazism: the logic of Germany's political evolution in those years relegated Marxist guidelines to the background. On the other hand, even in that extraordinary period the Comintern did not dare to revise its strategy, returning at best to the ideas and slogans of a united front – suffice it to recall Thälmann's candidature for the German presidency in the 1932 election.

Frequently, history runs counter to the theories of scholars and politicians, despite their confidence that they have succeeded in unravelling its laws. In the Comintern's strategy, Germany was assigned the role of a proving ground of a world revolution started by the Russian Revolution in 1917. In reality it became an area of quite different social experiments. Present-day historians in Germany are engaged in heated arguments about how close, and even interdependent, the personalities of Stalin and Hitler, and the ideologies of Bolshevism and National Socialism, were. They overlook, however, the main lesson of these twentieth-century tragedies: despite all the national, state and ideological borders, humanity is united and can learn from its mistakes. Having once been down with the malady of Communist dictatorship, humanity has acquired a lasting immunity to it.

The efforts of the Comintern were doomed to failure, and not only in Germany, from the moment it became clear that the Bolsheviks' victory in Russia was unlikely to be reversed in a short spell of time. At the same time, German history has given an appalling lesson of Nazism, showing that the bacterium of totalitarianism may have numerous variations and every time emerge in a new ideological attire. Perhaps this lesson is more topical today for Russia, which cautiously, and on its own, continues to get rid of the dominance of social utopias.

Notes

1 E. H. Carr, *The Bolshevik Revolution, 1917–1923*, III (London, 1953), p. 134.

2 A. Vatlin and M. Wehner, '"Genosse Thomas" und die Geheimtätigkeit Komintern in Deutschland, 1919–1925', *Internationale wissenschaftliche Korrespondenz zur Geschichte der deutschen Arbeiterbewegung*, 29: 1 (1993), 1–19.

3 V. I. Lenin, *Collected Works*, XXXII (Moscow, 1965), p. 167.

4 A. Vatlin, *Komintern: Pyervii Dyesyat Lyet* (Moscow, 1993), pp. 27–55.

5 RC 495/165/350, minutes of 7th ECCI Plenum, 1926.

6 RC 495/19/75, Lominadze to Comintern, 17 March 1927.

9

From Lenin's comrades in arms to 'Dutch donkeys': the Communist Party in the Netherlands and the Comintern in the 1920s

Gerrit Voerman

The Communist Party in the Netherlands, Communistische Partij in Nederland (CPN) did not originate in the wake of the Russian Revolution – as nearly all the other Communist parties did – but was founded in 1909, albeit under another name. This independent Dutch Marxist party was on friendly terms with Lenin, the leader of the Russian Bolshevists. After the October Revolution of 1917, the Dutch Communists expected this special relationship to be continued. Initially, they did seem to enjoy a special status, but they were soon treated just like an ordinary section of the Comintern.

The specific genesis of the CPN enables us to decribe clearly the loss of autonomy of this party after it had become a member of the Communist International. In 1919 the CPN joined the Comintern as a fully independent organisation, with a clear identity framed by its ten-year history. In 1930, the party was completely subordinated to Moscow, having lost nearly all characteristics by which it had stood out from the rest. In this chapter, this process of subordination of the CPN during the 1920s will be analysed. It will focus on the way the Comintern undermined the autonomy of its Dutch section. Three stages in the relationship between the CPN and Moscow are to be distinguished. After a short-lived period of partnership, the Comintern started to concern itself with the internal affairs of the CPN, first as an invited mediator, later as dictator without invitation.

Close contacts between Bolsheviks and Tribunists

During the first decades of the twentieth century, European social democratic parties were the scene of collisions between reformist groups and radical Marxists. In most countries, the Russian October Revolution of 1917 gave the impetus to a rupture between the two factions. In a few countries the split had come along earlier, as in Russia. In 1903 the Russian Social Democratic Party split into Mensheviks and Bolsheviks. Six years later in the Netherlands a group of orthodox Marxists – who were called 'Tribunists' after their oppositional paper *de Tribune* – broke with the reformist social democrats and founded a party of their own: the Social Democratic Party, Sociaal-Democratische Partij (SDP).

The SDP maintained close contacts with the Russian Bolsheviks. The latter were rather isolated within the international Socialist movement and were glad to welcome kindred spirits. After the split, Lenin backed up the SDP by advocating its admission to the Second International. He made the acquaintance of David Wijnkoop, the leader of most of the Tribunists. He also contacted Anton Pannekoek, Hermann Gorter and Henriette Roland-Holst, who together formed the so-called 'Dutch School' within international Marxism. These theoreticians made life difficult for Karl Kautsky, the 'pope' of the Second International. Though Lenin appreciated their contributions – especially Gorter's – he did not disguise his criticisms.

During the First World War, contacts became more frequent. To a certain extent Lenin was in need of his Dutch comrades, and he treated them like equals. In his struggle against the 'social chauvinists', he tried to establish closer links between left-wing internationalist groups. The SDP was one of the most obvious partners, for the Tribunists and the Bolsheviks were independent revolutionary Marxist organisations, as Lenin wrote to Wijnkoop in 1915; more or less the only ones in Europe.[1] At that time the Tribunists were not behaving submissively at all; on the contrary. In the summer of 1915, Wijnkoop and Lenin discussed the possibility of a joint declaration aimed against the imperialist war, which should be presented at the Conference of Zimmerwald (to be held in September). These plans, however, came to nothing. Wijnkoop and his fellow-leader Willem Van Ravesteyn decided not to participate, despite Lenin's insistence. The results of the conference confirmed Wijnkoop's expectations. In the so-called 'Zimmerwald manifesto' revolutionary Marxist views were conspiciously absent, as he made clear to Lenin in September 1915: 'to be honest, it is not clear to us how you . . . could sign the Zimmerwald manifesto . . . It contains a lot of old rubbish . . . We would never have voted for something like that, because our principles would us not have allowed that.' [2]

After the Russian Revolution in 1917, Wijnkoop and Van Ravesteyn again clashed with the Bolsheviks. Both SDP leaders advocated a continuation of the Russian war effort against Germany. By siding against Germany, they contravened the revolutionary Marxist principle of strict impartiality in what was considered to be an imperialist war. They also condemned the separate peace treaty of the Russians with Germany in Brest-Litovsk, after the Communist takeover. Within the SDP this position of Wijnkoop and Van Ravesteyn provoked an opposition, voiced by Pannekoek and Gorter, who criticised their pro-Entente orientation.

Special status: the Amsterdam Bureau

These differences of opinion with the Bolsheviks did not waken the admiration of the leaders of the SDP for the October Revolution. The change of name of the

Dutch party was an expression of this. In March 1918 the Russian Bolsheviks decided to call themselves the Russian Communist Party (Bolsheviks). The SDP followed this example a few months later and renamed itself the Communistische Partij in Nederland. The CPN was invited to attend the foundation of the Comintern in March 1919, but was not able to send a representative because of the international blockade of Russia. Therefore, Sebald Rutgers, a Dutch Communist living in Vilnius at that time, represented the CPN at the constituent congress.

The fact that Wijnkoop and Van Ravesteyn had not only held aloof from Lenin's efforts to organise an international revolutionary Marxist movement, but had also disapproved openly of the treaty of Brest-Litovsk, did not harm the relationship between the Tribunists and Lenin – which became clear in 1919. Threatened by the capitalist powers who were beleaguering and invading Russia, Lenin decided to create several outposts in Western Europe to facilitate communication between Moscow and the Communist groups elswhere. Yakov Reich (alias Thomas) was selected to establish a Western European Secretariat (WES) of the Comintern in Berlin, and Rutgers – who was still in Moscow – was asked by Lenin to set up a Branch Bureau in Amsterdam. For this aim, twenty million roubles were set aside.[3]

The main tasks of the Bureau were to establish contacts with Communist groups in Western Europe and America, and to prepare an international conference. According to Rutgers, Amsterdam was considered the best place to meet, since 'comrades in Holland were known by their revolutionary tactics of over ten years to express the essentials of the Comintern'.[4] In correspondence with Moscow's instructions, Wijnkoop, Van Ravesteyn, Gorter, Pannekoek and Roland-Holst were drawn into the Bureau. Apparently Moscow had dictated its personal composition without knowing about the deep disagreements among the leading Dutch Communists.

Contrary to the WES in Berlin, the Dutch Bureau had a hard time in establishing contacts with Moscow. It was not until May 1920 that Rutgers received new instructions after his departure from Moscow. Consequently, the Bureau was functioning without exactly knowing what was going on in the Comintern headquarters. This proved to be fatal when in February 1920 an international conference was held in Amsterdam. The Bureau framed a resolution which contained notions which were previously held by the Comintern itself, but which were now seriously deviating from the Moscow line. With respect to parliamentarianism, the Amsterdam Bureau stated the possibility of boycotting parliamentary action, instead of regarding participation in the bourgeois Parliament as necessary, as Lenin did. The second offence was the Amsterdam recommendation to avoid 'reactionary' trade unions.

Apart from these political mistakes, the conference was also a complete failure organisationally. Without taking into account basic rules of clandestine operations, the meeting was held in a hotel, where the police could keep an eye on the revolutionary representatives.

'Dutch donkeys'

So, ideologically and organisationally, the Amsterdam Bureau – and the only conference it arranged – failed. In April 1920, the Executive Committee of the Communist International (ECCI) revoked the mandate given to the Dutch and dissolved the Bureau. The decision explicitly referred to the deviating views concerning the trade union and parliamentary question.[5] The news fell like a thunderbolt for the Dutch. Rutgers wrote a letter to the ECCI, in which he disclaimed the accusations and stated that he had operated 'in the spirit of our Russian friends' like Lenin and Bukharin.[6] Poor communication with Russia had prevented the Dutch from taking note of the changing political line. In another letter Rutgers sneered that 'we in Amsterdam were at the least consonant with the earlier ideas in Moscow'.[7]

In his private correspondence, Rutgers accused Karl Radek of having discredited the Amsterdam Bureau, since it was dissolved soon after Radek had become ECCI Secretary. Rutgers wrote to Bukharin that he had never believed that the Russians would support Radek's 'opportunist' line in respect of Parliament and trade unions.[8] It is very likely that rivalry between Berlin (where Radek had stayed in 1919) and Amsterdam had played a role; in the resolution of the Amsterdam conference the WES was considered a section of the Dutch Bureau. Of course the Germans did not accept such a subordinate position. They had already frustrated the activities of the Amsterdam Bureau by withholding funds appropriated for the Dutch.[9] Moreover, Rutgers suspected the WES of not transmitting Comintern messages to Amsterdam.[10]

Apart from the dissolution of the Amsterdam Bureau by the ECCI, Lenin himself also settled accounts with the Dutch Communists with respect to their tactics and ideology in his pamphlet *'Left-Wing' Communism, an Infantile Disorder*. In this, he dictated the Bolshevik methods of centralisation and discipline to the Communist parties. The pamphlet was aimed to counter the growing number of doctrinaire left-wing Communists in Western Europe, who preached abstention from bourgeois-capitalist structures like Parliament and trade unions in favour of ideological purity. In his Russian manuscript Lenin explicitly criticised the Tribunists. He spoke about their 'absurd inventions' and their 'hopelessly poor' views on parliamentarianism – as expressed in the theses of the Amsterdam Bureau, which Lenin very conscientiously rebuked. 'The Tribunists, and the "Leftists" in general, argue . . . like doctrinaires of the revolution, who have never taken part in a real revolution', he wrote. This was unmistakenly true with respect to the Dutch, given their lack of clandestine experience at the Amsterdam conference. Lenin proposed that the ECCI should condemn the refusal to join the 'reactionary' trade unions 'and, in particular, the line of conduct of the Tribunists who – whether directly or indirectly, overtly or covertly, wholly or partly, it does not matter – have supported this erroneous policy'.[11]

Because of this verdict, the Dutch Communists gained a reputation as sectarians. Gorter and Pannekoek, however, stuck to their opinions. They became ideologists of left-wing communism, and broke with Lenin and the CPN and founded a new party. Wijnkoop, on the contrary, opted for retreat. In the summer of 1920, when he arrived in Moscow to attend the Second World Congress of the Comintern, he found out that in Lenin's *'Left-Wing' Communism* the Dutch Communists were treated badly. In a letter to Lenin he objected to the implication that the CPN in general was being held responsible for the political deviations of only a few party members – i.e. Gorter and Pannekoek. Wijnkoop was able to convince Lenin, for in the next edition the words 'Dutch Tribunists' were replaced by 'certain members of the CPN'.

So Lenin had given in, but he was certainly not convinced of Wijnkoop's political attitude. At one of the sessions of the Comintern Congress, he flew out at the Dutch leader who had been going against the grain quite frequently. 'Every one of Comrade Wijnkoop's speeches shows that he shares almost all of Comrade Pannekoek's mistakes. Wijnkoop has, it is true, declared that he does not share Pannekoek's ideas, but his speeches prove the opposite', Lenin stated.[12]

From his point of view, the Russian leader certainly was not mistaken. Wijnkoop, for instance, had warned against simply transferring the Russian revolutionary model to Western Europe. One should learn from the Bolshevist Revolution, but not follow it in a doctrinaire way. The Dutch party leader was also opposed to Moscow as the residence of the Executive Committee in favour of Italy or Norway. Referring to the international blockade of Russia, Wijnkoop feared that if the ECCI were to have its seat in Moscow, its members would lose contact with their own countries and would 'be guided by Russian information and thus by the Russian Executive'.[13]

As so often, Wijnkoop stood mostly alone in his opinion. The Dutch leader was criticised by Radek and Grigorii Zinoviev, secretary and chairman of the ECCI respectively. The former had called the Dutch Communists 'donkeys' because of the failure of the Amsterdam Bureau.[14] Zinoviev publicly humiliated Wijnkoop and delivered a heavy blow to the idea cultivated by the Tribunists that they were on equal terms with the Russian leadership as a result of their common past. Zinoviev stated that 'Comrade Wijnkoop is laughable, speaking on behalf of a party that has only 1,500 members after fifteen years of activity.'[15]

So the early foundation of the Dutch independent Marxist party, which its leadership liked to boast about, was no longer positively valued by the Russians. Before the Revolution the Bolsheviks had been willing to co-operate with the Tribunists when this was considered useful, partly because apart from the Dutch there were only very few partners to collaborate with. But in 1920 this situation was completely changed. While the Russians now had many parties they could rely on, Wijnkoop was still acting obstinately, thinking that he was indispensable.

Naturally, the arrogance of the Dutch leader disturbed Lenin, Zinoviev and

Radek, who were all scornful of the CPN. Lenin had set the tone by diagnosing the left-wing disease of the Tribunists, of which one of the main symptoms was turning away from the masses. Wijnkoop had tried to limit this diagnosis to Gorter and Pannekoek only, but Lenin found that he was affected as well. Zinoviev supplied the empirical evidence to Lenin's statement. Founded in 1909, the CPN had – compared to other Comintern sections – a long history, but unlike several other sections it had not developed into a mass party at all: it counted only 2,400 members in 1920. So theory linked up nicely here with practice: the CPN was branded as 'sectarian', an accusation which was to haunt the party for years – and which was usually related by its (Russian) critics to its early, if not premature, foundation.

The Comintern as mediator

At the Second World Congress in 1920 the twenty-one conditions of adherence to the Comintern were adopted. Reflecting Lenin's *'Left-Wing' Communism*, Bolshevik-style centralisation and discipline were imposed on the national party organisations. In principle, the sections were giving up their autonomy. 'All the decisions of the Congresses of the Comintern, as well as the decisions of its Executive Committee, are binding on all parties', the sixteenth condition stated. These conditions, which were also adopted by the CPN, laid the foundation of substantial Comintern interference with the affiliated sections.

Unlike the German party, for instance, the CPN initially could follow its own line in a relatively undisturbed way. It was not until the summer of 1923 that the Comintern involved itself in the Dutch section. Moscow did not act on its own, but was asked to intervene by a newly formed opposition which acted against the 'old' leadership consisting of Wijnkoop and Van Ravesteyn. Partly, this opposition was composed of youngsters who had joined the party after the October Revolution and who did not have the traditional respect for the old leadership of 1909. Another part consisted of members of the revolutionary syndicalist trade union, the National Labour Secretariat, Nationaal Arbeids Secretariaat (NAS). They protested against the CPN ignoring the revolutionary role NAS played in their eyes.

Early in 1923 both groups joined hands in a Committee for the Third International. Wijnkoop and Van Ravesteyn were criticised because of the dictatorial way they led the party, the deficient party organisation, their 'defeatist' opinions about a possible revolution in Germany, their incompetence with regard to the united front policy, their one-sided orientation on Parliament and, above all, their unwillingness to co-operate with NAS ('liquidationism'). The opposition also used the prematurity of the CPN as an argument against its leadership: because of the specific genesis of the party, Wijnkoop and Van Ravesteyn were *blasé*, thinking that 'they knew it even better than the Comintern'. Eventually, the opposition came to the same diagnosis as Lenin had come a few years earlier: sectarianism.[16]

The opposition claimed that the party leadership was not willing or not able to carry out the Comintern policy, but was only paying lip-service to it. Moscow was explictly asked to examine the case. The ECCI summoned delegations of the two factions to Moscow. Its principal aim was to prevent a rift within the party. An ad hoc 'committee on the Dutch question', presided over by Radek, looked at the problem. The fact that he, of all persons, was chairman, might have been a bad sign for Wijnkoop, given their collisions in previous years. The resolution of the committee, however, which was adopted by the ECCI, spoke in admiring words about 'the founders of the CPN', who had made great sacrifices to the proletarian cause. Yet, in the same breath, the finger was put on the weak spot of the specific origins of the CPN, which had not only brought about a poor anchoring of the party within the masses, but also a touchiness among its leadership. Neither did the opposition, however, get off without a scratch: the ECCI strongly condemned the formation of a fraction.

The resolution was framed in mild words and looked like a compromise. The Comintern seemed indeed to have made an attempt at reconciliation, but in the end the opposition got the best of it. Not only did the expulsions of some of its members by the party leadership have to be undone, but the opposition also obtained the right to publish in the party newspaper.[17] As a consequence, the opposition regarded the outcome as a victory; Wijnkoop, on the contrary, perceived it as a defeat. According to party secretary Jan Ceton, the leadership now 'had to protect communism despite Moscow'.[18] The decision was accepted since rejection would imply withdrawal from the Comintern; but in a long letter to the ECCI the leadership complained about the verdict. It charged the ECCI with 'grotesque nonsense' and 'complete ignorance of the Dutch situation' and called its decision 'destructive'.[19]

In these circumstances, it was not surprising that the Moscow agreement came to nothing. Consequently, the opposition formally organised itself again at the end of 1923. This time, it demanded the head of Wijnkoop. Again, the ECCI called both factions to Moscow 'at the request of both'. The consultations in March 1924 proved to be a repetition of earlier moves. In a letter to the CPN, the ECCI reformulated its criticism in a diplomatic way, but, just as in 1923, this could not conceal that the party leadership received most of the blame. The Comintern demanded freedom of criticism for the opposition within the party, and proportional representation within the leading bodies.[20]

The Comintern takes sides

After the second attempt at reconciliation had failed, Moscow decided to step in more seriously. Some personnel were allocated to the case of the CPN on a more permanent basis. In spring 1924 Max Hammer, a German representative of the Profintern, was sent to examine the case on the spot. Moreover, in April 1924 the Comintern for the first time sent a delegation to a Congress of the CPN. The Swiss, Stirner (whose real name was Edgar Woog) – who was in charge of the

Dutch question within the Comintern apparatus – and the Czech, Karel Kreibich, attended the meeting, and had a large say in the decision-making process.

The extended involvement of the Comintern in the CPN was accompanied by a change in tactics. Instead of mediating, as it had done before, Moscow was now openly taking sides at the party Congress. It was not the opposition, however, which could count on its support, but the party leadership. In the light of the previous verdicts of the ECCI, Stirner's speech came as a complete surprise. On the one hand, Wijnkoop had to give in with respect to the NAS. Stirner considered this trade union as a revolutionary factor with which the CPN had to co-operate. In the trade-union resolution, which was adopted by the Congress, the Comintern's view triumphed after Stirner had put Wijnkoop under strong pressure. This bitter pill for Wijnkoop was more than compensated for, however, by the fact that Stirner publicly let the opposition down: he called some of its publications a 'dagger stabbed in the back of the CPN'. At the same time, he praised the leadership by calling the Dutch section one of the 'most important' parties of the Comintern and 'one of the oldest, which had restored Marxism'.[21]

Consequently, the partly leadership appeared as the victor in the party strife; its prestige had been strengthened by Moscow's support. Moreover, the opposition had fallen apart. The NAS-inclined part, which was headed by Hendricus Sneevliet (a Dutch confidant of Lenin who had worked as a Comintern representative in China) seemed to have been somewhat pacified by the political rehabilitation of their trade union in the party resolution.

The other oppositional component, which had focused its criticism especially at Wijnkoop's dictatorship, left the CPN and founded a small dissident organisation. Its leader Jacques De Kadt wrote a bitter letter to the ECCI, in which he wondered if Stirner had acted in agreement with Moscow when he pitched into the opposition.[22] The representative of the German party at the Dutch Congress, Paul Schlecht, was also displeased with Stirner's siding with the party leadership. He wrote to Zinoviev that Stirner was wrong in presenting the CPN as one of the best in the Comintern.[23]

It remains a question as to what extent Stirner had acted on directives from the ECCI. Up till now, no evidence has been found that Moscow explicitly changed tack and opted for the party leadership. At any rate, Stirner's strategy seemed to have been aimed at ending the dragging party strife at minimal costs. This implied a pacification of both the NAS opposition and the party leadership at the cost of the breaking away of a – probably smaller – part of the opposition. Above all, the unity of the party had to be safeguarded as much as possible. By doing this, Stirner certainly acted in line with Moscow, for this principle had been the guideline as long as the Comintern had been involved with the CPN. Since the summer of 1923, Moscow had – though claiming neutrality – sided very cautiously with the oppositional groups, by pressing the leadership to meet their demands to some extent. In that way an oppositional split-off was prevented for the time being, but on the other side the leadership was not really called to order for not following the Comintern's demands. These tactics of half way concessions to both sides could not be continued, according to Stirner, for it resulted in a disorientation of the party's rank and file. The Comintern had to choose and had 'to bring victory to one side and to beat the other'. The question then was: which side had to be supported, the 'old' leaders or the opposition?[24] For Stirner, this was more a tactical than a political question. In his analysis, 'good elements' within the leadership – relatively young people who recognised Wijnkoop's obstinacy and who were in favour of collaboration with NAS – had allied themselves closely with the old leaders, because they feared Moscow would support the opposition. They would therefore never have joined hands with 'good elements' from the other side, that is, that part of the opposition in favour of the Comintern and Profintern. Stirner anticipated that a triumph of the opposition would result in a party split far worse than the small one which had occurred now after supporting the 'old' leaders.

Yet Stirner's compromise, which was adopted at the CPN Congress, was a fragile construction, since it rested completely on the armistice between Wijnkoop and the NAS opposition. If nobody was really willing to give in, the truce would not last long – which turned out to be the case. The NAS itself did not agree with the compromise and its oppositional members within the CPN continued to raise objections against Wijnkoop's faction, especially when the latter publicly boasted of its Comintern-blessed victory. Moscow also became convinced that Wijnkoop was misusing his victory and that he was not trying seriously to improve relations with the NAS.

The downfall of Wijnkoop

Slowly, but surely, the willingness in Moscow to get rid of Wijnkoop grew. Without doubt, the Fifth World Congress of the Comintern was important here. The Congress had met in the summer of 1924, and decided to impose the organisational model of the Communist Party of the Soviet Union (CPSU) on the sections. These had to be Bolshevised and based on factory cells. In general the Congress marked 'a turn to the left'.

In the autumn of 1924, Stirner wrote that 'it is now time to deal firmly with Wijnkoop's methods'.[25] He was backed by Heinz Neumann, who had come to Holland in October. His report to the ECCI was a screed of complaints about Wijnkoop. In many aspects it resembled the previous charges of the opposition. Neumann observed a 'complete passivity' in organisational affairs. Moreover, the CPN was still sectarian and resembled in no way a mass party. In addition, 'the party maintains a very unhealthy cult of its fifteen-year old history and tries to cover up its political non-activity with this tradition', according to Neumann. Wijnkoop was exercising 'a nearly monarchical dictatorship' and was provoking the NAS. The leaders of the NAS opposition within the CPN therefore strongly insisted on his departure. Neumann also thought this necessary. In line with Comintern policy since the Fifth World Congress, he suggested a swing to the left: a 'left, Bolshevist group within the party' had to be created. This group should settle accounts with Wijnkoop and restore good relations with NAS.[26]

After having backed the 'old' leaders against the opposition at the CPN Congress in April 1924, Moscow now sided with the latter against Wijnkoop. Instead of the previous frontal attack, this time silent diplomacy was preferred. The tactics Neumann suggested were consonant with Stirner's earlier analysis: Moscow should try to win over the 'good elements' of the leadership, after which a common front with the NAS opposition had to be forged against Wijnkoop. Stirner himself did not direct the project; he was temporarily replaced by Neumann. The representative of the Profintern, Hammer, who was still in Holland, had to bring the two oppositional groups together.

The campaign against Wijnkoop was accelerated by a speech he made in Parliament in November. Wijnkoop then played with the idea of a labour party, which would organise all workers – the Communists included. He had not consulted the party at all before he raised the subject. This was grist to the mill of the opposition, who accused him of acting unilaterally and wrong-headedly. Hammer, Moscow's eye in the CPN, called Wijnkoop's deed 'liquidationistic and opportunistic'. He wrote to Neumann that this question would be the kind of conflict 'by which Moscow has to step in'.[27] Hammer suggested a pincer movement: Wijnkoop had to be put under pressure from inside the party by the opposition and from outside by the ECCI. Indeed, Moscow sent a message in which it condemned Wijnkoop's parliamentary statements. Representatives of the 'old' leadership and of the new opposition were invited to come to Moscow for consultations during the meetings of the fifth ECCI Plenum.[28]

Gradually the rope around Wijnkoop's neck was tightened. In Holland, the oppositional groups came to terms with the 'rightist elements'; in Moscow, Neumann proposed that the ECCI replace Wijnkoop and Van Ravesteyn – at that time both Members of Parliament – with working-class candidates at the next national elections.[29] In April 1925 the conflict reached a show-down in Moscow at the Dutch Committee, presided by Neumann. Stirner and Hammer came out into the open against Wijnkoop. The latter charged the representatives of the Comintern with artificially constructing an opposition against him. Stirner hit back: Wijnkoop was unable to carry through the Comintern line in the Netherlands. Later, he would add that he had got the impression that Wijnkoop was in fact 'angry that Moscow was meddling with [his] affairs, that is the affairs of the CPN'.[30] Wijnkoop, however, repeatedly professed his loyalty to the Comintern. After long debates, the committee decided that the opposition would appoint the second party secretary, a parliamentary candidate and a member of the editorial board of *de Tribune*. Stirner, Hammer and the opposition had also urged the dismissal of Wijnkoop and his replacement by NAS-friendly leaders, but Otto Kuusinen – one of the leaders of the Comintern and a member of the committee – did not want to discuss this: 'Let me say beforehand that the Comintern will leave it to the CPN whether Wijnkoop will remain at the top of the party.'[31]

Despite the antagonism between the Dutch leadership and the Comintern, Moscow was still not willing to drop Wijnkoop. The risk of a party split was considered to be too large. Moreover, Moscow still respected the autonomy of the CPN with regard to the appointment of its leader. Yet despite the reservations of Kuusinen, Wijnkoop's fall was near, even if initially it did not look like that. At the Congress of the CPN in May 1925, the distribution of the important party functions between both factions by the ECCI was rejected by a small majority, after Wijnkoop had advised against it. Moreover, the delegates nominated Wijnkoop and Van Ravesteyn as the first two candidates for the national elections. Although the Comintern was asked to approve of this decision, the opposition handed in a motion in which the ECCI was asked to send a representative immediately. This motion was also adopted. So although there was not a clear majority within the CPN against the Comintern, there was a substantial, large minority which disregarded the decisions of Moscow and still took a rather independent stand.

The ECCI sent the Swiss, Jules Humbert-Droz, to the Netherlands. He was instructed to make sure that the Moscow resolution was going to be implemented, which he did. 'The question of international discipline was at stake and then one has to go to any lengths', Humbert-Droz wrote to Zinoviev.[32] In talks with the Comintern representative, Wijnkoop stuck to his opinion that Moscow was making a political mistake by supporting the opposition. He would no longer resist, however, and announced his resignation. A few days later the 'old' leadership retired.

In fact, it was not the Comintern in the first place, but Wijnkoop's oldest and closest comrade, Van Ravesteyn, who was responsible for Wijnkoop's retirement. Van Ravesteyn was not willing to accept the Comintern's compromise, which implied his resigning as a Member of Parliament. Wijnkoop, on the other hand would not let down his companion. As a result, they both disappeared, after having directed the party since 1909 and represented it in Parliament since 1918. Humbert-Droz suggested that both would be offered a job by the Comintern, because he thought it might be dangerous to leave these old leaders, who still had large support within the party, without work.

Indeed, both 'old' leaders became actively involved in the split the Comintern had tried so long to prevent. At the CPN Congress of 1926, their supporters assailed the legitimacy of the meeting and left the meeting. Thereupon, Wijnkoop, Van Ravesteyn and others were expelled and replaced by the leaders of the opposition. In October 1926 the old guard, directed by Wijnkoop, was involved in the foundation of a new Communist party, which was called 'CPN-Central Committee' – suggesting this organisation was the legal continuation of the CPN. The CPN-CC declared itself also loyal to the Comintern. In strength, it was not far behind the 'official', Comintern-recognised CPN. At the national elections of 1929, both parties won one a seat; Wijnkoop returned to Parliament.

Although the CPN-CC stressed its loyalty to Moscow time after time, its foundation and continuing existence is certainly to be regarded as an infringement of the discipline of the Comintern. Wijnkoop was not alone in being obstinate; he was supported by probably half of the Communist membership and electorate in the Netherlands. The party split therefore demonstrates clearly the imperfect state of the Comintern's control over the Dutch section in the mid-1920s – perhaps also because a small party like the CPN was not among Moscow's priorities.

Subordination

Of course the ECCI was not at all satisfied with the existence of two competing Communist parties in the Netherlands. Moscow's policy in the period 1923–26 had been aimed at maintaining the unity of the Dutch Communist movement, but this had proved to be a failure at long last. The inclusion of the revolutionary syndicalist NAS within that movement was also not fated to last long. In December 1925, after Wijnkoop's resignation, NAS had joined the Profintern. Soon serious problems arose after Moscow had demanded the dissolution of all the small NAS-affiliated trade unions (a policy which, ironically, Wijnkoop had previously advocated). Relations between NAS and the Profintern deteriorated rapidly, and at the end of 1927 the ties were cut. In the background, differences of opinion regarding Trotsky and his ideas also played a role. In May 1927, several NAS leaders – among them Sneevliet – had already left the CPN and the Comintern. Some time later they founded one of the first independent Trotskyist party organisations in Europe.

Around 1928, therefore, the Comintern-recognized CPN stood empty-handed. Both Wijnkoop and Sneevliet and their followers (NAS included) had left the party. In this situation, the ECCI could not think very highly of the leadership it had helped to install in 1925. Moscow also received alarming reports from its Statistical Information Institute in Berlin, directed by Varga. These reports stated that in order to prevent the Wijnkoop party from outstripping the Comintern one, the policy of the latter had to be drastically changed. A reshuffling at the top of the party was also recommended.[33]

It was not until 1929, however, that the Comintern again started to occupy itself seriously with the CPN. Compared with the mid-1920s, the Comintern had come even more under the control of the CPSU. The new radical line which was adopted at the Sixth World Congress of 1928 reflected the swing to the left that Stalin had made after he had defeated Trotsky. The end of the 'relative' stabilization of capitalism and the beginning of a 'third period' of revolutionary opportunities were proclaimed. Relations with social democracy became very tense after the Comintern had labelled it 'social-fascism'. Within the reformist trade unions 'red oppositions' had to be formed, which had to radicalise these organisations from the inside.

The new course of the Comintern brought about conflicts within the sections. Moderate leaders who were not willing to adopt the new line fully clashed with a more extreme wing – the former became known as the 'rightists' or 'conciliators'. In these conflicts in Western Europe, the Western European Bureau (WEB) in Berlin – founded in 1928 and soon to be headed by Georgii Dimitrov – played an important role. The establishment of the WEB was part of the process of increasing organisational discipline and centralisation of the Comintern, which went along with its political radicalisation. The powers of the WEB were extensive. It could give directives to the parties or send instructors to them. Normally the WEB had to consult Moscow in these matters, but in emergencies it could decide on its own.[34]

The WEB was Moscow's instrument to meddle with the conflict within the CPN in 1929–30.[35] As in other parties, the radicalisation of the Comintern after the Sixth World Congress led to a so-called 'right-wing danger'. The present leaders of the CPN – the same persons who had come to power in 1925 with the help of Moscow – were now considered to be the main exponent of this deviation. They were blamed for the electoral and organisational stagnation of the party. According to their critics, the leaders were too much focused on Parliament ('parliamentarism' and 'legalism') and too little on agitation and trade-union activism ('passivity').

Supported by Moscow, in 1929 a group of young intellectuals within the Political Bureau started to rebel against the leadership. In this period the WEB sent several instructors to the CPN, like 'Alarich' (Richard Gyptner, former secretary of the Communist Youth International (CYI) and secretary of WEB, who also called himself Magnus); Wilhelm Florin, a German Communist and member of the *Reichstag* since 1924; the English-speaking Ferguson and Neptun (alias Robert), nether of whom can be identified with certainty; and Silvio, a Swiss whose real name was Sigi Bamatter. He was the principal WEB instructor in the CPN in 1929 and early 1930.

The CPN was going to be a showcase in the Comintern. Judging from an article of the Czech Communist Reimann in *Inprecorr*, Moscow wanted to teach all sections 'how a small party, small in membership and weak with respect to its influence on the large proletarian masses can grow in size and power by a correct formulation and accomplishment of its political tasks'. The Dutch party was selected to be used in this 'public lesson'.

Initially, the strategy of the Comintern was to convince the dissenting leaders of the rightness of its new line. At the end of 1929, however, the conflict escalated. 'If it is true that the rightist danger takes shape as passivity and non-execution of adopted decisions, then the question of the improvement of the party leadership is the central question', one of the leaders of the opposition wrote.[36] Previously, Moscow had observed some right-wing elements in the Dutch party leadership, but still did not hold the view that there was an organised rightist faction.[37] In January 1930, however, this suddenly seemed to be the case. The Comintern clearly distinguished a rightist faction, led by the same person who had directed the opposition against Wijnkoop in 1924–25.

According to Silvio, he was a 'cunning opportunist, who was plotting against the decisions of the Sixth World Congress'.[38]

This time, Moscow did not wait as long as they had in the mid-1920s. The party strife then dragged on for years; now it was solved within ten months. No longer were delegations of the two rival groups called to Moscow; instead, a representative was sent to the Netherlands, and he was far more more energetic than Hammer had been in 1924–25. At that time, the Comintern, as Kuusinen had said, still allowed the CPN the right to select its own leader; now, the Political Secretariat of the ECCI issued a very detailed list of persons it wanted to be elected as members of the Central Committee, Political Bureau and Secretariat of the CPN. The party leadership had to be purged of all 'rightist, conciliatory and passive elements'. These had to be replaced by persons 'who since the tenth plenum have unconditionally represented the Comintern line'.[39] Moreover, Moscow suggested a certain Daan Goulooze as the new party secretary.

Goulooze was leader of the Communist Youth and had not taken a clear position in the party conflict. Silvio and the WEB, however, were strongly opposed to this choice of the highest body of the Comintern. Under the direction of Gyptner, secretary of WEB, his nomination as party secretary was cancelled – with the approval of Moscow, who gave the WEB *carte blanche*. Gyptner knew Goulooze from the CYI and did not have a high opinion of him. Some time later Goulooze publicly admitted that he had belonged to the group of 'reconciliators'. Because of his self-criticism, he was received back in favour and was elected a member of the Central Committee. Eventually his career would not be harmed by this *faux pas*: a few years later he became radiographic liaison officer between the CPN and the Comintern.

Instead of Goulooze, a rather colourless district secretary named Cornelius Schalker was appointed; he had not seriously committed himself to either faction, and stood fully on the side of the Comintern. He was relieved in 1938 by Paul De Groot, who was going to lead the party in a true Stalinist manner till 1977.[40]

Conclusion

As was the case with all the other parties in the Comintern, the 1920s were the years in which the gradual disappearance of the organisational and political autonomy of the CPN took place. In 1920 the expectation of a special status, based on pre-revolutionary co-operation between Tribunists and Bolsheviks, was knocked to pieces with the dissolution of the Amsterdam Bureau. Around 1925 the inclination towards independence of leaders like Wijnkoop, who had directed the party since 1909, was thwarted by the Comintern. They had to bend or break. Not having lost their own will, they decided to do the latter and to found a new party. At the end of the decade, the leaders who had replaced Wijnkoop with the help of the Comintern were also put aside by Moscow. They were not only not zealously carrying into effect the new radical line of the Sixth World Congress, but had also expressed some objections, after which the Comintern decided to get rid of them. This time, Moscow did not embark diplomatically on mediation and compromise, as it had done in the mid-1920s in order to prevent a party split, leaving the choice of the leader to the party. Now, Moscow simply appointed the leading functionaries itself, a selection based on the criterion of absolute political loyalty.

The year 1930 therefore marks the completion of the process of disciplining of the CPN by, and its subordination to, the Comintern. It is significant to note that after four party splits in the 1920s (in 1920, 1923, 1926 and 1927), none occurred during the 1930s. Even when the line of the Comintern was changed drastically, as in 1935 and 1939, there were no attempts to break away. Apparently the more critical spirits had left the party, leaving their place to Moscow-devoted, docile *apparatchiki*, out-and-out supporters of the Soviet Union.

The culmination of this process of extending the dominance of the Comintern within Dutch communism was the termination of the organisational discord which had existed since 1926. In the summer of 1930, Wijnkoop and his party returned to the Comintern-recognised CPN. This merger was facilitated by the departure of the leadership which had replaced Wijnkoop previously. Moscow directed the whole operation and decided to make a showcase of it, which had to demonstrate that Communist life outside the Comintern was not possible and that absolute loyalty should be practised. Wijnkoop therefore had to surrender unconditionally in public by confessing his political sins. He was pressed to make a self-critical statement in Parliament, in which he blamed himself for having pursued a wrong policy which objectively had led him to reformism: 'The Comintern was right to join a strong battle with this wrong policy and it was put in the right on all points without the least reserve, both by objective historical development and according to my own personal views', he declared. The once so obstinate founder and leader of the Dutch Communist Party had to humble himself in the dust before the Comintern was willing to receive him back into favour. The subordination of Dutch communism by Moscow was completed.

Notes

1 *Briefwisseling van W. I. Lenin met Hollandse communisten* (Moscow, n.d.), p. 15.

2 *Ibid.*, p. 39.

3 RC 495/1/1, protocol meeting ECCI, 28 September 1919.

4 RC 497/1/1, 'Statement about the Branch Bureau of the Communist International and the February Conference in Amsterdam', from Rutgers, 3 February 1920.

5 The decision of the ECCI was sent to Rutgers through Fritz on 12 May 1920 and was signed by Radek as secretary of the ECCI; RC 497/1/9.

6 RC 497/1/9, letter from Rutgers to the ECCI, 14 May 1920.

7 RC 497/2/8, letter from Rutgers to Winter (Berzin), 12 May 1920.

8 RC 497/2/2, letter from Rutgers to Bukharin, 15 May 1920.
9 RC 495/18/3, letter from Rutgers to Winter (Berzin), 20 December 1919.
10 RC 497/2/2, letter from Rutgers to James (Thomas = Reich), 28 May 1920.
11 V. I. Lenin, *'Left-Wing' Communism, an Infantile Disorder* (Moscow, 1970), pp. 34, 51–9.
12 *Second Congress of the Communist International: Minutes of the Proceedings*, 2 vols (London, 1977), I: 276.
13 *Ibid.*, II: 132
14 J. De Kadt, *Uit mijn communistentijd* (Amsterdam, 1965), p. 150.
15 *Second Congress*, I: 104–5.
16 RC 495/161/87, report of the 'Committee for the Third International', 20 April 1923.
17 RC 495/41/1, letter from the ECCI to the leadership of the CPN, 6 July 1923.
18 RC 495/72/11, shortened protocol of the meeting of the party council, 22 July 1923.
19 RC 495/172/65, letter from the CPN to the ECCI (end of July) 1923.
20 RC 495/41/1, letter from the ECCI to the CPN, 26 March 1924.
21 *De Tribune*, 16 April 1924.
22 RC 495/172/66, letter from the opposition to the ECCI (end of April) 1924.
23 RC 495/18/336B, letter from Schlecht to Zinoviev, 28 April 1924.
24 RC 495/18/336A, letter from Stirner to Hammer, 9 June 1924.
25 RC 495/18/336A, letter from Stirner to Manuel, 13 October 1924.
26 RC 495/18/336B, letter from Neumann to the ECCI, 26 October 1924.
27 RC 495/18/336B, letter from Hammer to Neumann, 7 December 1924.
28 RC 495/18/336A, letter from the ECCI to the Central Committee of the CPN, 13 December 1924.
29 RC 495/18/336B, H. Neumann, 'About the Dutch question', December 1924.
30 RC 495/18/397A, letter from Stirner to De Visser, 21 April 1925.
31 RC 495/41/4, protocol of the meeting of the Dutch Committee, 14 April 1925.
32 RC 595/18/394B, letter from Humbert-Droz to Zinoviev, 8 (18) May 1925.
33 RC 504/1/217, 'The city council elections and the efforts of NAS to split the CPN', 2 June 1927.
34 RC 495/20/795, 'To the Central Committees of the Communist Parties', 24 October 1928.
35 G. Voerman, 'De *coming men* van de CPN: Goulooze, De Groot en de Komintern (1929–1930)', in *Jaarboek 1994 Documentatiecentrum Nederlandse Politieke Partijen* (Gronigen, 1994), pp. 237–60.
36 RC 495/25/581, letter from De Vries (De Leeuw) to the party secretariat, 15 November 1929.
37 RC 499/1/8, letter from the WEB to the Central Committee of the CPN, 29 November 1929.
38 RC 495/28/44B, 'Concerning letter of comrade Bergsma', sent by Silvio, 28 November 1929.
39 RC 495/3/194, directives from the WEB to the CPN Congress, 6 January 1930.
40 G. Voerman, 'De Groot aan het bewind: De CPN en de Komintern, 1935–1938' *Politiek & Cultuur*, 50 (1995), 125–31.

10

The highpoint of Comintern influence? The Communist Party and the Civil War in Spain

Tim Rees

The Communist International took as its basic organisational model an idealised – if not mythologised – understanding of the role of the Bolsheviks during the Russian Revolution of 1917. There was to be a world revolutionary party, with its 'general staff' based in Moscow. The national Communist movements, known as sections in Comintern terminology, were to be entirely subordinate to the centre in a kind of command economy model of political action. An iron chain of control was postulated that stretched from the Executive Committee of the Communist International (ECCI) to the leaderships of individual parties and from them to the rank and file. Not only broad strategy but detailed tactics were to be decided by the Comintern and transmitted for local implementation. The ostensible goal was a world revolution that would extend that which had been achieved in the Soviet Union.[1]

The Spanish Civil War (1936–39) was the greatest opportunity, and proved the greatest test, of the ability of the Comintern to control the actions of individual parties in this way and to influence decisively wider political developments. There is no doubt that the Comintern rose to the challenge presented by the war, and that it sought to impose just such control in Spain, mobilising great forces to try and secure it. Nor could it have done otherwise. The Civil War represented just the kind of crisis in which the Comintern was supposed to offer decisive leadership and, moreover, it occurred at a time when the Communist International appeared to be in danger of becoming moribund. The desire to act was also matched by seemingly optimum conditions for the wielding of influence: the Communist Party of Spain, Partido Comunista de España (PCE) had a leadership that was chosen by the Comintern and which was thoroughly imbued with its methods and doctrines; the party participated directly in the wartime Republican government, holding a wide range of positions from ministers downwards; the USSR was the chief backer of the Republic, providing arms and military advisers, and Soviet agents and security services operated freely in Spain.[2]

Given these circumstances, it is not surprising that the self-image of the Comintern as a controlling force has long underpinned analyses of the part that the Spanish Communists actually played in the Civil War. The strategy and tactics pursued by the PCE are seen overwhelmingly by both critics and defenders as the result of Comintern direction. The nature of this direction is, in turn, portrayed as largely dictated by Stalin personally, following the needs of a Soviet foreign policy which sought alliances with the Western democracies against the threat of fascism. Accordingly, the popular front strategy adopted by the Seventh Congress of the Comintern in 1935 called for co-operation with other political forces to counter the rise of fascism and played down the revolutionary mission of the national sections. It was this policy that was applied in Spain, and to which the PCE apparently slavishly adhered.[3] The controversy that has ensued about the part played by the PCE in the war has largely concentrated on polemical attacks or defences of its policies during the war as either a cause of eventual Republican defeat or as the only sensible measures given the circumstances of the time.[4]

The broad nature of the positions taken by the party can be briefly summarised. A minority and marginal force before the outbreak of the war, the PCE grew to become a decisive force on the Republican side. Its rise to power occurred within the complex situation created after the army revolt of July 1936 that sparked off the Civil War. Conventional government was effectively decapitated by the attempted military coup and real power passed into the control of those social and political groups that successfully resisted the insurgents in large parts of the country. In some regions (notably Aragón and Catalonia) this allowed the supporters of the large Anarchist movement, the National Confederation of Labour, Confederación Nacional de Trabajo (CNT) and a smaller independent Marxist party, the Worker's Party of Marxist Unity, Partido Obrero de Unificación Marxista (POUM), to declare a revolution. Land and industry were collectivised and the conventional Republican state rejected. Instead, these forces advocated a revolutionary war effort, fought by militias, to defend and extend these gains.

This path was rejected by the Spanish Communists, despite their own theoretical commitment to revolution. They sided with the republican parties[5] and many Socialists who wanted to see a conventional war effort, using a centrally organised army, in defence of the social and political status quo of the reforming Republic of 1931–36. Accordingly, the PCE joined a new popular front government in September 1936 under the Socialist Largo Caballero. He was a compromise leader – in sympathy with revolution, but also in favour of recreating the machinery of the state and for central government control. Initially, this consisted of the establishment of a new Republican army and police forces, both of which were strongly supported by the PCE and largely armed with weapons supplied by the USSR from October 1936 onwards.

Increasingly, the state tightened its grip over the localities within Republican-controlled territory, bringing political power and the economy back under central direction. Tensions rose between those who advocated a conventional war and those who sought to defend and advance a decentralised revolution. These came to a head in May 1937 in Barcelona, when Communist police seized control of the telephone exchange from Anarchist militia, precipitating a short-lived war within the Civil War. This was resolved with some bloodshed in favour of the centralisers who proceeded to liquidate the revolution. Largo Caballero was ousted from power and replaced as Prime Minister by Juan Negrín, a right-wing Socialist. Collectives were dismantled by force and the remaining militias were incorporated into the Popular Army – to the detriment of popular enthusiasm for the Republican cause in the eyes of many. Even more divisively, members of the POUM – as well as some Anarchists – were singled out for harsh treatment. Denounced as 'Trotskyist' and 'objectively fascist' by the Communists, the party was declared illegal and many of its leaders were arrested. One of the most prominent, Andreu Nin, died under torture and others were arraigned for a show trial. Thereafter, the Republican side followed a conventional war effort until finally defeated in 1939.

This chapter does not seek to overturn this understanding of the nature of Communist activities, at least not in its broader outline, nor to return directly to the question of whether the PCE bore the greatest responsibility for the defeat of the Republic. Instead, it focuses on the origins of Communist policies and argues that the Comintern was simply unable to achieve the high level of control over the PCE – and hence over developments in Spain through it – that is assumed. The enormous efforts put to this end were often unproductive, if not actually self-defeating. Though, of course, Comintern forces did play a part – sometimes decisively so – in determining the positions taken by the PCE, this never amounted to constant central direction. Instead, patterns of authority and influence were shifting and uncertain in a fast-changing and complex political and military struggle. Far from demonstrating the smooth working of a centralised organisational model, tendencies towards confusion and tensions within and between every level of command were revealed by the Civil War. As a result, decisions were taken by many actors at different levels, often as ad hoc responses to pressing developments, rather than being simply dictated from the centre. Indecision and conflict also prevailed at crucial moments, particularly during the crisis of the summer of 1937. Ultimately, the PCE followed the lines that its leaders and their followers were predisposed to take anyway – though Comintern endorsement was sought, if only retrospectively, for their actions. There was no unthinking adherence to the wishes of the Comintern or to Stalin's wider objectives.

The transformation of the PCE

The fundamental reason for the relative failure of centralised control was the changed nature of the Spanish section with which the Comintern had to deal. Until the declaration of the democratic Republic in 1931 the PCE was a small party with a few thousand members at most, operating in a country that was at the margins of ECCI interest. It grew into slightly greater prominence for the Comintern with the establishment of the new regime, and increasingly so after the failed Asturian Rising of October 1934, for which the PCE disingenuously claimed the credit. Membership grew in the rising's aftermath, and by the eve of the Civil War had increased to some tens of thousands with the formation of a united youth movement, the United Socialist Youth, Juventud Socialista Unificada (JSU) with the Socialist Party, the Partido Socialista Obrero de España (PSOE), in April 1936.[6]

Although by no means the centre of Comintern attention, the activities of the PCE came under fairly close control before the Civil War. Until 1935, and the internal reorganisation of the Comintern, direction from Moscow (known as 'la casa' or 'home' in the parlance of the Spanish Communists) was largely left to the Roman Land Secretariat (RLS) under the control of Manuilsky (nicknamed 'Manu' by the Spanish delegation in Moscow),[7] and thereafter to his personal Secretariat. Influence over the party was strengthened in 1932 during the so-called Third Period of Stalinisation in the Comintern when the leadership of the PCE was ruthlessly replaced. This brought in a younger generation that included José Díaz (General Secretary), Jesús Hernández, Vicente Uribe, Antonio Mije, Manuel Hurtado, Dolores Ibarruri ('La Pasionaria') and Enrique Lister. All had attended the International Lenin School in Moscow (some also received military training at the Frunze Academy), and all were thoroughly versed in the central operations of the Comintern.[8] At the same time, the Argentine Communist, Vittorio Codovilla (known as 'Louis' or 'Medina'), was appointed in place of Jules Humbert-Droz as 'adviser' with orders to keep the PCE in line. Using the authority of the ECCI, Codovilla accomplished this task with great ruthlessness, leading Enrique Castro Delgado to describe him as 'the real head of the party'.[9] While he certainly imposed the Moscow line, Codovilla also wielded personal power as the interlocutor between the Comintern and the rest of the PCE leadership. This has led Antonio Elorza to identify such 'advisers' (also called 'instructors' or 'delegates') as key power-brokers in the Comintern organisational model, leading to an insightful comparison with absolute monarchy where middle men gained great influence by transmitting and interpreting policies, while also reporting back on their effects.[10]

With Codovilla as the linchpin, the leadership of the PCE carried out the often detailed instructions it received from the Comintern. This was made easier by the relatively stable political situation in Spain which allowed for considerable periods of consultation and investigation, sometimes in Moscow, before decisions were taken. The dependency of a weak party like the PCE on the financial and organisational support of the Comintern further reinforced this pattern of control. Not that there were no instances of friction with party leaders. Two good examples concerned the adoption of the popular front line in 1935, following the earlier policy of opposing the 'bourgeois' Republic, and over the formation of the JSU with the PSOE. But in both these, and other, instances conflicts were resolved in favour of the Comintern.[11] This pattern was reproduced further down the chain of command with the party leadership exercising close authority over the rank and file. Paradoxically, it was the relatively small size of the membership (for which the leadership was constantly berated by the RLS) which ensured that this was the case. In a party of only a few thousand militants, drawn from a very narrow stratum of the working class, many of whom were known personally by leaders, it was relatively easy to monitor their activities.

Ironically, after years of failure in Comintern eyes, it was the transformation brought about by sudden success that fundamentally undermined hierarchical control over the PCE. One self-imposed complication was provided by the formation of Catalan and Basque sections on the eve of the Civil War, and finally by the creation of the United Socialist Party of Catalonia, Partit Socialista Unificat de Catalunya (PSUC) under the leadership of Joan Comorera shortly after its outbreak.[12] While the Comintern tended to see this as simply a tactical move to attract Catalans and Basques to communism, it did serve in practice to make relations more difficult by creating greater organisational complexity within the Spanish section. However, what really altered the situation was the explosive growth of membership following the outbreak of the war. Although figures cannot be relied upon unreservedly, by June 1937 it was reported that the PCE had 301,500 members, the PSUC a further 64,000 and the Basque section some 20,000.[13] Ironically, the conditions for the growth of the PCE were provided by the fervently anti-Communist insurgent Nationalists who started the war. Just as the leadership had been unable to do much to increase the size of the PCE before the conflict, so the rush to join after its outbreak had equally little to do with their efforts. In many respects this was a general movement, as all the political parties in the Republican camp grew in size during the Civil War, and the PCE did not become the largest by any means. Beyond the appeal the party shared with other political forces of identifying with the Republican cause, it benefited from more specific attractions. It was closely identified with the defence of the Republic through a coalition approach – most specifically through the popular front alliance. In addition, the party was untainted with the failed policies of the previous governments of the Republic. Finally, it was associated with Soviet support for the Republican war effort and with the idea of military efficiency.[14]

As a result of this broad appeal it was not just the size of the party that changed, but also the nature of its membership. By the middle of the war the PCE and PSUC became something of a microcosm of the social coalition underpinning the Republican war effort. In January 1937 the party reported that although the majority of its members were classified as industrial workers or agricultural labourers, there was a significant representation of small peasant farmers, the middle classes and professionals.[15] The most controversial aspects of this change were the growth of middle-class support and the attraction of defectors from other working-class movements – leading to charges that the party was adopting a policy of cynical and aggressive recruitment to undermine its rivals. However, after a long period of weak support for the party it was difficult to turn away new members and almost impossible to regulate the tide of recruits. Even so, both developments were a source of some concern to the party leadership and to the Comintern, as a potential threat to the 'proletarian character' of the movement and as a source of conflict with other political parties. One result was the creation of small business and peasant organisations, the most important of which were based in Catalonia. Though often seen as an unscrupulous means to undermine the Anarchist CNT, it was also recognised by the leadership of the PCE as a means to channel such support into the Republican camp rather than see it lost to the Nationalist insurgents. Such bodies were also part of a general proliferation of organisations aimed at mobilising different sections of the population, which ranged from the Association of Antifascist Women (Asociación de Mujeres Antifascistas), led by Dolores Ibarruri, to the welfare associations of International Red Aid (Socorro Rojo Internacional).[16] Though it was difficult to turn converts away, the PCE wavered over the undermining of other parties in the Republican camp as it did not want to discredit the popular front framework. The party did pursue a policy of uniting all the parties (or at least the working class movements) on the model provided by the JSU and PSUC. However, when this campaign faced fierce resistance from the Anarchists and Socialists it was shelved. Instead the PCE continued to rely on a network of joint committees with the PSOE and its trade-union federation to co-ordinate activities.[17]

Inevitably, the dramatic change from a small, relatively homogeneous movement existing in stable circumstances, to a large, more varied party involved in a fast-changing military, social and political struggle had serious consequences for internal relations. It became enormously difficult for the leadership of the party, and hence for the Comintern, to keep control over the activities of the rank and file. An important reason for this was the great difficulty in keeping in touch with local party organisations and new developments on the ground. Communication and movement within Republican Spain during wartime were difficult, so party leaders often lacked knowledge of what was going on, impeding the free flow of information upwards that was so vital to the operation of the Comintern model of control. Not surprisingly, the party leadership faced a constant barrage of requests for reports on the situation in Spain following the outbreak of the war. This was also one of the main reasons why the Comintern dispatched Stepanov (real name Stoin Minev, also known as 'Moreno') and Ernö Gerö (known as 'Pedro') as additional advisers alongside Codovilla to the PCE in Madrid and PSUC in Barcelona, respectively, at the beginning of the conflict. A host of other visitors from the Comintern also appeared on temporary fact-finding missions, the most important of whom was André Marty who was a regular visitor as head of the Western European Bureau (WEB) in Paris and the organiser of the International Brigades.[18] Despite these helping hands, it proved impossible at times to keep up with the constant pressure for news.

Spanish leaders and Comintern delegates found themselves unable to keep up, to the point that they complained to Moscow about the overwhelming workload and sheer impossibility of keeping track of everything that was happening, despite constant forays to gather information. Not surprisingly, at crucial moments central direction almost broke down completely, in particular during the early months of the war, when the Republican state was swept away in the aftermath of the military rising, in the crisis of the summer of 1937 and during the final internal struggle following Colonel Casado's attempted anti-Communist coup at the end of the war.[19]

The result was that the initiative frequently passed to the local level in the absence of firm directions from above. Far from directing events, the party leaders found themselves responding to local initiatives and the rivalries that came with the power vacuum – a situation exacerbated by the growth in membership which brought new interests into the movement. One consequence was that even though the PCE had been formally committed to the popular front policy of the Comintern before the war began, giving it a clear lead to follow once the Civil War erupted, in reality the party was far from united. Local Communist groups took varied views of what the popular front meant in practical terms when faced with their own choices. In areas such as Andalusia, Castile and Extremadura, some Communists became involved alongside other Republican supporters in the seizure of fields and factories belonging to supporters of the military rising, formed militias to defend their districts and took part in committees set up to administer local affairs. In other regions, particularly Catalonia and Aragón, local party members tended to defend property rights and the existing Republican order.[20] Surprise developments were also a problem. The most striking example came with the events that precipitated the so-called May Days of 1937 which produced a virtual civil war within the Civil War and threw the government of Largo Caballero into disarray. No central order was given by PCE leaders for Communist police forces to seize the telephone exchange from Anarchist militiamen on 3 May 1937. The crisis that followed was unanticipated, and even local party leaders, particular Comorera and Gerö in Barcelona, found themselves racing to catch up with developments.[21]

The dilemmas of the party leadership

Responding effectively to the pressures and tensions of the Civil War, including those emanating from the party's followers, would have been difficult for the leadership of the PCE in the best of circumstances. However, under the Comintern model a strongly united body of leaders, aided by advisers and with clear directions as to strategy and tactics passed down from Moscow, was supposed to be able to cope with just such a task. In fact, none of these ideal conditions actually prevailed at the leadership level of the party for the greater part of the Civil War. Far from offering constant guidance, the actions and inactions of the Comintern tended to exacerbate the confused situation within which the party leadership had to operate. This in turn encouraged disunity and indecision amongst party leaders and Comintern advisers who were offered no clear lead from above.

The fundamental problem between the leadership and the Comintern was the lack of a reliable line of communication. Here, once again, the command model required a constant flow of accurate information and instructions for it to work. The leaderships (including advisers) of national sections had to supply up-to-date assessments of the situations in their countries to allow the central bodies of the ECCI to make their decisions. Policies had to be efficiently transmitted back and their effects then reported upon. Even in peacetime this was a difficult task; in wartime Spain it proved to be impossible for a number of reasons.

One problem was that the chain of command became confused by the Comintern's own actions. In particular, the appointment of additional advisers as a means of enhancing Comintern control in Spain was counterproductive. With Codovilla and Stepanov in Madrid, Gerö in Barcelona, and frequent visitors such as Marty, all speaking for the Comintern, the Communist International's authority was complicated rather than clarified. In addition, the status of the Spanish leaders of the party was never exactly clear. In practice, Codovilla's dictatorial tendencies continued in the Civil War, supplemented by Stepanov who shared a similar personal style. At the same time, after the reorganisation of 1935 the Comintern did not deal exclusively with its delegates and, in theory at least, the views of the leading Spanish figures were also sought.[22]

The other major reason for the difficulties of communicating effectively with the Comintern was physical – the means of secure communication were erratic at best. The most direct method was through the clandestine radio-telegraph station, built with some difficulty in the roof of a safe house in a working-class district of central Madrid before the war. It never operated entirely satisfactorily, but as the area in which it was located was under Francoist artillery and air bombardment for most of the war, it broke down frequently, and by the latter part of the war worked only intermittently. A great many messages never arrived or were only partially received. The alternative was to carry messages. However, couriers inevitably were slow, even when they were visiting Communists from other countries, and some messengers were intercepted by hostile security services. The final means was the well-established practice for instructors and leaders to make the long journey directly to Moscow for consultations.[23]

The result of these uncertain and delicate links to 'home' was that the leadership of the PCE was often left effectively without the 'guidance' of the Comintern. Often, it was the sheer speed at which events sometimes unfolded during the war that simply overwhelmed the system. Information and instructions passing to and from Moscow became instantly outdated or irrelevant, leading to further rounds of frantic message-sending to try to catch up. Such a situation occurred during the chaotic outbreak of the war, and again when the Giral government fell and Largo Caballero became premier in September 1936. The indiscriminate nature of the Comintern's bureaucratic demands for detailed knowledge also overburdened party leaders and instructors with paperwork. All requests for reports needed to be answered regardless of their true importance, leading to backlogs, not to mention the exhaustion and frustration caused to the writers. Thus, Gerö complained in February 1937 that it was simply impossible to keep up with the demand for news from the Comintern and Stepanov did the same a few months later. As well as these delays, however, there were complete breakdowns in communication that often occurred at crucial moments. Perhaps the clearest example came during the crisis of May and June 1937, when requests for instructions went unanswered.[24]

The absence of Comintern guidance meant that the party leadership was often unclear as to what was expected of it. However, it was the case that Communist leaderships, as good Bolsheviks, were expected to know implicitly what to do in any circumstances. Moreover, Comintern endorsement of any action taken by the leadership was certainly required, even if it was only sought retrospectively. It could thus be argued that, in effect, the PCE was following Comintern instructions despite the absence of direct orders.

This would require that Comintern policies should be capable of being easily and unambiguously translated into 'correct' decisions on the ground. Unfortunately, the popular front strategy applied in Spain did not fit these criteria, nor, probably, could any broad 'line' have done so, given the complexities of the Civil War. Even so, the popular front was particularly vague as a prescription for action. It was a compromise that stressed the need for broad political alliances against fascism, while downplaying revolution, without actually eliminating it as an aim for Communist parties. In general rhetorical terms it fitted the Spanish situation well, equipping the PCE with an approach to the war that was far more consistent than that of any other major political force within the Republican camp. However, what it might mean in any particular instance was not always clear to Spanish Communists. Did it mean that no revolutionary initiative was permissible even if the opportunity presented itself? What sort of alliances could be sought with political groups, such as Socialists, Anarchists and dissident Communists, which had been seen as deadly rivals for influence over the working class? Such questions had not been answered even though the existence of a popular front, in name at least, predated the outbreak of the war in Spain. In fact, it was more of a temporary electoral pact, predominantly brokered by the Socialists and middle-class republican parties rather than the Communists, instead of an alliance.[25] Not just the broad aims of the Comintern, but many of the apparently detailed instructions received in Spain were ambiguous, open to interpretation or simply outdated. Having orders from the Comintern was not the same as being able to carry them out, and seeking clarification was yet another source of frustration and delay in the relationship between Moscow and the PCE.

Not surprisingly, even a leadership as seemingly Stalinist as that of the PCE found itself on the horns of many dilemmas because of this uncertainty. In the end the leadership frequently had to improvise policy, taking local initiatives as the only way forward left open to them, dealing with any objections from the Comintern after the fact. This meant that, in practice, party leaders and Comintern advisers had a certain freedom of manoeuvre to do as they chose as long as they were able to defend any initiative as compatible with the general line emanating from the ECCI and as a response to any detailed instructions that might actually be received. At the same time, the difficulties of deciding on exactly the best tactics to meet the situation in Spain and to satisfy the Comintern provided the substance for debates and disputes among party leaders and advisers. These were always couched in the received categories of Communist discourse, but, inevitably, the leadership advocated policies that conformed to their personal opinions and collective prejudices. The possibilities for alternative interpretations of the situation in Spain and of Comintern policy also meant, of course, that personal and political rivalries could flourish amongst the advisers and Spanish leaders.

Far from seizing the initiative to reshape ruthlessly the Republican camp to their design, the leadership of the PCE was more tentative and indecisive in the face of the complexities of the Civil War. This was particularly so during the early stages of the conflict when dilemmas over policy were at their most acute and accurate knowledge of local developments was at its most scarce. Initially, party leaders took an optimistic view after it became clear that the military rising had not succeeded, seeing it as a re-run of the abortive Sanjurjo coup of 1932. They expected that the government would regain control fairly quickly and the political situation in Spain would return to normal.[26] Accordingly, the PCE was unprepared for the fall of the Giral administration at the end of August 1936 and unsure whether to support the formation of a coalition government under the Socialist, Largo Caballero. Initially, while appealing for a view from Moscow, Codovilla and a major part of the Politburo conservatively favoured the continuation of an abstentionist position. Only when it was clear that almost all the other political groups within the Republican side would join a new government did the PCE enter, gaining three ministerial positions. Comintern endorsement of this action as compatible with the popular front policy came when Stepanov arrived later in September bringing directives from Moscow. This was reinforced in October 1936 when the Soviet Union intervened militarily on the side of the Republic.[27]

In most accounts the PCE in government is portrayed as uncompromising in its defence of the status quo and counter-revolutionary in its actions. The fact that the party did not recognise that a revolution had taken place is seen as symptomatic of the blind obedience to Stalin's wishes that supposedly dominated its actions. However, it is evident that the Communist leadership was far from clear in its view of developments, and not merely perversely blinded by Stalinist loyalty in its attitudes to revolutionary possibilities. Revolutionary claims from the Anarchists and POUM were easily dismissed as ridiculous by PCE leaders because, by definition, the only authentic 'revolution' could be one declared and led by Communists. Initially, in the aftermath of the military coup and in the absence of any other information, party leaders assumed that only a breakdown in order had occurred. When local party and trade-union branches seized control in the Republican zone, this was seen, accordingly, as a temporary necessity that would be reversed when central government power was restored. Anything more than this was denounced as the actions of 'uncontrollables' amongst the ranks of the CNT. However, the PCE had to acknowledge, albeit grudgingly, that something more fundamental might be occurring when it became clear that local Communists were also participating in land and factory seizures in many areas.[28] Faced on the one hand with the need to support the popular front, and to respond to Comintern injunctions not to drive the middle classes into the hands of the Nationalists, and on the other hand with the desires of part of the rank and file of the party to seize the revolutionary opportunities that had opened up, the leadership of the party leadership prevaricated.

Rather than following its own path, the PCE responded by adopting the compromise position taken by the left wing of the Socialist Party: to favour both the popular front and the revolution.[29] Accordingly, the Communists did nothing to prevent party members from creating collectives, joining local committees or forming their own militias. At the same time they endorsed the need to defend the Republican status quo and to rebuild a Republican state: a policy given formal status in the letter from the Soviet leadership to Largo Caballero in December 1936 which laid out the views of the Soviet leadership towards the war.[30] In many respects it was natural for the PCE to take a particularly active role in the creation of new centralised institutions, particularly a state bureaucracy, police forces and army. There appears to have been no policy of Communist 'infiltration', as one was not needed. Communist ideology emphasised the importance of the state, and the Comintern, of course, was strongly imprinted with the notion of central control. However, once again, they were not alone in this view – it was common to the Socialist and republican parties as well. Given that the personnel for these institutions had to be drawn from the ranks of committed supporters of the Republic, it was also not surprising that members of the PCE figured prominently. In the end, though, this balancing act was unsustainable. The very act of recreating a central Republican state put its supporters on a collision course with those social and political forces that favoured a more wholeheartedly revolutionary approach to the war and, in the case of the Anarchists, a de-centralised one. It was a conundrum which Largo Caballero and his political faction were simply unable to solve, and over which the Socialist Party was to become fatally divided.[31]

Even without pressure from the Comintern to oppose the chief proponents of revolution, the PCE leadership would have faced the need to decide which way to throw the weight of the party in an inevitable clash of opinions. As it was, hostility to the Anarchists and, above all, to the POUM was constantly urged on the Spanish Communists from the highest levels of the Comintern. The clearest instances of this were two resolutions from the Presidium of the ECCI issued in December 1936 and February 1937 to the PCE, the latter calling for 'the complete and final crushing of Trotskyism [i.e. the POUM] in Spain'.[32] However, Comintern orders did not force the PCE into a course of action that it would not otherwise have followed. When PCE leaders apparently echoed the rhetoric of the Comintern in reports like those of the General Secretary, José Díaz, in March 1937, arguing that 'the POUM must be removed from the political life of Spain', they were not simply adopting the dictates of Stalin's Terror.[33] Spanish Communists had their own reasons going back to the 1920s for seeing the POUM as a deadly enemy. Leading figures in the POUM had been members of the PCE. Andreu Nin, in particular, had been the party's delegate to Profintern and while in Moscow had sided with Trotsky in the debates over the future direction of the Soviet Union. As a consequence, he spent a period under house arrest in the Hotel Lux, before being allowed back to Spain in 1930. Reports on his activities, and those of other 'dissident' Communists, were sent back to Comintern for years before the Civil War erupted. After the POUM was formed, and had became a party roughly equal in size to the PSUC in Catalonia, the antipathy of the Spanish section of the Communist International to a direct ideological rival was merely confirmed.[34] Yet, at the same time the PCE leadership actually showed a marked reluctance to take decisive action, seeking clarification from Moscow on how exactly they were supposed to proceed. Partly this was another case of confusion over how to translate a general principle into concrete action. But mainly it was a concern on the part of the party leaders that the PCE lacked the strength to act alone and a fear that any precipitate blow against the POUM would wreck the popular front approach to the war. Instead, a low level conflict with the POUM, and to an extent the Anarchists, in Catalonia bubbled away fuelled by local rivalries, serious enough to lead to assassinations on all sides.[35] In the end, it was this steadily growing tension, rather than a calculated strike delivered by the PCE on behalf of Moscow, which provided the background to the sudden eruption of open conflict in May 1937.

During the deep political crisis that now engulfed the Republican camp, the leaders of the PCE were largely bereft of the advice of the Comintern and by no means clear about how best to proceed. At a series of meetings of the Politburo the underlying differences between them were exposed in debates about the party position. Díaz (debilitated by the severe illness that was to dog the rest of his life[36]) and Hernández cautioned against precipitate action that might alienate the Anarchists and urged continuing support of the Caballero government. This view was opposed by the Comintern delegates. Codovilla and Stepanov, supported by the other Spaniards, argued instead that Caballero had finally become a complete liability and that action was needed to quell the 'counter-revolutionary putsch' against the Republic, as they termed the struggle in Barcelona. In fact the tide of opinion had been flowing against Caballero for some time, mainly due to the Republic's continual military defeats. Even before the May events, the PCE had begun to distance itself from the left of the PSOE, a move which included a critical speech from Hernández as a government minister, which he was later to argue he had been forced to make.[37] The paralysis of Caballero in the face of the current crisis confirmed the bankruptcy of his government, and undermined the positions of Díaz and Hernández. However, what finally persuaded the Communist leadership openly to oppose Caballero was the support of the right faction of the PSOE, led by Negrín, and the smaller republican parties for action. Caballero would no doubt have survived if his party had continued to back him, but it was Negrín who largely orchestrated his removal in negotiation with the other parties. This began with the withdrawal of the three Communist ministers from the government, and ended when the right-wing Socialists and republicans in the cabinet called for Caballero to resign. Negrín then formed a new administration in which the number of Communist ministers was reduced to two.[38]

With the compromise period of the wartime Republic now brought to a close, harsh actions were taken against the POUM and CNT following the May events. Far from moving unilaterally to crush the proponents of a revolutionary approach to the war – including Caballero's faction of the PSOE – the Spanish Communists acted only in co-ordination with their Socialist and republican partners in the national government in Madrid and with the Catalan republicans in the Generalitat (Catalan regional government). Nor were Communist leaders uniformly enthusiasts for this course, despite the further urgings of Comintern for decisive action once contact was restored with Moscow. Díaz and Hernández remained fearful for the future of Republican unity, arguing ineffectively for rapprochement with the CNT and POUM rather than confrontation, and afraid that the party risked alienating its own rank-and-file supporters who favoured a revolutionary approach. In the event, the brutality which Communist troops and police (as well as others) showed in quelling the street fighting in Barcelona, in the forcible dismantling of collectives and local self-government and, above all, in the campaign to suppress the POUM, once again owed far more to feeling on the ground than any dictates from Moscow. [39] Nor does it seem to have been the case that the Comintern ordered the arrest and torture of Nin, although Hernández gives an account in his memoirs of a meeting of the PCE leadership in June 1937 – minus himself and a bedridden Díaz – in which the detention of Nin was supposedly ordered.[40] All other evidence suggests that the leaders of the party, including the Comintern delegates, were unaware that Orlov had arranged the kidnapping of Nin with three unknown Spanish Communists who were members of the Republican Security Service, Servicio de Información Militar (SIM), acting either on his own initiative or under the orders of the People's Commissariat of

Internal Affairs, Narodny Komissariat Vnutrennikh Del (NKVD).[41] The main role of the Comintern in this affair was to order Gerö to produce, after the event, highly implausible, forged documents purporting to show collusion between the POUM and the Francoists. In other respects the PCE supported a 'legalistic' approach to the POUM, along with the other members of the governing coalition, involving 'show trials' of the leading figure of the movement and some Anarchists.[42]

Although the fall of Caballero is often portrayed as confirming the dominance of the PCE, in many respects it actually showed its dependence. By following the lead taken by Negrín, the party confirmed its minority status within the government coalition and the leadership showed the limits to their ability to take independent action. Support from the PCE was essential, but the decisive shift in government policy towards the centralisation of the war effort and the suppression of alternatives had its real origins within the divisions of the Socialist Party, which formed the backbone of the Republican government.[43] The position of the Communists was reinforced in the sense that the party became, even more than before, at the heart of the reconstructed state and military apparatus until defeat in 1939. Despite the relatively successful passage of the PCE through the crisis of the Republic, the failure of the party to seize the initiative, and clear signs of discord amongst the leadership evident in reports from Spain, greatly disturbed the ECCI. Conflicting versions of events that were received from the main Comintern delegates and from Marty, who was also present during the May–June period, further fuelled the concern that the influence of the Communist International over events was less than perfect. It was for these reasons that Palmiro Togliatti (known as 'Alfredo' or 'Ercoli') arrived in Spain in mid-July 1937, ordered directly by the General Secretary of Comintern, Georgii Dimitrov (nicknamed 'Dios' or 'God' by the Spaniards), to investigate the state of the PCE and, in particular, to assess the work of the Comintern representatives. As one of the most important figures within the central apparatus of the Comintern, with a knowledge of the PCE and its leaders (though not of Spain itself) that went back before the Civil War, he was well placed to intervene in the troubling Spanish situation.[44]

Once in Spain, Togliatti immediately set about imposing his authority, attending meetings of the PCE Central Committee and interviewing the leading figures in the party. In a series of reports to Moscow over the next few months he presented a portrait of the internal workings of the leadership which was critical of the lack of unity amongst the Spaniards and damning of the role of the Comintern delegates.[45] Far from many hands making light work, as the Comintern had intended, too many cooks were spoiling the broth. His final recommendations were transmitted in a report to the ECCI of 15 September 1937:

> my conviction has grown that it is neccessay to radically change the working methods of your 'advisers' that are here . . . there exists a group of comrades (Uribe,

> Dolores, Hernández, Girola) capable of leading the party and leading it well. It is necessary 1) that your advisers do not disorientate the Spanish comrades by pushing them down a mistaken path, either by the fabrication of improvised or incorrect theories, or by an innoportune political nerviousness which, united with that of the Spanish comrades, confuses little by little the party's tactics. 2) that your 'advisers' stop considering themselves the 'bosses' of the party, considering that the Spanish comrades are worthless, that they stop substituting for them on the pretext of doing things 'quickly' or 'better'. [46]

While attacking the tendency of Codovilla, Stepanov and Marty to be both domineering and competitive, Togliatti encouraged the Spanish leaders to express their own opinions about the progress of the war and the role of the Comintern in it.

On the basis of Togliatti's reports, Codovilla was removed from Spain, and Marty was ordered to concern himself with the International Brigades and not to interfere in party affairs directly. Though Gerö continued as representative to the PSUC, where he was well liked by the Catalan leadership, Togliatti effectively became the sole official link between the Comintern and the PCE, with Stepanov serving as his deputy – in effect, recreating the position that had existed before the outbreak of the war. The constant demands for detailed information and attempts at micro-intervention by the Comintern abated, making life a lot easier for the PCE leadership. Having dealt with this problem, he went on to take further measures to improve the inner workings of the party leadership. In particular, decision-making in the Central Committee became more open and collective in nature, encouraged by the sympathetic attitude Togliatti took towards the Spanish leaders following the injunction of Dimitrov 'neither to limit nor suffocate in any way the initiative or personality of the Spanish leaders'.[47] The fact that the party no longer faced any major decisions as to its direction during the war also meant that differences between the leaders became more muted. At the same time there were changes in the position of individual leaders that Togliatti pursued on behalf of the Comintern. Perhaps the most significant was the rise of Dolores Ibarruri as the most prominent public face of the party; a recognition that she was the only figure who possessed a charismatic appeal that went beyond the ranks of convinced Communists. She was clearly already being groomed as successor to the ailing Díaz, who retained the post of Secretary General but whose importance was in decline. The other main change concerned Hernández, who was conveniently removed as Minister of Education in a cabinet reshuffle in April 1938, and appointed as a Military Commissar.

Togliatti's other main influence on the PCE as chief Comintern delegate was to reformulate the language in which the party's role and the war itself were described. This married the current objectives of the Communist International with the realities of Spain, rationalising the position of the party as it had emerged by the end of 1937 and providing a flexible version of Communist ideology. The main plank was a redefinition of Communist war aims as the creation of a 'democracy of a new type', presenting the Republic not just in terms of the pre-1936 status quo, but as a 'regime with progressive features'. These slogans allowed the PCE to preserve its popular front approach while maintaining its claims to be working towards a socialist society – hence the continued use of the notion that the PCE was pursuing a 'Spanish revolution' with the caveat that Spain was not yet ready for fully fledged Bolshevism.[48] The government alliance with the Socialist right and republicans could be maintained – though this did not prevent the PCE pursuing a campaign against anti-Communist ministers such as Indalecio Prieto – and the middle-class elements in the party were reassured.[49] At the same time, the progressive claims for the Republic appealed to working-class and peasant supporters who favoured change and who (just as Díaz and Hernández had feared) had expressed some dismay at the attacks on collectivisation. Having dissolved Anarchist collectives in the middle of 1937, often handing back land and businesses to their original owners, the party proposed that the government 'nationalise' similar organisations that were under the control of Communists or Socialists and bring them under the direction of the state.[50] This also allowed overtures to be made to the CNT that led to the entry of Anarchist ministers to the government, even as the campaign against the POUM continued to unfold.[51]

By these means a delicate balance was maintained both within the PCE and in its relations with its political allies in the Republican camp that was to last until the end of the war. What was not possible, of course, was to eliminate the understandable resentments at what was perceived as Communist influence, even though these were, in reality, government policies. This led to another round of internal struggle with the so-called Casado coup and the final collapse of Republican resistance.[52]

Comintern and decision-making

Dispatching Togliatti to Spain was arguably the most important positive step that the Comintern made in its relationship with the PCE during the war. His actions helped create a measure of order out of a near-chaotic situation, they brought some stability to a party which had come to seem rudderless, and improved links with the Communist International. This was achieved by reversing many of the measures that Comintern had previously made, ironically with the aim of tightening its control over the PCE, and by recognising that centralisation of decision-making in Moscow could not work and was, in fact, often counter-productive. Such a 'hispanisation' of the Comintern's Spanish policy was made all the easier when the Civil War ceased to be so important for both the Communist International and the Soviet Union during 1938.

What is surprising is that it took the Comintern so long to act to regularise the situation in Spain. Though it is difficult to prove definitely just why this was the case, undoubtedly it was very hard for Comintern officials to break with a model of political control that was so entrenched within the whole ideology of international communism in the Stalinist period. Indeed, the problems that the Communist International actually encountered in its relations with the PCE encouraged a redoubling of misguided efforts rather than inducing a rethink – that is until a near breakdown was reached. The best example was again in the crucial area of information. Naturally, if the leaders of the PCE found it impossible to keep up with wider developments, so too did the ECCI. If anything, the confusion in Moscow was often even greater, as the Comintern suffered not only from news droughts when communications broke down, but also the opposite: information overload. This was because reports on Spain were received not only from the party leadership and advisers, but also from visiting Communists and, on a selective basis, via Soviet journalists, the embassy, military advisers and intelligence sources. These often contradicted themselves, leading to confusion. For instance, at the beginning of the war the Comintern was relying for information on German intelligence reports from Barcelona that had been obtained by the NKVD and on dispatches from Codovilla. The German sources suggested that the military rising was achieving a measure of success, while Codovilla misleadingly continued to suggest, in line with the view he had presented before the conflict began, that there was no serious threat to the Republic.[53] As we have seen, the response of the Comintern to both the lack of news and too much of it, was to ask for more, in the vain hope that some accurate and definitive version of developments was out there somewhere that would enable the system to work as it was supposed to.

The pattern of decision-making within the central apparatus over Spain also worked against centralised control by the Comintern. For the bureaucracy, the Civil War represented a much-needed opportunity to exert influence and keep busy at a time when the Communist International was in danger of becoming moribund.[54] The archives of the Comintern bear witness to the mountain of paper produced in the way of internal reports by individuals and special committees, usually of great length and often showing limited understanding of the situation in Spain. It is hard to be sure how much effect these actually had on the two figures within the Communist International who took the greatest responsibility for Spain on a day-to-day basis – Manuilsky, whose secretariat was responsible for the PCE, and Georgii Dimitrov, the head of the Comintern – but they indicate how cumbersome the machinery could be.

The effect of outside influences on the functioning of the Comintern is also hard to judge. The need to consult Stalin – nicknamed by the irreverent Spaniards 'Bigotes' (Moustache) – might also have slowed the taking of decisions, though again the evidence is inconclusive.[55] Certainly, until 1938 a weekly digest of reports from Spain, along with an assessment of the situation, was sent to Stalin. His 'advice' was frequently sought by Dimitrov, though we have no record of replies. In many cases, however, what was required was approval for actions already taken or for policies that were being proposed from within Comintern.[56] Telephone conversations and the contents of private meetings (easily arranged, given that the main Comintern buildings stood next to the Kremlin) are also unknown to us. In any event, Dimitrov and Manuilsky did not need to be reminded what the objectives of foreign policy were at any moment in time. What does seem to have been lacking was any well-co-ordinated approach to Spain by the Kremlin into which the Comintern was integrated. This mirrored the competition and confusion within the Soviet system at a time when the Terror was spreading – not least to the ranks of foreign Communists in Moscow.[57] Although some information was shared, the different Soviet agencies present in Spain seem to have worked largely on separate lines.

Conclusion

The Civil War revealed many inherent deficiencies in the Comintern approach to controlling the activities of member parties. No consistent chain of command operated in Spain connecting headquarters in Moscow with the party rank and file. In some respects, the reverse held true, with power flowing upwards rather than downwards, due, above all, to the difficulties of obtaining reliable information upon which to make decisions. There was also a corresponding tendency for each level of organisation to turn in upon itself. Though connected to the other layers, the party membership, leadership and central Comintern apparatus tended to become absorbed in their own version of affairs. Inevitably, how officials of the Communist International saw the war and the role of the PCE in it was quite different to the experiences of ordinary Spanish Communists. Similarly, instead of operating to a detailed strategy concocted in Moscow, as it was supposed to, the party rather stumbled through the war – at least until after the crisis point of mid-1937 when the direction of policy became set.

However, it would be equally untenable to write a history of the PCE during the Civil War that failed to acknowledge the role of the Comintern. The Communist International provided the general framework for the actions of the PCE through its policies, which, although clearly open to a great deal of interpretation, had to be adhered to. On occasions, its interventions made a difference, though not to the point of forcing the PCE to act in a way that it would not have done otherwise. Its existence also had a more intangible, but important effect on the PCE which gave it a crucial advantage over other political forces within the Republican camp. All the other main groups – particularly the PSOE and CNT – became fatally split over how and why to fight the war, divisions that became acute in the summer of 1937, while the PCE managed to stay united. As we have seen, this was not because there were no divisions within Communist ranks: internal conflict and vacillation greatly affected the party. Rather, this underlying unity – perhaps most evident amongst the leadership of the party – flowed in great part from the sense of belonging to a wider, special international movement with its own specific political culture, ideology and mission. The writings and memoirs of Communists, even those who became hostile to the cause, demonstrate the extent to which the self-image of discipline and direction perpetrated by Comintern was deeply felt. Perhaps, ultimately, it was not the reality of the controlling hand of Moscow that really mattered, but the power of the myth of that control.

Notes

1 The principles behind the Comintern are laid out in F. Claudin, *The Communist Movement: From Comintern to Cominform* (London, 1975), pp. 103–12; K. McDermott and J. Agnew, *The Comintern: A History of International Communism from Lenin to Stalin* (London, 1996), pp. 14–27.

2 For overviews of the role of the Comintern in Spain, see D. Cattell, *Communism and the Spanish Civil War* (Berkeley, Calif., 1954); M. T. Meshcheryakov, *Ispanskaya respublika i Komintern (natsional'norevolyutsionnaya voyna ispanskogo naroda i politika Kommunisticheskogo Internatsionala 1936–1939 gg.)* (Moscow, 1981) and 'Kommunisticheskaya Partiya Ispanii i Komintern', *Novaya i Noveishaya Istoriya*, 5 (1991); E. H. Carr, *The Comintern and the Spanish Civil War* (London, 1984); P. Broue, *Staline et la Révolution: Le cas espagnol* (Paris, 1993).

3 On Soviet policy and Spain, see M. T. Mescheryakov, 'SSSR i Grazhdanskaya Voina v Ispanii', *Otechestvennaya Istoriya*, 3 (1995), 83–95; J. Haslam, *The Soviet Union and the Struggle for Collective Security in Europe 1933–1939* (London, 1984), chap. 7; D. Cattell, *Soviet Diplomacy and the Spanish Civil War* (Berkeley, Calif., 1957); D. Smyth, '"We Are With You": solidarity and self-interest in Soviet policy towards Republican Spain, 1936–1939', in P. Preston and A. Mackenzie (eds), *The Republic Besieged: Civil War in Spain 1936–1939* (Edinburgh, 1996), pp. 87–106; M. Alpert, *A New International History of the Spanish Civil War* (London, 1994), esp. chap 12.

4 In addition to the overviews of Comintern actions (above), there is an extensive literature on the role of the PCE in the war, often polemical in nature, which it is impossible to list the whole of here. Contributions include memoirs from across the whole of the Republican political spectrum, including ones by unrepentant and repentant Communists, works by Francoist apologists eager to prove that a Communist plot was at work in Spain, and later studies often taking critical or supportive stances of PCE policy. All take it as axiomatic – whether for good or ill – that the PCE followed Soviet policy. The most comprehensive and sophisticated account, taking a negative view, is that of B. Bolloten, *The Spanish Civil War: Revolution and Counterrevolution* (Hemel Hempstead, 1991), which also offers a good guide to the literature. A far more nuanced picture is painted by H. Graham, 'War, modernity and reform: the premiership of Juan Negrín 1937–1939', in Preston and Mackenzie (eds), *The Republic Besieged*, pp. 163–96. Various views from within the PCE are provided by J. Díaz, *Tres años de lucha por la Frente Popular, por la libertad, por la independencia de España* (Paris, 1970); V. González, *Comunista en España y antistalinista en la URSS: Nuevas revelaciones* (Mexico, 1952); Jesús Hernández, *Yo fuí un ministro de Stalin* (Mexico, 1953); E. Castro Delgado, *Hombres made in Moscú* (Mexico, 1960); E. Líster, *Nuestra guerra* (Paris, 1966) and *Memorias de un luchador* (Madrid, 1977); D. Ibarruri, *They Shall not Pass: the Autobiography of La Pasionaria*

(New York, 1966) and *El unico camino* (Paris, 1967); J. Almendros, *Situaciones españolas: el PSUC en la guerra civil, 1936–1939* (Barcelona, 1976).

5 This word is used with a lower case to identify the middle-class, liberal political parties which had historically called themselves republicans, as opposed to upper-case Republican indicating all those forces that supported the Republic in the Civil War.

6 The Organisation Department of the CI, 'Report on the state of the Spanish Party n.d.' [1935], RC 495/25/622, gives a figure of membership of 20,000 for the end of 1935. According to the statistics for the earlier period of the Republic, the party experienced great fluctuations in membership from some 1,500 in 1930 to 19,489 in March 1933 (plus 11,275 in the youth movement) in March 1933. It then declined to a few thousand members before growing again after October 1934: see 'Statistics of the Spanish Communist Party', RC 495/25/615 and 'Report of the Spanish Delegation', RC 495/32/124a. The JSU had probably 40,000 members in April 1936, though many Socialists left shortly after unification in protest at PCE domination: see H. Graham, *Socialism and War: the Spanish Socialist Party in Power and Crisis, 1936–1939* (Cambridge, 1991), pp. 29–31. On the development of the PCE before 1930, see P. Pagès, *Historia del Partido Comunista de España* (Barcelona, 1978) and for its development under Republic, see R. Cruz, *El Partido Comunista de España en la Segunda República* (Madrid, 1987).

7 According to Dolores Ibarruri's private secretary, working as a translator in Moscow after October 1934: see Irene Falcón, *Asalto a los cielos: Mi vida junto a Pasionaria* (Madrid, 1996), p. 132.

8 On the replacement of the leadership, see the reports to the Politsekretariat on the party in RC 495/3/121 and the letter from the ECCI to the PCE announcing the 'exclusion of several opportunists' for failing to adhere to the Comintern 'line', RC 495/32/208; and the account of the ousted General Secretary, J. Bullejos, *La Comintern en España: recuerdos de mi vida* (Mexico, 1972), pp. 202–7. P. Pagès, 'Jules Humbert-Droz et les Origines du Communisme dans l'Etat Espagnol', in Centenaire Jules Humbert-Droz, *Colloque sur I'Intenationale Communiste. Actes* (Geneva, 1992), pp. 136–7 makes the point that in many respects the old leadership was thoroughly 'Stalinist' but was simply not compliant enough. Castro Delgado, *Hombres made in Moscú* gives a profile of the new party leadership at the time of the Civil War emphasising their subordination to Moscow.

9 Delgado, *Hombres made in Moscú*, p. 374. This viewpoint is also supported more recently by Ibarruri's secretary: see Falcón, *Asalto a los cielos*, p. 144. See also A. Elorza, 'Stalinisme et Internationalisme en Espagne, 1931–1939', in S. Wolokow and M. Cordillot (eds), *Prolétaires de tous les pays, unissez-vous? Les difficiles chemins de l'internationalisme (1848–1956)* (Dijon, 1993), p. 196. For a profile of the career of Codovilla, see B. Lazitch, *Biographical Dictionary of the Comintern* (Standford, Calif., 1986), pp. 77–8. Of Italian extraction, Codovilla's first name was frequently hispanised to Victorio.

10 A. Elorza, 'In the shadow of God: the formation of the Comintern's Spanish policy', in M. Narinsky and J. Rojahn, *Centre and Periphery: The History of the Comintern in the Light of New Documents* (Amsterdam, 1996) pp. 237–45.

11 In May and June 1936 Dimitrov, as General Secretary, felt the need to counter the reluctance of Spanish leaders to abandon a revolutionary and sectarian approach in meetings of the Comintern Secretariat and Presidium, stressing the need to con-

solidate the popular front approach and strengthen the Republic: see *Outline History of the Communist International* (Moscow, 1971), pp. 415–16; Meshcheryakov, 'Kommunisticheskaya Partiya Ispanii', 19–20.

12 The PSUC was composed of Catalan Socialists and Communists in a confederation on the same lines as the JSU, but quickly became dominated by the Communist leadership. See J. L. Martín i Ramos, *Els origens del Partit Socialista Unificat de Catalunya, 1930–1936* (Barcelona, 1977).

13 Figures reported at the June 1937 Plenum of the PCE, *Communist International*, 7, XIV (1937). For January 1937 the party reported figures of 249,140 (50,000 of them members of the PSUC alone), *Communist International*, 5, XIV (1937). Doubts about the figures arise in part because of the PCE's long history of overestimating its membership to try and appease the Comintern.

14 In many respects the grassroots history of the PCE still remains to be written.

15 The actual figures were: industrial workers 87,660; agricultural labourers 62,250; peasants 76,700; middle class 15,483; intellectuals and professionals 7,045; women 19,300, *Communist International*, 5, XIV (1937).

16 The best known of the small business organisations was the Catalan Federation of Small Commercial and Industrial Guilds and Organisations, the Federación Catalana de Gremios y Entidades de Pequeños Comerciantes e Industriales (GEPCI). Bolloten, *The Spanish Civil War*, pp. 81–7 makes the charge that the PCE sold out to the middle classes. The potential problems of the broadening base of the party are reported by the French Communist Raymond Guyot to Dimitrov: RC 495/74/199, 'Memorandum der Genossen R. Guyot zu den Spanischen Fragen', 21 December 1936.

17 This is not to deny, of course, that other parties felt themselves to be facing a sectarian Communist Party. On the joint committees and early Socialist reactions to the growth of the PCE, see Graham, *Socialism and War*, pp. 74–85 and *passim* for the development of Socialist hostility throughout the war. The suggestion that elections should be held in the Republican zone to legitimise the growth of party supported by Stalin, was also shelved: see Elorza, 'Stalinisme et Internationalisme', p.199. The later analysis of Tito, mentioned in Geoff Swain's chapter in this volume (chapter 13), that the PCE should have done more to take over other parties is also interesting in this regard.

18 For profiles, see Lazitch, *Biographical Dictionary*, pp. 137–8, 305–6, 36–7. Stepanov had a great deal of previous personal experience of the PCE, having been involved in the LLS and later as number two in Manuilsky's secretariat, which had responsibility for the PCE.

19 Reports to Dimitrov on the situation in Spain for 1936 and 1937 make it clear the extent to which the party lacked direction at crucial moments: RC 495/74/206.

20 In many respects the grassroots history of the Communists during the Civil War still remains to be written. Collectivisation, in particular, has tended to be identified wholly with the Anarchists, producing a large literature on the subject, and one which deals only sparsely with the other forces in the Republican camp. On the varied positions of local Communists, some details can be gleaned from L. Garrido González, *Colectividades agrarias en Andalucía: Jáen (1931–1939)* (Madrid, 1979) and N. Rodrigo González, *Las colectividades agrarias en Castilla-La Mancha* (Toledo, 1985); Julián Casanova, *Anarquismo y revolución en la sociedad rural aragonesa, 1936–1938* (Madrid, 1985).

21 The initiative to remove the telephone exchange from CNT control was taken by the police commissar for Barcelona acting under the authority of the Generalitat, Eusebio Rodríguez Salas, a member of the PSUC. See V. Alba and S. Schwartz, *Spanish Marxism Versus Soviet Communism: A History of the POUM* (New Brunswick, NJ, 1988), pp. 188–9 for details.

22 Codovilla, in particular, remained highly dictatorial in his attitude, much to the annoyance of the Spanish leaders and his fellow delegates. In October 1936 Marty complained to Manuilsky that Codovilla was failing to heed the directives of the Seventh Congress in 1935 which had called for greater consultation with domestic leaders of Communist parties. Instead, Marty argued, Codovilla treated the Spanish leaders as 'mere executive agents', and he stated that 'Comrade Codovilla considers the party to be his property': RC 495/10a/209, also cited in Elorza, 'In the shadow of God', pp. 240–1. J. Hernández, *Yo fuí un ministro de Stalin*, p. 22, offers a similar view of Codovilla and Stepanov.

23 RC 495/32/217 contains reports on the setting up of the clandestine radio station. Telegrams from and to Spain are to be found in various locations in the archive, particularly in RC 495/120/226–240. Visiting foreign Communists frequently reported their findings and passed on messages to the Comintern. See, for instance, Harry Pollitt's letter to Dimitrov of July 1937: RC 495/74/206.

24 See various reports to Dimitrov in RC 495/74/206 and Elorza, 'In the shadow of God', p. 243.

25 On the development of the popular front in Spain, see S. Juliá, *Orígenes del Frente Popular en España (1934–1936)* (Madrid, 1979) and 'The origins and nature of the Spanish popular front', in M. Alexander and H. Graham (eds), *The French and Spanish Popular Fronts: Comparative Perspectives* (Cambridge, 1989), pp. 24–37; P. Preston, 'The creation of the popular front in Spain' in H. Graham and P. Preston (eds), *The Popular Front in Europe* (London, 1987), pp. 84–105.

26 Codovilla's initial reports to the Comintern after the military rising began suggested that it was a minor difficulty that the government would quickly deal with: RC 495/74/206.

27 Hernández sums up the views of the party leadership in his unreliable memoirs: 'We decided that the revolutionary position was not to collaborate. Our decision was submitted to Moscow, with no little amazement we recieived the order to participate in the government', J. Hernández, *Yo fuí un ministro de Stalin*, p. 47. The Comintern's first directive to the PCE on 24 July 1936 vaguely urged the party to defend the Republic and gave it the option of joining the government if it seemed necessary. The Secretariat and Presidium only met to consider the situation in detail on 17 September 1936, deciding to establish the International Brigades and to define the war in terms of the defence of an 'anti-fascist state' under the banner of the popular front rather than for the establishment of Soviet power in Spain. See Carr, *Comintern and the Spanish Civil War*, pp.19–23.

28 The notion that only a breakdown in law and order had occurred was not simply fanciful. The situation in the Republican zone was chaotic in the early period and it was by no means as clear as Anarchist and POUM sources suggest that a revolution had actually taken place. See M. Seidman, *Workers Against Work: Labor in Paris and Barcelona during the Popular Fronts* (Berkeley, Calif., 1991) and Casanova, *Anarquismo y revolución* for useful correctives. On mixed PCE and Comintern views of the revolutionary possibilities presented in Spain, see A. Elorza, 'Storia di un

manifesto: Ercoli e la definizione del Frente Populare in Spagna', *Studi Storici*, 36 (1995).

29 For the position of the left-Socialists see Graham, *Socialism and War*, pp. 56–8.

30 For the text of this letter and Caballero's reply, see Carr, *Comintern and the Spanish Civil War*, pp. 86–8.

31 On the inevitability of a clash between these positions, Graham, 'War, modernity and reform', p. 191 makes a similar point. See also H. Graham, 'Spain 1936. Resistance and revolution: the flaws in the front', in T. Kirk and T. McElligott (eds), *Community, Authority and Resistance to Fascism in Europe* (Cambridge, 1997) and, on the crisis of the Socialist Party, *Socialism and War, passim*.

32 Details in *Communist International*, 2, XIV (1937). A steady stream of orders denouncing 'uncontrollables' (Anarchists) and the POUM as agents of fascism and Trotsky appeared throughout the war.

33 Quoted in *Communist International*, 5, XIV (1937).

34 In December 1936 the POUM claimed some 40,000 members. On the development of the POUM, see Alba and Schwartz, *Spanish Marxism Versus Soviet Communism*; R. Tostorff, *Die POUM im Spanischen Burgerkrieg* (Frankfurt, 1987); A. Durgan, 'The Catalan Federation and the International Communist Movement', in Humbert-Droz, *Colloque sur l'Internationale Communiste*, pp. 279–93. The POUM and its forerunners were something of an obsession for the Comintern. Although any rival claiming the mantle of the Bolshevik Revolution was clearly perceived as a threat, in fact, for a long period the Communist International wavered in its view of how best to meet it. Attempts were made to woo the dissidents back to the PCE, and it was only decided during the war that this was not a serious possibility. Reports on the POUM abound in the archives, but see especially that prepared for Manuilsky by unknown authors: RC 495/10a/336, 'Trotskyist Activity in Spain', 20 January 1937. The CNT was viewed far more sympathetically by the PCE, largely on the grounds that the Anarchists were misguided but could be brought around to correct thinking. The fact that José Díaz was a former Anarchist no doubt helped in sustaining this view.

35 See Alba and Schwartz, *Spanish Marxism Versus Soviet Communism*, pp. 186–8 on the growth of violent conflict. In December Nin was removed from the Generalitat as POUM representative, marking the only concrete success in marginalising the party before May.

36 Díaz died in 1942 while in exile in the USSR. His mental and physical health never really recovered from the experience of the Civil War, though nominally he remained in charge of a personal secretariat of the Comintern (jointly with Dolores Ibarruri). His death was officially described as a suicide, though there has been some speculation that he was actually murdered.

37 Ibarruri, *They Shall Not Pass*, p. 285 repeats the 'counter-revolution' formula. Though denouncing the Anarchists and POUM in her memoirs, nowhere does Ibarruri mention their suppression. For PCE meetings see Hernández, *Yo fuí un ministro de Stalin*, pp. 67–70. As Carr, *Comintern and the Spanish Civil War*, p. 39, also points out, Hernández's account is clearly suspect given that his list of participants at the meetings that decided on PCE policy towards Caballero include Togliatti who did not arrive in Spain until later. Díaz, *Tres años de lucha*, pp. 62–71, gives some clue as to Díaz's views.

38 For a recent reinterpretation of the role of Negrín, see Graham, 'War, modernity

and reform'. In a report to Manuilsky on 30 August 1937, shortly after his arrival in Spain, Togliatti criticised PCE leaders for overestimating their role in the fall of Caballero, 'forgetting that Prieto and the centrists had played a very important role in both the preparation and the solution of the crisis'. See P. Togliatti, *Opere*, 4, 1 (Rome, 1979), p. 270 Also quoted in Carr, *Comintern and the Spanish Civil War*, p. 91.

39 See the account of Hernández, *Yo fuí un ministro de Stalin*, pp. 128–48. Once again, the fact that Hernández places Togliatti at these meetings, and gives him a leading role, makes this version suspect.

40 *Ibid.*

41 The most comprehensive account to date is provided by the television investigation, 'Operación Nikolai', broadcast in November 1992. Falcón, *Asalto a los cielos*, pp. 142–4 repeats the view that the leaders of the PCE and PSUC were unaware of the arrest of Nin.

42 For an account from a POUM point of view, see A. Suárez (pseud. I. Iglesias), *El proceso contra el POUM: un episodio de la revolución española* (Paris, 1974). The need for 'legality' and co-operation with other Republican forces was stressed in reports and instructions to and from the Comintern to Togliatti: RC 495/12/94.

43 See Graham, *Socialism and War*, *passim.*

44 For an excellent recent overview of Togliatti's relationship with the PCE during the war see A. Agosti, *Togliatti* (Turin, 1996), pp. 225–43.

45 Reports contained in RC 495/74/212

46 RC 495/74/212, 'Togliatti to Dimitrov', 15 September 1937. This report is also reproduced in Togliatti, *Opere*, 4, 1, and Carr, *Comintern and the Spanish Civil War*, pp. 94–8.

47 Quoted in Agosti, *Togliatti*, p. 232. Falcón, *Asalto a los cielos*, pp. 150–1 gives an account of the different styles of Codovilla and Togliatti. She also argues (p. 160) that Dimitrov had personally told her that he valued the independent opinions of the party leaders, not just the Comintern delegates: ' "Say on my part to Pepe (José Díaz) and Dolores (Ibarruri) that I would like to receive proposals, independent opinions, criticisms, directly from them, independent of the reports that I receive from the delegates of the International. The delegates are one thing and the leaders of the party are another." ' She adds that Dimitrov gave her a code book for the use of Díaz and Ibarruri to send messages to him, but it was never used and she returned it to Moscow. It is clear, however, from the reports that Togliatti sent to Dimtrov that he remained very much the main point of contact with Comintern: see RC 495/74/212 and 220 for examples.

48 Togliatti was involved in elaborating this line on Spain even before he arrived: see Elorza, 'Storia di un manifesto' and Agosti, *Togliatti*, pp. 225–30.

49 On the fall of Prieto, see the report 'On the Struggle Between Negrín and Prieto', RC 497/74/214, stressing that the attack on Prieto was *not* just inspired by the PCE. See also Graham, *Socialism and War*, pp. 134–49.

50 As Communist Minister of Agriculture since September 1936, Vicente Uribe had already begun to elaborate the party line on collectives even before May 1937 through the creation of Local Agricultural Committees that were to decide on just which lands should be expropriated and on how they should be worked. This led, in some areas, to conflict with the Socialist Landworkers' Union, Federación Nacional de Trabajadores de la Tierra (FNTT). See Garrido González, *Colectividades agrarias;* Casanova, *Anarquismo y revolución* and Rodrigo González, *Las colectividades agrarias.*

51 B. Bolloten and G. Esenwein, 'Anarchists in government: a paradox of the Spanish Civil War, 1936–1939' in F. Lannon and P. Preston (eds), *Elites and Power in Twentieth Century Spain* (Oxford, 1990), pp. 153–178 provides a useful summary of the CNT's position on collaboration. Lack of sympathy for the POUM was a striking feature of Anarchist attitudes.

52 S. Casado, *Asi cayó Madrid* (Madrid, 1968) gives Casado's views of his actions.

53 German intelligence information is to be found in RC 495/74/198. Codovilla was eventually summoned to Moscow in September 1936 to give an account of the development of the war after his initial predictions proved false. See RC 495/74/206 for his early reports. One reason for Codovilla's optimism was that it was difficult for him to contradict the favourable impression of the situation in Spain that had been given at meetings of the Spanish Commission in January and May 1936 just before the outbreak of war: RC 495/10/3 and 6.

54 See E. H. Carr, *The Twilight of Comintern, 1930–1935* (London, 1982) for an analysis of the period just before the Civil War.

55 Hernández, *Yo fuí un ministro de Stalin*, p. 24.

56 Examples of Dimitrov's letters to Stalin for 1936–37 are in RC 495/74/201. See also Elorza, 'In the shadow of God', pp. 239–40.

57 For a recent view of the Terror and the Comintern, see K. McDermott, 'Stalinist Terror in the Comintern: New Perspectives', *Journal of Contemporary History*, 30 (1995), 111–30.

11

Nationalist or internationalist? The Portuguese Communist Party's autonomy and the Communist International

Carlos Cunha

This analysis focuses on the degree of autonomy which the Portuguese Communist Party, Partido Communista Português (PCP) had *vis-à-vis* the Communist International from 1919 to 1943, when the latter was disbanded. Was the PCP a 'nationalist' or an 'internationalist' party? Did its stance vary depending on the time period focused on? Did the party's position hinge on the types of issues or questions involved?

What has been clearly established is that the PCP's history is not a purely 'domestic' history. While, as discussed below, the party was formed without Soviet assistance, once it joined the Communist International it lost a significant amount of its autonomy, as Comintern officials increasingly meddled in PCP internal politics by dictating policy, manipulating leadership elections and often financing party activities. This analysis briefly examines the PCP's history until the 1940s.[1] The analysis is as accurate as possible to date, although new documents from Russian archives will continue to clarify the party's history.

Anarcho-syndicalist roots

When the Russian Revolution began in 1917, Portugal already had a lively labour movement. Ever since 1913, anarchists and syndicalists debated whether syndicalism alone could end worker exploitation. The PCP, therefore, did not surface to fill a void in worker representation, as it claims, but emerged instead into a field of contenders with which it had much more in common than not. The first Bolsheviks could be found at the extreme left of the Portuguese syndicalist movement. As a result of the successes of the Russian Revolution, the failure of the 1918 general strike, and the impasse which the syndicalist movement had reached, the movement split. One section moved towards reformism, and the other moved further towards revolution.[2]

The Portuguese Maximalist Federation, Federação Maximalista Português

(FMP) especially focused on the need for swifter revolutionary organisations. According to Pereira, from the start the maximalists were distinguished from the anarcho-syndicalists because they claimed to be Bolsheviks. The major difference was in their concept of the transition of the 'dictatorship of the proletariat' developed from Lenin, Stalin and others. The anarcho-syndicalists were more attached to Marx and Bakunin and criticised the authoritarian character of the Bolsheviks.[3] The FMP, especially through its official publication *Bandeira Vermelha* (*Red Flag*), emphasised that its attempt to bypass the lethargic revolutionary syndicalist movement was not an attempt to replace the syndicalist organisations. What the working-class movement needed was unity among the syndicalists, anarchists and maximalists. The FMP would leave to the syndicalist organisations the implementation of economic reforms, while it would be concerned with carrying out and then defending the revolution. Its activities would be focused on the political realm, while the syndicalists would be concerned with the economic realm.[4]

The FMP disbanded in December 1920 shortly after the arrest of its Secretary General. The official PCP history labels it a transitional party to that 'glorious' date of which the Communists are so proud:

> The Assembly which elects the leadership organs of the PCP is held in Lisbon on the sixth of March of 1921 in the home office of the Association of Office Workers. The Portuguese Communist Party is founded. Decades of suffering and struggle of the Portuguese working class, the lessons of the great victories of the international working class, the teachings of Marx, Engels, and Lenin all converged on the PCP. With the party's foundation the Portuguese working class finds its firm and secure vanguard.[5]

At the time of its founding the PCP was to be a federalist and decentralised organisation with the following goals:

(a) The organisation of workers on the triple base of political, syndicalist and co-operativist resistance.
(b) Unconditional support to the General Confederation of Workers, Confederação General do Trabalho (CGT).
(c) International understanding and action among Communist parties and syndicalist organisations.
(d) Collaboration of technicians, specialists and scientists with the working classes.
(e) Preparation and promotion for the complete emancipation of the indigenous peoples of the colonies.

The ultimate objective of the party was the socialisation of 'the means of production, circulation, and consumption, that is, the radical transformation of the capitalist society into a Communist society', which was to be achieved through a radical revolution when conditions were ripe.[6]

As with the FMP, relations at the start between the CGT and PCP were fairly good. However, rifts which had begun under the FMP eventually intensified to the point of outright rhetorical hostility, which led the PCP and CGT to drift apart. One reason was that many Young Syndicalists joined the newly formed Communist Youth, Juventudes Comunistas (JC). In addition, the CGT accused the PCP of dividing the labour movement. This allegation intensified after the PCP's publication of the Comintern's twenty-one conditions in 1921 and its proclamations that the syndicalist movement should reserve activity to the economic sphere and leave the political arena to itself. The party leaders were especially blunt in stating that on balance the syndicalist movement's political successes were negative and that syndicalist leaders were misguiding the workers. What was needed was an end to the sectarian divisions that split the movement and a shift toward a unitary organisation. The movement should be fighting for a decrease in the high cost of living for all rather than trying to increase workers' salaries.[7]

According to Pereira, the FMP received warm support from the syndicalist organisations because it emphasised working alongside them rather than trying to undermine them. The FMP also benefited from the novelty of the Russian Revolution, which had subsided by the time the PCP was formed. The repression of Russian Anarchists led the Anarchist press to push for a clear distinction between Anarchists, maximalists, Soviets, and Bolsheviks. The acceptance of the PCP as an extra-syndicalist organisation ended as the party inched toward competition with the 'bourgeois' parties in the political arena. Participation in elections, Parliament and government, and alliances with other parties or groups were taboo for the Anarchists and the syndicalists. In fact, if 'official' PCP historians want to emphasize the party's uniqueness *vis-à-vis* other labour parties and movements, it would have to be in the realm of terminating a twenty-year tradition of exclusive devotion to syndicalist activity when it began experimenting with parliamentary tactics.[8]

Pereira's analysis of the often microscopic ideological divisions which distinguished the diverse political parties and movements of the first republic and made the Portuguese labour movement distinctive can help us understand the complex evolution of the PCP in its early years. He insists that the key to understanding the complex ideological threads which bind the various movements lies in the organisational rather than the ideological sphere. Because the PCP, and communism in general, evolved from grafts of the indigenous labour movement rather than as a result of the Communist International, and because communism emerged outside the spawning grounds of the social democratic left from which sprouted most European Communist parties, the 'original' PCP was endowed with singular characteristics when compared to the rest of the international Communist movement. As communism developed spontaneously out of the Portuguese labour movement, it found only two organisational vehicles available through which it could conduct its activities. One was the republican (bourgeois) political organisational model, and the second was the anarchist model pursued by several different Portuguese labour organisations.

Both options had unfolded within Portugal to fulfil the needs of the working classes as representational or 'channelment' vehicles *vis-à-vis* bourgeois capitalism.[9]

Reflecting the labour movement, Portuguese communism was severely fractionalised. The Communists had their advocates of reformism, of revolutionary syndicalism and of Bolshevism. As a result, early communism oscillated between the two indigenous vehicles of worker 'representation', with the first Bolsheviks forming autonomous groups represented by certain magazines and newspapers. Communism as represented by the FMP and PCP, therefore, was highly decentralised and federalist in nature as was still evident at the first party Congress held in 1923.[10]

The PCP and the Comintern in the 1920s

The first Communists adhered to a melange of ideological strains and were accustomed to lively internal debate, external discussion with rivals, and a loose organisational structure. The problems which underlay the various conflicts until the 1929 reorganisation focused not on ideological differences, but on attempts to impose an external Bolshevik type of organisation, with all its trappings, on a decentralised organisation with a higher degree of autonomy inherited from anarco-syndicalism. This is not to say that ideological, tactical and political differences did not accompany the organisational problem, but they were not the major issue.[11]

The PCP leaders, therefore, as well as the active militants until the purges of 1926, were old, seasoned syndicalists with fifteen–twenty-five years' experience, including those of the 1910–12 syndicalist struggles. Furthermore, they either participated in or had close connections with republican movements and 'civil revolutionary' activism, masons, 'anarchist interventionism,' the Carbonaria, conspiratorial movements, the Radical Party, and the Democratic Left.[12]

Despite the internal divisions, the major confrontation came not from within the PCP, but from the JC which had been formed independently. The JC was much more cohesive than its parent, the PCP. The majority of its members had come either from the Young Syndicalists or the Socialist Youth and brought to the JC a tradition of political extremism, violence and criminal activity, such as counterfeiting, terrorism, bombings and the elimination of enemies. Their experiences and views differed radically from the traditions to which the PCP members were accustomed. They were not concerned with the internal democratic debates which older PCP members had experienced in the syndicalist movement and which, the latter felt, were a crucial aspect of democratic centralism. Because the JC had been officially acknowledged by the Communist International, the leaders assumed recognition gave them a power similar to 'judicial review', whereby their interpretation of the Comintern directives was the correct interpretation. To the JC, 'democratic centralism' meant the ability to expel members who disagreed with the leadership; the open debate which still occurred within the parent was sacrilegious. Their view was that the party should be centralised and ultra-conspiratorial in the mould of secret societies or terrorist groups which allowed a few individuals total control. Discussion was minimised and disagreement intolerable. At times, JC leaders seemed more concerned with personal power than applying Comintern directives because when their views were questioned they disregarded both the directives and the rules of democratic centralism.[13]

The confrontation between JC and PCP leaders erupted at the latter's first Congress in 1923. The norm was for JC members to join the PCP as they aged. José de Sousa, a former JC leader, became a PCP leader prior to 1923. In addition, the JC's views were mirrored by Caetano de Sousa, another PCP leader. Towards the end of 1922 Caetano de Sousa and Pires Barreira (Secretary of the JC) left for Moscow to participate in the Fourth World Congress. At the time, the PCP showed little evidence of the Bolshevisation process that the Comintern expected of its affiliated parties.[14]

When they departed, the confrontation between the two Communist groups had already begun. According to Jules Humbert-Droz, when Caetano de Sousa and Barreira returned from Moscow they had misinterpreted Comintern directives as giving them licence to purge the party. In their excitement to apply their interpretation of the Comintern's twenty-one conditions on a heterogeneous party, they risked destroying it. The JC created a re-organisational committee; but in keeping with the JC's undemocratic nature, the committee did its work in secret. The majority of PCP members, from the directive organs down to the rank and file, were not consulted. The Central Committee (CC), which was set up by the JC fraction, was rejected by the majority of the party that regrouped around Carlos Rates, their choice for General Secretary.

The result was two competing PCPs. The JC group continued purging anyone who disagreed with it and soon found that its PCP-SCI had been reduced to abysmally low levels. (The JC group attached to the party title the words 'International Communist Section' to distinguish itself from what it considered the illegal PCP.) It literally disbanded the PCP by proclaiming that it would cease activity until the Communist International intervened and resolved the dispute. Meanwhile, the majoritarian Rates group continued publishing the party organ, *O Comunista*, analysing the Portuguese situation through its interpretation of Comintern directives, and strengthening the party organisationally.[15]

In August of 1923, Humbert-Droz found himself compelled to resolve the dispute. Despite all of its imperfections, he sided with the Rates faction. It was better to maintain the party's small, heterogeneous base intact and force its adherence to the Comintern's twenty-one conditions later than to risk weakening the party any further. Humbert-Droz also sided with Rates's group because of the JC's terrorist and criminal activities through the Red Legion and because Caetano de Sousa's expulsion of dissenters had reduced his party to a minuscule level. Droz feared that Caetano de Sousa's and Barreira's heavy-handedness, intransigence and sectarianism would not allow Comintern control of the group.

With Humbert-Droz's support, the newly reorganized PCP bypassed the original JC and formed a rival 'official' JC organisation. Caetano de Sousa was frank when he told Humbert-Droz that he had no interest for the syndicalist activity which the Comintern required of the Communists. His major concern was in the political realm. As a result, Caetano de Sousa found that his group had neither support nor influence either among workers or in the syndicalist movement.[16]

In a December 1923 speech to the CC, Humbert-Droz emphasised that the party had to convince the anarcho-syndicalists that only PCP tactics could be victorious. Merely seizing the factories and economic base of the nation was not enough without conquering political power. Neither would social democratic methods work because only through revolution led by a disciplined PCP following Comintern methods could the workers seize power.[17]

Increased internal acceptance for parliamentary activity showed a de-emphasis on immediate victories or revolution and a PCP shift toward social democratic tactics, contrary to the years of anti-parliamentarianism of the Portuguese labour movement. In the end, the distinction between the PCP and other labour groups was the evolution toward 'bourgeois' politics. The move away from anarchism and syndicalism delivered a severe blow to the 'maximalist' tendency within the party.[18]

The PCP's decentralised nature is evident during the three years between the first and second (1926) party congresses. During this short period the party increased its syndicalist activity; formed alliances with the Radical Party, the Democratic Left, the Socialist Party, Partido Socialista Português (PSP) and the CGT; struggled with a bid for accelerated Bolshevisation, which led to internal conflicts and purges of most historical leaders; created a shortlived Popular Agrarian Party; took part in the elections of 1925; and participated in various attempted military coups – all of which helps explain why it diminished in strength to near non-existence by 1927.[19]

Rates's policies were partially to blame for the organisation's decline. The leaders were convinced that the Russian Revolution's momentum would deliver the Portuguese government to the PCP on a silver platter. All that the party need do to create a 'Soviet' nation was to issue revolutionary decrees and control the government which would implement them. When the passive strategy to gain governmental control failed, Rates turned increasingly to the many bourgeois putsch attempts between 1924 and 1925.[20] He believed Portugal was ripe for a Russian-style revolution; but the new Comintern representative, Dupuy, insisted that a 'united front' was the correct path since the 'subjective' conditions necessary for a successful revolution (a Bolshevised, well-disciplined PCP through which the Communist International could control the revolution) had not accompanied the 'objective'.[21]

According to Pereira, Portuguese excitement over Russian successes slowly dissipated after the Communist International's imposition of the united front policy on the PCP.[22] The policy sapped the party of its revolutionary energy and left it ill-prepared for the approaching years of clandestine existence. The united front strategy was the final stand for a group of aged syndicalist leaders who had been at the forefront of the Portuguese labour movement. Although Rates and his group were forced to pursue bourgeois tactics, they were later stripped of their leadership positions and were blamed for incorrectly analysing the Portuguese situation even though they were following Comintern orders. Because the bourgeois parties with which the PCP was competing had similar ideological views, the PCP became increasingly indistinguishable from its rivals. By the end of the Republic many Communists had rejected the PCP for other parties (especially for Democratic Left (Esquerda Democrática) and the Radical Party).[23]

Rates did not dominate the party until 1926, as the 'official' historians would have us believe. After his visit to the Soviet Union in the summer of 1924, his power waned; and by the end of that year, he no longer played a determining role. In 1925, he had been replaced as the General Secretary by Ferreira Quartel.[24]

Pereira claims that the PCP's analyses during Rates's leadership provided an accurate account of the Portuguese situation, while avoiding the ideological or dogmatic blinds which were putting a bias on analyses of the rest of the global labour movement. Rates's views held the worst as well as the best features of the labour movement. He epitomised the generation of militant workers who emerged from the 1910–12 strikes and disappeared during the first few decades of the dictatorial 'new state'. His judgements were full of the contradictions which might be expected from a self-taught man, but they were also free of the dogmatic constraints which coloured the analyses of others. His was a realistic assessment of the Portuguese situation. He had been a revolutionary syndicalist, a maximalist, a Communist and a co-operativist. His influence was evident in the major debates on Portuguese communism from the 1913 controversy concerning the revolutionary potential of the syndicalist movement to the 1923–24 palaver concerning the need for syndicalist unity and the role of the peasant in the Portuguese revolution.[25] Rates was purged not only for his disdain of a centralised and disciplined party, but also because he thought for himself and was a product of the generation which emphasised the free expression of ideas and opinions. He wrote what he thought and felt with little regard to ideological discipline (which helps explain why the official PCP organ *O Comunista* is so lively from 1923–24 and so dull from 1925–26).[26]

By 1926 the same JC members who had been purged or suspended after the 1923 confrontation took control of PCP leadership positions from older comrades entrenched in the syndicalist tradition. By late 1924 the Communist International had reinstated them with full privileges, and by the end of 1925 they held key positions. A quick glance at the CC membership of International

Red Aid (an ancillary organisation) shows the resemblance with the 1923 CC of the JC. The internal changes were a tactical move by the Comintern to 'Bolshevise' the party. The same intransigence and sectarianism which earlier led Humbert-Droz to purge the Caetano de Sousa faction were now valuable assets welcomed by Dupuy and, later, Vittorio Codovilla, the new representatives of the Communist International.[27]

The 'Bolshevisation' of the PCP, claims Pereira, was accelerated in the second half of 1925, and its effects were already evident at the 1926 Party Congress. The large decline in membership which followed the Bolshevisation was largely a result of the party's emphasis on discipline and centralism. The reorganisation of 1925 imposed certain conditions of membership which many of the Communists were unwilling to accept (for example, like Rates they preferred the internal open debate which they expected of the syndicalist tradition). Furthermore, the party was faced with the contradictions that Comintern affiliates faced throughout the world. In applying directives imposed from above designed to achieve Comintern international goals, the party often neglected its obligations to the Portuguese. The directives often conflicted with, yet took precedence over, the party's analyses of the domestic situation. This is apparent when we compare the first and second congresses: while the first discusses many Portuguese national problems, the second merely appears to be a translation of directives which could have been written for any Communist party in the world. Rates's original analyses were also cleansed from *O Comunista* and replaced with ideological arguments that lacked references to original Portuguese problems.[28] This meant that the purges which accompanied the Bolshevisation of the party resulted in a minuscule, unstructured, unorganised PCP which was unprepared to combat the forthcoming military dictatorship, for the coup would occur before the new leadership had the chance to rebuild the party it had just destroyed.

In 1926 a rightwing military coup ended the first Portuguese Republic and began the regime which would postpone the Second Republic until 1974. According to Pereira, the coup was not the major factor in the catastrophic decline of PCP strength because repression did not intensify until a few years later. The coup did, however, alter the ideological and political context within which the party had to function, which in turn required new tactics. The new hostile environment fed the Bolshevisation process which created a new type of Communist that epitomized the militant of the 1930s. He was still radical, as under the JC; but the realities of the day required an increased discipline, an acceptance of political about-turns, and less debate than even he had been accustomed to. He was not yet the 'perfect' Stalinist, who epitomised the party after the 1940–41 reorganisation, but he was, nevertheless, more disciplined than his predecessors. He developed a better understanding of the value of administrative and bureaucratic solutions. Slowly, the commitment to the working-class movement that the members stubbornly protected in the early 1920s was replaced by the ideal that the 'party' was 'above' or more important than the movement. The members became much more pragmatic and much less ideological.[29]

After the coup the PCP carried on its activity, especially in Porto where *Bandeira Vermelha* continued to be published uncensored. The party participated in both bourgeois republican putsch attempts against the new military dictatorship. The first putsch of early February 1927 resulted in a wave of repression which was mainly directed at republicans and the labour movement. The PCP also took its share of punishment, as many militants were imprisoned and others hid in the provinces. In March 1927 the PCP was reorganised by José de Sousa and Silvino Ferreira, but the party's activities did not change. On 20 June the PCP participated in a second abortive putsch and bore the brunt of a new wave of repression.[30]

The Portuguese delegation to the tenth anniversary of the Bolshevik Revolution returned to Portugal in November of 1927 with the task of reorganising the PCP once again. The newly reorganised party, however, was primarily devoted to the development of cadres and was inactive and increasingly isolated.

A PCP cell of naval arsenal workers, where Bento Gonçalves was a member, demanded that the party either renew its syndicalist activities or face a new reorganisation. When the CC did not respond, the cell decided to take action, even though the former had the backing of the Comintern. The successful reorganisation of 1929 ended the phase which focused on immediate revolution. The second phase, which began under Gonçalves's leadership,[31] focused on defensive tactics because of the repressive atmosphere under which the party worked. Its goal was to achieve partial victories that would ultimately lead to the overthrow of the fascist regime through a national and democratic revolution. The new focus required tactics which included a shift from the worker–peasant alliance to the formation of united fronts and electoral participation whenever possible.[32]

The major factors behind the PCP's disastrous decline from 3,000 members in 1923 to only 49 members in 1929 cannot be blamed only on Rates and Humbert-Droz, as the PCP claims. It is true that Rates's turn to putschist tactics with the bourgeois republicans led to a decline in members, but so did the Communist International's policies. With each reorganisation the party hemorrhaged through voluntary disassociation or expulsions.[33]

The PCP, during its early years, was weak in grassroots membership and was basically an 'elite' party. It was a predominantly male organisation with minuscule female participation. It was also primarily urban, centralised in Lisbon, and was not yet strong, as in later years, in either the Alentejo or Setúbal.[34]

The PCP in the 1930s

The Communist International continued to intervene in party affairs throughout the 1930s until the PCP was expelled from the organisation in 1938–39. After the 1926 coup, the PCP was the only party which resisted fascism and

Table 11.1 *PCP membership in the 1920s*

Year	*Number of members*
1921	400–1000 PCP
	260 JC
1922	2,900*
1923 (early)	3,000
1923 (November)	500
1924	700
1928	70
1929	49**

Notes:
* 1,072 of whom were paying dues
** The PCP claimed there were only 40 members
Source: J. P. P. Pereira, *Problémas da História do PCP* (Lisbon, 1982), p. 12.

continued its activities underground. According to the PCP, Bento Gonçalves played a decisive role in the 1929 reorganisation which transformed a legal party into a clandestine party. He struggled with the persistent internal anarchist tendencies, to connect the party with the working classes, and to bolshevise the organisation. He helped form the directive organs, the ancillary mass organisations and the diversified clandestine press necessary to implement the party's covert strategies. The successful transition to a clandestine party eventually attracted working-class confidence and catapulted the PCP to become the workers' vanguard.[35]

The 'official' historians claim that the reorganisation found the party in dire straits in terms of its clandestine experience, ability to combat repression, ideological preparation and finances. The few members who remained in the reorganised party were mainly militant workers with long years of experience within the syndicalist movement. When it became evident that the fascist regime could only be overthrown by an invigorated popular movement led by strong, well-organised, combative political organisations, the leaders worked in that direction. Amongst the unitary or partisan organisations which they set up were the Revolutionary Organisation of the Armada, Organização Revolucionário do Armada (ORA), the League of Friends of the USSR, and the League Against War and Fascism.[36]

In order to improve links with the working classes the leaders focused on conducting strikes and demonstrations which supported worker grievances (especially during 1931–32).[37] In September 1930 they set up the Inter-Syndical Commission to counter government attempts to control the unions. The Commission quickly contested and replaced the CGT as the major representative of the revolutionary syndicalist movement which had been exploited for decades by Anarchists.[38]

In 1933 the PCP's Gonçalves outlined the party's progress and evaluated its deficiencies at the twelfth Executive Committee of the Communist International (ECCI) Plenum. The reason for the major difficulties within the party was that its organisational strength was much weaker than its actual influence. The party's cadres were primarily young, inexperienced individuals who still harboured anarchist tendencies and occasionally resorted to terrorist activity. The party's major tasks in 1933 were:

(a) To purge the anarchist tendencies which remained within the party.
(b) To strengthen the bonds between the agricultural labourers and the industrial workers by creating a strong unitary organisation.
(c) To shift the basic organisational unit to the factory cell from the neighbourhood cell.
(d) To continue strengthening its activity in the syndicalist movement.
(e) To devote more time to the problems of the agrarian poor.

Gonçalves criticised the Communist International for not being more supportive because, although small, Portugal played an important role in international communism.[39]

In the mid-1930s the major role of the PCP, as dictated by the Communist International, was to entrench itself in the society as a clandestine organisation and, if possible without imperilling itself, to enlighten and prepare the masses for the inevitable revolution.[40] Social democracy, a label which was also applied to the bourgeois 'collaborators' (the anarchists), was considered the primary obstacle to developing a revolutionary movement, especially during 1929–33. It was 'social fascism', to be combatted through the workers' unitary front, an attempt to wean Socialist workers away from their social fascist leaders.[41]

While in theory the leaders' interpretation of the Comintern's class against class tactics dominated PCP strategy from 1928 (the Sixth Communist International Congress) to 1935 (the Seventh Communist International Congress), in reality the Portuguese proletarian base was small, and the party often worked alongside the bourgeois elements. Although leaders opposed participation in bourgeois putsch movements, which they labeled 'reviralhista', militants continued to take part (as is evident from the number of Communists imprisoned after the 1931 putsch).[42]

The increased repression of 1932 and the arrests of several PCP and JC leaders led to decreased distribution of the party press. After Gonçalves's return from prison in 1933 the leaders intensified their shift from mere agitation and theoretical discussion to mass political action (such as general strikes) through the organised class movements to fulfil workers' economic and political demands and end repression.[43]

A comparison of the tactical shifts discussed above with the decisions made at the twelfth ECCI Plenum shows a close correlation and will help reveal why the shift occurred when it did. Throughout Europe, class struggles for economic and political reasons were numerous as the Great Depression approached its most difficult years. The grave crisis was reflected in the polarisation of the classes, which was paralleled by the increasing strength of Fascist and Communist parties. The ECCI analysed the increasing turmoil throughout Europe and concluded that the Communist parties needed to organise the workers, strengthen the unity of the working classes (especially between the employed and the unemployed), and fight for the fulfilment of workers' demands even if it meant the expulsion of sectarian tendencies within the party.[44]

This helps explain the party's increased involvement in syndicalist strikes and insurrectional activity to block the dictatorship's efforts to replace free unions with state-dominated ones. According to Gonçalves, after such an attempt in June 1933, International Red Aid set up the first unitary front to combat the government's moves which brought together the central Anarchist, Communist, reformist and independent organisations.[45] By 1934 the leaders praised the party's successful syndicalist strategy by declaring that membership of the Inter-Syndical Commission had increased to 25,000, as compared to 15,000 in the anarco-syndicalist CGT and 5,000 in the Socialist unions.[46] This meant the PCP increased Inter-Syndical Commission membership by 67 per cent in only one year because at the twelfth ECCI Plenum the party claimed the ISC had only 15,000 members.[47]

The unitary front's call for general strikes and demonstrations in the nation's industrial centres led to the protests of 18 January 1934 against the government decrees. In Marinha Grande, a two day general strike evolved from demonstrations to insurrectional attempts. With the support of the populace, the insurrectionists were able to seize control of the city and overpower the police forces for a few hours. These errors, which the PCP leaders claim were committed by the Anarchists as well as anarchist tendencies within the PCP, undermined the front's policies and destroyed the campaign to stop the fascistisation of the unions. However, it did display to the masses that they could demonstrate against fascism so long as they maintained unity.[48] The PCP leaders also concluded that the party should focus on organising partial strikes because total strikes and insurrectional attempts could lead to backlashes from the government.[49]

One result of the repression which followed the January demonstrations was that all PCP activities became clandestine. Prior to 1934 the party was able to continue legal, quasi-legal and illegal activities, partly as a result of disorganised censors and police. Nevertheless, in 1935 the PCP began to make inroads into the Alentejo, the Algarve and Marinha Grande.[50] Party membership had also climbed to more than 400 by this date.[51]

At the Seventh Comintern Congress (1935) which abandoned the class against class strategy in favour of the popular front strategy, Gonçalves proclaimed that PCP leaders had been suggesting the need to attract petit-bourgeois intellectuals who were dissatisfied with the dictatorship and republicans who had turned their backs on putschist attempts, and had been building a united anti-fascist popular front that would include the Anarchist and syndicalist movements. Creating a united front did not include allowing members of those groups into the party because purging the PCP of sectarian and opportunistic views was also a goal, along with reinforcing and widening party strength by defending working-class interests. The leaders were especially interested in developing stronger links with peasants, the unemployed, women and youths, who had all received relatively little attention up until then.[52]

As clandestine activity progressed, the party's directive organs destabilised because of repression, imprisonment and disorganisation. The Central Committee coexisted with other directive organs, such as the Executive Central Commission and the Secretariat. After waves of repression it was not uncommon to find cadres or even militants directing the organisation, so it is often difficult to determine which of the organs was running the party at a given time.[53] The arrests of Secretariat members in the mid-1930s (Gonçalves, José de Sousa and Júlio Fogaça) profoundly affected party activity. Nevertheless, a Central Committee was formed in 1936 which included Alberto Araújo and Manuel Rodrigues da Silva (who also belonged to the Secretariat) as well as Pires Jorge and Alvaro Cunhal, the Secretary General of the JC in 1934.[54]

Despite setbacks, activity continued. *Avante!* began publishing weekly until 1938. The party supported the Republican forces in Spain, and many members joined the fighting. One of the PCP's proud, historical landmarks is involvement through its ancillary association ORA in the 1936 mutiny aboard three Portuguese warships to prevent their helping Franco's troops.[55]

The PCP has martyred Gonçalves, but Pereira claims that José de Sousa, who was in charge of the syndicalist sector, and Júlio César Leitão were the ones who reorganized the PCP into a clandestine party in 1929. According to Francisco Ferreira, an exPCP member, Gonçalves was very intelligent, but a bad organiser with little initiative or motivation. When compared to de Sousa's activity, Gonçalves's endeavours are dwarfed. Although the differences between the two leaders were already apparent in the late 1920s, by the end of the decade they were more pronounced. De Sousa focused more on propaganda and agitation at the syndicalist level, while Gonçalves focused on imposing centralised hegemony on the party. These differences could even be seen in the party press. While Gonçalves's sectarian group had to make a tremendous effort to publish the 3,000 copies of *Avante!* on schedule, de Sousa appeared to have a much easier time publishing the much more numerous party affiliated, syndicalist-related publications.[56]

The years 1939–41 were difficult ones for the PCP not only because of increased domestic repression, but also because of problems within the party spurned on by the Nazi–Soviet pact and other foreign actions. A split among Tarrafal's (Cape Verde) Communist prisoners resulted in the PCP's expulsion of de Sousa's Group of Disassociated Communists (GCA) by Gonçalves's Organisation of Tarrafal Communist Prisoners because of the former's circulation of texts that were highly critical of party activity from 1929 to 1935.[57]

The division could be traced back to Gonçalves's attempt to impose Comintern directives on the party after he returned from the Seventh World Congress. He moved to disband the clandestine Inter-Syndical Commission, through which the party channelled most of its syndicalist activity, and to work through the corporative syndicates controlled by the government. His attempts infuriated the more radical syndicalist members within the PCP, even though his imprisonment prevented him from carrying out the change. As the 'inter-syndicalists' and anarchists were arrested from 1935 to 1937 they took to Tarrafal the vestiges of an internal split which had never been resolved.[58]

The final break centered around the *política nova* (new policy) pursued by Gonçalves within Tarrafal, and the *política de neutralidade* (politics of neutrality) pursued by the reorganised PCP of 1941. Both of these policies revolved around the official PCP position toward the Second World War, which was categorised by Gonçalves as an inter-imperialist struggle similar to the First World War. He claimed that the party's position was to place Portugal's independence above partisan differences and to maintain a position of neutrality in the war. Gonçalves went so far as to present the Tarrafal prison officials with a document outlining these views and offering the PCP's co-operation in achieving both goals. The collaboration was unacceptable to the syndicalists who increasingly criticised Gonçalves until they were expelled from the party in 1941. Goncalves's support came primarily from ORA to which most of the prisoners belonged.[59]

The divisions were not limited to Tarrafal. At home the PCP was also struggling. In 1939 the Communist International broke relations with the PCP, so in terms of Comintern affiliation, Portugal did not have a Communist party. Relations were apparently cut because of the PCP's position on police arrests. From 1939 to 1941 two Communist parties struggled to attract the support of the Comintern (each labelling the other revisionist).[60]

The reorganisation began in 1940 with cadres recently released from Tarrafal. The official leadership of the party (Velez Grilo and Vasco de Carvalho) found itself confronted by a reorganised PCP in which Júlio Fogaça and Alvaro Cunhal played leading roles.[61] The indications are that the PCP aligned with the GCA, while the reorganised PCP sided with Gonçalves. The Grilo group immediately followed the Comintern's directives and declared the need for national unity after Hitler attacked the Soviet Union, while the 'reorganisers' continued their policy of neutrality.[62] Despite the reorganisers having wrested control of the party from Grilo, the latter continued publishing its own *Avante!* until 1945, when the group faded away.[63]

The reason little is known of the *política nova* is that the reorganisers extinguished references to Gonçalves's position because after the USSR's entrance into the 'imperialist struggle' his martyrdom would have been dealt a blow. The reorganised PCP used its powers to maintain a favourable image of its two 'cults of personality', Gonçalves and Cunhal, his successor.[64]

As we have seen, the 1929 reorganisation continued the PCP's metamorphosis into a better organized and Bolshevised party, essential for successful clandestine operations. After the 1934 insurrectional strikes, the Bolshevik influence strengthened. The metamorphosis helps explain why it is difficult to find pre-1929 PCP members among the party ranks at any level after 1929 (and this is especially true after the 1940–41 reorganisation). In effect, the parties of 1929 and 1941 were different from the PCP of 1921.[65]

The PCP in the 1940s

The reorganisation of 1940–41 finally brought the party under orthodox Communist control. Although Soviet support was denied to the newly reorganised party at first, the new leaders continued the party's Stalinisation. The enforcement of democratic centralism and insistence on the dictatorship of the proletariat became entrenched.

The PCP's link to the Comintern during the reorganisation of 1940–41 was through the American Communist Party. Fogaça described in his letters to the Comintern the reasons behind the PCP's reorganisation, which included arrests of cadres, a lack of conspiratorial work and suspicions that even the leadership had been infiltrated. The Comintern had been aware of these problems as early as 1939 when it cut off relations with the PCP. Fogaça was upset that the Comintern ignored the PCP despite its reorganisation and attempts to get Comintern recognition.[66]

The reorganisation had not been easy because the former leaders (like Vasco de Carvalho, Velez Grilo and Francisco Sacavem) had been reluctant to give up their positions. In addition, the suspicious arrests of many of the best militants complicated matters. Nevertheless, the party tried to continue its work. With information from its imprisoned leaders and members, it uncovered and purged suspected informers. The reorganisation was carried out so secretively and successfully that many leaders only learned of the newly reorganised party when they were denounced as unworthy of mass support.[67]

As additional proof of the successful restructuring, Fogaça emphasised that after one year of activity the party had not suffered from any new imprisonments. He claimed the party had not yet reached a significant influence among the masses (especially the peasants), but it had gained the confidence of the 'revolutionary proletariat', and the party leadership was primarily working class. Despite the legacy which the new PCP inherited, he claimed it was making daily gains among the workers. The new party was made up of disciplined, revolutionary militants and leaders devoted to the principles of international communism. Even if the Communist International had never given the party much attention or support before or after this latest reorganisation (for which Fogaça delivered a long, scathing criticism of the Comintern), the new party would prove its commitment through future successes. The new PCP was committed to Bolshevisation and was doing all it could to uncover its enemies and become a mass party. If errors were made, it was only for lack of experience and not for lack of revolutionary spirit.[68]

Fogaça also discussed the hardships of beginning and maintaining a clandestine press without the necessary resources because the economic hardships of the workers made it difficult for them to fund party activities. He asked the Comintern for money, although he emphasised that the party would continue the presses and the struggle whether or not help arrived.[69] In August 1941, after a two-year shutdown stemming from repression, *Avante!* reappeared.

The 'official' history, a product of the 1940–41 reorganisers who had firm control of the party by the third PCP Congress held in 1943, conveniently ignores the second PCP headed by Grilo and the rival *Avante!* which it published, the 'zigzag' policies pursued by both PCPs as they mirrored Soviet policy shifts concerning the Second World War, and the reorganisers' adherence to the 'neutrality' politics even after a year of Nazi attacks on the Soviet Union. With the disappearance of Grilo's PCP in 1945, the 'reorganiser party' was able to continue its activities virtually free of internal opposition. The party moved to reopen or strengthen its links with the international Communist organisations which replaced the Comintern. For the first time in its history, the PCP created a stable clandestine leadership which maintained a hegemonic organisation and pursued co-ordinated policy until a new wave of repression began in 1949.[70]

The 1940s were a period of increased growth resulting from the anti-fascist alliance between the Western democracies and the Soviet Union, the shortage of food from grain speculation and sales to both sides of the war (which caused unrest at home and serious difficulties for the regime), the collaboration with domestic antifascist forces and the organisational strength of the reorganised party. During this time the PCP reached its clandestine era membership apex, rising from 1,200 members in 1943 to around 4,800 in 1946 and approximately 7,000 in 1947. [71]

Conclusion

The degree of autonomy which the PCP had *vis-à-vis* the Communist International varied depending on the period in question. At times, the PCP was a nationalist party pursuing its preferred tactical path and ignoring orders sent to it by the Comintern. At other times, it was clearly internationalist and followed closely the Comintern directives. The party's position hinged on the types of issues or questions involved.

The PCP's history is not purely domestic. Comintern officials regularly meddled in PCP internal politics by dictating policy, manipulating leadership elections and often financing party activities. New documents from Russian archives will continue to clarify the party's relationship to the Communist International.

Notes

1 Some of the information included in this paper was covered much more extensively in C. Cunha, *The Portuguese Communist Party's Strategy For Power, 1921–1986* (New York, 1992).

2 See excerpts from *Bandeira Vermelha*, in J. G. P. Quintela, *Para a História do Movimento Comunista em Portugal: 1. A Construção do Partido (Primeiro Periodo 1919–1929)* (Oporto, 1976), pp. 88–153.

3 J. P. P. Pereira, *Questões Sobre o Movimento Operário Português e a Revolução Russa* (Oporto, 1971), p. 22.

4 *Bandeira Vermelha*, in Quintela, *Para a História do Movimento Comunista em Portugal*, pp. 108–12.

5 *60 Anos de Luta* (Lisbon, 1982), p. 24.

6 *O Comunista*, 1 (16 October 1921), in Quintela, *Para a História do Movimento Comunista em Portugal*, annex.

7 *Ibid.*, pp. 95, 131–35.

8 J. P. P. Pereira, 'O PCP na Primeira República: uma História por Revelar', *Diário de Notícias* (13 May 1980), 7.

9 J. P. P. Pereira, 'Bento Gonçalves Revisitado', *Diário de Notícias* (11 December1979), 15.

10 *Ibid.*

11 *Ibid.*

12 J. P. P. Pereira, 'O PCP na Primeira República: Membros e Direçcao', in *Estudos sobre o Comunismo*, 1 (September–December 1983), 13.

13 Pereira, 'Bento Gonçalves Revisitado'.

14 Quintela, *Para a História do Movimento Comunista em Portugal*, pp. 50–3.

15 *Ibid.*

16 *Ibid.*, pp. 48–53

17 *O Comunista*, 7, in Pereira, *Questoes sobre o Movimento Operário Português e a Revolução Russa*, annex.

18 Pereira, 'O PCP na Primeira República: uma História por Revelar', 7.

19 Pereira, 'O PCP na Primeira República: Depois de 1923', *Diário de Notícias* (27 May 1980), 7.

20 *Ibid.*

21 *O Comunista*, 27, in Quintela, *Para a História do Movimento Comunista em Portugal*, p. 226.

22 The emphasis here is on 'united front' to distinguish it from 'unitary front'. While the former would imply an electoral or formal unity for participation in bourgeois democratic politics, the latter would focus on a unity of workers for syndicalist and revolutionary activity.

23 Pereira, 'O PCP na Primeira República: Membros e Direçcao', 14.

24 The CC published its note purging Rates from the PCP in *O Comunista* (25 October 1925). Rates circulated an emotional response to his expulsion which provides considerable insight into the internal dynamics of the CC at the time: see RC 495/179/3.

25 Rates's documents nos. 12 and 13 in Pereira, *Questões Sobre o Movimento Operário Português e a Revolução Russa* (Oporto, 1971), annex.

26 Pereira, 'O PCP na Primeira República: Depois de 1923'.

27 Pereira, 'O PCP na Primeira República: uma História por Revelar'.
28 Pereira, 'Bento Gonçalves Revisitado'.
29 Pereira, 'O PCP na Primeira República: Membros e Direçcao'.
30 Quintela, *Para a História do Movimento Comunista em Portugal*, pp. 71–2.
31 On Bento Gonçalves, see *60 Anos de Luta* for the official view, and Pereira, 'Bento Gonçalves Revisitado', for a more critical and realistic view.
32 Quintela, *Para a História do Movimento Comunista em Portugal*, pp. 73–4.
33 J. P. P. Pereira, 'Contribuição para a História do Partido Comunista Português na I República (1921–1926)', *Análise Social*, 17: 67–8 (1981), 695–713; and Pereira, *Problemas da História do PCP* (Lisbon, 1982), p. 12.
34 Pereira, 'O PCP na Primeira República: Membros e Direçcao'.
35 *60 Anos de Luta*, p. 40.
36 *Ibid.*, p. 44.
37 'Intervenção de "António" na XII Reunião Plenária da Internacional Comunista', *Estudos Sobre o Comunismo* (1983), 29–30.
38 'A Reorganização do PCP em 1929', *Bandeira Vermelha* (25 April 1974).
39 'Intervenção de "António"', 31.
40 'Apontamentos duma Entrevista com Firminiano Cansado Gonçalves', *Estudos Sobre o Comunismo* (1983), 37–8.
41 J. A. Nunes, 'Sobre Algúns Aspectos da Evolução Política do Partido Comunista Português após a Reorganização de 1929 (1931–33)', *Análise Social*, 17: 67–8 (1981), 720.
42 *Ibid.*, 721–4.
43 *Ibid.*, 728–9.
44 *Ibid.*, 729–30.
45 'Intervenção de "António"', 29–30.
46 *60 Anos de Luta*, pp. 45, 47.
47 'Intervenção de "António"', 29–30.
48 J. A. Nunes, 'Da Política "Classe Contra Classe" ás Origens da Estratégia Antifascista: Aspectos da Internacional Comunista Entre o VI e o VII Congressos (1928–1935)', in *O Fascismo em Portugal* (Lisbon, 1982), pp. 69–70.
49 'A Reorganização do PCP em 1929'.
50 *Ibid.*
51 *60 Anos de Luta*, pp. 48–9.
52 Nunes, 'Da Política "Classe Contra Classe" ', p. 71.
53 Pereira, *Problemas da História do PCP*, p. 9.
54 *60 Anos de Luta*, pp. 48–9. For biographical information on Alvaro Cunhal in which the 'official' biography is contrasted with the 'real', see R. Rodrigues, 'Cunhal: o ABC dos Comunistas Portugueses', *O Jornal* (23 July 1982), 2–4. For the official biographies, check *Avante!* prior to elections.
55 *60 Anos de Luta*, pp. 48–9.
56 Pereira, *Problemas da História do PCP*, p. 9; and Pereira, 'As Primeiras Series do *Avante!* Clandestino', *Estudos Sobre o Comunismo* (1983), 23.
57 Pereira, *Problemas da História do PCP*, p. 13.
58 *Ibid.*
59 F. Rosas, 'O PCP e a II Guerra Mundial', *Estudos Sobre o Comunismo* (1983), 3–22.
60 Pereira, *Problemas da História do PCP*, p. 16.
61 A. Ventura, introduction to 'Documentos sobre uma Tentativa de Contacto entre o

Bureau Político do PCP (Júlio Fogaça) e a CI em 1941', *Estudos sobre o Comunismo*1 (September–December 1983), 23.

62 Rosas, 'O PCP e a II Guerra Mundial', 5.

63 Pereira, 'O PCP na Primeira República: Membros e Direçcao', 23.

64 Pereira, *Problemas da História do PCP*, p. 13.

65 Pereira, 'Bento Gonçalves Revisitado', 15.

66 J. Fogaça, 'Carta ao C.E. da Internacional Comunista (July 15, 1941)', in 'Documentos sobre uma Tentativa de Contacto entre o Bureau Político do PCP (Júlio Fogaça) e a CI em 1941', *Estudos sobre o Comunismo*, 1 (September–December 1983), 26. For additional analysis of the PCP from the 1940s to the 1960s, see D. L. Raby, *Fascism and Resistance in Portugal* (New York, 1988).

67 Fogaça, 'Carta ao C.E da Internacional Comunista', 26

68 *Ibid.*, 27–8.

69 *Ibid.*,

70 Pereira, *Problemas da História do PCP*, pp. 12.

71 *Ibid.*, pp. 10, 16.

12

The Communist Party of Greece and the Comintern: evaluations, instructions and subordination

Artiem Ulunian

The special nature of the relationship between the Communist International and foreign Communist parties has given rise to many myths and rumours, but a clear picture was unattainable so long as access to the original archival materials of both the Comintern and the Communist parties themselves was impossible. But even since the opening of the secret holdings, many questions remain on the agenda. This chapter concerns the relationship between the Comintern and the Greek Communist Party (known as the Socialist Workers' Party of Greece, Socialistik Ergatikon Komma Ellados (SEKE) until 1924 and the Kommunistikon Komma Ellados (KKE) thereafter). Particular reference will be made to the Comintern's evaluations of the situation in Greece and within the party, to the Comintern's instructions to the party, and to the realisation of those instructions on the part of the Greek Communists.[1]

The penetration of socialist ideas brought new elements into the balance of Greek political forces in the late 1860s. 'Historical' political parties, created around prominent Greek politicians and based on a vast clientele, were challenged by new untypical political organisations with different ideological and organisational principles. Until autumn 1918 there was no centralised Socialist party in Greece, because the various left-wing organisations, clubs and groups represented different ideological trends and could not come to agreement between themselves. One such group, Federation, which operated in Thessaloniki, did manage to establish contacts with and gain membership of the Socialist International. But regardless of their differences, from the very beginning the Socialist organisations demonstrated political and ideological radicalism, frightening the authorities and attracting the lower and middle classes of Greek society.[2]

The *coup d'état* in Russia in October 1917 brought the Bolsheviks to power with an ideology based on world revolution. A special role in the fulfilment of such a revolution was assigned to the revolutionary movement, which would be led by parties ideologically and theoretically akin to the Bolsheviks. Thus, as early as 13 December 1917 the Soviet Council of People's Commissars issued a secret decree on assistance 'to the left-wing internationalist labour movement in all countries'. Ambitious plans of world revolution would be realised, it was believed, so long as the Soviet Bolsheviks rendered organisational, ideological and financial support to their friends abroad.

Meanwhile, three years of world war had split the international Socialist movement. The Russian Bolsheviks occupied the leading place among those who had opposed the 'imperialist war' from the start. Their slogan 'to convert imperialist war into Civil war' was not pure propaganda, but reflected what they saw as their political mission. Some Western European social democrats supported that extremist plan, and sought to destroy the 'oppressive bourgeois regime' with international revolutionary actions. At a Pan-Hellenic Socialist Congress (17–23 November 1918) the delegates managed to establish SEKE, and adopted a political programme similar to the Erfurt Programme of the German Social Democrats. This agreement to unite into a single party came despite the fact that members of the different groups at the Congress had shown contradictory approaches to political and social problems. The participants at the Congress were divided, essentially, into two wings. The majority supported traditional social democratic values; the minority backed the radical Bolsheviks.

On 24 January 1919 Moscow announced the establishment of the Third, or Communist, International through the press and radio. This news reached Greece, but was met with caution by local Socialists, since it was not known whether there were any Western Europeans among the Comintern's founders. However, the newly created organisation took serious steps to contact possible followers within Western social democratic parties and 'national revolutionary organisations' in the oriental and colonial countries. In the latter half of April 1919 a Foreign Board was organised under the auspices of the Central Committee of the Ukrainian Communist Party. It aimed to undermine the military forces of those countries taking part in anti-Bolshevik intervention in southern Russia. Since the Greek army was participating in this anti-Bolshevik offensive, a group of local Greeks was organised at Odessa. One of the members of the group, P. Toboulidis, made frequent illegal trips to Greece on intelligence matters and to pursue anti-militarist agitation.[3] In Constantinople, meanwhile, the International Unity of Workers, dominated by ethnic Greeks, had also been formed. Its leaders, S. Maximos, N. Zakhariadis, N. Tryachev and Kh. Katev, contacted the Greek Department of the Foreign Board in Odessa and the SEKE in Greece. Political and military changes in the Balkans were carefully scrutinised in Moscow. At the session of the Executive Committee of the Communist International (ECCI) Bureau which took place on 5 August 1919, N. Bukharin and K. Berzin (the latter already an important figure in the Soviet secret services) were ordered to deliver theses on attitudes to parliamentarism, 'depicting in them the necessity to use the parliamentary struggle for the establishment of Soviet rule'.[4] In the context of possible revolution in Italy, ECCI's view of the importance of the Balkan peninsula in plans for world revolution increased.

The region was considered to be one of the beach-heads for spreading revolution on the continent. At its session of 11 December 1919 the ECCI Bureau discussed the problem of 'addressing the Communist groups in the Balkans in connection with imminent events in the Balkans'.[5] It decided 'to suggest all Balkan groups select active functionaries from their ranks and send them for a week in the Balkans'.[6]

Meanwhile, divisions within the SEKE leadership had seen a sharpening of the conflict between the left pro-Bolshevik radicals and the champions of traditional social democracy of the Western type. Among SEKE Central Committee members, those who advocated the 'left course' were led by D. Ligdopoulos, M. Sideris, Sp. Komiotis and the party secretary, N. Dimitratos. They all resigned their posts, demanding that the party take a much more left-wing orientation. At first, the rightists took the opportunity to replace them with their own moderate followers, like P. Dimitratos, A. Tsalavoutis and Fr. Petrouska. But the leftists soon counter-attacked with a demand that the SEKE enter the Comintern. On 25 November 1919, at the second session of the party's governing body, the National Council, they managed to persuade the delegates to vote for a document approving preparations for 'the establishment of tight links with the Comintern'.[7] This decision to join the Comintern immediately raised the issue of the nature of SEKE's connections with the Comintern in political, ideological and structural terms. Ligdopoulos was designated as SEKE representative at future Comintern congresses. Meanwhile, A. Ivanov, an envoy of the International Propaganda Department, had arrived illegally in Greece from Russia and contacted the leaders of the left-wing faction. With the assistance of the well-known Serbian Socialist, S. Markovitch, he managed to stay in Thessaloniki, where 'he carried out party activity in the workers' centre by organising Communist evening meetings with the participation of selected revolutionary workers, with whom [he] talked about Soviet Russia, workers' and peasants' councils, about their organisation and about the Communist Party'.[8]

It was the contacts of the Soviet emissary with Ligdopoulos and Komiotis which had triggered the activity described above, which was aimed at establishing tight relations with the Balkan 'radical brothers' within congenial Socialist parties as they passed through the process of splitting into pro-Bolshevik and pro-social democratic wings. A conference of Balkan Socialists, organised under the auspices of the Bulgarian 'narrow' Socialists (that is, the Communists), aimed to create a Balkan Communist Federation affiliated to the Comintern. Ligdopoulos represented the SEKE at this conference on 2 January 1920, and later he went on to Moscow to provide the Comintern with information about the situation in Greece and within the SEKE.

The Second Comintern Congress, held between 19 July and 7 August 1920, was more representative than its predecessor. Despite the lack of official SEKE representatives, the party's interests were championed by Ligdopoulos and a member of the Russian Communist Party, O. Alexakis.[9] The report on the

Communist Movement in Greece, delivered in French to the Congress's Presidium, was both brief and generalised, omitting detailed discussion of the current balance of forces within the SEKE leadership and referring only to past disagreements between the left and right.

At the Congress, the Comintern's President, Grigorii Zinoviev, put forward bluntly the idea of converting the Comintern into a world government after the establishment of the 'International Soviet Republic'.[10] He emphasised the importance of the 'second row' countries, such as the Central European and Balkan states, for future revolutionary activities.[11] All the resolutions adopted at the Second Congress were binding so far as national sections (that is, Communist parties) were concerned. They included resolutions on the tasks of the Comintern, the role of Communist parties in the proletarian revolution, national and colonial issues, conditions of admission to the Communist International, its statutes, and so on.

On 21 September 1920 a specially convened session of the ECCI took place. In the presence of Zinoviev, Bukharin, N. Shablien, J. Reed and Gurvitch, Ligdopoulos (under the pseudonym 'Nikdopoulos') delivered a short report on the Greek Communist and labour movements. (The bulk of the report had already been submitted to the Comintern in written form.) Touching upon SEKE policy, Ligdopoulos stressed that 'we had a programme based on an old one, but we have cancelled it and have appointed a commission to work out a new [programme] according to the principles of the Third International'. The Greek representative promised to carry out purges of 'opportunist elements' in the SEKE at its next party congress.[12] Thus, after a short discussion, the Greek party became a full member of the Communist International.

In April 1921 the Central Committee of the Soviet Communist Party adopted a resolution on the establishment of a new special training body, to be called the Communist University of the Workers of the East (KUTV). The KUTV was meant to train cadres of Asian Communists, whether from the Soviet party or foreign parties. The latter were trained in so-called 'foreign groups', created in 1922. There was a separate Greek faculty, or Greek Branch, which started its work in 1923.[13] In November 1921 the Communist University of National Minorities of the West (KUNMZ) was established; in 1928 a Greek section was established to train functionaries of the KKE and Greek nationals from the USSR.[14]

By the spring of 1921 the process of fragmentation of the SEKE leadership into several groups was well under way. The main controversies in the developing intra-party debate were the party's links with the Comintern, its strategy and tactics under Greek national conditions, the country's agrarian problem, and evaluations of Central Committee activity. There was much division on these issues in the party's regional organisations, heightened by the preparations for the next international congresses of the Comintern and the Communist Youth International (CYI). Three factions emerged, led by members of the SEKE Central Committee and those close to the party and trade-union leadership. The first, a radical leftist group under the leadership of N. Sargologos and A. Papanastassiou, accused the Central Committee of 'right deviation' and demanded the strengthening of illegal activity, including armed insurrections. The second, led by Y. Kordatos, G. Georgiadis, A. Benaroyas and P. Dimitratos, demanded the revision of the whole strategy and tactics of the SEKE, particularly with regard to the agrarian problem, relations with the Comintern, and party policy on the national scene. They sought, essentially, to convert the SEKE into a traditional legal political party. The third group of leading members of the SEKE, represented by Ar. Sideris, Al. Kouriyel and N. Dimitratos (the party secretary), supported a programme of social reform and co-operation with traditional parties in order to gain victory in elections.

Leaders of all three factions were sent to the Third Comintern Congress in Moscow (22 June to 12 July 1921). At the same time, the ECCI, with the assistance of the Balkan Communist Federation, sent a new representative, Iv. Chonos, to the Central Committee of the SEKE. He replaced N. Maximov, who had left for Sofia to inform the Comintern of the situation in Greece.[15]

The victory of the Kordatos–Georgiadis group, which resulted in the former becoming the party's secretary, did not help to resolve the problems that existed within the party leadership. Moreover, it worsened relations with the left wing. However, Kordatos reported to the ECCI on behalf of the Central Committee that the party conference had adopted resolutions closely in line with Comintern decisions, and the Comintern representative also gave Moscow a favourable impression of the conference, stressing that the party's decisions were 'consistent with the situation which we have and are appropriate to the methods we have at our disposal'.[16]

So far as electoral tactics were concerned, the pragmatic Kordatos–Georgiadis faction stated that a 'united electoral front of workers and authoritative labour and peasants' organisations' should be built up. They took the view that co-operation during elections was not the principal problem facing the party. They also rejected the left's view that any co-operation with other parties during the general elections was inadmissible.[17]

Attempts to achieve compromise and reconciliation between the left and right wings and to strengthen unity in the highest circles of the party came to fruition when T. Apostolidis was elected as party secretary.[18] Simultaneously, a document adopted by the new Central Committeen, 'Information to Party Members', stressed that the committee 'would guide the party by methods legitimised by the will of all its members'. The Comintern emissary, Chonos, gave an absolutely different picture of the newly elected Central Committee, however. In his secret report to the Presidium of the Balkan Communist Federation, he wrote that 'the party's leadership is weak and theoretically unskilful. It demonstrates lack of activity and organisational abilities.'[19] Ideological and individual compromises had brought the theoretical discussions to a conclusion on the basis that the terms 'proletarian dictatorship' and 'workers'-peasants' government' meant, essentially, the same thing.[20]

By early 1924 there had developed, in the 'headquarters of the world revolution', a serious crisis. This was rooted in the intra-party strife in the Soviet Communist Party where, after the death of Lenin, leading figures had intensified their bids for power. At a session of the CYI executive on 14 January, it was stated that 'the Balkan section of the Comintern inquires of the Balkan Commission about information as to whether it had received any messages concerning contradictions within the Greek party and youth organisation'.[21] The CYI secretariat instructed Lambrev (who had been sent to Greece as its representative at the Congress of the Greek Communist Youth Organisation, (OKNE)), '1) to carry out the principal struggle against the right-wing trends in the [OKNE] organisation which seeks to cancel the Comintern tactical line; 2) . . . to carry out a severe struggle against left-wing mistakes; 3) to transfer organisational activity onto the road of practical youth problems.'[22] Continual intra-party conflict had affected the OKNE. As the Balkan Secretariat of the CYI reported:

> [the forthcoming OKNE congress] should make an important decision in the field of organisation (transfer of the centre to Athens, reorganisation on the basis of industrial cells, liquidation of the professional groups, intensification of activity in the agricultural regions and among national minorities, etc.), then opposition in the organisation should be liquidated and finally, relations with the party should be settled.[23]

This last point related to the fact that 'although the CC [Central Committee] of the Organisation had been maintaining neutrality in the factional feud it had been opposing the present Central [Committee] and had been in sympathy with those expelled from the party'.[24]

The situation in the Balkans continued to draw the Comintern's attention. Political developments in Bulgaria and Yugoslavia testified to the increasing right-wing pressure upon centrists and the left. In Albania, the short-lived 'democratic revolution' had been suppressed by the monarchists. Greece occupied a significant but not central place among those countries on the peninsula where the balance of right-wing and centrist forces was equal. The Comintern and its organisations took steps to advance Communist activity in the region. On the part of the Greek Communist leaders, there was some optimism about the party's prospects. These leaders included P. Pouliopoulos, S. Maximos and T. Mangos, who were the Greek delegates to the Fifth Comintern Congress (17 June–8 July 1924). On their arrival in Moscow they delivered a report, 'On the Situation in Greece', to the Profintern's Executive Bureau. The report's basic conclusion was that 'from early May 1923 there was a permanent offensive of capital'; failures in trade-union activity were explained by the fact that 'it had been difficult to direct the work of the revolutionary organisation because there had not been a Communist Party in Greece'.[25]

The Fifth Comintern Congress brought about serious corrections to the existing ideological and propaganda guidelines of international communism.

The resolutions and directives adopted testified to the fact that both the intra-Comintern regime and administrative methods within the member parties were being strengthened. Once again, the aim of Bolshevising the parties was approved. The resolution 'On the Report of the ECCI' stressed that it was inadmissible to convert united front tactics into 'something more than revolutionary agitation and mass mobilisation', or 'to use the slogan of the workers' and peasants' government not for propaganda for the proletarian dictatorship but for the purpose of organising a bourgeois-democratic coalition'.[26] Despite traditional rhetorical statements of an irreconcilable attitude towards both right deviationism and leftism, there was obvious evidence of condescension towards the latter.

Among the specific political problems that the Greek Communist Party had to handle was the 'Macedonian Question'. The Comintern insisted that the party adopt a special resolution on this issue, admitting the idea of autonomy for the region because of its ethnic composition (bearing in mind the Leninist slogan of granting nationalities the right to self-determination pending full independence). In September 1923 Chonos, as Comintern representative in Greece, delivered a detailed report to Moscow on the party's neglect of Moscow's orders on this matter. In his message he quoted the party's words, 'that without having money to make the party ready for illegal activity we cannot declare our support for Macedonian autonomy in the press since we would have been immediately banned and we would have lost everything'.[27]

Regardless of the party's stance on the Macedonian question, however, it was clear that Communist activity would soon have been curbed by the authorities. In a secret cable a Comintern agent resident in Vienna wrote that 'it is obvious as we had supposed that there will be a period of illegal activity. I am writing to comrades . . . and calling them here immediately to make them ready for going underground'.[28]

At the same time, the Comintern maintained surveillance of the situation within the party. Two of the Comintern's highest officials, D. Manuilsky and B. Smeral, were sent illegally to the party's third Congress (November–December 1924: it was at this Congress that the party's name was changed from the SEKE to the KKE). Their task was to clarify the situation and to give a detailed plan for KKE activity. The ECCI set the party the following tasks: to isolate the right-wing trend within the party and to secure the return of left-wing elements, who had organised a parallel Communist Union; 'to strengthen the party leadership and to establish strong authority'; to provide 'permanent and durable links with the Comintern either by monthly written reports or by sending a party representative to Moscow'; and to guarantee the strengthening of the ideological and political guidelines of the party's programme by stressing 'Bolshevik principles'. As the CYI's informer reported to Moscow, 'the youth has taken up a good stand and skilfully criticised the Central Committee'.[29] The efforts of the Comintern emissaries resulted, at least, in significant changes in the upper echelons of the party, where members of the left-wing trend were now in the majority. The new leadership readily published the report on 'The Situation within the CP of Greece' which had been composed in the Comintern. It appeared in the central party newspaper *Rizospastis* without even the usual signature of 'Central Committee' or 'Presidium of the Congress'.[30]

Developments within Greece during the early part of 1925 were characterised by enduring, permanent crisis. The KKE's official analysis painted a very black picture of the government. The party made statements on the semi-fascist nature of the ruling duumvirate of Mikhalakopoulos and Kondylis, and argued that the only way out of the situation was the establishment of a workers' and peasants' government.[31]

In the context of unstable conditions in the early summer of 1925, the concepts of revolution and political struggle were integrated into the party programme. The party's task was to 'preserve the revolutionary situation', which meant struggling against the 'monarcho-fascist bloc', and fighting for trade-union unity, organisation of the peasants, and the creation of a united front of workers, peasants and refugees. At the same time, probably for the first time in the party's history, there was an official declaration to the effect that the party must 'use the second type of reaction [social democracy] against fascist and espionage elements and to disclose to the masses when it rejects co-operation and helps fascist elements'.[32]

Moscow followed Balkan developments closely, with a view to strengthening the labour movements there and perhaps counting on the possible co-ordination of action, either at a national or a regional level. With this end in view, on 16 June 1925 the Profintern Secretariat adopted a resolution 'On the Balkan Bureau'. This resolution defined the technical functions of the newly created secret body situated in Vienna, and stated that the latter's political task was 'to be in touch with the Presidium of the Balkan Communist Federation'.[33]

Meanwhile, events in Greece were developing in a dramatic fashion. On 25 June 1925 General Pangalos, the leader the military movement, removed the Mikhalakopoulos government in a *coup d'état*. The KKE was banned; membership of the party was declared to be high treason. For its part, the Executive Bureau of the Profintern cabled to the KKE Central Committee rather firm instructions on the strategy and tactics of the trade-union movement, and demanded their execution:

> [T]he whole energy of reactionary [governmental and non-Communist syndicalist] forces in Greece will be aimed in the nearest future on the one hand at the destruction of progressive organisations from above and, on the other, simultaneously, at penetration into destroyed and weakened organisations. . . . [The KKE should therefore aim] not only to preserve its influence on the masses [but] to oppose in the trade union movement, with Leninist, Bolshevik, revolutionary tactics, all trends which seek to infiltrate themselves into the revolutionary masses of the Greek proletariat, and to increase and to make this influence broader, subjugating new masses.[34]

In the process, the whole of the party's previous line towards the trade unions was denounced, because the 'formal replacement of the trade union leadership in the trade union centres actually represents anti-Leninist, anti-Bolshevik tactics, and is fundamentally opposed to all decisions of the Comintern on the direction of the trade union movement'.[35] A new policy was promulgated along the lines discussed at a meeting between the Profintern Executive and the Central Committee of the KKE on 8 September 1925. This contained five points: the posts of party and trade-union centre chiefs were to be combined; vertical and horizontal structures were to be established for the syndicalist commissions; three persons approved by Profintern were to be appointed to places on the Central Syndicalist Commission; legal and illegal activity was to be carried on through the Communist fractions; and the party and trade-union press were to be separated.[36] But the most important instruction dealt with the separation of the KKE from the trade unions. Such a 'formal separation' was necessary to eliminate the possibility of the reactionaries destroying the trade-union movement on the pretext of 'curbing' communism.[37] The KKE's Central Trade Union Commission readily accepted the Profintern instructions.[38]

During the presidential election campaign on 11 April 1926, the KKE actually sided with the monarchists who supported Demertzis as the rival to Pangalos for the post. But the KKE's ideological and political thesis was advanced in an excessively complicated manner, as with the phrase 'the menace to the working people stemmed and stems from Pangalos and Demertzis'.[39] Close to this evaluation was the slogan worked out jointly by Moscow's emissary, Korzokov (who became a member of the KKE Politbureau under the pseudonym Evtikhiadis) and the KKE secretary, Khaitas. According to its authors, the slogan of 'left democracy' or 'real democracy' explained the necessity of the 'transitional period' on the path to the immediate establishment of the 'workers' and peasants' government'. All the corrections that were made in the ideology and politics of the party were the result of the theoretical searchings of that group in the party leadership who sought, as they saw it, to work out tactical guidelines applicable to national conditions. The reasons for the adoption of this new conception of the revolution were revealed by Korzokov in a message to the Comintern, where the innovations had been criticised as opportunistic. Korzokov insisted that the slogan should not be characterised as opportunist because of the situation in the KKE leadership. The Comintern's evaluation of the slogan as mistaken, he wrote, 'would have seriously beaten many comrades. Even without this act the locals look at me with suspicion.' Korzokov tried to assure his sponsors in Moscow that the slogan 'left democracy' or 'left democracy under the guidance of the proletariat' had essentially 'the same nature as the Bolshevik slogan had in 1905'.[40]

For its part, the KKE had tried to forecast the next developments in Greece in order to define its aims for future. Its evaluation of the situation was concentrated in the statement that 'in Greece there has not been such a defeat or retreat of the working class as we had in Germany, Bulgaria, etc., thus the spirit of the working class has not been destroyed'. In this regard, clearly, the author of the message did not agree with Badulescu, the leading expert on the Balkans, who told the ECCI of the 'political tiredness and apathy of the working class' in Greece.[41]

Comintern tactics towards the central organs of the KKE had been set forth in a letter from Korzokov to Smeral, the Comintern official responsible for Central Europe. He stated that the Comintern should provide support for the KKE Central Committee 'so far as that is not to open fire against them' but that 'at the same time we should take up measures to compose such a Central Committee which would guarantee correct guidance'.[42] Meanwhile, the situation in Greece was getting worse. The political and economic stabilisation promised by Pangalos had failed to materialise. Korzokov wrote in his report to Moscow that 'at the present moment events of great importance are becoming imminent; the situation is developing in a similar way to that in Poland and they want to involve our party in this adventure'.[43] Greek officers were divided into several groups. One of them comprised followers of Eleftherios Venizelos, Prime Minister for much of the period, under the leadership of General Plastiras and expressed the views of the conservative military establishment. Another group was under the guidance of General Kondylis and the republican Guard Colonel, Zervas: they shared left ideals and part of their group 'was under the ideological influence of the Communist Party', with 'some of its representatives' envisaging 'a future plot as a united military and people's insurrection with a view to the creation of a government under the leadership of the Communist Party which would be left-wing democratic in form and workers' and peasants' in nature'.[44]

Mass strikes in July 1926 and intensifying social and political instability were favourable to military conspirators. On 22 August, Kondylis carried out a *coup d'état* which made him Prime Minister with Admiral Koundouriotis as President. Soon afterwards, Kondylis was speaking, as Korzokov noted, in 'radical and socialist terms, thus some newspapers characterised him as a Bolshevik'.[45] Once in power, however, Kondylis could not garner any serious support, and began to govern in an equivocal manner, trying to be on friendly terms with both left and right. This policy was viewed with suspicion by his erstwhile supporters in the army. In a letter to the Comintern on 9 September, Korzokov reported that 'adventurous officers came suggesting the carrying out of a *coup d'état* in our [KKE] favour, but we considered this proposal provocative and stated that we would not support their insurrection, but that in the case of their victory we would evaluate them upon their deeds'.[46] At the same time, he evaluated KKE behaviour negatively, stressing that the party had been 'lagging after events'.[47]

Meanwhile, the split within the international Communist movement between pragmatists, on the one hand, and a left-wing, revolutionary-oriented minority, on the other, was becoming increasingly apparent. The Soviet leadership, where the contending factions had divided into two blocs behind Stalin and Trotsky, tried to exert influence on Comintern politics and ideology. By 1927 the Communist International had been converted into the tool of the Soviet Communist Party. Meanwhile, the intra-party strife in the USSR drew the attention of those within foreign Communist parties who sought to define their own path in their own particular countries. The KKE was not immune from this process, which was common to the whole of international communism, and three groups emerged within the party's leadership. The first, clustered around Pouliopoulos, supported 'ideas of the national peculiarities of Greece', and blamed the Comintern for its mismanagement in 'Greek affairs'. The second group took shape under the influence of Maximos, and demanded more independence from the Comintern. Finally, there was a third group, smaller than either of these others, which combined a strongly pro-Comintern line with some features of left extremism. This group's leadership, consisting of Khaitas and Korzokov, was close to the highest circles of the Communist International.

The Comintern had decreed that a party Congress should be held to unite the shattered leadership of the KKE and to strengthen its 'Bolshevik' nature. This Congress took place between 25 March and 5 April 1927. In order to exert its influence on events, the Comintern sent a delegation to the Congress. The delegation's tasks were defined by the ECCI as follows:

(a) To define the contents and nature of the party's mistakes and especially each of the groups. We shall not permit the use of the factional mistakes of one group by the others.
(b) It is necessary to determine in detail the party's tasks for the future in order to work out the political platform for the future activity of the C[entral] C[ommittee] and the whole party.
(c) On the basis of the two former points, to concentrate the best elements of the party for active party work.[48]

Meanwhile, the delegation's plan regarding the existing factions was as follows:

> Don't allow all the opposition groups and elements to unite by opposing and dividing different views inside oppositional groups. Thus to some extent we render support to the Maximos group in its struggle against the rather right-wing group of Kordatos and Apostolidis. Above all we have taken efforts to produce an abyss between Maximos and Comrade Pouliopoulos, [and] we have managed to achieve some results in this field.[49]

The world economic crisis which swept over the leading industrial nations of Europe and the USA in the late 1920s and early 1930s gripped the Balkans with the whole of its force. Besides dire economic consequences, it brought about serious ethnic disorders in many countries. Ethnic problems combined with economic and social difficulties made a serious impact upon political developments in Greece, Bulgaria, Yugoslavia and Romania. For its part, the Comintern sought to take advantage of every crisis within the 'capitalist encirclement' and to use it in the interests of the 'world proletariat'. In addition, of course, and equally, the strategic interests of the USSR were a major consideration for the chiefs of the Communist International. On 6 June 1931, at a session of the ECCI Presidium at which KKE leaders participated, Otto Kuusinen, one of the Comintern's leading figures, delivered a report 'On the National Liberation Movement of the Oppressed Peoples in Europe'. He stated that:

> the correct tactics of the Communist Party determine . . . self-managed and active work [in] preparation for national insurrection; a permanent fight among the working masses to win influence for the CP; [and] compulsory interlinking between national liberation slogans and the important economic and political class demands of the workers and peasants.[50]

These words were, in effect, the next instructions to the KKE as to how it should act in the ongoing Macedonian problem.

The strengthening of Communist parties' positions depended upon their ability to concentrate their activity upon particular problems on the national scene. Intra-party conflict had weakened the parties, so the Comintern, keen to revive them, tried to eliminate any serious discussions within party ranks. The Comintern believed that in Greece, where the political situation had been far from stable, there was a serious prospect of wide-scale social and political disorder leading to ultimately favourable consequences. But there was severe intra-party strife within the KKE between those demanding a general strike and their opponents who favoured a mass political strike: in other words, between those who favoured immediate revolution and those who wanted a series of steps in the same ultimate direction, but with thorough preparation.

The first serious step by the Comintern to try to clear up the Greek situation was the session of the ECCI Presidium held on 8 September 1931. This session was convened to approve a draft letter to the party membership on the situation within the party. The Comintern was represented by, among others, leading figures such as B. Kun, V. Kolarov, D. Manuilsky and M. Tskhakhaya. The Greek side was represented by A. Khaitas, Vornos and Siandos. In a rough and arrogant manner Kun and Manuilsky verbally chastised all the invited Greek 'guests'. It became clear that the Communist International was keen to change the leading figures in the KKE. Although no special resolution on the matter was adopted at the session, the process of 'selecting' a new leadership began. The 'Open Letter to KKE Members', dispatched by the Comintern Presidium in December 1931, talked about the necessity to 'unite' and to concentrate on political and social problems, rather than continuing with unprincipled and mistaken intra-party strife. At the fourth Plenum of the party in the same month a new leadership was officially elected; this included N. Zachariades as general secretary, as well as Y. Ioannidis, Y. Mikhailidis, V. Nefeloudis, St. Sklavenos, G. Konstantinidis and L. Stringos. This new leadership had been selected in Moscow and included people well known to the Comintern through their having been trained in the Soviet Union.[51]

The KKE had to seek an ideological and political direction that could achieve success within Greece. As the crisis in Greece intensified, and with the vast majority of the population expressing discontent with the government's use of a 'strong hand' to curb economic disorder, the party tried to find ways to take advantage of the situation. Moscow paid particular attention to the theoretical thesis of the KKE, and a special session of the ECCI Political Secretariat was held on 9 July 1933 to determine the party's ideological programme. Kuusinen, Reno, Ioannidis, Knorin and Piatnitsky were all active participants in the discussion. The Greek side suggested that the 'forthcoming revolution' would be proletarian in form, but this view was rejected as mistaken by the Comintern leadership. The Greeks' thesis was therefore replaced by another one in which the future revolution was described as 'bourgeois-democratic transforming quickly into proletarian'.[52]

Under the influence of Soviet concerns, the Comintern underwent subtle changes in early 1934. These changes, which, though real, were hardly perceptible in the Communist International's official propaganda, affected the KKE. The party interpreted Moscow's talk of united political action against the 'bourgeois regime' as a call for a 'united front of the left'. In some ways, it hinted at possible union with forces which had recently been considered in Communist circles as 'agents of the bourgeoisie within the labour movement'. On 5 October 1934, the party signed a secret agreement 'On Joint Actions during the Period of Military Fascist Dictatorship' with the Agrarian Party, the Socialist Party, the Workers' Socialist Party, the United General Trade Unions of Greece, the General Trade Unions of Greece, and the independent trade unions. The programme of action outlined in this document combined, first, political methods to obstruct right monarchist forces from establishing an authoritarian regime, and, second, the use of trade-union power to defend the economic and social rights of the workers.[53]

The new line ushered in at the Seventh Comintern Congress (July/August 1935) demanded the creation of 'people's fronts' against fascism. This offered a new opportunity to the Communists, who might now be able to reach power on the crest of a wave of anti-fascism. So far as the KKE was concerned, it was hoped that this stage would serve as a bridge to the ultimate reward of general political domination in the form of the dictatorship of the proletariat. Despite their obvious weakness, Greek Communists cherished serious hopes that power could be seized at an opportune moment.

In August 1936, however, General Metaxas established an authoritarian military dictatorship. The KKE was immediately banned and forced to go underground. Metaxas's Minister of Public Security, Maniadakis, used unorthodox methods to undermine Communist activity. He arrested the leaders of the party but then organised a new Central Committee, known as the Provisional Leadership. This new body was met with suspicion on the part of some Communist activists, but many party members did not suspect provocation and worked under the guidance of the 'Provisional Leadership'. Meanwhile, there was growing dissatisfaction with the Metaxas regime on the part of many civilian politicians and some of the military. Although the military insurrection in Crete in July 1938 was suppressed, the KKE Political Bureau believed that the spread of this anti-dictatorial uprising 'could . . . create serious prerequisites for the rapid spread of the events all over the country'.[54]

All the attempts of KKE functionaries to contact anti-Metaxas forces in Greece and abroad failed, though, because the majority of the opposition did not want to support links with the Communist Party: it was known to be a radical force, 'sponsored from abroad', with a programme of establishing dictatorship along Soviet lines. Some exiled KKE emissaries, notably in France, were able to gain information regarding the situation in both the opposition camp and in Greek ruling circles. They sent their cipher cables and letters to Moscow. In early 1939, on the basis of their information, V. Kolarov prepared special notes on the Greek situation for Manuilsky. In these notes Kolarov wrote of 'the approaching fall of Metaxas'.[55] In turn, Manuilsky composed a memorandum to Dekanazov, the Deputy Foreign Minister of the USSR and a close associate of Beria in the NKVD. In this memorandum, Manuilsky wrote without hesitation of having already solved the problems which would arise imminently:

> in the case of a *coup d'état* the Communist Party, jointly with the left wing of the anti-dictatorial bloc, were to act as a third force, struggling not only against the Metaxas dictatorship but against the establishment of a dictatorship under Italian pressure. It will take advantage of the confusion stirred up by the armed struggle in the ruling camp in order to arm the masses in their fight for a democratic republic.[56]

These ideas found their way into the recommendations sent by Comintern Secretary, Georgii Dimitrov, to the KKE representative in June 1939. He stressed that:

> in our opinion the Plastiras putsch [long forecast by the KKE] is a conspiracy on the part of Mussolini and reactionary Panhellenic circles in Greece. The ostensibly anti-dictatorial programme is only a bait for the masses. It is a pity that our party does not see clearly the real purpose of this clique. It is necessary to warn the party quickly and to take measures to unmask this dangerous gamble of Plastiras. Our line consists of [the establishment of] a national front on a democratic basis for the defence of the country's independence, against foreign aggression and for the establishment of a Balkan bloc on the basis of peaceful co-operation against the menace of invasion by Germany and Italy.[57]

Further instructions were addressed to the party leadership on 14 July 1939. These comprised a detailed secret resolution of the ECCI Secretariat 'On the Balkan Bloc of Defence' plus a 'Platform of the Movement for a Balkan Bloc'. The Greek party was ordered to recognise the fact that 'the principal enemy is the Fascist Rome–Berlin Axis which acts in Greece mainly with its Italian wing'.[58] The final sentences of this secret message read as follows:

> If an offensive against Greece on the part of the Fascist aggressors (Mussolini, Hitler) takes place during the reign of the dictatorial Metaxas government, then . . . there could not even be hesitation that we spare our weapons against it, if it carries out resistance to aggression then we will fight with all our forces against the Fascist armies, that principal enemy invading Greece. . . . Whether or not it [the Metaxas government] demands any formal declaration against Communism [the 'repentance declaration'] during mobilisation it will not change our stance.[59]

In the early hours of 28 October 1940 the Italians attacked Greece. Mass protests of Greeks against this act of aggression followed, and the imprisoned KKE General Secretary, N. Zakhariadis, issued a statement demanding support for the efforts of Metaxas in repulsing the invaders. However, he soon changed his mind, and defined the war, not as one of national liberation, but as an imperialist struggle, and demanded the taking up of arms against the dictatorship.[60] This ostensibly unexpected change can be explained by reference to the Comintern. More than a year had passed since the instructions of July 1939. The Nazi–Soviet Pact and the consequent changes in Soviet foreign policy had transformed the line taken by the Comintern. The characterisation of the war as a struggle between rival imperialisms dominated Soviet propaganda and official evaluations. The minutes of a session of ECCI on 10 January record the statement that 'the present war is not one of Greek national liberation'. Moscow was not interested in stirring up its German partner and sought to escape any policy that could be directed against Berlin.

After the German invasion of the Soviet Union, the Communist International immediately changed its views and hence its guidelines to foreign Communist parties. Despite the hardships of war, and the concomitant disruption of communications, the Comintern did manage to maintain or re-establish links with some Communist parties. But Greece was not at the forefront of the Comintern's attention. Moreover, the KKE had lost contact with Moscow in the late spring of 1941. Soon, however, the Soviets decided to resume their links with the party, and with the Greek resistance movement, about which Moscow knew little. In mid-December 1941 the Intelligence Administration of the Red Army General Headquarters asked Dimitrov 'to select right away for our [Intelligence] disposal two, or at least one, Greek under your control with organisational abilities and [who is] strong-willed who we need urgently to send to carry out very important illegal work'.[61] But at the time the Comintern did not have any such people at its disposal, and the request was therefore not fulfilled.

Before October 1942 there was no news on the situation in Greece. Moscow had firm contacts with the majority of Communist parties behind the front line, but Greece fell from the Comintern's view completely because of the difficulty of maintaining contacts with dispersed Communists and the complete uncertainty of the situation after May 1941 when Greece was occupied by joint Italian, German and Bulgarian forces.

In the autumn of 1942 some attempts were made by the Communist organisation within the Greek army to contact the Soviet secret services. The secretary of the organisation, Spithakis, wrote a short message in broken Russian to inform Moscow of the fact that the National Liberation Front, Ethnikón Apdeftherotikón Métopon (EAM), which was the major resistance organisation, had been organised and led by the Communist Party. Spithakis was particularly concerned with rumours he had picked up, according to which 'the Soviet Union does not recognise the National Front and does not any longer recognise the Communist Party'.[62] Meanwhile, the armed struggle within Greece against the Nazi invaders was getting more active than ever before. EAM gained the upper hand in the situation and the pro-Communist forces became much stronger. Non-Communist resistance groups tried to obtain support from the Western Allies and to neutralise their opponents. Soviet intelligence reported to Dimitrov that the British were particularly important:

> British counter-intelligence follows intensively the activity of the Communist parties in Britain, its colonies and all countries of the world. . . . It is known that Britons seeking to take advantage of the situation are trying to establish direct contacts and to subordinate to their influence some active members of the party getting in touch with them under the pretext of the activisation of the anti-fascist struggle.[63]

Despite all the efforts of the Comintern to contact the KKE, regular relations had not been established between the Communist International and the leadership of the party or that of the pro-Communist EAM. Moreover, the weak grasp of Comintern officials in regard to Greek affairs can be seen in the statement of Comintern 'experts' that 'the central leadership of the Greek CP is extremely weak and needs regular help on our part. It can be assumed that the current antifascist movement of the Greek people against the German invaders is not under the guidance of the KKE.'[64]

By the spring of 1943, Stalin and his close colleagues were moving to take serious steps in the interests of Soviet foreign policy and to strengthen the anti-German alliance. In disbanding the Comintern, Moscow tried to calm the Western Allies, but it sought simultaneously to restructure Soviet links with international Communism. The Greek Communist Party had not been able to re-establish its links with Moscow until the very moment of the dissolution of the Communist International; and, in fact, KKE activity during the war period was not guided from Moscow, and so represented an example of independence during a crucial period.

Notes

1 For fuller details, see A. A. Ulunian, *Kommunisticheskaya Partiya Gretsii: Aktualnie Voprosi Ideologii i Vnutrennei Istorii* [*The Communist Party of Greece: Problems of Ideology and Intra-Party Relations*] (Moscow, 3 vols, 1992–94).

2 The early period of the Greek Socialist movement is covered in detail in the classic

work by Y. Kordatos, *Istoria tou Ellinikou Ergatikou Kinimatos* (Athens, 1956). On different trends within Greek socialism in the late nineteenth and early twentieth centuries, see G. Leon, *The Greek Socialist Movement and the First World War: The Road to Unity* (New York, 1976); C. Jecchins, *Trade Unionism in Greece: A Study in Political Paternalism* (Washington, 1967).

3 B. Tsikoula, 'I Oukraniki Ekstrateia kai to SEKE', *Neos Kosmos*, 1 (1967).

4 Russian Centre for the Preservation and Study of Contemporary Historical Documents [hereafter RC], 495/1/1a, minutes of ECCI Bureau, 5 August 1919.

5 RC 495/1/1a, minutes of ECCI, 11 November 1919.

6 *Ibid.*

7 'Report on the Second Session of the National Council of the SEKE' was received in the Comintern in mid-December 1919.

8 RC 495/18/58, report by a member of the Russian Communist Party to ECCI.

9 There is no reference to this fact in either the published official proceedings of the Second Comintern Congress or in the *Soviet Historical Encyclopedia*. Details of Ligdopoulos's presence at the Congress can be found in M. Shedio, *Syndomi Istoria tou KKE* (Athens, 1988), p. 40.

10 *Second Congress of the Comintern* (Moscow, 1934), p. 11 (in Russian).

11 *Ibid.*, p. 604.

12 RC, 495/1/12, minutes of ECCI, 21 November 1920.

13 On the history of the KUTV, see N. N. Timofeyeva, 'Kommunisticheskiy Universitet Trudiashchiksia Vostroka (KUTV): Tsentr Ideynoy Podgotovki Kommunisticheskih i Revolutsionnih Kadrov Vostoka' (unpublished Ph.D. dissertation, Moscow, 1988).

14 RC, 529/1/22, draft of the 5th anniversary of the University of National Minorites of the West, January 1926.

15 RC 495/18/75, message from Maximov to the Central Committee of the Bulgarian Communist Party, n.d.

16 RC 534/7/232, Kordatos to Profintern, 4 April 1922.

17 Communist Party of Greece, *Episma Keimena* (Athens, 1973), p. 259.

18 *Ibid.*, p. 324.

19 RC 509/1/50a, Chonos, 'Information on the Party Congress', n.d.

20 A. Katsoukali, *I Proti Dekaetia tou KKE, 1918–1928* (Athens, 1979), p. 130.

21 RC 533/3/75, minutes of CYI Executive Committee, 14 January 1924.

22 RC 533/4/41, minutes of CYI Executive Committee, 31 January 1924.

23 RC 533/5/32, monthly report of the Balkan Secretariat of the CYI Executive Committee, February 1924.

24 *Ibid.*

25 RC 534/3/79, minutes of Profintern Executive Bureau, 13 June 1924.

26 *Kommunisticheskiy Internatsional v Dokumentak: Resheniya, Tezisy i Vozvaniya Kongressov Kominterna i Plenumov IKKI, 1919–1932* (Moscow, 1933), p. 395.

27 RC 509/1/50a.

28 RC 533/5/32, information from 'Oskar' in Vienna to the CYI Executive Committee, 28 July 1924.

29 RC 533/4/48, 'Shnayder' to 'Robert' in the CYI Executive Committee, 4 December 1924.

30 This document was worked out by several Comintern bodies and was based on information and secret reports from Comintern agents in the party, the trade unions and OKNE.

31 To KKE.T.2.S.4. Resolution of the KKE executive committee on the political situation, 18 February 1925.
32 RC 534/3/116, minutes of Profintern Secretariat, 16 June 1925.
33 *Ibid.*
34 RC 534/6/64.
35 *Ibid.*
36 *Ibid.*
37 *Ibid.*
38 RC 534/7/232, letter from Central Trade Union Commission of KKE to Profintern, 17 October 1925.
39 To KKE.T.2.S.123.
40 RC 495/69/113, Korkozov to Comintern Balkan Secretariat, 28 January 1926.
41 RC 495/69/113, Korkozov to Smeral, 29 June 1926.
42 *Ibid.*
43 *Ibid.* In 1926 the Polish Communist Party had supported and welcomed the military *coup d'état* carried out by Marshal Pilsudski. As soon as Pilsudski was established in power, however, the Comintern declared his regime fascist and condemned as mistaken the line which had been taken by the Polish party. Pilsudski went on to ban the party, and his regime was characterised by persecution of Communists and other left elements.
44 RC 495/69/114, 'Letter of information', 1926.
45 RC 495/69/112.
46 RC 495/69/112, 'On the letter to the KKE'.
47 *Ibid.*
48 RC 533/4/104, report of the CYI delegation to the CYI Exeecutive Committee on the third Party Congress, 10 April 1927.
49 *Ibid.*
50 RC 495/2/148.
51 For details of the process, see Ulunian, *Communist Party of Greece*, I: pp. 282–300.
52 See 'Agenda of the Politsecretariat session', 9 July 1933.
53 To KKE.T.4.S.87–9, open letter addressed by the KKE and the United GTUWG, 9 September 1934.
54 RC, 495/74/172.
55 RC 495/10a/319.
56 RC 495/10a/320.
57 RC 495/74/172.
58 *Ibid.*
59 *Ibid.*
60 For details on this, see Ulunian, *Communist Party of Greece*, II: pp. 413–20.
61 RC 495/74/175, Iliychev to Dimitrov, 15 December 1941.
62 RC 495/74/173a, Spithakis to ECCI, September 1942.
63 RC 495/74/56, Fitin to Dimitrov, 17 March 1943.
64 RC 495/74/174, Plyshevsky and Georgiyev to Dimitrov, 26 March 1943.

13

Tito and the twilight of the Comintern

Geoffrey Swain

In the very twilight[1] years of the Comintern, from 1940–43, the Yugoslav Communist Party, Komunistička Partija Jugoslavije (KPJ), led by Tito, donned the mantle held by the German Communist Party in the 1920s and the French Communist Party in the 1930s, the mantle of *primus inter pares* among Communist parties, the status of Moscow's favourite child. The KPJ achieved this distinction because, after many vicissitudes, it learnt under Tito's leadership to be truly 'Bolshevik'. Tito successfully resolved the contradiction between legal activity and illegal organisation that his predecessors had found insurmountable; in so doing he negotiated the contradictory pressures emanating from Moscow between 1937 and 1939. Thus, when with the outbreak of the Second World War the Comintern needed a new operations base outside Russia, it naturally turned to the strategically sensitive Balkans and the KPJ; the 'Bolshevik' KPJ served as a role model for all Communist parties in Hitler's new Europe.

Tito's negative experience of the popular front, both in Yugoslavia and in Spain, meant he readily endorsed the radical line of the 1940s Comintern; the demand for a people's government, and in particular the lesson of the Spanish Civil War that a new revolutionary government needed to be constructed from below, stood at the heart of KPJ policy at this time. When, during the winter of 1940–41, it looked as if the Balkans might drag the Soviet Union and Nazi Germany into premature conflict, this policy was repudiated by the Comintern, but once that conflict had begun, Tito's Leninist path of insurrection and revolution was resumed. The abolition of the Comintern meant that Tito could continue to support revolution in the Adriatic and Aegean through a vestigial regional Comintern organisation, until Stalin decided this no longer suited his purpose.

Coming to terms with illegality

It took the KPJ more than a decade to come to terms with its illegal status. It had begun life as a legally organised mass party with widespread popular support and its own traditions, frequently antipathetic to the ideological and organisational straitjacket implicit in the Comintern's famous twenty-one conditions. A powerful reformist faction, centred around the KPJ's first Secretary, General Sima Markovic, was sceptical about accepting guidance from Moscow and remained loyal to the German and Austrian Marxist tradition; thus the party leadership had great difficulty getting the twenty-one conditions endorsed. Although the KPJ was dissolved after the November 1920 elections, and its parliamentary delegation arrested in the summer of 1921, the Communist-run Independent Trade Unions were allowed to continue their existence – in 1921 serving as a cover for the Independent Workers' Party which fought that year's elections – and the reformist party leadership clung to the belief that the ban on the party was purely temporary and that, in the meantime, too close contact between the Independent Trade Union leadership in Belgrade and the exiled party leadership in Vienna could put at jeopardy the continued existence of the trade unions. The party leadership in Vienna saw the Belgrade leadership's attitude as indiscipline, and in the ensuing rows the Executive Committee of the Communist International (ECCI) had to intervene more than once.[2]

In May 1926 the ECCI lost patience with the Yugoslavs and described the party as 'paralysed and transformed into a permanent debating club'.[3] The logical solution was to skip a generation and select a new leadership uncompromised by factional strife. Thus the ECCI welcomed Tito's initiative when in March 1927 he began a campaign in Zagreb, based around the Zagreb Independent Trade Union, for the formation of a 'workers' front' opposed to the factionalism of the right reformist trade-union leaders in Belgrade and the left faction in charge of the party hierarchy. Meeting in February 1928, the eighth Conference of the Zagreb Party Organisation sent a letter, signed by Tito, calling on the ECCI to intervene in the party's affairs; that it willingly did and the letter was discussed during the Sixth Comintern Congress in July 1928. The result, endorsed by the fourth Party Congress in Dresden in November 1928, was the final suspension of the reformists and the official end of the factional struggle which had nearly destroyed the party in the 1920s.[4] But no sooner had the ECCI intervened than the situation in Yugoslavia changed dramatically. On 6 January 1929 King Alexander dissolved Parliament and established his personal dictatorship; at the same time all parties and all trade unions were closed down.

Alexander's coup discredited the reformists in the KPJ and the party took a dramatic lurch to the left. It asserted that the only 'solution of this crisis for the working class and peasantry is armed struggle', and a month later called for the 'armed revolutionary struggle' to start at once. Although in May 1929 the Politburo suggested the armed insurrection was no longer imminent, the Central Committee resolved in October 'to go from defence to attack . . . and prepare the masses and the Party for armed insurrection'. Again, it was the Comintern which intervened to restore a more coherent and effective line: on 7 December 1931 ECCI officials and the party leadership met in Moscow,[5] but there were further false starts before, in spring 1932, Milan Gorkic emerged as the new dominant party figure. Gorkic, a successful Comintern operative, had been on the ECCI Commission which in spring 1928 considered Tito's letter against factionalism: he attended the fourth Party Congress in Dresden, where he was elected to the Central Committee, but was apparently out of sympathy with the leadership of 1929–30 and spent that time as a roving Comintern agent, visiting Great Britain among other places. In April 1932 the ECCI appointed him to a new three-member temporary leadership, the sole survivor of the 1928 Central Committee,[6] and he was given the job of reviving the party's fortunes more or less from scratch.

In November–December 1933 Gorkic travelled to Yugoslavia to prepare for the fourth Party Conference; in the process, in July 1934 he co-opted Tito to the temporary leadership.[7] Although he did not attend the fourth Party Conference held in Ljubljana in December 1934 in person, there was no doubt that he was the dominant personality in the five-member Politburo established by it.[8] Gorkic's success in reviving the fortunes of the KPJ was most clearly marked in the content of the official journal *Proleter*. Although in September 1930 the incorrect use of the slogan 'armed uprising' had been criticised,[9] it was with Gorkic's appointment that the alternative of 'working with the masses' became a *Proleter* hobby-horse. Back in 1929 the first issue of *Proleter* published an article entitled 'We will win over the masses', which suggested that, unless the masses were won over, the armed uprising would degenerate into a disorganised and unsuccessful rebellion; the key task was, without waiting for party directives, to use one's own initiative and respond to the day-to-day demands of the masses, combining work in the illegal sphere with work in the legal sphere.

These concerns then disappeared from the pages of *Proleter* until May 1930, when the question of work in the masses was again raised. After October 1930 the journal always put the question of the 'armed uprising' in the context of long-term mass activity among the working class, and occasionally articles like one of February 1932 reminded members not to ignore the possibilities offered by legal struggle. However, with Gorkic's emergence as *de facto* leader, the content of *Proleter* dramatically changed. In an article of September 1932 entitled 'The Communist Party at the head of the revolutionary struggle of the masses', the author made clear that the KPJ had to break out of the cell mentality to which it had become confined, and base its work in the factories: armchair revolutionaries plotting revolution in smoke-filled rooms were no longer appropriate; the party would only be a mass party when it was linked with the masses. Thereafter, this became *Proleter*'s perpetual refrain, its most articulate expression perhaps being the article 'The Organisational Tasks of Our Party' of December 1932, which suggested that initiative should be transferred to the rank and file in the factories, with the party organisation helping members rather than dictating to them.[10]

Work among the masses meant competing with the Socialists and, in the Comintern context of 1932–33, working for the 'united front from below', i.e.

ignoring the Socialist Party leadership and trying to win a majority of workers to the Communist side. Gorkic always interpreted this slogan imaginatively: in September 1932 *Proleter* suggested that joint action with the Social Democrat rank and file, rather than permanent confrontation with them, was the way forward. By October 1932 *Proleter* was criticising the sectarian policy of the Spanish Communist Party, which had failed to profit from the overthrow of the monarchy in 1931; the journal stressed that the 'united front from below' allowed for the formation of 'militant accords' with members of reformist trade unions for specific if limited campaigns.[11] Clearly, Gorkic was keen to push the concept of the 'united front from below' to its very limits, and this became even clearer in the aftermath of Hitler's triumph in Germany. In April 1933 *Proleter*'s editorial called 'For United Struggle against Fascism' and 'held out a brotherly hand to all workers and social democrats in reformist organisations'. While the editorial was careful not to go beyond the Comintern appeal 'For a united front of the proletariat', Gorkic immediately took up the suggestion that the Communists reach 'concrete agreements in individual countries' by proposing joint campaigns with both the Yugoslav Social Democrats and the reformist trade unions, a call repeated in subsequent issues.[12]

Once preparations for the Seventh Comintern Congress had begun, Gorkic became an enthusiastic supporter of those working to change the 'united front from below' to the 'united front from above', or the popular front. In 1932 King Alexander had re-legalised some trade unions and established a new non-parliamentary assembly; in 1933 the KPJ decided to boycott the elections to this assembly, but in July 1934 the party criticised this decision to boycott and in August *Proleter* praised the sort of 'action unity' reached between the French Socialists and Communists; by January 1935 the paper was praising the Spanish Communist Youth for achieving unity with their Socialist colleagues. The fourth Party Conference in December 1934 stressed that the party's call for united action with the Socialists was in line with the French popular front already formed and the 'worker–peasant alliance' established in Spain; for the first time it stated publicly that unity would be reached 'from above', in talks with Socialist leaders, not only 'from below'. The clear target for such talks was the next assembly elections due in May 1935.[13]

Gorkic held talks with the Socialist leaders in January and February 1935. Although an agreement on joint action in the trade unions seemed feasible, negotiations for an electoral agreement broke down over who should head the electoral list. To break the deadlock, Gorkic made a dramatic concession which, while clearly in line with the new spirit of the popular front, appeared to contradict traditional Leninism: the agreed Politburo line was that the party should fight the elections as an independent entity, but in cooperation with other groups; Gorkic did an about-turn and proposed that the party should merge its candidates with those of the Socialists into a single opposition list.[14] An electoral pact with the Socialists was one thing, a policy of a single opposition list was quite another. After all, in Tsarist Russia Lenin had more than once warned of the dangers of such a tactic: there was not, he had argued, simply an authoritarian regime and an opposition, but an authoritarian regime, a false liberal 'opposition', and a genuine workers' opposition; in the 1912 State Duma elections it had been Lenin's Menshevik opponents who had talked of a single opposition list.[15]

Although the Central Committee criticised the conduct of the May 1935 elections,[16] Gorkic saw no need to change his enthusiastic endorsement of popular front type policies. He was to repeat the proposal for a single opposition list with the Socialists throughout his period as party leader. Prospects for such an alliance improved in the autumn of 1935 when Gorkic himself visited Yugoslavia in October to try to finalise an agreement;[17] but success eluded him and in April 1936 a Central Committee meeting adopted a series of resolutions critical of the talks.[18] In support of the popular front policy, the ECCI quashed these resolutions and summoned the whole leadership to Moscow in August. Gorkic's policies were endorsed, but Gorkic himself was criticised for not having sought Comintern intervention earlier.[19] When he returned from Moscow to Vienna in December he did so with the right to veto all KPJ decisions,[20] and having already instructed Tito to reach a deal with the Socialists for that month's local elections. In a letter to Tito, Gorkic stressed the need for agreement at any cost, whether officially or unofficially and no matter what name was given to the list; it was essential, he felt, that a united left should become an active part of the opposition organized by the 'bourgeois' parties; the 'old socialist' idea of a 'third block' was rejected. Gorkic seemed unaware that, in 1912, Lenin himself had advanced the idea of a 'third block' and advised against joint oppositional activities with the bourgeoisie.[21]

While not critical of the negotiations *per se*, Tito was clearly worried by the logic of reaching an agreement at any price. The Socialists insisted that the illegality of the KPJ was a major stumbling block to an agreement, and Tito told Gorkic in November 1936 that much of the current talk about relations with the Socialist Party could only be described as liquidationist.[22] Liquidationism meant abandoning or 'liquidating' the underground committee structure of the party in an attempt to legalise it and thus make easier an alliance with the liberals by distancing the party from its radical leadership in exile. It was a term used by Lenin to describe the views of the majority of his Menshevik opponents in Russia during the years 1907–14. The Menshevik view of Tsarism was that there were essentially only two political groupings in the country; supporters of the Tsar and supporters of the opposition; the Russian Social Democrats should, therefore, be ready to cooperate with any opposition alliance which might emerge. Liquidator Mensheviks argued that this would be facilitated if the Social Democrats concentrated their activity on the trade unions, legalised after 1905, and rebuilt the party on a semi-legal footing, abandoning the centralised hierarchy of underground committees.[23]

That Gorkic became a liquidator during his negotiations with the Socialists there can be no doubt. Not only did he call for a united opposition, but he wanted to facilitate this by legalising the KPJ and thus overcome the Socialists' fear of association with an illegal organisation. To this end, he drew up lengthy proposals aimed at completely transforming the party's organisational structure. At his first meeting with the Central Committee on returning from Moscow in December 1936 he called on all those in exile who were in contact with Yugoslavia to study the question of the relationship between legal and illegal work. All Gorkic's correspondence with the Comintern in the spring of 1937 made clear that radical changes were at the front of his mind.[24] He proposed legalising as many party leaders as possible by involving them in the legal and semi-legal trade-union work so essential for working-class unity. This would inevitably mean the demise of 'deep underground commanding committees', which showed little activity and were increasingly irrelevant; 'we must be brave enough to recognise this', he wrote in January 1937, 'and draw the logical conclusions, which are not', he insisted, 'liquidationist.' The old technical apparatus should be abolished, the party rebuilt from below, and the party leadership legalised in Yugoslavia.[25]

Unfortunately for Gorkic, the Comintern did not agree that these proposals were not liquidationist. He was warned by the KPJ representative in Moscow that he should take care not to commit any sort of 'silliness' by appearing to favour liquidationism. The impression 'here', he was told, was that the proposed reorganisation would indeed be 'silly'. Gorkic stuck to his guns and took a detailed statement on party reorganisation when summoned to Moscow at the end of June 1937. This repeated the call for the legalisation of the party and the abolition of the technical apparatus; it described the underground cells as irrelevant.[26] The Comintern had also begun to worry about his repeated calls for the KPJ to follow the tactic of a single opposition, and criticised his letter dated July 1937, issued just before his departure, calling for all anti-government elements to be part of the same list in local elections.[27] Gorkic never returned from that visit to Moscow. One of the many victims of Stalin's purges, he was arrested as a British spy, a charge related in some way to his Comintern work in Britain.[28]

Tito Bolshevises the KPJ

It would not be until January 1939[29] that Tito was finally endorsed by the Comintern as KPJ secretary, and November 1939 before his position as party leader was unassailable. In the interim he would have to navigate through a minefield of constantly changing Comintern policies. During the autumn of 1937 the Comintern clearly wanted him to take a firm line with the Socialists – something paralleled by developments in Spain – but no sooner was this embarked on than – again paralleling events in Spain – the Comintern wanted further concessions to the Socialists; while at the same time Stalin issued his *Short Course* history of the Bolshevik Party, which paid no attention at all to the popular front. Unendorsed as party secretary, Tito was prey to a number of machinations,[30] but his actions were always consistent with the struggle of an orthodox Bolshevik against liquidationism. In December 1937 the Politburo agreed to confront the liquidator danger, while retaining legal work at the centre of attention, by establishing party cells in mass organisations.[31]

Tito would not have contradicted Gorkic's view that the underground had become discredited, but rather than abandoning it he concentrated on reforming it, making it more secure and more in tune with workers' needs. He concentrated on trying to break down the old 'superconspiratorial' three-man cell structure – in which student revolutionaries had debated the pros and cons of the dictatorship of the proletariat – and establish party cells within the legal workers' movement. Cells in the trade unions would become the responsibility of the trade-union commission, operating under the control of the Central Committee.[32] The results of this reorganisation were visible almost at once. At the April Congress of one of Yugoslavia's major trade-union federations, the URSS, seven of the fifteen members of the new executive were Communists. That same year Communists took control of the URSS Construction Workers' Union, Textile Workers' Union and Woodworkers' Union, while the powerful Zagreb regional board of the URSS Metal Workers' Union was in their hands.[33] When summoned to Moscow in autumn 1938, Tito could stress that progress had been made in the trade-union sphere without weakening the party and making excessive concessions to the Socialists.[34] Tito's principles for the December 1938 assembly elections brought this out clearly. Although over the summer the Socialists and Communists had come to an understanding about some joint activities, Tito insisted that the Communists were not committed by this arrangement to following the tails of the Socialists in the elections. He believed the party should put up a separate list and issued an instruction from Moscow to this effect. In Croatia, however, the party refused to accept this ruling and did not put up a separate candidate.[35] Tito condemned them angrily as 'capitulators and liquidators',[36] and when he returned to Yugoslavia in spring 1939 he was determined to finish with them. At three meetings of the Central Committee between March and May 1939, all leading liquidators were expelled and in June the Croat party was severely criticised.[37]

Finishing off the Croat liquidators fitted well with the Bolshevising cult under way in Moscow associated with the publication of Stalin's *Short Course* history of the Bolshevik Party, a volume Tito had avidly read; it did not sit so comfortably in the overall context of adapting the popular front policy to an ever worsening international situation. The spring of 1939 saw the final collapse of the Spanish Republic when unity against fascism at any cost was the order of the day. Spring 1939 also saw the final dismemberment of Czechoslovakia, when Hitler had successfully pandered to the repressed national aspirations of the Slovaks; in this context an attack on the activities of Croat Communists seemed inopportune. For both reasons the Comintern could see very good reasons for Tito showing indulgence towards his wayward Croat comrades, and Tito soon found himself balancing on a very slack tightrope as he sought both to assert his authority as party leader and satisfy the Comintern.

A resolution on the KPJ's defence policy was almost his undoing. In March 1939 the KPJ issued a statement on defence which appealed to the Comintern in terms of its forthright defence of Yugoslav territorial integrity, but which also rang alarm bells. Far from seeking alliances with other opposition groups to help preserve and defend that integrity, the statement verged on the revolutionary: only a people's government, it argued, a truly democratic government, would be capable of defending the country.[38] Franco's victory in the Spanish Civil War, the Central Committee stressed in an open letter published at this time, proved that the officer corps was inherently disloyal and reactionary, and that the time had come to put the Yugoslav armed forces at the service of the people.[39] This view, which seemed to imply that political change not far short of revolution was the only way Yugoslavia could play a role in the defence of peace, caused great concern in Moscow. Tito was immediately summoned to Moscow to face the capital charge of Trotskyism; but he delayed his departure and by the time he arrived there the Molotov–Ribbentrop Pact had been signed, the Comintern had turned sharply to the left, and the slogan of a people's government had become official policy. Tito had no difficulty adapting to this new line when reporting to the Comintern on 26 September,[40] and on 23 November 1939 the charge of Trotskyism was rejected and Tito's work endorsed.[41]

The model party at peace

The Molotov–Ribbentrop Pact completely changed the priorities of the Comintern. If the prospect of a German revolution had hypnotised the Comintern in the 1920s and the diplomacy of the popular front beguiled it in the 1930s, so in the 1940s the strategic importance of the Balkans forced the Comintern to concentrate its activities on Yugoslavia. The Pact had made the Balkans an area where both Nazi Germany and Soviet Russia felt they had legitimate interests. While in Yugoslavia, Tito had created a party which, it seemed, had found the Communists' philosopher's stone; it could operate effectively underground.

Tito returned to Yugoslavia early in 1940 to prepare for the fifth Party Conference. During the spring, summer and autumn of 1940 conferences were held of all the national and regional parties. These developments were welcomed: the Czech Comintern emissary Jan Sverma returned favourably impressed from the second Slovene Party Conference held on 31 December–1 January 1940;[42] and an even more positive assessment was given by Franz Honer, an Austrian Comintern emissary, after meeting Tito on 5 May 1940.[43] Quoting Stalin's *Short Course*, the KPJ continued to argue that an illegal party could win mass support if illegal work were correctly combined with legal work: every legal opportunity had to be exploited, but under the guidance of the party hierarchy. This lesson was repeated in the Comintern journal, the *Communist International*, which published a statement at this time from the British, French,

German, American and Italian parties calling for detailed study of the *Short Course* to help formerly legal parties like the Spanish and the French adapt to the new exigencies of life underground.[44] The results of correctly combined legal and illegal work were impressive in Yugoslavia: after two general strikes in Split in autumn 1940 the government decided to close down the communist-influenced URSS.[45]

During 1940 the KPJ could claim with some justification to be the model for the new illegal Communist movement, the party to which the old legal parties of the popular front era could turn for advice. That claim was reinforced by the Comintern's decision to use Zagreb as the base for its new radio transmitter for communications with the Italian, Swiss, Austrian, Czechoslovak, Hungarian, Greek and Yugoslav parties; its operator was to be Tito's ally Josip Kopinic.[46] The transmitter operated throughout the war and was the only continuous outlet for Communist liaison. Evidence survives to establish that the Yugoslavs were in regular contact with Greece, Italy, Bulgaria and Austria throughout the war, and via Italy contact with France was claimed in 1943.[47] Another sign of its new role was the Comintern's decision of July 1940 to relocate the foreign base of the Italian Communist Party to Yugoslavia rather than France. This gave the Yugoslavs a kudos in the international Communist movement they had never experienced before, although providing the expected support in terms of printing-presses and personnel severely stretched the KPJ, and resulted in considerable tension between the two parties; at one point Tito was so exasperated with the Italians that he asked Dimitrov for the power to 'control their work'.[48]

Like other Communist parties that had been the one most favoured by Moscow, the KPJ found itself in an ambivalent position once the Comintern line began to be modified as the defence needs of the Soviet Union evolved. Tito had favoured the slogan of a people's government since early 1939, but when it came to endorsing this at the fifth Party Conference in October 1940, Dimitrov was far from certain. By that autumn the Molotov–Ribbentrop Pact had outlived its usefulness: Hitler had annexed much of Western Europe, Stalin had annexed the Baltic states, and all eyes were on the Balkans where Stalin had established diplomatic relations with Yugoslavia in June and incorporated Bessarabia into the Soviet Union in July. When on the eve of the fifth Party Conference Tito asked the Comintern to rule on whether the slogan 'a genuine people's government' should be endorsed – it had been used regularly in party documents in July and August 1940[49] – the Comintern rejected the slogan as inappropriate, explaining that it could be interpreted as a call for the dictatorship of the proletariat, something which would isolate the party from the masses and provide hostile powers with a justification for interfering in Yugoslav affairs.[50] The conference, held illegally in Zagreb on 19–23 October 1940, nevertheless endorsed the policy of a 'people's government': the final resolution made clear that the war had opened up the perspective of the 'revolutionary overthrow of imperialism' and 'new victories for socialism'. The 'decisive battle' lay in the 'near future'.[51]

This clash between Tito and Dimitrov over the slogan 'a people's government' was the first of many which occurred during the Comintern's twilight years, but the essence of these clashes was always the same. For Tito, the notion that the Second World War was an 'imperialist war' was not simply the product of Stalin's diplomatic *realpolitik*, but the result of a deeply held conviction based on his own experience of politics in the 1930s. For many Communists the Spanish Civil War had been positive proof that there was little real distinction between the German government and the British government: the Nazis were openly and aggressively imperialist; but 'democratic' Britain remained an empire, and, through its policy of non-intervention, had allowed democracy in Spain to be smothered. For many Communists, particularly those interned in the prison camps of 'democratic' France after Franco's victory, the experience of the Spanish Civil War showed that the whole tactic of the popular front had been misconceived.

Among the tasks allocated to the KPJ by the Comintern from 1940 was the return of disillusioned Spanish Civil War veterans from internment camps.[52] Back in 1937 Tito had played an important role in sending Yugoslav volunteers to Spain; he was later in Moscow for the greater part of the Comintern's inquest into the Spanish Civil War and discussed the verdict with Yugoslav volunteers taking refuge in Moscow.[53] That inquest produced a report implicitly, yet bitterly, critical of the popular front policy. It concluded: 'to defeat the enemy in a popular revolution, it is essential to destroy the old state apparatus, which serves reaction, and replace it with a new apparatus which serves the working class.' The 'people's' character of the revolution had to be recognised organisationally; keeping the old system had led to all sorts of problems, with reactionaries remaining in control of key posts.[54] For Tito, these lessons of the Spanish Civil War were crucial. The essence of his concept of revolution was that success could only be guaranteed if a new state apparatus was constructed under 'proletarian hegemony'; he believed not in the 'popular front from above', which in the case of Spain had meant simply the formation of a coalition government, but in the 'popular front from below', a new form of government in which Communists retained control behind the façade of coalition. The KPJ's New Year communiqué for 1941 echoed the call for proletarian hegemony, via the 'popular front from below', and, again ignoring the advice of the Comintern, it firmly called for a 'genuine people's government'.[55]

By the spring of 1941 Tito had resuscitated another Communist slogan from the past, that of the armed uprising. Tito's report on 'The Strategy and Tactics of the Armed Uprising' was probably delivered to the Zagreb party school held at the end of February and early March 1941. The report concentrated on the importance of party leadership: in Vienna in 1934 the workers had taken up arms, but with no leadership they had been crushed. The party should not allow the uprising to break out 'spontaneously, beyond its organisation and leadership'; the 'hegemony' of the working class in the national revolutionary situation was essential. The key to a successful uprising, Tito argued, was to act offensively, even if momentarily on the retreat: an uprising needed to unleash the revolutionary energy of the masses. Controlling that revolutionary energy, however, meant electing a single central staff which would lead the uprising. Equally, the party should form its own armed formations; Spain had shown that armed units should not be based on the trade union, but be under central party control from the start. The key lesson of the Spanish Civil War also formed part of the report. The revolutionary army should disarm the gendarmerie and overthrow the old pattern of local government. They should then call mass meetings to elect a new form of local government which would at once begin to implement the party's programme.[56]

While such radical policies fitted well into the Comintern ideology of the Second World War as an imperialist war, pregnant, as the First World War had been, with revolutionary opportunities, it was far from acceptable to the Comintern at a time when the nature of the Second World War seemed about to change and any sign of Soviet adventurism in the Balkans could provoke a Nazi attack on Stalin's Russia. The Balkan situation became even more tense at the end of March 1941 when popular demonstrations led to the overthrow of the pro-Axis government in Yugoslavia and the opening of negotiations between the newly established government and the Soviet Union about a possible defence pact. Dimitrov urged Tito to be cautious and not to confuse the growing anti-Axis movement in Yugoslavia with a revolution that was still a long way off. Tito decided to ignore this advice and organise his party on the assumption that resistance to the Nazis would result in the social transformation of Yugoslavia.[57] As a result Tito was accused of Trotskyism for a second time and plans were laid in May to depose him;[58] but after the Nazi invasion of the Soviet Union on 22 June 1941 and the transformation of the Second World War into the Great Patriotic War, all such opposition to Tito was dropped and he was encouraged to make what use he could of the rump of the Comintern apparatus to organise resistance to Hitler.

The model party at war

Yugoslav predominance in the affairs of the Comintern was at its height during the first year of the Great Patriotic War. In June 1941 Tito informed Dimitrov that he was planning an insurrectionary partisan war and asked for Dimitrov's comments. The latter was enthusiastic: 'The time has come', he wrote, 'when Communists should arouse the people to open struggle against the occupier.'[59] The journal *Communist International* took up the cause of the Yugoslav partisans enthusiastically. It argued from the start of the Nazi invasion of the Soviet Union that the people of occupied Europe would play a crucial role in winning the war; to report such developments it started a regular feature entitled 'The United Anti-Hitler People's Front'. This gave its first coverage to the Yugoslav partisans in September 1941. They were credited with opening a 'new front', while in the same issue the French Communist Party leader Maurice Thorez stressed that the moment was right for the French party to launch a similar uprising. By December 1941 Yugoslavia was described as no longer being an occupied country, but a country at war with the Germans. By the spring of 1942 the Yugoslav partisans were being held up as a model, and all other resistance movements urged to follow their lead.[60] This pro-Yugoslav line dominated *Communist International* throughout the summer of 1942. The July issue stressed that it had now been 'proved' that partisan war was not a question of terrain: 'the source of partisan strength is not nature, but the people'.[61]

Enthusiasm for partisan warfare was not the same as enthusiasm for the sort of social revolution Tito preached. From the start of the Nazi occupation Tito saw its revolutionary potential, and was determined that the Communist Party should have the leading role in the resistance. His only discussions with other party leaders in Yugoslavia were held in terms of the Communists having hegemony, for from the start Tito was determined to base the resistance around new liberation (popular front) committees.[62] These liberation committees were open to all, and elections were held to them throughout liberated territory, but they were firmly under Communist control. While at local level the committees might be responsive to local needs, with delegates being elected for a six-month term, higher up the hierarchy of committees real power was delegated to a 'plenum' or even a 'narrow committee' of that plenum; these bodies remained under Communist control, and since higher committees had powers to dissolve lower committees, hegemony was assured.[63]

For all the prominence given to the Yugoslav partisans, the Comintern remained suspicious of Tito's revolutionary agenda. Although as early as December 1941 the Comintern had asked for details of the partisan leaders so their names could be publicised, they never were.[64] Unlike Maurice Thorez, Tito never wrote in the *Communist International*. The Yugoslav party was never referred to by name as the organiser of the partisans, who were always described as 'patriots' and few details of the partisans' social policies in liberated territories ever emerged. This concern over the nature of events in Yugoslavia continued throughout 1942. In February the Comintern suggested that the Yugoslav partisans issue an appeal to the resistance movements in France and Czechoslovakia, but the idea was cancelled after protests from the Yugoslav government-in-exile. Subsequently, Dimitrov was bombarded with stories originating from the government-in-exile about the 'Trotskyist' activities of Tito, and Tito was quizzed as to whether it was not his radical policies which were responsible for the break with Mihailovic. In these exchanges Dimitrov was as much baffled as angry about Tito's domestic policies.[65]

By autumn 1942, after Winston Churchill had visited Stalin in Moscow in August, the Comintern became increasingly wary of Tito's policies and began a campaign against 'sectarianism'. This was implicitly critical of Tito's determination to use the resistance to establish a new revolutionary state structure. On 9 August Dimitrov instructed Tito to change the name of his 'proletarian' brigade, since it was fighting for the people as a whole, not just the workers. Similarly, Tito had made it clear he favoured the establishment of a new Yugoslav government to replace the government-in-exile; however, on 13 November the KPJ was told that its planned Anti-Fascist Council for the National Liberation of Yugoslavia (AVNOJ), elected from liberation committees from the whole of the country, could not be used to appoint a new government.[66] In February 1943 the Comintern dropped a broad hint that Tito should instead form some sort of coalition government.[67]

In May 1943 Stalin followed through the logic of the anti-sectarian campaign by dissolving the Comintern. Where diplomatic relations with his Allies might be at risk, Stalin wanted to signal that Communist parties were no longer what they had been, no longer controlled by Moscow, and quite willing to become junior partners in a 'bourgeois' coalition government. To any Communist veteran of the Spanish Civil War it had been the Communists' willingness to play the game of junior partner in a bourgeois coalition that had led to disaster. Tito's new state constructed around liberation committees and under Communist hegemony was a conscious response to that 'lesson of the Spanish Civil War'. The dissolution of the Comintern was therefore a blessing for Tito. It meant that he could ignore Dimitrov with virtual impunity, but continue to use the KPJ's position as *primus inter pares* to guide the policies of other parties. Indeed, discussion at the ECCI meeting which dissolved the Comintern positively encouraged him to do so, since it was suggested there that, in future, rather than enforcing one rigid line, the formally dissolved Comintern should encourage the regional collaboration of parties with similar prospects and problems.[68]

Thus, if in November 1942 Tito had been prepared to listen to the Comintern's advice against declaring AVNOJ a government, when the second Conference of AVNOJ met on 29–30 November 1943 he had no hesitation in declaring the formation of a new Yugoslavia headed by AVNOJ, ignoring all blandishments from Moscow.[69] And, wherever Yugoslav influence could be felt, Communist parties not only pursued the path of partisan insurrection, but also Tito's policy of hegemony through the popular front from below. In places as far afield as Corsica, during 1943, and Slovakia, during 1944, the policy of insurrection and Communist hegemony was implemented through Communist-dominated national fronts modelled on Yugoslavia's liberation committees and AVNOJ.[70] In areas under direct Yugoslav influence the process was particularly marked. The Albanian Communist Party was instructed in August 1943 to break off relations with the nationalist resistance movement there and follow the Yugoslav model,[71] and from October 1943 the KPJ used its representative with the Greek Communists to encourage the formation first of a liberation army, the National Liberation Front (EAM), and then in March 1944 of a liberation assembly modelled closely on AVNOJ.[72] In Bulgaria, links between Tito and the former Comintern official Shteryu Atanasov, parachuted to join Tito in September 1943, were such that the Bulgarian partisan army produced propaganda which put praise for Tito above praise for the Red Army.[73]

Over the summer and autumn of 1944 Tito's influence continued to be felt among the partisans of German-occupied northern Italy, who established the Liberation Committee for the North of Italy on Titoist principles; it was typical that Luigi Longo, the leader of the Italian partisans, should be a veteran of the Spanish Civil War and should have communicated with Dimitrov via Zagreb rather than the Italian Communist Party headquarters in Rome, where a bourgeois coalition government was being formed.[74]

For a few heady months in the summer and autumn of 1944 Tito must have felt that his revival of an informal regional Comintern, as bequeathed by the ECCI, was going to succeed in establishing revolutionary regimes throughout the Balkans and beyond. The realities of the post-war world were brought home to him by Stalin. In January 1945, after Yugoslav support for the Greek Communist insurrection of December 1944 – which prompted Churchill's dramatic Christmas Day visit to Athens – Stalin felt it necessary to bring Tito to heel. He was told that the KPJ should concentrate on domestic matters and avoid international disputes; in March 1945 this was formalised into a specific promise by the KPJ Central Committee not to undertake any foreign policy initiatives without prior consultation with Moscow. In a related move, the post of liaison officer between the KPJ and the Greek Communist Party was abolished, ending a physical symbol of the KPJ's regional Comintern role.[75] But during the Second World War, in those twilight years of the Comintern, Tito did much to reinvigorate and rejuvenate the Communist movement which had seemed to lose direction after the defeat in Spain. He revived the movement by re-establishing those certainties of Bolshevism: the underground party organisation, proletarian hegemony and armed insurrection. And he used the vestigial Comintern organisation to do what had seemed impossible for the Comintern leaders of the 1920s and 1930s, to carry out a Communist revolution and spread the Soviet system beyond the confines of the Soviet Union. Ironically it was the dissolution of the Comintern which made this possible.

Notes

1 The phrase 'twilight of the Comintern' was used by E. H. Carr, *The Twilight of Comintern, 1930–35* (Basingstoke, 1982). Since the Comintern was arguably at its strongest during the Spanish Civil War, the term 'twilight' seems far more appropriate to the Comintern in the 1940s.

2 This account is taken from S. Cvetkovic, *Idejne borbe u KPJ, 1919–28* (Belgrade, 1985), and I. Avakumovic, *History of the Communist Party of Yugoslavia*, I (Aberdeen, 1964).

3 Avakumovic, *History*, pp. 79, 84.

4 Cvetkovic, *Idejne borbe*, pp. 200–9; Avakumovic, *History*, p. 92.

5 Avakumovic, *History*, p. 95.

6 N. Jovanovic, 'Milan Gorkic: Prilog za Biografiju', *Istorija 20 veka*, 1 (1983), 25–37.

7 Jovanovic, 'Gorkic', 38–43.

8 Avakumovic, *History*, p. 99.

9 See *Proleter*, March 1929, July 1929, December 1929 and September 1930.
10 See *Ibid.*, March 1929, May 1930, October 1930, February 1932, September 1932 and December 1932. Whether Gorkic wrote 'We must win over the masses' before his transfer to other duties is a matter of speculation. The article on the party's organisational tasks was in line with the review of KPJ activity at the twelfth ECCI Plenum in September 1932; see *Proleter*, January 1933.
11 See *Proleter*, July 1931, September 1932 and October 1932.
12 See *Ibid.*, April 1933 and June 1933.
13 See *Ibid.*, July 1934, August 1934, September–October 1934, January 1935 and February–March 1935.
14 M. Bosic, 'Aktivnost KPJ na stvaranju jedinstvene radnicke partije 1935. godine', *Istorija radnickog pokreta, Zbornik radova III* (1966), 134–8.
15 For the Russian State Duma elections, see G. Swain, *Russian Social Democracy and the Legal Labour Movement, 1906–14* (Basingstoke, 1983), pp. 133–57.
16 See *Proleter*, July–August 1935.
17 Jovanovic, 'Gorkic', pp. 45–6; and Bosic, 'Aktivnost KPJ na stvaranju', 148–51.
18 Bosic, 'Aktivnost KPJ na stvaranju', 161–7.
19 Archive of the Yugoslav League of Communists Central Committee, Belgrade [hereafter, ACK], KI 1936/434.
20 Jovanovic, 'Gorkic', 51.
21 ACK, KI 1936/279, 1936/364, and 1936/379 (1936/304 shows that the purge trials starting in Moscow also hampered an agreement); and I. Jelic, 'O nekim problemima stvaranja narodne fronte u Hrvatske, 1936', *Historijski zbornik* (1976–77), 538–41.
22 J. B. Tito, *Sabrana djela* (hereafter, *Works*), (Belgrade, 1977), I, pp. 40–1; and ACK, KI 1937/121.
23 Lenin's controversy with the liquidators is explored in Swain, *Russian Social Democracy*, pp. 57–80.
24 ACK, KI 1937/121, 1937/161; and Jovanovic, 'Gorkic', 51. See also M. Djilas, *Memoirs of a Revolutionary* (New York, 1973), p. 259.
25 ACK, KI 1937/61, and 1937/121.
26 *Ibid.*
27 ACK, KI 1937/55, and 1937/82.
28 For more details on the events surrounding Gorkic's arrest, see Jovanovic, 'Gorkic', 53–4; and G. R. Swain, 'Tito: the Formation of a Disloyal Bolshevik', *International Review of Social History*, 2 (1989), 248–71.
29 S. Clissold (ed.), *Yugoslavia and the Soviet Union, 1939–73: A Documentary Survey*, (London, 1979), p 115.
30 For details, see Swain, 'Tito', 254–61.
31 ACK, KI 1938/3.
32 R. Colakovic, *Pregled istorije Saveza Komunista Jugoslavije* (Belgrade, 1963), pp. 248–50; and I. Jelic, *Komunisticka Partija Hrvatske*, 2 vols (Zagreb, 1981), I, p. 229.
33 Colakovic, *Pregled*, pp. 220–8; and Jelic, *Komunisticka Partija Hivatske*, p. 153.
34 Tito, *Works*, IV, p. 144.
35 Tito, *Works*, IV, p. 55; and M. Bosic, 'Komunisticka Partija Jugoslavije u parlemantarnim izborima 11 Decembra 1938', *Istorija radnickog pokreta, Zbornik radova II* (1965), 322–54.
36 Tito, *Works*, IV, p. 141.

37 *Ibid.*, V, p. 5; and Djilas, *Memoirs*, p. 302.
38 Tito, *Works*, IV, p. 165.
39 See *Proleter*, May 1939.
40 Tito *Works*, V, p. 25.
41 Clissold, *A Documentary Survey*, p. 155.
42 Djilas, *Memoirs*, p. 340.
43 Tito, *Works*, V, p. 203; and *Izvori za istoriju SKJ: peta zemaljska konferencija KPJ*, (Belgrade, 1980), p. 247.
44 See *Proleter*, 1, 1940; and F.Fürnberg, 'Ein geniales Lehrbuch der Bolschevistischer Taktik', *Die Kommunistische Internationale*, 3:4 (1940).
45 P. Damjanovic, 'Peta zemaljska konferencija u svetlost pripremanja KPJ za ustanak', *Jugoslovenski istorijski casopis*, 1–2, 85; and Jelic, *Komunisticka Partija Hrvaske*, I, pp. 410–13. See also *Proleter*, 7:8 (1940).
46 V. Cencic, *Enigma Kopinic*, 2 vols (Belgrade, 1983), I, p. 128.
47 Telegrams relating to the affairs of other Communist parties appear throughout a collection of documents published in Belgrade which began life as *Izvori za Istoriyu SKJ: Dokumenti Centralnih Organa KPJ, NOR, i Revolucija 1941–5*. Two volumes were published in Belgrade in 1985 and many others prepared for publication in the KPJ archive, but the process was never completed. They are cited here as *Izvori* with the date of the document. *Korespondenca Edvarda Kardelja in Borisa Kidrica* (Ljubljana, 1963) also contains several telegrams to the Italian Communist Party in particular.
48 Cencic *Enigma Kopinic*, p. 129; U. Massola, 'La direzione del Pci in Italia, 1940–43', *Critica Marxista* (March/April) 1976, 157; and U Massola, *Memorie*, (Rome, 1972) p. 90. An English account of some of these matters is E. R .Terzuolo, *Red Adriatic: The Communist Parties of Italy and Yugoslavia*, (London, 1985). For Tito's move to take control of the Italian Party, see *Izvori*, 11 July 1942.
49 For examples of use by Tito, see *Works*, V, pp. 132, 149.
50 *Ibid.*, VI, p. 203.
51 *Ibid.*, pp. 205, 225–226.
52 For details, see G. Swain, 'The Cominform: Tito's International?', *Historical Journal*, 35:3 (1992), 650.
53 B. Maslaric, *MoskvaMadridMoskva* (Zagreb, 1952), pp. 95–6.
54 J. Diaz, 'Ob urokakh voiny ispanskogo naroda', *Bol'shevik*, 1 (1940), 31, 34.
55 Tito, *Works*, p. 126.
56 *Ibid.*, pp.151–81.
57 For Dimitrov's telegram to Tito, see *Ibid.*, p. 215; for Tito's commitment to social transformation, see accounts of the 'May Meeting' of the KPJ Central Committee in 1941, in particular in English S. Clissold, *Djilas: the Progress of a Revolutionary* (London, 1983), p. 48.
58 The details are in Swain, 'Tito', 266–7.
59 *Izvori*, June 1941. Tito was being slightly dishonest here. The uprising had already started.
60 B Voinich, 'Boevoy primer Yugoslavii', *Communist International* (Russian edition), 3 and 4 (1942).
61 'Edinyi antigitlerovski front narodov', *Communist International* (Russian edition), 5 and 7 (1942).
62 Thus, although in mid-August 1941 other parties were invited to join a national liberation committee, it was made clear such a committee would not be based on

parity and compromise, but unity under Communist leadership; see B. Petranovic, *Revolucija i kontrarevolucija u Jugoslaviji, 1941–45*, 2 vols (Belgrade, 1983), I, p. 216. Tito's terms for a deal with his nationalist rival Mihailovic were similar; liberation committees had to be extended to areas controlled by Mihailovic, see M. Wheeler, *Britain and the War for Yugoslavia* (New York, 1980), p. 88.

63 Petranovic, *Revolucija i kontrarevolucija*, II, pp. 59–61. See also Tito's 'Letter to the Serbian Provincial Committee of the KPJ, 22 July 1944', reproduced in V. Dedijer, *Novi prilozi za biografiju Josip Broza Tita*, 5 vols (Rijeka and Belgrade 1984), I–II, p. 1077.

64 *Izvori*, December 1941.

65 *Ibid.*, 13 February 1942, 22 March 1942 and June 1942.

66 *Ibid.*, 9 August and 13 November 1942.

67 *Ibid.*, early January 1943.

68 V. Vlahovic, 'L'internationalisme à l'oeuvre', *Est et Ouest*, 16–31 (May 1959), 8.

69 B. Petranovic, *AVNOJ: Revolucionarna smena vlasti* (Belgrade, 1976), pp. 91–3.

70 See Swain, 'Cominform', 645.

71 N. C. Pano, *The People's Republic of Albania* (Baltimore, 1968), p. 52.

72 J. C. Loulis, *The Greek Communist Party, 1940–44* (London, 1982), pp. 91–103.

73 N. Oren, *Bulgarian Communism: the Road to Power, 1934–44* (New York,1971), p. 202 ff.; and Sh. Atanasov, *Pod znameneto na partiyata* (Sofia, 1962), p.145 ff. For documents putting Yugoslav support before Red Army support, see *V'or'zhenata borba na B'lgarskya narod protiv fashizma* (Sofia, 1962).

74 Swain, 'Cominform', 648, 651.

75 B. Petranovic, 'Tito i Staljin, 1944–46', in *Jugoslovenski istorijski casopis* (1988), 151, 158–9; C. Strbac, *Jugoslavija i odnosi izmedju socialistickih zemalja: sukob KPJ i Informburo* (Belgrade, 1984), p. 75.

Part III

The parties and the Comintern: the Americas and Asia

14

The Communist International and the American Communist Party

Hugh Wilford

Ever since the end of the Second World War, American scholars have engaged in a heated, often vituperative controversy about the history of American communism. In the summer of 1995 this controversy entered a new, public phase, with the publication of historical documents from Russian archives attracting extensive coverage from such newspapers as the *Wall Street Journal* and the *Washington Post*, and comment from a variety of right-wing pundits. Indeed, the historiography of American communism seemed set to cause yet another skirmish in the United States's much-publicised 'Culture Wars'.[1]

It would be no exaggeration to say that all arguments about the history of American communism could be reduced to a single question: the relationship of the Communist Party of the United Stated of America (CPUSA) to the Comintern. The earliest scholarly historians of American communism, the post-Second World War 'orthodox' school, portrayed the CPUSA as entirely, and disastrously, subordinated to the Comintern. The next historical generation, the contemporary 'revisionists', tend to downplay the Comintern's role in favour of domestic aspects of the American Communist movement. Recently, however, the revisionists have been challenged by 'neo-orthodox' scholars, who reassert the overriding importance of the Comintern, and cite records in Russian archives to support their case.

The purpose of this chapter is to provide a critical survey of the scholarship of the various historiographical schools in an attempt to illuminate the relationship between the CPUSA and the Comintern. The first section briefly rehearses the main events in the history of the American Communist movement from its inception to the end of the Second World War. Subsequent sections examine the claims of, respectively, the orthodox, revisionist and neo-orthodox schools. The chapter concludes with some reflections on the implications for study of American Communism of Comintern records, and some suggestions concerning future research in this area.

A brief history of the American Communist movement, 1919–45

The origins of the American Communist movement lay in the left wing of the American Socialist Party (SP). By the late 1910s the SP had alienated a wide variety of radical groups with its preference for electoral politics and its failure to appeal to recent immigrants. The Bolshevik Revolution gave discontented Socialists an issue around which to unite. A series of internal conflicts ensued, leading to the fragmentation of the SP in 1919, and the subsequent emergence of the language-federation-dominated, hardline Communist Party of America, and its rival, the relatively moderate, English-speaking Communist Labor Party. The Red Scare of 1919–22 drove these organisations underground, where they continued to fight each other. Both sought recognition from the Comintern as the legitimate face of American communism, only to be instructed to abandon their differences and merge. This they eventually did in 1921, forming the Workers (Communist) Party, which was renamed the CPUSA in 1929.[2]

The 1920s was a bad decade for American communism. A few gains were made, such as the creation of cadres in some industrial unions, and the stabilisation of party institutions like the *Daily Worker*. For the most part, though, the movement lost strength and support. Party leaders repeated the SP's error of alienating radical immigrants' groups. Ethnic and regional divisions threatened party unity. Perhaps most damagingly, the leadership singularly failed to address the contradiction between communism's massive unpopularity in America and the Comintern's united front strategy, which required Communists to move above ground and work within established organisations. In view of these problems it is hardly surprising that major initiatives during the 1920s, like the creation of a farmer-labour movement, did not succeed. However, the Comintern's reversion to an ultra-leftist strategy in the wake of Stalin's rise to power did not ease the Americans' plight, leading as it did to the defection of Trotskyist James Cannon and the expulsion of moderate deviationist Jay Lovestone.

The future still appeared bleak for the CPUSA as it entered the 1930s. The revolutionary isolationism enjoined by the Comintern proved profoundly inappropriate to American conditions; factional strife persisted, as did ethnic divisions, and a series of violent demonstrations discredited the Communists in the eyes of many sympathisers. Considering this background, the rout of Communist presidential candidate William Z. Foster in the election of 1932 was only to be expected. However, there were signs of change. The San Francisco general strike of 1934, an increase of activism in ethnic communities, and a marked shift of rhetoric in the party press, all signified the emergence of a new mood of realism. This of course coincided with the promulgation by the Comintern in 1935 of an international popular front against fascism. In accordance with Comintern directives, the CPUSA threw in its lot with reformist elements like President Roosevelt's Democratic Party and John L. Lewis's Congress of Industrial Organisations. Although a minority of Communists, already concerned by reports of Stalin's domestic policies, perceived the popular front as unprincipled and opportunistic,[3] the majority welcomed it. The result was a period of unprecedented popularity and influence. By the late 1930s party membership had reached 65,000, and there were numerous 'fellow-travellers' in many walks of American life.

Then came the Nazi-Soviet Pact of 1939, and an accompanying shift in Comintern policy back towards ultra-leftism. Immediately, the array of front organisations that party workers had laboriously constructed during the late 1930s collapsed, and the CPUSA experienced a calamitous loss of members and support. However, the Nazi invasion of the Soviet Union in 1941 permitted a return to a democratic front strategy, and a revival of Communist popularity. Indeed, that year saw CPUSA membership reach an all-time high of 85,000, and the beginning of a thoroughgoing 'Americanisation' of the party by its leader Earl Browder. The war years were in many ways the best of American Communists' lives. Popular hostility towards communism was lower than ever before, reflecting a general decline in anti-Soviet feeling. The CPUSA could boast a thriving educational programme, an increasingly vibrant press, and important connections in leading industrial unions. Nevertheless, these gains proved ephemeral. The year 1945 witnessed Browder being replaced as leader by Foster, and the first stirrings of the Cold War both at home and abroad. The late 1940s and 1950s were to see American communism reach its lowest ebb.

Orthodoxy

Such, then, are the main events in the early history of American communism. How have historians interpreted them? How, in particular, have historians portrayed the relationship between the CPUSA and the Comintern? Scholarly debate concerning American communism began in earnest during the 1950s (earlier studies of the subject, of which there were several, were partisan and unreliable).[4] Most significantly, the 'Fund for the Republic', founded in 1953 with a grant from the Ford Foundation, sponsored a series of ten studies entitled 'Communism in American Life'. Although obviously conditioned by the excessively anti-Communist atmosphere of 1950s American society, these studies were notable for their variety of subject-matter and approach. The first and most influential of them was Theodore Draper's *The Roots of American Communism* (1957), which was followed a few years later by his *American Communism and Soviet Russia* (1960).[5]

These works shared two basic assumptions. First, Draper believed that the hierarchical, vanguardist nature of party organisation meant that 'the top leadership is, in all important respects, the only part that makes effective decisions. In its main line, therefore, a history of the Communist Party is chiefly a history of its top leadership.'[6] This conviction is reflected in the two works' narrative structure, which consists fundamentally of a detailed, if forceful, account of the activities of party elites. The tone throughout is one of ironic, almost mocking detachment. Second, both volumes advance the claim that 'whatever has changed from time to time, one thing has never changed – the relation of American Communism to Soviet Russia'.[7] According to Draper, the subordination of American Communists to their Soviet counterparts was irreversibly established in 1921, when the various factions obeyed the Comintern's order to merge into one organisation and go above ground, and this subordination was conclusively demonstrated in 1929 by the defeat of Jay Lovestone. 'After ten years, nothing and no one could alter the fact that the American Communist Party had become an instrument of the Russian Communist Party'[8] (for Draper the Comintern and the Soviet Communist Party were practically indistinguishable). From that point on any appearance of independence or spontaneity on the part of American Communists, such as during the popular front phase of the late-1930s, was deceptive, the result of cynical manipulation by Moscow. It is perhaps worth mentioning at this point that Draper was himself a former Communist – during the 1930s he had belonged to the National Student League, and briefly worked as foreign editor of the *New Masses*.[9]

Revisionism

Draper's two books dominated historians' perceptions of American communism throughout the 1950s and 1960s. Gradually, however, a younger generation of scholars, crucially influenced by the social and political upheavals of the late 1960s, as well as by the writings of Marxist historians like E. P. Thompson and Eugene Genovese, began to challenge the orthodox school of Communist history. While Draper's description of the factional feuds of the 1920s was still generally accepted as authoritative, his claims about American communism after 1930 were vigorously contested, as was his disregard for ordinary party members.

In the latter respect, revisionist historians, using such techniques of social history as oral interviews, have attempted to recreate the life experiences of the rank and file, showing how communism interacted with the daily round of working and family lives, and giving particular notice to previously neglected groups, like women and African-Americans. The other characteristic feature of the 'new' history is its assertion that, in addition to being the wing of an international movement, the CPUSA was also the projection of an authentic domestic radicalism, commanding widespread support, engaging with organic indigenous struggles, and often displaying considerable initiative of its own, not least during the popular front period and the Second World War. In particular, revisionist historians, while not always disputing the orthodox claim that CPUSA policy was controlled by the Comintern, nonetheless direct attention to the ways in which American Communists interpreted the Moscow line in light of peculiar national and local conditions according to their own specific needs and interests. To quote the exemplary revisionist study of American communism during the Second World War by Maurice Isserman, the new history 'has depicted the Party as, at certain times and places, flexible, imaginative, principled, rooted in neighbourhoods and workplaces, and enjoying genuine popular support'.[10]

Neo-orthodoxy

The revisionists have not had it all their way. Recently, Theodore Draper himself has rejoined the historiographical battle with a series of polemical review articles in the *New York Review of Books*.[11] In them, Draper scathingly criticises the tendency of the new history to privilege the daily lives of American Communists over their political beliefs and activities. This he views as a ruse to distract attention from the CPUSA's unpleasant political history. 'A good deal of recent work on American Communism', he alleges, 'deals with Communists by leaving out the Communism or making it innocuous.'[12] However, his main objection to revisionism is not what he calls its rank-and-file 'favouritism',[13] but rather its failure to acknowledge the authority of the Comintern in CPUSA affairs. For example, he notes the degree of importance attached to the late 1930s by the new historians (he jokingly describes the popular front as 'the long-awaited apotheosis of American radicalism'[14]), and then goes on to point out the brevity of this phase – it amounted to less than one-sixteenth of the party's entire history – and the circumstances in which it ended – a humiliating volte-face ordained by the Comintern – concluding: 'it cannot be seen as more than a short, aborted interlude. As such, its significance for any basic generalisation about the Communist movement is strictly limited.'[15] Draper is similarly dismissive towards claims made about the 'Americanisation' of the CPUSA during the war years.[16] Along the way he accuses the revisionists of disguising opinions as facts, of lacking the scope and ambition that characterised his own work and that of other orthodox scholars, and of hanging on to their own radical pasts by means of the academic study of communism.

Meanwhile, Draper's protégé Harvey Klehr has fought a determined rearguard action against revisionism, seeking to reinstate leadership and the Comintern as the central concerns of American Communist history. His monograph on the CPUSA during the 1930s, for example, de-emphasises the significance of the rank and file and 'American conditions'.[17] Likewise, his recent text-book history of the American Communist movement, co-authored with John Earl Haynes, basically consists of a Draperian-style narrative of the actions of party elites, and constantly stresses the influence, both institutional and psychological, of Soviet communism. To quote the Introduction:

> Every era in the history of the American Communist movement has been inaugurated by developments in the Communist world abroad. The Russian revolution led to the formation of the first American Communist Party. Soviet pressure led to the abandonment of an underground strategy. Comintern directives led American Communists to an ultra-revolutionary posture during the late 1920s. Soviet foreign policy needs midwifed the birth of the Popular Front in the mid-1930s. The

> Nazi–Soviet Pact destroyed the popular front in 1939, and the German attack on the Soviet Union reconstituted it in 1941. The onset of the Cold War cast American Communists into political purgatory after World War II, and Nikita Khrushchev's devastating expose of Joseph Stalin's crimes in 1957 tore the American Communists apart.[18]

As might be inferred from this excerpt, Klehr and Haynes's opinion of the influence of Moscow in the USA is unremittingly negative. While the example of Soviet communism might have provided American Communists with some psychological strength, the CPUSA's subordination to the Comintern condemned it to constant disruption and ultimate impotence. 'American communism', the authors conclude, 'is a sad tale of wasted commitment and wasted life.'[19]

This resurgence of orthodoxy has been given greatly added impetus by recent revelations concerning Soviet funding of American communism. One of these resulted from a 1991 criminal investigation by the Russian Prosecutor-General into the use of Soviet government funds by the Soviet Communist Party for subsidies to foreign Communist parties. In the course of this investigation a set of documents purporting to be correspondence between the Soviet Politburo and American Communist leader Gus Hall were released to the *Washington Post*. These letters indicated that during the 1980s the CPUSA had received approximately $20 million from the Soviet Communists, before Hall's criticisms of Gorbachev's reforms in 1989 led to the termination of this support. (They also revealed Hall to have had an extremely poor understanding of American politics, including as they did confident predictions by him of a revolutionary uprising on the eve of Ronald Reagan's re-election in 1984.)[20] Not surprisingly, publication of these documents was greeted by right-wing American commentators with ill-concealed glee.[21]

More significant for the early history of American Communism is the recent opening up of Comintern archives. Fragmented evidence of Comintern funding of the CPUSA existed prior to this event – the testimony of embittered ex-Communists, the findings of American government investigations, and so on.[22] However, Comintern files at the Russian Centre for the Preservation and Study of Contemporary Historical Documents contain extensive and conclusive documentation of regular Soviet subsidies to American Communists. These began as early as 1919, and included a single disbursement to John Reed in January 1920 (when he arrived in Soviet Russia as delegate of the Communist Labor Party) of over 1 million rubles. Further payments followed throughout the 1920s. For example, a 1923 report from the Communist Party of America acknowledges receipt of $30,950 in December 1921 and $49,429 in June and July 1922; a 1926 report from party leader Charles Ruthenberg acknowledges receipt of $14,864 from June to September of that year; and so on.[23] (These and other records from the Comintern archives are reproduced in *The Secret World of American Communism*, by Klehr, Haynes and Fridrikh Igorevich Firsov.[24])

Conclusion

Evidently, the new availability of Comintern records is set to transform our understanding of American communism and its relationship with the Soviet Union. The first signs suggest that these documents will lend support to the claims of orthodox and neo-orthodox scholars that the affairs of the CPUSA were dictated by the Comintern. The evidence relating to funding is incontrovertible. As Klehr and Haynes state: 'One can no longer take seriously any scholarship on American communism that does not recognise the role and significance of Soviet funding.'[25]

That said, the documents produced so far do not prove that the CPUSA was utterly beholden to the Comintern. On the question of funding, for example, the possibility should be considered that some American Communists used Soviet money for their own, domestic purposes, in ways not envisioned by the Comintern, that is – *appropriated* it. Indeed, a literal case of appropriation occurred in 1924 when Armand Hammer, an American courier entrusted with $16,000 for transport to the USA, kept $7,000 for himself, until forced to part with it by Charles Ruthenberg.[26] Moreover, it is possible to overstate the generosity of Comintern funding. As the figures quoted earlier suggest, the 1920s saw a considerable reduction in Soviet grants after the revolutionary expectations of 1919–20 had faded. Comintern files contain numerous and insistent begging letters from American Communists. For example, a 1928 cable from Jay Lovestone reads in part: 'Bukharin Molotov Insist you execute your promise rendering immediate substantial financial assistance. . . . Cable money immediately.' [27] In any case, as Klehr and Haynes themselves point out, the chief source of American Communists' loyalty to the Soviet Union was psychological, not financial, dependence.

Just as one should be wary of exaggeration of the significance of Soviet funding, so one should be sceptical of recent claims based on Comintern documents about espionage carried out by American Communists on behalf of the Soviet Union. Certainly documents reproduced in Klehr *et al.*'s *The Secret World of American Communism* indicate that many CPUSA members were willing to spy for the Comintern. But this is not the same as proving that they were in fact spies. As Maurice Isserman shows in a review of the book, Klehr *et al.*'s interpretation of some documents purportedly proving espionage is questionable.[28] Even Arthur Schlesinger Jr., the eminence grise of American liberal anti-communism, has seen fit to reprimand the authors of *The Secret World* for sensationalising this issue.[29]

In short, despite the triumphalist declarations of some conservative commentators, the Comintern archives have not proved the orthodox case, or disproved the revisionist. What I would like to suggest is a synthesis of the two approaches, one which acknowledges Comintern control of the CPUSA, while at the same time remaining sensitive to the specificities of the American reception of Soviet directives, incorporating the best features of both political and social history. A model for this synthetic methodology has recently been provided by Robert Cohen's excellent study of the American Communist student movement during the 1930s, which handles the interaction between external influence and American conditions with exemplary deftness, and gives equal attention to leadership and rank and file.[30] Of course, it should not be forgotten that the CPUSA belonged to an international movement and accepted orders from the Comintern. On the other hand, it should be remembered that the history of American communism is not just an episode in the history of communism: it is also part of American history.

Notes

1 See M. Isserman, 'Notes from Underground', *The Nation*, 12 June 1995, 846–56.

2 A useful brief survey of CPUSA history is contained in Mari J. Buhle, P. Buhle and D. Georgakas, *Encylopedia of the American Left* (New York, 1990). The best recent single-volume treatment of the subject is H. Klehr and J. E. Haynes, *The American Communist Movement: Storming Heaven Itself* (New York, 1992) (see below).

3 For example, a group of New York-based Jewish intellectuals associated with the journal *Partisan Review*, including Sidney Hook, Philip Rahv and James T. Farrell, broke with the CPUSA in favour of anti-Stalinist Marxism and cultural modernism. This group would later rise to positions of extraordinary political and cultural prominence in the USA. See H. Wilford, *The New York Intellectuals: From Vanguard to Institution* (Manchester and New York, 1995).

4 See Maurice Isserman, 'Three Generations: Historians View American Communism', *Labor History*, 26 (Fall 1985), 518–23.

5 T. Draper, *The Roots of American Communism* (New York, 1957) and T. Draper, *American Communism and Soviet Russia: the Formative Period* (New York, 1960).

6 Draper, *American Communism and Soviet Russia*, p. 4.

7 *Ibid.*, p. 5.

8 *Ibid.*, p. 440.

9 J. P. Diggins, *The Rise and Fall of the American Left* (New York, 1992), p. 309.

10 M. Isserman, *Which Side Were You On?: The American Communist Party During the Second World War* (Wesleyan University Press, 1982), pp. ix–x. Other works by revisionist or new historians include: M. Naison, *Communists in Harlem during the Depression* (Urbana, 1983); F. M. Ottanelli, *The Communist Party in the United States from the Depression to World War II* (New Brunswick, 1991); and M. E. Brown, R. Martin, F. Rosengarten and G. Snedeker (eds), *New Studies in the Politics and Culture of U.S. Communism* (NewYork, 1993).

11 T. Draper, 'American Communism Revisited', *New York Review of Books*, 9 May 1985, 32–7; 'The Popular Front Revisited', *New York Review of Books*, 30 May 1985, 44–50; and 'The Life of the Party', *New York Review of Books*, 13 January 1994, 45–51.

12 Draper, 'Life of the Party', 46.

13 Draper, 'Popular Front', 47.

14 *Ibid.*, 44.

15 *Ibid.*

16 See his comments about Isserman, *Which Side?*, in Draper, 'Communism Revisited', 32–3.

17 H. Klehr, *The Heyday of American Communism: the Depression Decade* (New York, 1984).
18 Klehr and Haynes, *Communist Movement*, p. 4.
19 *Ibid.* p. 182.
20 The letters are reproduced in J. E. Haynes and H. Klehr, '"Moscow Gold," Confirmed at Last?', *Labor History*, 33: 2 (1992), 279–93.
21 See, for example, E. Breindel, 'Moscow Gold', *Commentary*, 94: 6 (1992), 46–8.
22 See Haynes and Klehr, '"Moscow Gold"', 279–81.
23 J. E. Haynes and H. Klehr, letter, *Labor History*, 33:4 (1992), 576–7.
24 H. Klehr, J.E. Haynes and F.I. Firsov, *The Secret World of American Communism* (New Haven and London, 1995).
25 Haynes and Klehr, letter, 578.
26 *Ibid.*, 577. See also Klehr, Haynes and Firsov, *Secret World*, pp. 26–30.
27 Quoted in Haynes and Klehr, letter, 577. Much is made of Comintern stinginess by M. Kempton, 'Notes from Underground', *New York Review of Books*, 13 July 1995, 29–34.
28 Isserman, 'Notes from Underground', 848–56.
29 A. Schlesinger Jr., 'The Party Circuit', *The New Republic*, 29 May 1995, 39.
30 R. Cohen, *When the Old Left was Young: Student Radicals and America's First Mass Student Movement 1929–1941*, (New York, 1993).

15

From Caribbean backwater to revolutionary opportunity: Cuba's evolving relationship with the Comintern, 1925–34

Barry Carr

The revolutionary moment of 1933

The late 1920s and early 1930s witnessed important worker and peasant mobilisations in Central America and the Caribbean. The most dramatic of these occurred in Cuba. In the first ten days of August 1933, a spectacular urban and rural worker insurgency, culminating in a massive general strike in Havana and other major cities, contributed to the overthrow of the dictatorial regime of Gerardo Machado. The popular insurgency also determined the fate of the reformist Grau San Martín government which briefly ruled Cuba between 4 September 1933 and 10 January 1934. In August, September and October 1933, field and mill workers seized several dozen sugar mills and estates and, in a number of cases, inaugurated peasant councils or soviets.[1]

The inauguration of Grau's reformist 'Government of 100 Days' failed to halt the popular mobilisations which in part were driven by the Cuban Communist Party, Partido Comunista de Cuba (PCC), and its allies. Without a mass base capable of defending its programme – partly the result of the bitter hostility shown by Cuban Communists – the reformist government was unable to consolidate its position. Finally, the combination of an aggressively hostile and interventionist United States administration in alliance with Fulgencio Batista secured the collapse of the Grau government in the middle of January 1934.

In spite of their early weaknesses, the Cuban Communists *were* major protagonists in the events of 1933. Moreover, in 1933 the PCC confronted the most substantial revolutionary opportunity seen in Latin America before the 1950s. Although the Communists' role has been greatly exaggerated and simplified by successive generations of Cuban and foreign historians, the controversial actions of the PCC did help shape outcomes at a number of key conjunctures between August 1933 and January 1934.

The PCC was a major actor in the extraordinarily rapid mobilisation and unionisation of sugar workers in the period 1932–34 and its cadres also influenced important sectors of the workforce in Havana and major regional cities. Second, the party, with its working-class base, was at the centre of the Havana general strike of 1–10 August which helped topple Machado, although the PCC neither initiated the strike nor did it direct the movement. In fact, when the party called for a general strike on 4 August 'the workers were already on strike', noted a Comintern envoy.[2] In mid-strike the PCC leadership agreed to negotiate with the now desperately isolated Machado and, in return for the legalisation of the party and other concessions, offered to use its influence to order a return to work. Havana workers did not heed the strike committee's call, and the origins and impact of the 'August mistake' became the centre of what is still a highly sensitive issue in Cuban historiography. The second half of this chapter tries to unpack this important conjuncture and, in doing so, assess the degree of involvement of the Comintern and its institutional and human actors.

Finally, the major political ruptures initiated by the 1933 Revolution – the fall of Machado and then, following the Sergeants' Revolt of 4 September, the creation of the revolutionary government led by Grau San Martín – encouraged Cuban Communists to accelerate their assault on the new administration. The party denounced Grau and his legislative initiatives as 'social-fascist'. It also manoeuvred to undermine the regime's legitimacy by renewing calls for a deepening of the agrarian and labour insurgency.

The PCC's enemies on both the right and left condemned the party's myopia in the closing months of 1933. Historians have argued that the Cuban Communists' refusal to acknowledge the revolutionary opportunities opened up by the government deprived it of the social base that could have mobilised to frustrate the intervention of the Batista-led army and the United States and, thereby, 'rescue' a 'frustrated' social revolution.

The debate and some preliminary conclusions

The early history of Cuban communism has not been the subject of adequate research. Brief treatments can be found in Aguilar, Benjamin, Karol, Thomas and Sims.[3] There are also a number of polemical, journalistic accounts. The single most detailed treatment to date is a study written by Cuban exiles which contains a mass of extremely useful detail embedded in a furiously anti-Communist narrative.[4] Curiously, no major book-length study on the PCC has been published in Cuba, although, since 1959, Cuban activists and scholars have produced a large and often well-researched literature – consisting of articles, as well as specialised monographs on the party's development in particular conjunctures and regions.[5]

Conditions now exist for the preparation of well-documented studies of Cuban communism. Certainly, the Comintern archives (at the Russian Centre for the Preservation and Study of Contemporary Historical Documents) in

Moscow contains a much more complete collection of PCC materials than that held in the Instituto de Historia in Havana – judging by this author's examination of the detailed index to the Fondo Primer Partido Marxista Leninista in the summer of 1996. In what ways do the recently opened Comintern archives throw light on these controversies and, more generally, on the first years of Cuban communism (1925–34)?

The Comintern archives are crucial for reconstructing the history of Cuban communism – at all spatial levels (national, regional and municipal). While their focus is on political strategy and tactics, they are also helpful for capturing elements of the quotidian social and cultural life of the party. However, and this is a point which needs underlining, the most valuable 'raw ingredients' now available in Moscow for historians are made up of the materials generated within Cuba by the PCC – copies of which were sent to the Comintern (to the Caribbean Bureau in New York as well as to Moscow) – and of the reports of Comintern and Profintern representatives in Cuba, rather than of the documents and discussion generated outside Cuba by the organs of the Comintern apparatus itself (in New York and in Moscow).

The early years of Cuban communism

Initially, the PCC was a 'backwater' organisation. It was established relatively late (in 1925) and its fragility can be observed in the frequent changes in the party's leadership in its first five years. In spite of the instability visible 'at the top', Cuban communism attracted a small but often outstanding group of individuals. Students, intellectuals, skilled workers and artisans played a key role in the early years – among them, Julio Antonio Mella.

Jewish working-class immigrants constituted an important nucleus in these early years and the Jewish community, mostly Polish, Romanian and Russian artisans, provided the party with several important cadres, the most celebrated being Fabio Grobart, a Polish Communist who arrived in Cuba in 1924 at the age of 19.[6] There was a Jewish workers' group represented at the founding Congress in August 1925 and materials were translated into Yiddish for the newly arrived immigrants. The Yiddish-speaking Jewish workers had their own language group within the PCC during the party's first decade. Within the broader Jewish community the Communists worked through a leftist Jewish organisation, founded in early 1926, known as the Kultur Farain (Unión Cultural Hebrea), a cultural organisation with an active musical, theatrical and sporting life which attracted young immigrant workers, above all, especially those from the Askenazi immigrant community, most of whom worked in shoe factories and the needle trades, many of them owned by Jewish businessmen.[7]

Spanish immigrants also constituted an important part of the PCC's early membership, especially during the party's founding years when the anarchist and syndicalist culture of many Iberian workers did not block involvement with the nascent Communist organisation.[8] Spanish workers were to be found in skilled sugar-mill work, on the railroads and bus lines and among the militant fishermen whose strikes peppered the late 1920s and 1930s. Chinese workers also constituted an important nucleus in the early PCC. A progressive Chinese political organisation, the Alianza Protectora de los Obreros y Campesinos (founded in 1927), established relations with the Communist Party and several of its members entered the PCC in 1928–29. Far from this being an oddity, the strong overseas-born contingent within the early PCC was simply a reflection of the heavy presence of immigrants in the overall Cuban workforce.

Rubén Martínez Villena's position as legal counsel for the National Labour Confederation of Cuba, Confederación Nacional Obrera de Cuba (CNOC) gave him unrivalled opportunities to build support for the left and for the PCC within a variety of unions – including printing workers, stevedores, bus drivers, *cigarreros*, textile workers and shoemakers.[9] The PCC also managed to establish an important base within this newly founded national labour federation, and in the Labour Federation of Havana, Federación Obrera de Havana (FOH), by weakening the influence of the Anarchists and anarcho-syndicalists. However, the pernicious influence of libertarian ideas was not easily eliminated, in spite of the simplistic evolutionary arguments of those who saw the birth of the Soviet Union and the foundation of Communist parties as a death blow to the anarchist tradition.[10] In 1932, Anarchists and Communist dissidents (some of them influenced by Trotskyist ideas) wrested control of the FOH away from Communists.

The first six years of the PCC (1925–31), however, were characterised by a number of severe weaknesses. The Central Committee met in a highly irregular fashion; its first Plenum was not held until mid-1931. The extraordinary turnover of members of the Central Committee did not help. As late as May 1931 the Comintern/Profintern representative 'Juan' reported that none of the members of the Central Committee could draft political materials and that the party's literature was written either by a student or by a Jewish comrade ('Hova') in Yiddish and then translated into Spanish. In a comment which tells us as much about the cultural world of European revolutionaries as it does about the nature of Cuban society, 'Juan' reported that the PCC's organisation in Catalina de Güines (in Havana province) contained comrades who carried amulets to protect themselves against the police.[11]

The PCC's relationship with the Comintern in Moscow and with other Latin American parties, especially the Mexican Communist Party, Partido Comunista Mexicano (PCM), during its first five years was extremely fragile, a product of infrequent communications which led to an almost total ignorance in Moscow of Cuban conditions. This gave the Machado government's secret service an opportunity to create a 'phantom' Communist party which caused great confusion in Moscow for a short period in 1928–29.[12] This incident should alert historians to the dangers of teleology – especially the assumption that the high degree of centralisation developed by the Comintern in the middle and late 1930s was present from the very beginning.

Finances were always a crisis-point. In January 1933 the PCC had only one paid official.[13] Most of the party's members were unemployed – so income from *cuotas* (dues) was virtually non-existent. Funds promised by the Comintern were insufficient and frequently did not arrive. There were constant, plaintive notes about this delicate issue in the PCC's correspondence with the Comintern.[14] The PCC leadership, in fact, felt completely abandoned: 'We had the sensation that the party was completely abandoned, dependent on its own resources and without international links with anyone.'[15] The arrival of 'Juan' from Mexico in 1930 helped facilitate international links with both the US Communist Party (CPUSA) and the Caribbean Subcommittee of the Profintern's Latin American labour federation – CSLA.[16] A representative of the Caribbean Subcommittee of the CSLA eventually worked in Cuba for four months in 1931.[17]

In June 1932 'Juan' was still bemoaning the weaknesses of the PCC – and especially of its union department – at a time when the revolutionary situation was clearly sharpening. Arrests were playing havoc with the CNOC and the identity of virtually all the members of the Central Commitee who were at liberty was known to the police. The PCC had lost 90 per cent of its safe houses – most of them in the Polish-Jewish *barrio* and in the middle-class Havana suburb of Vedado. It lacked a regular press outlet until 1931 when *El Trabajador* appeared.[18] A shortage of cadres impeded maintenance of international links, and the party was often frightened to send its best cadres overseas for fear that they would not or could not return. The party also underestimated the political potential of Antillean migrant workers from the British West Indies and from Haiti, who (in 1929) were described as having 'a cultural level below that of Cuban workers and no tradition of struggle or organisation . . . they are docile material ready for exploitation'.[19] As late as September 1932, the Caribbean Subcommittee of the CSLA acknowledged that its weakest work was among Caribbean immigrant workers and it urged the CPUSA to use its influence within the Marine Workers' Industrial Union to circulate propaganda and provide secure travel for Comintern and Caribbean party cadres.[20] This was one area in which the Comintern and Profintern's 'third period' line would drive the Cuban Communists in a new direction – the struggle to promote alliances between Cuban and Antillean workers and develop a Cuban version of the CPUSA/Comintern's call for black self-determination including the creation of 'black belts' in areas where a black population predominated.

Nevertheless, the Comintern archives provide us with a glimpse of some of the obstacles which stood in the way of cross-national and cross-colour lines. There were frequent reports of white nervousness concerning the impact of massive recruitment of blacks. A 1932 report on youth work in the PCC reported that the party had not organised dances in Havana for a year because negroes would have participated; the Santa Clara branch of the Young Communist League, Liga Juvenil Comunista (LJC), moreover, had suggested not recruiting more members since half their membership was already negro.[21] The unrest in the sugar industry soon changed the situation. By the end of 1933, the party's energetic involvement in the sugar strikes and occupations following the collapse of the *machadato* resulted in the recruitment of more black workers and a growing emphasis on black and mulatto figures in leadership.

More seriously, the Cuban sugar sector, the most highly proletarianised segment of the Cuban labour force, was not initially well represented in national labour organisations. At the first Congress of the CNOC in Camaguey in August 1925 only one sugar sector delegation was present, the Sugar Industry Workers Union of Puerto Padre, Unión de Trabajadores de la Industria Azucarera de Puerto Padre.[22] The party explained its poor performance by reference to the seasonal nature of sugar production and the surveillance of employers.

This weak penetration of the sugar industry was a reflection of a more general problem – the narrow geographical focus of the PCC at the close of the 1920s. In 1929, the party was concentrated mostly in Havana and in a handful of towns in other parts of the island such as the port cities of Manzanillo, Cienfuegos and Cárdenas.[23] There was a critical shortage of active cadres. Many of the most energetic early Communists had been deported or were forced to flee. Most serious of all were the departures of Antonio Mella and of Rubén Martínez Villena. The situation had deteriorated to such a point that in July 1930 the PCC leadership was obliged to plead with the leaders of the CPUSA for help in locating its exiled members and facilitating their return to the island.[24] As a result, and after discussions with Martínez Villena (who had been living in New York since May 1930), Jorge Vivó returned to the island where he became General Secretary of the PCC. The forced exiles and persecution of party members greatly hindered the PCC's ability to comprehend and respond creatively to the drama of the last three years of the *machadato* and the rapidly unfolding events of the 1933 Revolution.[25]

Nevertheless, by the end of 1929 the PCC had recovered sufficiently for it to be able to establish relations directly with the Comintern rather than using the Mexican Communists as a go-between.[26] It could boast of its influence in the 20,000-member CNOC (where two of the three *secretarios* on the Executive were party members) – and in the Havana-based FOH, and of a certain presence in the railroad union, Hermandad Ferroviaria, and among bakery workers, *zapateros* and drivers.[27] The party's mobilising capacity was demonstrated in the successful general strike launched on 20 March 1930 in which nearly 200,000 workers took part, paralysing Havana and the provincial port city of Manzanillo.[28] The PCC's cadres played an important role in organising the event even though the party could not claim to direct worker mobilisations at this time.

The party's willingness to embrace an armed uprising led some PCC leaders to consider supporting the insurrectionary plans being hatched by the Unión Nacionalista (UN), the most important bourgeois opponent of Machado. Members of the party's Central Committee met regularly with the Nationalist

Union (UN) leadership to establish its 'revolutionary' objectives. Although the party was sceptical of the UN's intentions, for several years individual Cuban Communists harboured illusions about the viability of Communist participation in a UN armed insurrection.[29] Here is one of many cases in which there is no correspondence whatsoever between the PCC's conduct and the ultra-left and sectarian directives of the Comintern during its third period. Comintern warnings about the dangers of putschism and collaboration with bourgeois opponents of the Machado regime were completely incapable of arresting the PCC's interest in exploring opportunities for armed uprisings alongside socially conservative warlords (*caudillos*).

But in the year following the March 1930 general strike, partly under the influence of directives from the CPUSA and the Comintern's Caribbean Bureau, the PCC and the CNOC changed tack. The party 'renewed' its Central Committee, and directed more attention to agrarian and agro-industrial matters. Intensifying the drive to organise the most proletarianised segments of Cuban society was certainly consistent with the strategy of the Comintern's third period and the effort to penetrate the sugar sector is definitely one example of Comintern directives shaping the direction of the Cuban Communists' strategy. However, the disastrous impact of the depression on the incomes of both field and mill workers was in any case promoting sugar worker mobilisations, many of which were spontaneous and or inacapable of being 'guided' by the Communists.

The decision was also made to organise agricultural and industrial workers in the same body. This apparently provoked differences of opinion and went against Profintern guidelines, another example of the CPP's readiness to ignore Comintern advice.[30] But the crucial decision to shift resources and energies towards organising the sugar labour force had now been made.[31] Preparations for the founding of a national organisation of sugar workers began in February 1932 and the first national sugar union, Sindicato Nacional Obrero de la Industria Azucarera (SNOIA) took formal shape at a December conference.[32] The manifesto of the conference emphasised the importance of the 'worker–peasant social alliance'.[33]

The SNOIA/CNOC and PCC intersected the first great wave of sugar strikes which accompanied the beginning of the spring grinding season in February 1933. But Comintern and Profintern evidence makes it clear that while the party had cells and members at many mills, the initiative in striking was not necessarily taken by the PCC's own cadres. Thus at Nazábal mill, where a major strike and a short-lived occupation occurred in February 1933, the initiative was taken by field workers rather than by workers in the mill in which there was a party cell. On the Nazábal strike committee there was not a single party member even though the strikers sought the advice of the CNOC and the PCC in the nearby town of Encrucijada.[34]

On the other hand, PCC influence could be crucial. Another of the combative regions in early 1933 was the area around the 'red' city of Manzanillo in south-western Oriente. A strong movement also arose in the Tacajó mill in northern Oriente which was later to be a springboard for the penetration of Báguanos and Santa Lucía mills and the Preston and Banes mills of the United Fruit Company.

The PCC won new supporters among mill workers and field workers as a result of these actions. By mid-1933 it had increased its strength fourteen times. Party membership increased from 350 in 1930 to 3,800 at the beginning of 1933, a figure which nearly doubled by April 1934 (6,000), when the party claimed to have 1,300 members in Oriente province alone.[35] Between the fall of Machado and the end of 1933 the LJC claimed to have increased its membership from 1,000 to 3,000, organised in fifty workshop cells (*células de empresa*).[36]

The PCC and the 'revolutionary opportunity': July 1933–January 1934

The third period of the Comintern dominated the environment within which the PCC and CNOC operated in 1933–34: the sectarian tone of the discourse is evident in the pronouncements and actions of the Cuban Communists during the whole of 1933. However, ironically, the hard-line practice and line of the Comintern was changing during the second half of 1933 exactly at the moment when Cuban Communists were confronted with an important test of political maturity. The thirteenth Plenum of the Executive Committee of the Communist International (ECCI) in late 1933 inaugurated a transitional period in which the Comintern began to reassess its analysis of fascism and slowly and unevenly started to consider ways of promoting co-operation between Communist-led and 'reformist' workers. No echoes of this rethinking (which eventually led to the popular front) are visible, however, in the words or actions of the Cuban Communists.

The general strike of July–August 1933

The strike that toppled Machado began modestly enough on 27 July among drivers and conductors of a small Havana bus company, who were angered by the extorsionist tactics employed by the Mayor of Havana. It quickly spread to workers on the electric tram services and to dockworkers; two days later, tramway and ferry-boat workers, typographers, shop employees and journalists had joined in. Hire car and taxi drivers struck next.[37] By 1 August, Cuba was without any transport at all; the strike was 'general' by 4 August when all newspapers also ceased publication. [38]

Only banks and government offices continued to function; 90 percent of the city supported the strike according to the British Embassy.[39] Few groups of workers remained on the sidelines, the most important of these being the personnel of the Havana electricity utility who were still loyal to one of the now tottering pro-Machado union federations. Outside Havana the strike was less solid, but life was paralysed in most of the big cities, such as Santiago where a general strike began on 7 August.[40] In Camaguey city streetcar and railroad workers began the strike and, as in other locations, the strike committee took charge of traffic in streets and the distribution of food and resources for the city's population.[41] In Cienfuegos the town council virtually disappeared and the strike committee 'practically controlled the city', organising its own food supply system for hospitals and working-class suburbs.[42]

Machado, as part of a last-minute effort to weaken the mediation efforts organised by the US envoy Sumner Welles, accentuated his 'nationalist' and 'anti-imperialist' rhetoric and tried to rally his own Liberal Party. He also attempted to neutralise the strike and present himself in a progressive light by reaching an understanding with the strike leaders with whom he had requested talks from early August. The strike committee met twice with Machado's Minister of the Interior and with Machado himself. At a meeting on 8 August with the CNOC strike committee (which was dominated by members of the PCC), Machado agreed to meet all the strikers' demands, release all the remaining political prisoners, recognise the legality of all trade unions and, most importantly, legalise the PCC.[43] That day, in a cable to the *New York Times*, Machado claimed that, 'in an interview held today in the palace with the strike committee, which has not vacillated in coming before the Cuban Government authority, I have approved their demands and they have offered to renew the transportation service tomorrow.'[44] According to one of the Comintern's representatives ('Comrade Bell') Machado's secretary shook hands with the head of the strike committee, saying, 'you fellows and I will save the fatherland'.[45]

Martínez Villena termed Machado's offer acceptable. It was a sign, he argued, that the 'bloody tyrant . . . felt weakened and wanted to dialogue with the working class'.[46] The PCC and CNOC immediately (8 August) ordered what was interpreted as a return to work. More accurately, they called on members to resume work once their economic demands had been met – in other words, a staggered resumption. The justification was that the strike did not represent 'the final struggle for taking power' and that its objective was not the overthrow of the 'bourgeois-imperial regime' or even (and here the point was made very bluntly), Machado's government. Machado, the strikers were told, would be toppled not by strikes, but by an 'insurrection of the masses equipped with rifles and machine-guns' prior to the creation of embryonic soviets.[47] Anticipating strong opposition, the PCC warned workers not to be misled by slogans demanding a continuation of the strike. The CNOC's call made during a series of consultations with different unions was angrily rejected by striking workers in Havana.

According to Blas Castillo, a railroad worker and a member of the PCC's Central Committee, Martínez Villena summoned a meeting of the Central Committee to discuss Machado's offer. Also present at the meeting was a Comintern delegation – which included a representative of the Profintern and an envoy from the Caribbean Bureau of the Comintern in New York (almost certainly the 'Mariano' mentioned in Comintern documents) as well as an

'Albert Moro'.[48] The Caribbean Bureau representative roundly condemned the PCC's decision to call off the strike and attacked the Cuban party's obsession with privileging the struggle against US intervention over the broader struggle to prepare the way for the launching of soviets and the inauguration of a 'worker and peasant government'. However, Martínez Villena argued that the international delegates did not have the right to vote on the questions, a position which was attacked by Jorge Vivó, the Party's General Secretary. The Central Committee, on Martínez Villena's insistence, voted to accept a return to work.[49] Subsequently, Vivó was removed from office at the end of August and replaced (in December) by Blas Roca, a young mulatto shoemaker from Manzanillo, and a member of the PCC since 1929.[50] The Comintern representatives were incapable of preventing Vivó's demotion – another incident which reveals the limited authority and power exercised by the Comintern. [54]

The PCC leadership quickly recognised the disastrous implications of the decision, although there is disagreement over how widely the recommendation of a return to work was disseminated outside Havana.[52] Although some unions urged their members to go back to work, the general strike kept its momentum even after Machado's fall on 12 August and right through the first days of the interim Céspedes government, which was installed when Machado fled to the Bahamas. It was only when transport workers – streetcar workers, taxicab drivers, Hermandad Ferroviaria members and employees of the Havana Electric Railway Company – returned to work on 15 August that the last fires of the general strike were extinguished.[53]

The PCC's volte-face in early August (the 'August mistake') was used by the PCC's enemies (especially Anarchists and the dissident Socialists and Marxists of the FOH) as evidence of Communist treachery. The FOH launched particularly savage attacks on the Communist-led CNOC, especially when a delegation from the CNOC visited President Céspedes a few days after he took office and asked him to ratify the agreements signed with Machado in his last days in office.[54] There were also armed clashes between supporters of the two labour organisations; one of them, on 27 August outside the offices of the FOH in Zulueta Street, was particularly bloody, with a toll of one death and eight workers injured.[55]

PCC apologists (like Raúl Roa and Lionel Soto) have argued that the mistake was a collective one – this was also the view of Martínez Villena when the PCC conducted its post-mortem on the crisis – and have blamed the disaster on faulty political readings of the strike by the party leadership as well as external intervention, in particular a message received from the Caribbean Bureau of the Comintern which contained the ambiguous order 'Delay Final Sale'.[56] The message, allegedly, arrived shortly before the decision to recommend a return to work was taken. Martínez Villena interpreted the message as meaning 'don't hasten the fall of Machado until the PCC is ready to replace him', a position which seemed to reinforce his own view that a weakened Machado was better than US intervention.[57]

The PCC's errors, it has been argued, were the result of mistaken directives flowing from the Comintern's class against class line which made understandings between Communists and other anti-imperialist forces impossible. Anything that was not directed by the PCC could not, by definition, be revolutionary. This was linked to the false belief that a weak Machado would be better than a strong bourgeois substitute or a US intervention which the PCC predicted was the inevitable outcome if the strike was maintained. This was the theory of the 'lesser evil' ('*mal menor*') developed by Martínez Villena.

The PCC's behaviour during August 1933 was also probably adversely affected by a severe internal dispute which had resulted in the expulsion of leading cadres in 1932 and early 1933 and the creation of a Communist 'opposition'. The dissidents challenged the PCC leadership's analysis of Cuban society and its conclusion that a transition to socialism was an immediate possibility. Arguing that Cuba was still a semi-colonial and fundamentally agrarian society with a weak working class and a swollen public sector bureaucracy, the oppositionists called for an agrarian revolution and a strategy that involved closer links with the petite bourgeoisie.[58] An additional problem was the disruption of the party's leadership caused by the arrests of two of its key leaders, Jorge Vivó and Joaquín Ordoqoui, in April.[59] Moreover, the party's dominant figure, the much-revered poet and lawyer Rubén Martínez Villena, had been out the country since September 1930, returning to Havana in late May 1933. In very poor health and knowing that he could only live for a few months, Martínez Villena was unfamiliar with the dynamic of Cuban politics in the last years of the *machadato*.[60]

The soviets episode

The 3 August 1933 programme of action of the PCC, issued before the fall of Machado and during the general strike, called for the establishment of a 'Soviet government of workers and peasants' and urged workers and peasants to 'form self-defense groups which will defend your mass action from the attacks of the armed forces'.[61] Three days later, the manifesto calling on Havana strikers to return to work called for an armed insurrection and the establishment of Joint Action Committees, Comités Conjuntos de Acción – 'the embryonic form of soviets'.[62] But the references to a 'soviet government' and 'self-defence groups' stopped short of calling for the formal establishment of soviets defined as organs of dual power. It was only in the middle of August that the Central Committee of the PCC held a Plenum in which it decided to further radicalise mass struggle by launching the slogan demanding the creation of worker and peasant soviets supported by soldiers and sailors.

Why was the soviets slogan issued at this time? Did it have antecedents in Cuba or elsewhere in Latin America? The concept was looser than its powerful historical pedigree might suggest. The Comintern's third period is clearly a crucial international framework and there were (confused) attempts to launch soviets in Vietnam and elsewhere. At the June 1929 meeting of Latin American

Communist parties in Buenos Aires, Jules Humbert-Droz ('Luis') argued that there could be a smooth transition from certain kinds of strike action to soviet power. If civil and administrative power in a region crumbled in a particular region where a revolutionary strike was under way, the strike committee could decide to take power by occupying public buildings and establishing committees to administer not only the strike, but also public life.[63]

Interestingly, the CPUSA, in an important letter to the PCC in early November 1930 criticising its tactics until that date, urged the party to emphasise the immediate demands of the masses and link them to broader slogans like the establishment of soviets, and 'the creation of Armed Workers Corps, and possibly small armed guerrilla groups round and out of which a Workers and Peasants Army may be developed'.[64] The PCC, however, with tiny resources, had difficulty in implementing even a small portion of these suggestions. Rather, until the end of 1930, as we have seen, it had flirted with the idea of throwing its support behind the many plans for armed action implemented by the bourgeois opponents of the Machado regime.[65] The PCC had made preparations for intervention in a putsch in October 1930, an ill-thought-out decision which led to the removal of the party's leadership that month.[66] Several years earlier (during the second half of 1928), from his base in Mexico, Julio Antonio Mella had tried, unsuccessfully, to organise and equip a military uprising in conjunction with the anti-Machado oppositionists of the Unión Nacional.[67] Thus, the Cuban Communists were not implacably opposed to insurrectionary action. However, the CPUSA and the Caribbean Bureau of the Comintern sternly criticised these early efforts to support military actions by Machado's bourgeois opponents.[68]

We should not exaggerate the significance of the PCC's late-August decision to launch a struggle for soviets. Communication difficulties and the PCC's organic weaknesses made it difficult for Havana directives to penetrate down to the base of the party. The PCC, as a recent study has noted, 'did not have enough cadres to exercise effective control over the broad masses'. The same study argues that the organisational work of the SNOIA during the August–September strike wave 'had tailed actual events' mainly due to the breathtaking speed with which the strike movement spread.[69]

In the military defence of the mill occupations, too, some of the strikers' actions went far beyond the expectations of the Communist cadres within the SNOIA. A somewhat worried 17 September report by the Communist fraction within the National Bureau of the SNOIA noted that the enthusiastic creation of Red Militias in some areas of Oriente province went beyond the SNOIA's recomendation to establish self-defence brigades.

The soviets episode was greatly facilitated by the party's newly won freedom to operate free of the worst abuses of the *machadato*. After the fall of Machado, the PCC's activities were no longer automatically repressed. For the first time local sections of the PCC and Young Communist League were able to open legal headquarters, although police arrests of Communists were still common. In working-class suburbs of Havana, Communists held open-air meetings attended by thousands of workers.[70] At the end of August both the PCC and the red flag were legalised.[71] Radical workers reshaped the urban landscape in ways which symbolized the arrival of a new order. In the port suburb of Havana, Regla, workers and students renamed the main street after Julio Antonio Mella.[72] In the old 'red centre' of Cruces, where sugar strikes were under way by the end of August and where a worker-dominated Joint Action Committee had taken control of the town government, a group of 1,500 men on horseback and several thousand people on foot marched from the town to the plantations led by the local Communist Party and the municipal band playing a selection of revolutionary tunes.[73]

With the establishment of the Grau/Guiteras government, tolerance of the PCC turned into a fragile and brief honeymoon. The party operated above ground without extreme harassment from army and police (except in sugar areas), and, together with its affiliates, was even given former *machadista* houses for offices. For example, the PCC itself was able to use the building formerly used by the *machadista* paper *El Heraldo de Cuba*.[74] The national headquarters of the International Workers' Defence, Defensa Obrera Internacional, was set up in a Havana house once owned by the *machadista* Treasury Secretary, Averhoff. Another elite house was used by the Anti-Imperialist League, Liga Anti-Imperialista, and the Pioneros, the PCC youth organization.[75] The national teachers union also received a new central office, a sumptuous home owned by Machado.[76]

The politicisation and radicalisation of the atmosphere in Havana became more intense in September as the air was filled with slogans calling for revolutionary revenge, radical unionism (and in particular the unionisation of the previously unorganised) and anti-imperialism (strengthened by the growing and visible US naval presence in Cuban waters).

Antonio Guiteras, the most left-leaning of the cabinet members, repeatedly offered to collaborate with the CNOC and the PCC. Shortly after his appointment as Secretary of the Interior, Secretario de Gobernación, Guiteras offered to establish a permanent link between the CNOC and his own office and he reportedly offered the Communist Party a hundred positions in the National Police and the opportunity to help create an armed workers' militia supplied from the Gobernación ministry. The CNOC and the Communist leadership turned down all these offers, even though party members, especially in Oriente, had managed to work with *guiteristas* in 1932 and 1933, another example of the dangers of assuming that Comintern policy and directives were automatically translated into behaviour at the local level. Nevertheless, as far as the party's national leadership was concerned, the PCC's hostility to Guiteras was in line with the ultra-leftist line of the Comintern, which saw the Grau-led government as a monolithic bloc with fascistic leanings.[77]

The situation changed dramatically after a 29 September massacre which marred the burial of Mella's ashes in Havana. Whatever Guiteras' own views and individual responsibility might have been, neither he (nor Grau) condemned the action, and the army's brutality was interpreted by the left as a declaration of war by Batista and his army allies. The PCC hardened its position throughout the island, armed with the proof that its own sectarian ultra-leftist views on the Grau government had been confirmed by the blood spilled on 29 September. In its proclamation after the massacre the PCC urged its members to 'build Communist cells in barracks and on navy ships'.[78] The PCC and the CNOC also launched an appeal for a general strike, although the action fizzled out for lack of preparation.[79]

As the US ambassador Sumner Welles continued to cultivate Batista as part of his campaign to undermine the Grau San Martín government, the army commander's anti-Communist pronouncements became more frequent and pronounced. In his report of a 7 October conversation with Batista, Welles reported the army strong man's promises to 'proceed immediately with a firm hand' in all of the American sugar plantations where labour troubles existed, by arresting and removing all Communist leaders and by using the troops to restore order wherever it was necessary.[80] While Batista's promises may have been designed to please the USA, the army soon after began to move against the mill occupations with great vigour. There were army massacres at Jaronú (27 October) and Senado (18 November) mills.[81] On 27 October Batista declared 'we will have a *zafra* [sugar harvest] or there will be blood' in an interview with mill owners, administrators and *colonos* and in the presence of President Grau. The declaration was a warning to those elements who would try and stop the next *zafra* .[82] Army repression, worker exhaustion and the resignation of the Grau administration in mid-January 1934 drastically weakened the working-class insurgency.

Conclusion

Historians are still struggling with a mass of contradictory models which attempt to measure and explicate the Comintern's relationship with 'its' national sections. Traditional models of Comintern–Latin American Communist party relations have tended to be overly simplistic: reductionist explanations still abound which present the history of particular Communist parties as a series of incidents in which they passively respond to Comintern directives. The importance of 'contingency', the logic of local as well as of international developments, the weaknesses of the Comintern apparatus – these are just some of the issues that need to be considered in any evaluation of Comintern–Cuban relations.

The Comintern did realise the significance for the prospects of an anti-imperialist revolution of events in Cuba – and the unique conjuncture of the anti-Machado insurrection and the worker–peasant insurgency of August–December 1933 – hence the scale of its presence in Cuba in 1932–34 when Comintern, Profintern, Peasant International (Krestintern) and Youth

International representatives worked in Havana. This was the most substantial Comintern presence seen in Latin America.[83]

The Comintern did shape the Cuban party's overall ability to exploit the opportunities unfolding in the course of 1933 – in the general sense that its third period (class against class) project made it almost impossible for Cuban Communists to exploit opportunities to build alliances with non-Communist reformists – such as those represented in the governments that replaced Gerardo Machado – the interim administration of Carlos Manuel Céspedes (12 August to 5 September) and, more importantly, the 'revolutionary government of 100 days' – headed by Grau San Martín whose cabinet included many progressives (Antonio Guiteras is the best-known example) committed to a programme of anti-imperialism and advanced legislation in social, labour and agrarian matters.

However, at the quotidian level the shaping impact of the Comintern and its envoys was greatly limited. A major problem was inadequate and out-of-date information at moments of rapid political change – for example, during the anti-Machado general strike. The Comintern Bureau in New York was painfully dependent on news published in the mainstream press, despite the intense correspondence between it and the Central Committee of the Cuban party and the Comintern envoys in Havana. The minutes of the New York-based Bureau reveal the frustration of its members who complain endlessly of 'silences' from Havana. 'We are unaware of . . .' is one of the most frequently encountered tropes in the Comintern Bureau's correspondence. [84]

National Communist parties did not necessarily implement Comintern advice. The PCC stubbornly refused to follow many of the directives of the Comintern, especially the advice and intervention of the Havana-based Comintern representatives who attended most meetings of the party's highest organs (the Central Committee and Political Bureau), and even drafted some of the party's documents. The old Spanish colonial slogan '*Obedezco pero no cumplo*' ('I obey but I don't follow through') seems to describe much of the PCC's responses to the Communist International.

Why was this the case? It is clear that nationalist sentiments were partly involved. 'We are tired of hearing your views and tattle', was a characteristically bitter response by one Central Committee member after the Comintern representative 'Juan' criticised the PCC's performance during the Havana general strike.[85] Martínez Villena, the party's most respected leader, accused the Comintern apparatus of deliberately backing Central Committee members who opposed the party's interpretation of the the general strike.[86] The prestige enjoyed by Comintern representatives is frequently underlined by historians of national communisms. But in the Cuban case it was Martínez Villena, the leading opponent of the Comintern's line on the general strike, who enjoyed prestige and authority – a point conceded by one of the Comintern representatives.[87]

The impact of 'accidents' should also not be underestimated. The best-informed Comintern representative in Havana, 'Juan' (normally based in Mexico) was seriously ill in bed with a high fever during some of the most crucial episodes in early August. Moreover, the party's ability to make decisions was influenced by curious incidents. The son of the distinguished journalist and historian Ramiro Guerra, Machado's private secretary, was also a member of the PCC's leadership, and passed on 'confidential' news from his father which some Central Committee members suspected was designed by Machado to 'sow panic' among the PCC leaders and influence the party's policy in the middle of the general strike.[88]

Notes

1 Barry Carr, 'Mill occupations and soviets: The mobilization of sugar workers in Cuba 1917–1933', *Journal of Latin American Studies*, 28 (1996), pp. 129–58.

2 RC 534/4/477, report by 'Juan', 29 August 1933.

3 L. Aguilar, *Cuba 1933* (Ithaca, 1972), pp. 84–6, 121–4, 144–7, 183–6; J. Benjamin, *The United States and Cuba: Hegemony and Dependent Development* (Pittsburgh, 1974), pp. 61–5; K. S. Karol, *Guerrillas in Power* (New York, 1970), pp. 63–98; H. Thomas, *Cuba or the Pursuit of Freedom* (London, 1971), pp. 575–81, 596–8, 605–6, 618–19, 656; H. Sims, 'The Cuban sugar workers' progress Under the leadership of a black Communist, Jesús Menéndez Larrondo, 1941–1948', *MACLAS: Latin American Essays. Vol. VI* (Middle Atlantic Council of Latin American Studies, 1993), 9–21.

4 J. García Montes and A. Alonso Avila, *Historia del partido comunista de Cuba* (Miami, 1970).

5 A small selection would include: A. García and P. Mironchuk, *Los soviets: obreros y campesinos en Cuba* (Havana, 1987); O. Zanetti *et al.*, *United Fruit Company: Un caso del dominio imperialista en Cuba* (Havana, 1976); J. Portilla, *Jesús Menéndez y su tiempo* (Havana, 1987); O. Portuondo Moret, *El soviet de Tacajó: experiencias de un estudiante de los 30* (Santiago de Cuba, 1979); U. Rojas, *Las luchas obreras en el central Tacajó* (Havana, 1979); L. Soto, *La revolución de 1933* (Havana, 1979) vols 1, 2, 3; O. Cabrera, 'La Tercera Internacional y su influencia en Cuba (1919–1935)', *Sociedad y Estado*, 2 (Enero–abril 1989), 51–9; I. Figueroa, 'El compañero Rubén', *Santiago*, 16 (December 1974), 95–149; F. Grobart, 'Testimonio: preguntas u respuestas sobre los años 30: Fabio Grobart en la Escuela de Historia', *Revista de la Universidad de la Habana*, 200:3 (1973), 128–57.

6 F. Grobart, *Un forjador eternamente joven* (Havana, 1985), pp. 14–19. Also see the file of correspondence between Jewish organisations, the Machado government and the police authorities. Archivo Nacional Cubano (hereafter, ANC). Secretaría de la Presidencia. 100/15.

7 On Jewish immigrant workers see Margalit Bejarano, 'The deproletarisation of Cuban Jewry', *Judaica Latinoamericana: Estudios Histórico-Sociales* (Jerusalem, 1988), and M. Kula, 'Those who failed to reach the United States: Polish proletarians in Cuba during the interwar period', *Polish American Studies*, 46:1 (1989), 19–41.

8 X. Neira Vilas, *Gallegos en el golfo de México* (Havana, 1983), pp. 17–19, 32–7, 60–2, 104–5; 122–30.

9 R. Roa, *El fuego de la semilla en el surco* (Havana, 1982), pp. 308–9.
10 T. Camiñas Lemes, 'El anarquismo en el movimiento obrero cubano hasta 1917. Algunos criterios para su periodización', *Santiago*, 60 (1985), 177–97.
11 RC 495/105/75, report of Comrade Juan to the Caribbean Secretariat, May 1931. The 'Hova' mentioned in this document is also referred to as 'Joba' in other correspondence and is probably the *nomre de guerra* of Fabio Grobart who worked in the Latin American Secretariat of the Comintern during 1933. RC 495/105/75, 'Sampedra for the CC del PCC to Estimados Camaradas', 5 November 1933. In this letter, the Cuban party requested the return of 'Joba' from Moscow.
12 RC 354/ 7/ 380, Arturo L. Carbonell to M. Siminin, 7 May 1929.
13 RC 495/105/91, 'La situación economica de Cuba', January 1933, no author.
14 RC 354/ 7/380, unsigned letter from Havana, 15 May 1929, 'Informe Sobre el Primero de mayo y el Congreso de Montevideo'.
15 *Ibid.*
16 RC 534/7/382, 'Extracto del Acta de la Junta del CC del 2 de abril de 1931'.
17 RC 534/4/431, 'Informe sobre Cuba', signed Emil and Arturo, 20 February 1932.
18 For part of 1928 the Mexican Communist paper *El Machete* disseminated the Cuban party's manifestos and documents. Roa, *El fuego*, p. 322.
19 RC 354/7/389.
20 RC 534/4/427. Anonymous report addressed to 'Herrn Alexander', 10/9/1932. No title.
21 RC 495/105/61, 'Report on the Work in Cuba and Mexico Given to LAB', 19 July 1932 signed 'Eduardo'.
22 F. Grobart, 'El movimiento obrero cubano de 1925 a 1933', *Cuba Socialista*, 6:60 (1966), 94.
23 ANC Fondo Especial, 75/15, 'Hacia las luchas decisivas por el poder soviético. Resolución sobre la situación actual . . . adoptada por el Segundo Congreso del PCC celebrado a fines de Abril de 1934', p. 23.
24 United States National Archives (hereafter, USNA) RG 84, Havana Embassy Post Records. 1933, Part 15. 800B. Secretary General of the PCC Comité Central Ejecutivo, 15 July 1930 to PCUSA. This was one of a number of documents intercepted by Machado's Policía Secreta Nacional and furnished to the US Embassy in Havana. See also Roa, *El fuego*, p. 417.
25 Cabrera, 'La Tercera Internacional', p. 59.
26 Roa, *El fuego*, p. 375.
27 RC 534/7/380. 'Informe resumen sobre la CNOC'. The most prominent Communist working in the railway sector was Joaquín Ordoqui.
28 Roa, *El fuego*, pp. 398–411 and García Montes and Alonso Avila, *Historia del partido comunista*, pp. 106–07.
29 RC 534/7/380. 'Informe sobre el primero de mayo y el congreso de Montevideo', 15 May 1929; 534/7/382, 'Extracto del Acta de la Junta del CC del 2 de abril de 1931'.
30 Roa, *El fuego*, p. 445. For the Profintern's warning about not confusing 'peasants' with agricultural (wage) workers, see 'Por la organización sindical de los trabajadores agrícolas (Resolución adoptada en la Conferencia Sindical Latino-Americana de Abril)', *El Trabajador Latinoamericano*, 1:3 (1928).
31 *El Trabajador*, 15 October 1931, 'El viraje del P. hacia los obreros agrícolas de los ingenios'.

32 'Llamamiento de la comisión pro-organización del sindicato de obreros de la industria azucarera', in *El movimiento obrero cubano, Documentos: Tomo II*, pp. 265–73.

33 Sections of the Manifesto are reproduced in Soto, *La revolución de 1933*, II, pp. 151–55.

34 RC 495/105/77, PCC Comité Central to CD de Santa Clara, 30 March 1933.

35 ANC, 'Hacia las luchas decisivas', p. 24.

36 ANC, Fondo Especial, 31/2, 'Convocatoria para el primer congreso nacional de la Liga Juvenil Comunista de Cuba', *Juventud Obrera*, 12 (12 January 1934), 5.

37 Soto, *La revolución de 1933*, pp. 234–5.

38 *Diario de la Marina*, 28 July, 31 July, 4 August 1933.

39 British Foreign Office records in the Public Records Office (PRO-FO) A/6072/255/14/No. 74, Mr. Grant Watson to Sir John Simon, Havana, 9 August 1933.

40 F. Fuentes, 'La huelga general', *El Trabajador*, II: 8 (9 September 1933), 5; USNA, RG 59, 837.00/3669, Sumner Welles to Secretary of State, 16 August 1933.

41 *Indice Histórico de la Provincia de Camaguey* (Havana, 1970), pp. 178–9

42 V. Rovira González, M. E. Olite Montesbravo, *Cienfuegos durante la República neocolonial 1902–1935* (no place or date of publication), pp. 46–7.

43 RC 495/105/70, Acta del CC del Partido Comunista de Cuba 29 de agosto de 1933. Soto, *La revolución de 1933*, vol. 2, pp. 328–9. A. Lamar-Schweyer, *How President Machado Fell* (Havana, 1938), p. 143. According to the labour boss Eusebio Mujal (who had been a Communist for a short while in the late 1920s and early 1930s), the Communists present at the meeting were the CNOC Secretary General César Vilar and the CNOC cigar worker Vicente Alvarez. Thomas, *Cuba or the Pursuit*, p. 618.

44 *New York Times*, 9 August 1933.

45 RC 495/105/69, report of Comrade 'Bell' on the Situation in Cuba, 3 October 1933.

46 Interview with Blas Castillo in *Pensamiento crítico*, 39 (1970), 197. Castillo's version of Martínez Villena's views is confirmed by Comintern documents.

47 *El Trabajador*, II: 7 (13 August 1933), 2–3. 'A los obreros y a los campesinos pobres y medios', signed by the Mesa Ejecutiva of the CNOC and the Political Bureau of the Communist Party Central Committee. The only extant collection of *El Trabajador* is located in the Instituto de Historia in Havana.

48 This individual is possibly Alberto Moré, one of the exiled Cuban Communists resident in New York in the early 1930s. See Roa, *El fuego*, p. 416, for a brief reference to his meeting with Martínez Villena in 1930.

49 See the interview with Blas Castillo. Castillo, however, does not specify the date on which the Comintern delegation intervened. The Comintern records allow for a much more detailed reconstruction.

50 On Vivó's removal, see RC 534/4/477, report by 'Juan', 30 August 1933. On Roca, see *Daily Worker*, 15 January 1934. See also C. Massón Sena, 'El II Congreso del primer partido marxista leninista en Cuba', *Revista de la Biblioteca Nacional José Martí*, 80: xxxi (1989), 189. Blas Roca's chief rival was 'Fabio' (Grobart?) who had just returned from Moscow. With some prodding from 'Juan', the Central Committee of the PCC, opted for a 'Cuban' rather than a 'foreigner'.

51 RC 495/105/68 'Johnny' to Comrades, 4 September 1933. 'It was impossible for me to stop that [i.e. Vivó's removal as General Secretary] because the hysteria went [*sic*] so much high.'

52 Lolo De la Torriente, *Mi casa en la tierra* (Havana, 1956), pp. 269–70. Compare J. Tabares del Real, *La revolución del 30: sus dos ultimos años* (Havana, 1973), p. 135. Later, the PCC blamed the August error on 'syndicalist residues' in the party. 'La influencia del anarco-sindicalismo en nuestro partido', *Bandera Roja*, II: 13 (18 April 1934); Partido Comunista Cubano, *Por un 12 de agosto revolucionario* (Havana, 24 July 1934), p. 2.
53 *New York Times*, 14 and 16 August 1933.
54 *Cuba Today*, 10:134 (14 August 1933), citing *El País*.
55 *Diario de la Marina*, 28 August 1933.
56 For a (very timid and incomplete) post-mortem examination of the 'August mistake', see *Bandera Roja*, II: 5 (5 January 1934).
57 Soto, *La revolución de 1933*, vol. 2, p. 388.
58 For a rare personal insight into the inner disputes within the PCC during 1933, see ANC Fondo Donaciones y Remiciones, 673/9. Bertha Dardet to Ofelia Domínguez, 15 May 1933.
59 *Daily Worker*, 8 April 1933.
60 Between October and December 1933 the 'Casa Matriz' (i.e. the Comintern Executive in Moscow) worked hard to force the PCC to acknowledge its errors – and to rectify its 'opportunistic' behaviour.
61 M. Kaye and L. Perry, *Who Fights for a Free Cuba* (New York, 1933), pp. 35–6.
62 'A los obreros y a los campesinos', in *El Trabajador*, II: 7 (13 August 1933).
63 Secretariado Sudamericano de la Internacional Comunista, *El movimiento revolucionario latinoamericano: Versiones de la Primera Conferencia Comunista Latinoamericana Junio de 1929* (Buenos Aires, 1929), p. 93.
64 'Letter of the Central Committee of the CPUSA to the Central Committee of the CP of Cuba, November 6, 1930,' *The Communist*, 10: 1 (1931), 70.
65 For comments on the Cuban Communists' relations with the Unión Nacionalista made by 'Juárez' (at the 1929 Buenos Aires conference of Communist parties), see Secretariado Sudamericano de la Internacional Comunista, 'El movimiento revolucionario latinoamericano', pp. 125–7.
66 Partido Comunista de Cuba, *El partido comunista y los problemas de la revolución en Cuba* (Havana, 1933), p. 31.
67 On Mella's plans for an armed action in Cuba, see Roa, *El fuego*, pp. 292–7, 309, 312–13, 322–3, 350–1.
68 'Letter of the Central Committee of the CPUSA', pp. 69–70.
69 F. López Segrera, *Sociología de la colonia y neocolonia cubana 1510–1959* (Havana, 1989), pp. 113–14.
70 *Daily Worker*, 21 August 1933.
71 *Ibid.*, 31 August 1933.
72 *Ibid.*, 23 August 1933.
73 *Ibid.*, 4 September 1933, report dated 29 August.
74 The building was taken away from the Communist Party on 22 September. See *Cuba Today*, 10: 169 (23 September 1933) citing *El Mundo*.
75 *Daily Worker*, 26 September 1933; J. A. Tabares del Real, *Guiteras* (Havana, 1973), p. 282.
76 B. Exposito Rodríguez, *Apuntes del movimiento de los trabajadores de la educación 1899–1961* (Havana, 1985), p. 155.
77 Tabares del Real, *Guiteras*, p. 282. On Communist links with *guiteristas* prior to

August 1933, see the case of Holguin. Rafael Soler, 'Francia y los revolucionarios del oriente cubano', in Jean Lamore (ed.), *Les français dans l'Orient Cubain* (Bordeaux, 1993), pp. 67–76.

78 Soto, *La revolución de 1933*, vol. 3, pp. 162–73.

79 ANC Fondo Especial 79/13, Partido Comunista de Cuba, 'Sobre la huelga general del primero de noviembre', no date.

80 Sumner Welles to Cordell Hull, 7 October 1933, in *Foreign Relations of the United States 1933*, V, pp. 477–8.

81 On the Senado massacre, see the letter published in *Bandera Roja*, 54 (5 January 1934) (reproduced in González Echevarría, *Orígen e desarrollo*, pp. 124–6.)

82 For Batista's declaration, see *Adelante*, 1: 40 (28 October 1933), 1.

83 The international representatives who visited Cuba included: 'Juan', 'Bell' (a member of the Caribbean Bureau of the Comintern, maybe Tom Bell, British Communist) and Rafael Carrillo (former General Secretary of the Mexican Communist Party). RC 500/1/10. BC al Sec del C y SA, 5 October 1933.

84 RC Caribbean Bureau, 500/1/11. Reunión del BC, 13 August 1933.

85 RC 534/14/477, report by 'Juan' on a meeting of the Central Committee of the PC, 29 August 1933.

86 RC 534/4/477, report by 'Juan', 30 August 1933. Martínez Villena's comment was that the envoys 'did not impress us so much with their arguments as with the positions they held'.

87 RC 495/105/68, 'Johnny' to Comrades, 4 September 1933. 'Villena exercises an absolute control over the majority of the CC members who are politically much inferior to him and who have an exceptionally exaggerated reverence for him.'

88 See RC 534/4/477 for comments of the Central Committee member 'Pablo' as reported by 'Juan' in the minutes of the Committee's 29 August 1933 meeting. Guerra's role is also outlined in RC 500/1/12. BC al CC del PCC, 31 October 1933.

16

The Comintern, the Chinese Communist Party and the three armed uprisings in Shanghai, 1926–27

S. A. Smith

Introduction

On 9 July 1926 the Guomindang (GMD) launched the Northern Expedition of the National Revolutionary Army (NRA) from Guangdong in south China. Its aims were to reunify the country under a single government by conquering the warlord armies and, ultimately, to regain sovereignty from the foreign powers which had grabbed privileges in China since the Opium Wars of the 1840s. The NRA fought effectively, its rapid success due in part to the fact that many warlords threw in their lot with it. In late November the GMD set up a national government in Wuhan in central China, and by mid-December the NRA controlled the major towns of central and southeast China. Military success raised the political prestige of the GMD to unprecedented heights, yet exacerbated political tension between its left and right wings, and between the GMD and the Chinese Communist Party (CCP), with which it had been allied since 1923. The tension had its roots in the deepening contradiction between the national and social revolutions.

The CCP and left GMD used the Northern Expedition to carry out a remarkable political and ideological mobilisation of the rural and urban masses. By spring 1927 more than fifteen million peasants were organised into peasant associations which fought to reduce rents and interest rates; whilst in urban centres workers launched strikes and joined labour unions. This created widespread popular support for the GMD, but provoked a reaction among local elites. In the countryside, gentry, officials and militarists put up fierce resistance to the peasant movement, whilst in the towns merchants and industrialists agonised over how to deal with industrial unrest. The right wing of the GMD believed that the aim of the Northern Expedition was to strengthen China by uniting her people, not to deepen social division by unleashing class conflict. And since most officers in the NRA came from gentry families, they looked askance at the way in which the national revolution was fuelling a social revolution. By contrast, the Communists and the GMD left believed that the national revolution should be carried out in the interests of the workers and peasants, rather than the bourgeoisie. Although mass mobilisation bolstered the political influence of the left, which dominated the new national government, military might lay in the hands of Chiang Kai-shek, supreme commander of the NRA and spiritual leader of the right. By the end of 1926, the left, uneasily aware of its vulnerability to a military backlash, searched for ways to preserve unity in the nationalist camp.

In Shanghai the conflict within the united front was played out to deadly effect. In this city of 2,700,000 people, there were up to 800,000 working people, including 250,000 factory workers. As the Northern Expedition advanced, the Communist-led Shanghai General Labour Union (GLU) managed to organise most of the city's workforce. By March 1927 it claimed that 502 labour unions, with 821,280 members, were affiliated to it.[1] Simultaneously, the CCP developed into something like a mass party. On 10 January 1927 there were 3,075 Communists in Shanghai; by 4 April there were 8,374.[2] At this stage, Shanghai was under the control of the warlord, Sun Chuanfang, and the Central Committee (CC) of the CCP, which was based in the city, hoped to use its influence over the labour movement to launch an uprising that would seize control from Sun's forces. The calculation was that if they could defeat Sun prior to the arrival of the NRA, this would strengthen the hand of the left in its stand-off with Chiang Kai-shek. On 24 October 1926, in alliance with the GMD, it attempted to carry out a first 'uprising', which proved a botched fiasco. Almost four months later, as advance units of the NRA's eastern route army, led by Bai Chongxi, prepared to capture Hangzhou, it made a second attempt. On 18 February the GLU called a general strike to prepare the city for the entry of the NRA, its somewhat vague aim being to create a democratic citizens' government.[3] The general strike which ensued was the largest ever witnessed in Shanghai, with a total of 420,970 employees stopping work between 19 and 22 February.[4] The Communist CC, shocked by the savagery of the terror unleashed by Sun Chuanfang's commander, vacillated as to whether to turn the general strike into an armed uprising, aware that Bai Chongxi intended to await reinforcements before advancing on Shanghai. It was not until 21 February, the third day of the strike, that it resolved on an uprising, by which time the strike was running out of steam. Badly led and lacking a clear objective, the insurgents failed to demoralise the warlord troops, and on the evening of 23 February the CC called off the uprising.

Sun Chuanfang turned for assistance to the warlord, Zhang Zongchang, whose northern troops entered the city during the first days of March. After two failures, the Communists prepared furiously for a new assault, expanding and training the armed workers' pickets. On 18 March the eastern route army of the NRA finally reached Songjiang, thirty kilometres from Shanghai, whereupon the CC called a third strike and uprising to commence on Monday, 21 March.[5] On that day at noon 200,000 workers came out on strike and pickets seized police stations and other strategic points. They met fierce resistance in Zhabei district, where 3,000 of Zhang's troops were holed up, and it was not until the following afternoon that they finally overcame the northern forces. Around 322 were killed and 2,000 wounded in what became known as the third armed uprising.[6] The workers' pickets won without the assistance of the NRA, which did not enter Shanghai until the afternoon of 22 March. They had deliberately delayed their entry at the request of Niu Yongjian, head of the GMD's Jiangsu Special Committee, who was in cahoots with Chiang Kai-shek. The CCP and GLU used their victory to set up a provisional municipal government, which promised to institute a swathe of social and economic reforms. On 26 March Chiang Kai-shek arrived in Shanghai to find the streets patrolled by armed pickets. Chinese businessmen, the secret societies and the foreign authorities in the International Settlement and the French Concession, alarmed by the Communist victory, offered Chiang money and personnel to deal with the revolutionaries. On 12 April 1927 gangsters, backed by troops of the NRA, ransacked the headquarters of the pickets and arrested and killed scores of Communists. Thus was the united front torn asunder.

By June 1927 the scale of the disaster suffered by the CCP was horrifyingly evident, causing bitter recrimination within the CCP and the Executive Committee of the Communist International (ECCI). The latter, guided by the Politburo of the Soviet Communist Party, had imposed the united front policy on a reluctant CCP. It calculated that China faced not a socialist revolution, but a national revolution against imperialism and warlordism, and that the GMD was the main force capable of achieving this. It thus insisted that members of the CCP join the GMD on an individual basis – the so-called 'bloc within' – and work within it to promote the national revolution, whilst taking care to maintain the political independence of the CCP and its capacity to organise the working class. From 1923 the Politburo poured massive amounts of military, financial and organisational aid into the GMD and the NRA. The success of the left in winning positions within the GMD, the Canton government and the NRA, led ECCI increasingly to conceive of it as a 'popular', or even a 'worker–peasant', party. Most of the leadership of the CCP did not share this optimistic view, since they were uncomfortably aware of the influence of the right wing within the GMD. And on at least three occasions prior to 1927 (in October 1924, September 1925 and again in June 1926), Chen Duxiu, general secretary of the CCP, called on the ECCI to permit the CCP to withdraw from the 'bloc within'. Each time, the ECCI refused.[7]

From the spring of 1926 both the ECCI and the Politburo became increasingly alarmed at the dictatorial and reactionary policy pursued by Chiang Kai-shek, but a fundamental reconsideration of the united front strategy was ruled out by the fact that it had became a bone of contention in the struggle taking place within the Soviet Communist Party between Stalin and the United Opposition, led by Zinoviev, Kamenev and Trotsky. The Northern Expedition thrust to the fore the problem of reconciling social unity in the interests of the national revolution with the promotion of the interests of the proletariat and the peasantry. The United Opposition denounced what Trotsky called the tendency of ECCI to substitute 'clever manoeuvres and good advice within the GMD' for independent mass organisation.[8] And when the united front ended in debacle, it claimed to have been vindicated. Stalin, the Politburo and the ECCI denied responsibility, heaping blame on the CCP for failing adequately to carry out Moscow's instructions. At the August 1927 emergency conference of the CCP, Chen Duxiu was made scapegoat for the disaster, and accused of pursuing a policy of 'right opportunism'.

This chapter reopens the question of the respective responsibilities of the ECCI and the CCP leadership for the events of April 1927. It seeks first to reconstruct policy differences within the ECCI, the CC and the Shanghai Regional Committee (SRC) of the CCP during the period of the three armed uprisings, using material that has only recently become available, in order to strip away the patina of retrospective denigration and distortion. Second, it examines briefly the policies that were actually carried out by the Communists in Shanghai, in order to compare their practice with the precepts of the ECCI. In particular, it is concerned to assess the validity of the charge of 'right opportunism'. This was levelled, as we have seen, by those eager to absolve the ECCI of responsibility for the bloodbath of 12 April 1927, who averred that the CC had deliberately ignored or distorted the revolutionary line laid down by the ECCI. But it was also a charge echoed by Trotskyist critics, who argued that the CCP's 'right opportunism' arose precisely because it had implemented Moscow's line all too faithfully.

The seventh ECCI Plenum

On 13 December 1926 the CC of the CCP met for a special meeting in Wuhan to discuss the political crisis in the united front, which had been brought to a head by the success of the Northern Expedition. Chen Duxiu observed that 'most political and military power is now in the hands of the right' and that Chiang Kai-shek was behaving in a very 'right-wing' fashion, and predicted that he might do a deal with the imperialists. At the same time, he accused elements in the CCP of 'infantile leftism', for seeking to monopolise positions of power within the GMD and in the mass movements. In order to reduce the widening gap between left and right, he proposed, first, to 'unite military power with the mass movement', as a way to develop the popular base of the struggles against warlordism and imperialism and to strengthen the left wing of the GMD; and, second, to fight the right wing through the GMD left in base organisations as well as central organs of the party. Less vaguely, and more contentiously, he proposed that certain curbs be placed on the mass movements: in particular, he suggested that agitators in the peasant movement concentrate on reducing rent and interest rates, rather than on land confiscation; and that workers' pickets be prevented from inflicting 'excesses' on traders and small producers.[9] These policies were in line with those hitherto advocated by ECCI, and were approved by both of its senior representatives in China, M. M. Borodin and G. N. Voitinsky, who attended the meeting.[10] It was these decisions, however, that would later be used as the main evidence to substantiate the charge of 'right opportunism'. For at the very moment the special meeting was taking place in Wuhan, the seventh Plenum of the ECCI was closing in Moscow, and had decided to shift its Chinese policy in a more radical direction.

The seventh ECCI Plenum, which met from 22 November to 16 December 1927, set forth a perspective of 'anti-imperialist dictatorship of workers, peasants and the petty-bourgeoisie' for the CCP, suggesting that the agrarian revolution could provide the impetus for the development of the national revolution in a non-capitalist direction. According to Cai Hesen, CCP representative on ECCI, this forced the party to choose between 'an alliance with the bourgeoisie and one with the peasantry'.[11] The most substantial leftward shift in policy prescribed by the Plenum was with respect to the peasant movement, a subject outside the purview of this chapter. For, as Bukharin declared in his keynote address, 'the most serious mistake which has been made by the CCP, not withstanding the general correctness of its line, has been insufficient attention to the peasant question'.[12]

Close examination of the debates at the seventh Plenum, including those in the commission set up to work out theses on the Chinese question, suggests that the new trail blazed was neither so clear-cut nor so consistent as Cai Hesen maintained. The eastern section of ECCI was so badly divided that it failed to produce a set of theses for the Plenum, whereupon a special commission was established. This considered no fewer than four different draft theses and two reports, and proved equally divided.[13] Its members were Stalin, Bukharin, F. F. Raskol'nikov, director of the eastern section of ECCI, P. A. Mif, A. S. Bubnov, head of the Political Administration of the Revolutionary Military Council and leader of a mission to China in spring 1926, B. A. Vassiliev, deputy head of the eastern section of the ECCI, three members of the CCP, Tan Pingshan, Cai Hesen and Ren Bishi (also general secretary of the Communist Youth League), Katayama Sen, M. N. Roy and William Gallacher, who chaired the commission.[14] This commission made little progress until 30 November when Stalin intervened to knock heads together.[15]

The commission agreed that the Chinese Revolution was entering a new phase, but there was no consensus as to its political and economic nature. Mif averred that the bourgeois-democratic revolution was growing into 'an immediately socialist revolution', whereas Raskol'nikov insisted that the tasks of the national revolution had not yet been achieved. The theses approved by the Plenum contended that the revolution was at a turning point and could develop along one of two paths: either rule by the bourgeoisie, with backing from the militarists, or rule by the workers, peasants and petty bourgeoisie. The drafting commission also disagreed as to the extent to which the proletariat was hegemonic within the revolutionary bloc. The concept of the hegemony of the proletariat in the national revolution had first been outlined at the CC Plenum of the CCP in May 1924, but it had never been clear whether it was something to be striven for – possibly a very long-term goal – or an already established fact. Nor was there accord as to whether proletarian hegemony should be exercised through the GMD or via independent working-class organisations and the CCP. In the drafting commission Roy claimed that the 'proletariat is the dominating factor in the revolution', whereas Tan Pingshan insisted that the 'hegemony of the proletariat in the Chinese revolution is not sufficiently guaranteed'.[16]

The drafters also disagreed as to what the departure of the national bourgeoisie from the national liberation struggle would signify for the character of a reunified national state. Mif insisted that a form of Soviet government was inevitable; but the final theses stated only that the 'revolutionary state will not be a purely bourgeois-democratic state but will represent a democratic dictatorship of the proletariat, peasantry, and other exploited classes', a formulation endorsed by Stalin.[17] Such a state would institute a 'period of transition to non-capitalist (socialist) development'. Some in the commission believed that this transition would be constrained by China's underdevelopment and by the ability of the state to take control of the economy, whilst others opined that it was eminently feasible, given support from the Soviet Union.[18]

In sketching the possibility of a non-capitalist path for the national revolution, the seventh Plenum went beyond the perspective within which the Comintern had hitherto worked. Yet the concrete implications of the changed perspective were left ambiguous. The final theses devoted only three of twenty-eight paragraphs to discussing the united front policy. The CCP was enjoined to transform the GMD into a 'genuine party of the people', into a 'solid revolutionary bloc of the proletariat, peasantry, urban petty bourgeoisie and other oppressed layers' by 'systematic and decisive struggle with the right wing of the GMD', by strengthening and closely co-operating with the left wing and by criticising the vacillations of the 'centre'. This was simply a reformulation of tactics first elaborated at the May 1924 Plenum of the CC.[19] What the theses failed to address were the issues which had become critical during 1926: how to define the 'centre' and 'right' of the GMD; whether or not a GMD left existed separate from the Communists; what the balance of class forces within the national revolution now was. Significantly, whereas the July 1926 CC Plenum had classified Chiang Kia-shek as 'new right', drafters of the ECCI theses assumed that he was still part of the 'centre'.[20] Moreover, the theses failed to address two burning questions that were exercising the CCP, which had been raised in Tan Pingshan's report to the Plenum. Was it possible that the GMD might conclude an alliance with the bourgeoisie and 'limit the political freedoms of the people under a military dictatorship'? And if the 'military dictatorship of the centre' continued, might 'the revolutionary petty-bourgeois elements' need to form a new party?[21] The principal change in policy *vis-à-vis* the united front was to direct the CCP to penetrate the apparatus of the national government in order to use it for the purposes of land confiscation, lowering of taxes, consolidation of the peasant committees, etc.[22] Ren Bishi expressed the CC's doubts on this score, fearing that participation in government might compromise the independence of the CCP.[23] In fact, Communists had never had difficulty acquiring positions of authority within the GMD, yet so far this had done little to transform it into a 'genuine party of the people'. Ironically, this was largely due to the highly centralist structure imposed on the GMD by Borodin. As Tan Pingshan hinted, the 'workers and peasants risk being conditioned by the constitution and becoming indifferent to their class interests'.[24]

In his speech to the drafting commission Stalin stressed the 'special role of the military factor' as one of the 'advantages' of the Chinese Revolution. Later, Mao Zedong would cite this as evidence of Stalin's sapience, but N. Nasonov, a member of the Far Eastern Bureau (FEB) of the ECCI, Ren Bishi and Tan Pingshan objected to the formulation. Significantly, it was the one recommendation which did not find its way into the final theses, showing that Stalin had still not acquired quasi-papal infallibility.[25] The theses merely called on the CCP to pay greater attention to military matters, mainly by stepping up political work inside the NRA. There was no call for the CCP to create its own armed force, though this had been an issue raised by the CC after Chiang Kai-shek's first move against the party on 20 March 1926. In effect, the Plenum fatally overestimated the revolutionary character of the NRA.[26]

M. N. Roy, who upheld a consistently 'left' position in the drafting commission, was sent to China to oversee the implementation of the seventh Plenum's theses. The theses arrived in late January, before he did, and it appeared as though the CC responded positively to them.[27] Its resolution conceded that in the past the party had drawn too sharp a line between the national and the proletarian revolutions, and pledged henceforward to strive to go beyond the capitalist stage.[28] In fact, the theses irritated some on the CC. Peng Shuzhi, who had recently published an article arguing that 'China's revolution will move directly from a national revolution to a proletarian revolution', referring to this as 'continuous revolution' (*yongxu geming*), allegedly said that the theses differed little from current policy.[29] And at the Fifth CCP Congress in May 1927 Peng, Luo Yinong and others were said to have argued that it was the ECCI, not the CC, which in the past had made a rigid distinction between the national and socialist revolutions, in order to justify co-operation with the national bourgeoisie.[30] By contrast, Qu Qiubai, infuriated by what he took to be the complacency of the majority, championed the new ECCI line. In March he published a pamphlet which argued that the revolution was still in the bourgeois-democratic stage and that the agrarian revolution was the key to carrying it forward in a socialist direction. He criticised Peng (and implicitly Chen Duxiu) for assuming that the proletariat was already hegemonic in the national revolution, and for denying any role to the national bourgeoisie.[31] Thus, despite the somewhat extravagant self-criticism of the CC – its resolution stated that hitherto the party had 'obstinately clung to a logical error' – the response of the majority to the ECCI theses was probably lukewarm. And this seems to be borne out by its decision to remit them to branches for discussion, on the grounds that they 'will have a huge influence on the political fate of our party and we should not blindly accept them unless all comrades understand their full significance'.[32]

Conflict within the CCP was a pale shadow of the conflict that existed among the Russian advisers supposedly responsible for ensuring that the party stuck to the agreed line. In China the Comintern was in the unusual position of working with two parties, rather than with the one, since the GMD had affiliated to the Comintern as a 'sympathising' party in the spring of 1926. Correspondingly, there was a division of responsibility between Borodin, the Soviet government's aide to the GMD, and Voitinsky, chair of the FEB of the ECCI in Shanghai and principal aide to the CCP. Throughout 1926 policy was prey to disagreements between the two men. Basically, Voitinsky thought the 'bloc within' strategy misguided, but followed the Moscow line, in urging the CCP to work within the GMD but to ensure that it had an independent base in the masses.[33] Borodin, by contrast, was optimistic that the Communists could gain control of the GMD and spent much time politicking among the different factions of the GMD, NRA and Canton government. During the Northern Expedition he leaned towards a dual strategy of intensifying the peasant movement whilst seeking to gain control of the national government in Wuhan. He saw a split within the GMD as inevitable, but was bullish about the chances of defeating Chiang Kai-shek.[34] Voitinsky was more fearful of the strength of the right wing, and in February 1927 he quarrelled with Borodin for gratuitously antagonising Chiang.[35] Back in September 1926 Voitinsky and the FEB had called for the removal of Borodin, but the Politburo had turned down the request and made Borodin senior Soviet representative in China.[36] As if this were not enough, however, the FEB itself was terribly split, with M. G. Rafes, secretary of the FEB, and N. Fokin, representative of the Communist Youth International in China, convinced that Voitinsky was an 'opportunist' who was not up to the job.[37] A. Albrecht (a pseudonym of A. E. Abramovich), who was responsible for organisational work, wrote to I. A. Piatnitsky, secretary of the ECCI, on 25 February 1927, saying of Voitinsky, 'having no soul, he destroys everything that is vital. He runs around in small circles, bragging and intriguing.'[38] Voitinsky was accused of not allowing the FEB to discuss the political line, preferring to square things directly with Chen Duxiu, and of covering up the CC's errors.[39] Although the FEB tried hard to maintain a common front in its dealings with the CC, it is hardly surprising that the latter 'avoids as far as possible actually meeting with us'.[40]

Communist activity during the three armed uprisings

Just five days before the Communists seized control of Shanghai, in a letter of 17 March 1927, addressed to the ECCI, three representatives of the FEB, N. Nasonov, a participant in the seventh Plenum drafting commission, Albrecht and Fokin made a swingeing attack on the CC. They claimed that 'there is directing the party a group which resolutely pushes the party to the right in the direction of liquidationism, which is supported by Voitinsky'. They diagnosed this deviation as 'an inclination to brake the mass movement and deliver it to combinations at the top, going so far as trade-offs and compromises which in a revolutionary situation are tantamount to menshevism'.[41] They directed their strictures, in particular, at Luo Yinong, secretary of the SRC, Peng Shuzhi and, more guardedly, at Chen Duxiu. Their testimony has been taken by historians as different as Harold Isaacs and Jean Chesneaux as proof that the CC and SRC were indeed practising 'right opportunism', and that this was not just a charge trumped up post facto. If one examines the specific evidence adduced to support the charge, however, it begins to look specious. Lack of space dictates that the evidence can be examined only in the briefest terms.

1 The Shanghai Communists were accused of overestimating the revolutionary role of the bourgeoisie and of failing to appreciate the potential of the working class. Cai Hesen claimed that Luo Yinong 'believed fervently in the bourgeois character of the revolution'.[42] It is true that on 9 October in the run-up to the first armed uprising Luo told the SRC that the 'merchants should play the main part . . . the proletariat must avoid taking a leadership role, for if it is eager to lead the revolution, this will alarm the imperialists and cause them to attack or even massacre us.'[43] But this was also the position taken at this stage by the FEB.[44] And when the uprising aborted, Luo reversed this position. At a meeting of district party secretaries on 25 October, he said: 'We now know that the capitalists have no real force, so we will not again exaggerate this. In the next Shanghai movement we must resolutely affirm that only the working class can be the driving force, there is no one else.'[45] By the time of the third armed uprising, the aim of the SRC, as stated in its resolution of 17 March, was that the 'workers and revolutionary petty bourgeoisie should aim to seize power'.[46]

Chen Duxiu probably felt that the CCP should co-operate as far as possible with Niu Yongjian and the GMD, since execution of the armed uprisings behind the façade of the united front would maximise its popularity. Yet after the failure of the second uprising he accepted that the CCP could not be hamstrung by the demands of the GMD and should plan the next uprising alone.[47] He personally chaired thirty of the thirty-one sessions of the special committee set up to organise the uprising.[48]

2 The third uprising succeeded in defeating the northern warlord forces, but failed to establish a revolutionary democratic government. In a declaration of 11 April the CC stated that the stillbirth of the government had been due to 'lack of firm, perspicacious, class-conscious leadership' and, in particular, to a failure to appreciate that the large capitalists had already gone over to the counter-revolution.[49] Later, such self-criticism would be seized upon by ECCI as proof that the CC itself recognized its 'right opportunism'. Yet the evidence of the meetings of the SRC shows that they placed few hopes in the bourgeoisie.

The aim of the third armed uprising was to summon a citizens' assembly of 1,200, two-thirds of whom should be workers elected from their workplaces. This was to choose an executive which would function as the provisional municipal government. Niu Yongjian expressed total opposition to this scheme, and it is true that the SRC made some cosmetic changes concerning the composition of the executive, with a view to conciliating the GMD.[50] Secretly, however, it cleaved to its objective, as is evident from its resolution of 17 March: 'We hope that the Shanghai citizens representative assembly will become a soviet (*suweiai*) of the revolutionary people of Shanghai. The working class must form its main body, because without the workers as a backbone it cannot be the soviet of the national revolution.'[51] On 22 March an exultant meeting of the citizens' assembly elected an executive of nineteen, among whom were nine or ten Communists. In an effort to impose a united front character on this organ, various representatives of the GMD and the elite were elected in absentia. This provisional municipal government agreed to consider the demands put forward by the GLU on 16 March.[52] On 24 March the Wuhan government recognised the new government, but on the proviso that its members be selected by the GMD party organs from a list of twenty-two drawn up by the citizens' assembly. The Communists ignored this stipulation.[53] When the municipal government was formally inaugurated on 29 March, Chiang Kai-shek pronounced it 'contrary to the party system of government' and refused to support it. Six members, on whom the CCP relied to give it a pan-class character, immediately resigned.

Given that it had popular support, Harold Isaacs argued that the municipal government should have gone ahead and ruled in the interests of the masses.[54] However, it had neither money nor administrative apparatus to do so. Although the Wuhan government actually sent a commissar to claim revenue, it found the municipal government penniless.[55] More seriously, it had no force at its disposal comparable to that wielded by Chiang Kai-shek. Immediately the NRA entered the city, Niu Yongjian appointed the GMD rightist, Zou Jing, chief of police, and Chen Duxiu could only issue a written protest.[56] Soon Chiang Kai-shek reinstated police superintendents who had been ejected during the uprising.[57] On 8 April the fate of the government was sealed when Chiang banned the press from reporting its activities and appointed Wu Zhihui to head a new Provisional Political Committee of Shanghai.[58] It was lack of power, not bourgeois ideology or failure of political will, that wrecked the chances of the provisional government.

3 Isaacs also accused the GLU of 'doing its best to avoid "open" struggle. It tried to limit the strike movement and to keep the pickets within strict bounds.'[59] This charge is echoed by Chesneaux, who suggests the GLU was culpable in not recognising the seriousness of the threat facing the labour movement and in seeking to appease Chiang Kai-shek.[60] Pointing to the fact that the workers were armed, Isaacs argued: 'there appeared to be no serious obstacle to the swift expansion of the numbers and armaments of this force. The entire

working population, flushed with their recent victory, was ready to follow the orders of the GLU.'[61] Yet if we look at the activities of the leadership, whilst it certainly wavered, it prepared as best it could for a clash with Chiang. As early as 25 March a meeting of five hundred activists was told to ensure that the pickets resisted any assault by the GMD right. A plan was drawn up to offer all workers eight-hour training courses as pickets, and advanced training to one hundred leaders.[62] On 31 March came the famous telegram from the ECCI calling on the CC to prepare a campaign among the masses against the right, but not to unleash open struggle, and to hide or bury weapons rather than give them up.[63] On 6 April the SRC declared: 'There are many who advocate that the GLU should temporarily hide its arms. This is a suicidal policy . . . Of course we must not use our arms provocatively, but we cannot avoid clashes or bloodshed.' It resolved that the arming of workers should continue, that everything should be done to rally popular support, and that if Chiang tried to disarm the pickets, they should call a strike.[64] A declaration of the CC on 11 April said that a conflict with Chiang was inevitable and that only a decisive struggle led by the proletariat could liberate Shanghai from the 'new warlord' government, but it warned that an immediate frontal assault would lead to the destruction of the revolutionary forces. It called for propaganda in support of the GMD Central Executive Committee, a unified national government, a citizens' assembly and a strengthening of armed workers' defence. This was certainly a rather weak prescription, but it reflected the CC's powerlessness rather than any failure to appreciate the parlousness of its predicament.[65]

4 Later critics berated the CC for making no attempt to mobilize the NRA. According to Isaacs, 'there was no visible reason to suppose that the city workers would not make common cause with the Nationalist soldiers now in occupation'. He suggested that the majority of soldiers were sympathetic to the workers and that 'only a few' backed Chiang Kai-shek.[66] The first division, commanded by Xue Yue, was regarded as the most revolutionary, so it came as no surprise when Chiang Kai-shek announced that it would soon be sent out of the city. Immediately, on the evening of 23 March, the CCP began to agitate to have the first division stay and to encourage workers to volunteer to join it. The GLU continued the campaign over the next days.[67] On 28 March Chiang ordered the first division to move to Longhua, whereupon, it is alleged, Xue went to the Communists and offered to arrest him as a counter-revolutionary. Chen Duxiu and Voitinsky are said to have temporised, advising Xue to feign illness. It is on this incident that the case for the feasibility of an armed rebellion against Chiang rests. The most reliable source on the incident suggests that the left had 'overwhelming influence' among NRA divisions in Nanjing and Suzhou and that these would have come to the assistance of mutineers in Shanghai. But even if one discounts the time that it would have taken for these divisions to get to Shanghai, other evidence suggests that they may not have been as revolutionary as is claimed (why should Chiang send the unreliable first division to the supposedly revolutionary hotbed of Nanjing?).[68] Moreover, although there was

sympathy for the workers among the soldiers of the first (and second) division, it does not follow that given a fighting lead from the Communists, they would have rebelled against Chiang Kai-shek. Leaving aside the question of Xue Yue's own political reliability and his capacity actually to arrest Chiang, there is no evidence that large numbers of the rank and file mistrusted Chiang. At the end of March Major-General Sir John Duncan, commander of the British Shanghai Defence Force, received intelligence that three-quarters of the 12,000 NRA soldiers were loyal to their leader.[69] And even in the first and second divisions, where revolutionary sentiment ran high, there were few signs that this extended to deliberately disobeying orders. On the very day that Xue Yue professed undying loyalty to the labour unions, for example, the third unit of his first division, with the active co-operation of British forces, disarmed irregulars in Zhabei who had fought against the northern warlord forces.[70] Underpinning Isaacs's analysis are two doubtful premises. First, there is an inappropriate analogy between the NRA and the Russian army in 1917. In that year the Bolsheviks and Left Socialist Revolutionaries were able to win the support of soldiers because the army had suffered three years of defeat. By contrast, in the spring of 1927 the NRA was a victorious army in which the morale of the soldiers was high. It would not have been easy to persuade them that Chiang Kai-shek was a traitor to the revolution.[71] Second, Isaacs overlooks the nature of the NRA. Many units of the NRA differed little from those of the warlords, with officers bound to their commanders by ties of personal loyalty, and the ranks made up of impoverished peasant mercenaries. We cannot assume that there was an affinity based on common class interest between the soldiers and revolutionary workers.

5 Finally, the Communists are accused of sowing illusions in Chiang Kai-shek and of making unseemly compromises to keep in with him. The most notorious example of this is the joint statement made on 5 April by Chen Duxiu and Wang Jingwei, leader of the GMD left who had just returned to China. Reaffirming the necessity of the united front, this proclaimed that the GMD 'has demonstrated to the whole world that it does not have the slightest intention to expel the CCP . . . and suppress labour unions'.[72] The best complexion that can be put on the statement, which Chen later described as 'shameful', is that it was designed to play for time and to prevent Wang ganging up with the right. It may have confused workers, but it did not inhibit preparations that were under way against the perceived likelihood of a coup. On 1 April Luo Yinong told a meeting of district secretaries that they were working for the overthrow of Chiang and called on them to expand party membership to 18,000 within ten days.[73] Four days later, he told activists that: 'Chiang Kai-shek is the focus of all the reactionary forces . . . As soon as Nanjing has fallen [Chiang entered that city on 9 April], he will settle accounts with the CP.' [74]

None of this is intended to deny that the CC vacillated during these crucial days. But it was in the forlorn hope that a clash with Chiang Kai-shek could be averted, rather than in a belief that he could be drawn to a revolutionary position. Chiang, for his part, cleverly exploited the uncertainties of the CC by emitting conflicting signals. On 28 March he told Zhao Zijing of the GLU that he 'sincerely approved' the general strike in support of the NRA and disclaimed any intention to disarm the pickets. On 30 March he had a cordial meeting with Zhou Enlai, to whom he once again expressed his distrust of Borodin. And on 6 April he presented to the pickets a silk banner for their part in liberating the city from the warlord forces.[75]

If one reviews the record of the CC from November 1926 to April 1927, it is hardly one of far-sighted and vigorous leadership. Its conduct of the first and second armed uprisings was inept, and even after the triumph of the third uprising it showed a degree of indecisiveness and conciliation. Nevertheless, the general charge of 'right opportunism' does not hold water. Despite the criticisms that were made by the ECCI representatives in Shanghai, the regional committee of the CCP pursued a policy that was broadly in line with the one they recommended. If such labels have any meaning, it was a 'leftist' policy, designed to shift power in favour of the proletariat and urban petty bourgeoisie through a Soviet-style government. It showed no illusions in the progressive political role of the national bourgeoisie, orienting decisively towards the working class. Of course, the regional committee and the CC compromised: but never out of myopia or credulousness; only in the vain hope of delaying or preventing their own destruction. In particular, there is no evidence to substantiate the charge, made by both Stalinists and Trotskyists, that they undertook measures that actively weakened workers' defences in order to keep Chiang Kai-shek sweet. In an appallingly difficult situation they did their best to strengthen the pickets and to ensure that the most revolutionary divisions of the NRA stayed in Shanghai. If they failed, it was not for want of revolutionary will, but because the balance of forces was tipped hopelessly against them.

Conclusion

Was the Comintern to blame for the disaster of 12 April 1927? At the deepest level, there can be little doubt that China represents a shocking instance of interference and manipulation by the Comintern. After all, it was the policy of the united front, foisted on a reluctant CCP, which led ultimately to the slaughter. Moreover, it was the logic of the struggle between the United Opposition and the Stalin–Bukharin majority which prevented Moscow from changing its policy. Had the CCP withdrawn from the united front after the 20 March incident of 1926, when Chiang's political tendencies became evident to all but the most self-deceiving, it might have been spared the bloodshed that was to come. Yet if the basic course of CCP policy was determined by Moscow, Communists on the ground were by no means as constrained by the ECCI line as many have supposed. Communist practice in Shanghai was far from being a carbon copy of Comintern precept. The vigorous pursuit of armed insurrection (complemented by a Red Terror, which there has been no space to discuss) was not a policy to which either Borodin or Voitinsky gave vigorous backing. It did have the broad support of the FEB representatives in Shanghai, yet local leaders were not beholden to these tiros (Mandalian was 26 years old, Nasonov was 25, and Fokin was 28). Peng Shuzhi on the CC, Luo Yinong on the SRC and the GLU leaders, in particular, had been sceptical of the revolutionary proclivities of the national bourgeoisie long before the seventh Plenum made such a view acceptable. If their policy was a distortion of Comintern policy, it was in the direction of a left not a right deviation. And one could argue that in relying principally on the proletariat and their own forces, the Shanghai Communists were pursuing a policy little different from that which was belatedly advocated by the left opposition of the Russian Communist Party.

How were the CCP leaders able to pursue a relatively independent line, given the centralised, bureaucratic nature of the Comintern? First, as we have seen, the very highest levels of the Communist movement were at sixes and sevens. Even if the debates at the seventh Plenum suggest a serious effort to grapple with Chinese complexities, the outcome was one of political fudge. Second, ECCI and Politburo directives were calculatedly general and ambiguous, so that Moscow could claim credit for or repudiate CCP activity, according to outcome (what Isaacs called 'double-entry book-keeping').[76] Yet this also allowed the CCP considerable leeway in interpreting what it called the 'abstract' (*chouxiang*) character of ECCI directives.[77] Third, CCP leaders were able to create political space for themselves by taking advantage of the bitter divisions that existed among Comintern agents in China: between Voitinsky and Borodin and between Voitinsky and the FEB. Finally, with Moscow far away and so ill-informed, and finding themselves in a political situation that changed so fast, the CC and Shanghai regional committee were, willy-nilly, forced to rely on their own initiative and experience.

In conclusion, we cannot ascribe the failure of working-class revolution in Shanghai in April 1927 exclusively, or even mainly, to policy errors on the part of the Comintern. These undoubtedly aggravated the predicament of the CCP, but they did not create it. The brute reality was that a national revolution based on the workers and peasants, and capable of proceeding in a socialist direction, could not have succeeded in 1927 because the balance of military and political forces was so overwhelmingly skewed against it. If ECCI policy had been more flexible, the debacle of April 1927 might have been avoided, yet the absence of an army and the inability to control and defend territory would still have ruled out the kind of revolution favoured by Communists of virtually all stripes. This is not to fall into a bleak determinism – different policies could have helped produce a different outcome – but it is to insist that people do not make history in situations of their own choosing. In retrospect, what is most striking is not the extent of conflict within the Comintern and the CCP, but the failure of all parties to that conflict to appreciate just how overwhelmingly the odds were stacked against them.

Notes

1 *Shanghai zonggonghui baogao* (Shanghai, 1927), p. 13.

2 Xu Baofang and Bian Xingying (eds), *Shanghai gongren sanci wuzhuang qiyi yanjiu* (Shanghai, 1987), p. 53. (Hereafter *Sanci qiyi yanjiu.*)

3 *Sanci qiyi yanjiu*, p. 39; *Xiangdao*, 189 (28 February1927).

4 *Strikes and Lockouts in Shanghai since 1918* (Shanghai, 1933), p. 52. (Chinese language appendix).

5 Zhou Qisheng (ed.), *Shanghai gongren sanci wuzhuang qiyi* (Shanghai, 1987), p. 347. (Hereafter *Sanci qiyi.*); Zhou Shangwen and He Shiyou, *Shanghai gongren sanci wuzhuang qiyi shi* (Shanghai, 1987), p. 147.

6 D. A. Jordan, *The Northern Expedition: China's National Revolution of 1926–28* (Honolulu, 1976), p. 116.

7 Gui Xinqiu, 'Chen Duxiu he gongchan guoji zai guo-gong hezuo wenti shang de fenqi', *Shehui kexue zhanxian*, 3 (1991), 16–22.

8 L. Trotsky, 'The Chinese Communist Party and the Kuomintang', in Peng Shu-tse intro., Lee Evans and Russell Block (eds), *Leon Trotsky on China* (New York, 1979), p. 115.

9 *Zhonggong zhongyang wenjian xuanji*, vol. 2 (Beijing, 1989), pp. 561–68. (Hereafter ZGZYWJXJ).

10 On 17 October 1926 Voitinsky, chair of the Far Eastern Bureau of the ECCI in Shanghai, was pressured by the other members to send a telegram to the Politburo calling for a radicalization of tactics, to which the Politburo replied on 29 October: 'the intensification of struggle against the Chinese bourgeoisie and gentry in the present stage is premature and extremely dangerous'. VKP(b), *Komintern i natsional'no-revoliutsionnoe dvizhenie v Kitae. Dokumenty*, vol. 2, 1926–27 (Moscow, 1996), p.498.

11 Cai Hesen, 'Istoriia opportunizma v Kommunisticheskoi Partii Kitaia', *Problemy Kitaia*, I (1929),16. The Chinese original is in *Gongchan guoji yu Zhongguo geming ziliao xuanji, yijiuerwu nian-yijiuerqi nian* (Beijing, 1985), pp. 541–83.

12 *Puti mirovoi revoliutsii: sed'moi rasshirennyi Plenum ispolnitel'nogo komiteta Kommunisticheskogo Internatsionala, 22 noiabria–16 dekabria, 1926.* Stenograficheskii otchet (2 vols, Moscow, 1927), I, p. 106.

13 *Ibid.*, II, p. 356.

14 A. I. Kartunova, 'Kitaiskaia revoliutsiia: diskussii v Kominterne', *Voprosy istorii KPSS*, 6, (1989), 61.

15 If one compares the final theses with Stalin's speech to the drafting commission, they follow his directions almost to the letter. See J. V. Stalin, 'The Prospects of the Revolution in China', *Collected Works*, vol. 8, January–November 1926 (Moscow, 1954). The theses on the Chinese question are translated in R. C. North and X. J. Eudin, *M. N. Roy's Mission to China: The Communist-Kuomintang Split of 1927* (Berkeley, 1963), pp. 131–45.

16 Kartunova, 'Kitaiskaia revoliutsiia', 67.

17 *Ibid.*, 62–3, 67–8; *Kommunisticheskii Internatsional i kitaiskaia revoliutsiia: dokumenty i materialy* (Moscow, 1986), p. 94. (Hereafter *Kommunisticheskii Internatsional*).

18 Kartunova, 'Kitaiskaia revoliutsiia', 64.

19 ZGZYWJXJ, I, (Beijing, 1989), pp. 338–41.

20 *Kommunisticheskii Internatsional*, pp. 99–100.

21 *Puti mirovoi revoliutsii*, I, p. 404; Yang Yunruo and Yang Kuisong, *Gongchan guoji he Zhongguo geming* (Shanghai, 1988), p. 159.
22 *Kommunisticheskii Internatsional*, pp. 98–9.
23 Kartunova, 'Kitaiskaia revoliutsiia', 69. The CC's slowness to accept the policy was later cited as more evidence of its 'right opportunism'.
24 *Puti mirovoi revoliutsii*, I, p. 410. See too Jiang Hongying, 'Gongchan guoji guanyu Zhongguo dageming zhanlüe de genben shiwu', *Zhonggong dangshi yanjiu*, 6 (1989), 89.
25 Kartunova, 'Kitaiskaia revoliutsiia', 62; Stalin, 'Prospects', p. 379.
26 *Gongchan guoji he Zhongguo geming* (Wuhan, 1987), pp. 129–30.
27 Voitinsky said on 21 January that he only just received the resolution of the seventh Plenum and that it was being translated into Chinese. VKP(b), *Komintern*, II, p. 606.
28 ZGZYWJXJ, III, (Beijing, 1989), pp. 19–23.
29 *Xiangdao*, 184 (21 January 1927), 1951; Cai Hesen, 'Istoriia opportunizma',16.
30 Cai Hesen, 'Istoriia opportunizma', 17; T. Mandalian, 'Pourquoi la direction du PC de China n'a-t-elle pas rempli sa tâche?' in Pierre Broué (ed.), *La Question chinoise dans l'Internationale communiste (1926–27)* (Paris, 1965), p. 281.
31 Qu Qiubai, *Zhongguo geming zhuyi zhi zhenglun wenti* (Wuhan, 1927).
32 ZGZYWJXJ, III, pp. 19–23; Huang Xiurong, *Gongchan guoji yu Zhongguo geming guanxi shi* (2 vols, Beijing, 1989), I, p. 314.
33 VKP(b), *Komintern*, II, p. 188.
34 ZGZYWJXJ, II, pp. 422–30, 559, 571–7; H. J. van de Ven, *From Friend to Comrade: The Founding of the Chinese Communist Party, 1920–1927* (Berkeley, 1991), pp. 202–13; *Gongchan guoji he Zhongguo geming*, p. 120; Yang Xiaoren, 'Shankhaiskie sobytiia vesnoi 1927g.', *Materialy po kitaiskomu voprosu*, 13 (1928), 11–12.
35 Chang Kuo-t'ao, *The Rise of the Chinese Communist Party, 1921–27: Volume One of the Autobiography of Chang Kuo-t'ao* (Lawrence, Kans., 1971), pp. 567–8.
36 VKPb, *Komintern*, II, pp. 439, 484.
37 *Ibid.*, p. 138.
38 *Ibid.*, p. 629.
39 *Ibid.*, p. 558.
40 *Ibid.*, p. 627.
41 'Lettre de Shanghai', in Broué, *La Question chinoise*, p. 53.
42 Cai Hesen, 'Istoriia opportunizma', 14.
43 *Sanci qiyi*, p. 6.
44 VKPb, *Komintern*, II, p. 477.
45 *Ibid.*, p. 48.
46 *Ibid.*, p. 326.
47 Ren Jianshu, 'Chen Duxiu yu Shanghai gongren sanci wuzhuang qiyi', *Dangshi ziliao*, 1982, 4 (13), p. 71.
48 *Sanci qiyi yanjiu*, p. 49.
49 ZGZYWJXJ, III, p. 36.
50 Zhou Shangwen and He Shiyou, *Shanghai gongren*, pp. 98, 193.
51 *Sanci qiyi*, p. 326.
52 *Shenbao*, 23 March 1927, p. 9; *Sanci qiyi yanjiu*, p. 75.
53 *Sanci qiyi yanjiu*, p. 75.
54 H. Isaacs, *The Tragedy of the Chinese Revolution* (Stanford, Ca.1961 [orig.1938]), p. 167.

55 Yang Xiaoren, 'Shankhaiskie sobytiia', p. 20.
56 Zhou Shangwen and He Shiyou, *Shanghai gongren*, p. 245.
57 *Ibid.*, p. 246; Yang Xiaoren, 'Shankhaiskie sobytiia', p. 16.
58 Tien-wei Wu, 'Chiang Kai-shek's April 12 Coup in 1927', in F. G. Chan and T. H. Etzold (eds), *China in the 1920s* (New York, 1976), p. 155.
59 Isaacs, *Tragedy*, p. 168.
60 J. Chesneaux, *The Chinese Labor Movement 1919–1927* (Stanford, CA,1968), pp. 368–9.
61 Isaacs, *Tragedy*, p. 146.
62 Zhou Shangwen and He Shiyou, *Shanghai gongren*, p. 263.
63 VKPb, *Komintern*, II, p. 658.
64 *Sanci qiyi*, p. 449; *Sanci qiyi yanjiu*, p. 99.
65 ZGZYWJXJ, III, pp. 35–8.
66 Isaacs, *Tragedy*, p. 168,
67 *Sanci qiyi yanjiu*, p. 89.
68 Yang Xiaoren, 'Shankhaiskie sobytiia', 20. Pavel Mif's account is confused, since he mistakes the 26th corps for the first and second divisions. P. Mif, *Kitaiskaia revoliutsiia* (Moscow, 1932), p. 99.
69 N. R. Clifford, *Spoilt Children of Empire: Westerners, Shanghai and the Chinese Revolution* (Hanover, NH, 1991), p. 246.
70 *Shenbao*, 27 March 1927, p. 11.
71 C. Brandt, *Stalin's Failure in China, 1924–27* (Cambridge, Mass., 1958), p. 159.
72 Warren Kuo, *Analytical History of the Chinese Communist Party*, I (Taibei, 1966), pp. 424–46.
73 *Sanci qiyi yanjiu*, p. 228.
74 *Sanci qiyi*, pp. 445–6.
75 Zhou Shangwen and He Shiyou, *Shanghai gongren*, p. 250.
76 Isaacs, *Tragedy*, p. 117.
77 ZGZYWJXJ, III, p. 19.

17

Peasants and the Peoples of the East: Indians and the rhetoric of the Comintern

Wendy Singer

The most revolutionary politics in India in the 1930s grew out of Indian peasant movements to which are owed the achievement of some degree of land redistribution and the abolition of most of the excesses of the landlordism soon after independence. Their success stemmed in many ways from the masterful and effective uses of revolutionary, in fact Communist, rhetoric. To the British government of India and also to the mainstream nationalists in India, the control or suppression of peasant uprising presented a major political challenge and the perception that peasant activists were part of an international Communist movement amplified their threat. When protestors sang:

Dekh kaise dhandeli	Look at the state of the world
Hai muti, ye char su	all around us
Chuste hai amir	The rich suck
up garib kar lahool [1]	the blood of the poor

they echoed the rhetoric of communism and evoked its symbols. In fact, the second verse of this marching song from 1930s protests celebrates the colour red, which is not only an image of communism, but an auspicious colour in Indian culture as well:

Lal inqilab se	From the red revolution
Ho gya jahan ilaqa	So is this whole place –
zamin asman lal	the land and the sky – red.
Dekh lal aft ab?	See the red sunrise?
utar nisan inqalab	Join the call of Revolution.

However, while the peasant movement intentionally had not capitalised on Communist rhetoric, the Communist Party of India (CPI) and the Comintern in the very same period failed to embrace the growing agrarian movement.[2] This chapter argues that Indian Communists floundered in the 1920s and 1930s because both external pressures from the Comintern and internal disputes derailed them from agrarian politics. Yet ironically, the writings of Communists and Communist ideology prevailed as central to peasant activists and to the overall image of peasant movements.

This chapter is part of a larger study of Indians in the Comintern. It argues that because Communists in India and outside defined too narrowly who were their comrades, they weakened the position of CPI *vis-à-vis* India's agrarian politics. This was true until 1942, when other events propelled the CPI to prominence. It is ironic that at the time that the Comintern was waning internationally, international communism finally came to its own in India.

But my primary concern is with the failings of the Comintern in India in the 1920s and 1930s. Using agrarian policy as a lens through which to study the relationship between the Comintern and Indian Communists reveals not only key weaknesses in the Communist movement but also missed opportunities for organising rebellion, if not revolution.

This is a new approach benefiting from materials I recently examined in Moscow and also a re-examination of other published materials from a point of view that focuses on agrarian issues.[3] Most scholarship on Indian communism and the Comintern dwells on the role of key figures in Indian communism, such as M. N. Roy, or on the ways in which Comintern misunderstood Indians. Both of these are valuable and valid approaches.[4]

Nevertheless, records in Moscow allow reinterpretation of the history of Indian communism because, first, correspondence that has long been lost in India due to repression of the CPI is available in Moscow and, second, Comintern documents show that there were some representatives abroad with considerable knowledge about agrarian relations and even agrarian politics in India.

This evidence shows that vacillations in Comintern policy on Indian peasants reflected similar confusion among Indian Communists and both contributed to misinterpretations of growing grassroots movements in India. As a result, while peasant organisations in India were marching forward, Communists in India failed to get into step. In 1928 when the Comintern was dismissing Roy for exaggerating the strength of Communists, everyone – even Roy – was underestimating the extent to which Communist ideology and propaganda were already filtering into grassroots politics. Therefore, this chapter explores ironies of misunderstanding.

These ironies of misunderstanding exacerbated the complex vacillation in Communist attitudes toward the growing peasant movement. I will follow this argument through several steps by focusing on the process of 'Defining Indian Communists' from four different perspectives. The first, which is called 'Which Indian parties were allies?', provides some examples of the Comintern's search for revolutionary movements in India, although repeatedly they fell back on the Indian National Congress (INC). The second, 'Supportive agents or outside infiltrators', describes the process of communication between Indian Communists and the Comintern and its implications on the movement. The third, 'The Comintern as mediator', shows the Comintern in Moscow as a potential source for mediating – and perhaps creating – disputes among other Communists who came to India. It focuses on juicy correspondence about an American agent who alienated a variety of Indian party activists. And finally, the fourth, 'Advice from the colonies', illustrates the double meaning of the word 'colonies' as it applied to Indians in the Comintern. Indian Communists sought the Comintern connection as an alternative to British colonialism, but their relationship to the Comintern and to the Communist Party of Great Britain (CPGB) in many ways undermined that effort.

Defining Indian Communists, 1928–32

The shifting definition of Indian Communists from 1928 to 1932 reflects events both inside the Comintern and among the Indian left. The Executive Committee of the Communist International (ECCI), the Eastern Commission and the Indian Commission of the Comintern, and the CPGB, which had several subgroups interested in India, all attempted to define and, therefore, shape Indian Communists and Indian communism. In a sense, the debates within the Comintern over whether or not to support the INC – the importance of which became palpable after the China affair – derailed Communists in India and outside from the opportunity presented by peasant organisers who (though they did not necessarily adopt the name Communist) were already sympathetic to their ideology.

Disagreements in the Comintern over who were Communists also illustrates British repression of Indian revolutionaries and the consequent disruption in communication, which has also limited the resources available for historical analysis. G. Adhikari, a scholar and member of the CPI who has expertly edited a critical collection of Communist papers, expressed his frustration with the amount of material lost through repression.

> As the party has been for the best part of its over 40 years of existence a target of repression, its offices, leaders and workers have been subject to searches, raids, confiscations, and arrests, it has not been able to preserve a continuous record of its activities and development, either at the central – all-India – or the state or provincial level.[5]

That same repression also limited and complicated forms of communication in the late 1920s. All correspondence had to be produced in code and sent by messenger to its destination. A reply required another courier. And meetings had to remain secret with constant vigilance for government infiltrators – an obvious obstacle to party growth.

With the senior, and often most talented, leaders arrested in the Meerut Conspiracy Case in 1929, the organisation of the party devolved to more junior, inexperienced comrades. Madhu Limaye, a key long-time Socialist, in his sophisticated and well-researched history of the relationship between Indian

Communists and Socialists, suggests that this new leadership was also more sectarian – closely aligned with the directions of the CPGB and ECCI of the Comintern. This was in part the case because Communists needed external support to survive government repression.

The link to the international Communist movement potentially provided Indian Communists with a needed source of funds, revitalisation after the decimation of party ranks in the Meerut case, and legitimacy. Indian Communists cultivated that connection in three ways: first, they regularly sent reports to the Indian Commission (whether or not they received recognition for them) to underscore the organised hierarchy of which they were a part; second, they sent agents to Europe and welcomed or (at least acknowledged) agents of the Comintern in India; and, third, they used the Comintern as a mediating force in local disputes.

However, in each instance it remains clear that there was no common voice among Indians. Rather, some Indian Communists argued against Comintern theses, complained about insufficient support from Moscow, roundly criticised agents of the Communist International whom they considered inept, and disregarded some Comintern policies altogether. Often, they corresponded with the Comintern as individuals rather than as an affiliated party. Others, as Limaye suggests 'showed the greatest deference to the Comintern and its CPGB deputies'.[6]

To the Comintern, therefore, Indian Communists appeared disorganised, divisive, and dependent on international intervention. Periodically, even from 1928 to 1932, members of the ECCI called for the formation of an Indian Communist Party – six to ten years after the founding of the CPI. For example, Molotov, writing in 1930, called Indian Communists 'primitive and sporadic'.[7] To see the origins of this impression, one can look at reports from Indians themselves:

> What is lacking in India is a Communist party. India has no party in any sense and what has been made known or spoken of till now were mere bluffs of interested parties. Not only is there no party in India but the present Communist movements is heavily encumbered with police agents and adventurers. Undoubtedly there are good elements but their number are few and rare. The first task should be to clean the movement of doubtful elements.[8]

Cleaning the movement in India required redefining who were Communists. It would be too simple to suggest – as some contemporary scholarship has done – that the Comintern served only as a force of Soviet foreign policy and only Indian revolutionaries who fitted the Stalinist line were considered 'Communists'.[9] Rather, a variety of factors influenced the defining of who were 'real Communists'. Comintern records, for example, show that the Communist International badly needed a colonial and Asian victory. With China seeming a remarkable policy failure, India was a potential success.

Also, the 'suggestions' above came from India, in a telegram through Berlin.

In fact, Berlin was a major clearing house for Indian Communists who sought refuge among the large expatriate community there. Berlin provided an independent site for dialogue between Indians and the Comintern. The 'suggestions' cited here represent one mode through which Indian Communists and the Indian Commission of the Comintern through expedient means were trying to gauge not only the ideological purity of Indian Communists, but also which Indian revolutionaries would win.[10] To do this they evaluated the parties and organisations forming in India, including the Workers' and Peasants' Party (WPP), the INC, the Kirti Kisan Party and the Nawjavan Bharat Sabha.

Which Indian parties were allies?

By analysing peasant interests in the form of reports to the Comintern, Indian Communists competed for legitimacy in this international arena. The contents of the reports represent a continuation of the debate about the condition of Indian peasants and their potential for rebellion, showing differences of opinion that persisted among Indian leftists. One report entitled 'Some Suggestions for the Indian Commission' countered published accounts that were produced in Moscow. Written about 1930, it concurred that peasants

> which form the bulk of the nation are notoriously in a condition of great poverty and backwardness. The land of the country from which the peasants derive their living is in the hands of three main agencies, the landlord, including state rulers, the government, and religious institutions all of which demand their quota from the cultivators. All suffer from gradually increasing demands of the Government for direct taxes as well as from indirect taxation, e.g. salt and other imported goods

Then the writer continues with a vision of peasant mobilisation that was much more pessimistic than Roy's had been a few years earlier (and hence closer to the Comintern line):

> Peasants have taken hitherto little part in politics. At the height of the non-cooperation Movement, the peasants joined in large numbers, but on the abandonment of the policy of non-payment of taxes out of regard for the interests of the landlord class, which at any rate in its lower strata was strong in the Congress, they left again. Many peasant societies were then in existence, especially in UP [Uttar Pradesh] but if radical they were ruthlessly suppressed and those now in existence are small and under moderate guidance.[11]

Yet, despite this pessimism, the author comes to a conclusion similar to Roy's that the Congress was not working in the interests of peasants and that 'the future of the country, its economic development, education, culture and the well-being of the masses depend upon the rapid development of this mass movement of the exploited millions united and guided by the Workers' and Peasants' Party'.[12] This was particularly significant because an official Comintern document published in 1928 ordered the WPP be disbanded. The workers' and peasants' parties were under attack from Indian Communists who opposed Roy, as well as from Comintern representatives who wanted greater connections with the INC. But a main force arguing against the WPP was the CPGB. As reflected in the suggestions submitted by the CPGB:

> Action of All-Empire Communist Party and Comintern should be: Liquidation of all present 'workers' and peasant parties'. Such mixing up of classes is not luministic, it had its value in 1923, but that stage is passed. Such mixing of classes inevitably subjugates the movement to Nationalist opportunists and adventurers. The workers should have one party and this is the CP. Just now the legal appearance of the Communist Party is possible it may not last another two years but as long as such is possible this must be utilised to its fullest extent.[13]

This report from a group within the CPGB roundly criticised the Workers and Peasants Party tactics that Roy had initiated in 1928. The WPPs were legal parties – established at a time when the British government of India was arresting anyone remotely connected to communism on charges of an international conspiracy. In fact, the WPP tactic had not succeeded very well; they had very small membership. Nevertheless, calls to disband the WPP came largely from the CPGB – including from its Indian members. The ECCI capitulated and ordered them to be disbanded. However, the directive from the ECCI had no effect: the WPPs continued in their limited way for years afterwards and the CPI worked with them.[14]

While the All-Empire Communist Party focused its attention on the potential – or lack of potential – of the WPP, another report addressed two parties in the northwest of India, namely the Kirti Kisan Party and the Nawjavan Bharat Sabha. Its author, 'Comrade from Peshwar', one of the muhajirs who had formed the CPI in Tashkent in 1920, argued that Kirti Kisan (literally, the agrarian peasant party) and Nawjavan (New Soldiers of India organisation) more accurately reflected the interests of Indian masses than did the bourgeois INC. This position contradicted the proposition of the Fifth Congress of the Communist International which called for Indian Communists to work within the INC:

> Masses are not taking a good interest toward Congress Movement. In Punjab for example ... peasants are not taking part in it at all. In frontier provinces very little. The Congress has started this movement in order to suppress the rising revolutionary movement of the workers and peasants. But the masses are also more or less aware now.[15]

The author, a comrade from Peshwar, therefore, concurred with Roy's thesis, and this in 1930 after Roy had been expelled from the Comintern. He also complained that other Communists 'lost credibility among peasant groups' because they advocated joining the Congress Programme. In other words, the comrade from Peshwar constructed his argument against Congress based on his own abilities to gauge the revolutionary capacity of the masses.

What he wanted from the Comintern was continued support for his efforts in the northwest frontier, a part of what is now Pakistan. He knew that other groups in the area were also vying for Comintern support and pleaded his case based on his better understanding of what peasant activists would do. He wanted to reopen an overland route from India to Moscow in order to send students for training, and considered the Kirti Kisan Party and the Nawjavan Bharat Sabha as sources for identifying young revolutionaries. He also wanted financial support from the Comintern to bring these parties into the Communist fold, as he said 'before they side with Congress'.[16]

The comrade in Peshwar wanted to define Indian communism as an alternative to the INC. His position, which was outside the published directives of the Comintern, also suggested that Communists in India could rival Congress with sufficient support from abroad.

Supportive agents or outside infiltrators?

The travel of Communists and revolutionaries back and forth to Europe (and America) provided necessary contact for Indian revolutionaries. But it also complicated the process of defining who were Communists in India and what direction the movement should take. The traffic, moving in different directions, followed a variety of routes. Just as the comrade in Peshwar wanted to send more Indians for training through overland routes to Moscow, other CPI workers in Bombay and Madras used ships and the cover of the seamen's union to send students to Europe. One proposal recommended a systematic selection of ten to fifteen students from each province to study abroad.[17]

In addition, the Comintern sent representatives to India to 'help' in party work and organisation. With or without their explicit direction, many came from the CPGB. Also, rivals of Roy sent agents to check up on Roy and on the expansion of the movement in India. One of them, writing from France in 1932, expressed frustration that so many seamen were still Royists, even though Roy had been expelled from the Comintern in 1929.

Despite the fact that Communist visitors in India came with agendas of their own, which often conflicted with the work of the CPI, travellers to and from Europe provided an essential lifeline. They served as couriers of information, funds and publications. For example, the process of international communication is intricately portrayed in the form and content of letters from Indian Communists – 'Rebel Against Sabotage' and Misra – who worked in Bombay and Madras. The letters themselves, of course, are one form of international contact; they reached Comrade Mazooth, an Indian working for the Comintern in Moscow, by the hand of an agent who, the Rebel said, 'will explain in detail his personal experiences with our Bombay people'. So both the letter and the agent provided the message. Within the first letter, marked March 1932, the Rebel also referred to a couple who were sent to Moscow to bear witness to the work going on in the Bombay CPI. Furthermore, the Rebel's narrative itself described his own international journey carrying the messages of communism to various ports:

> I left you on 8 December 1930 though the decision was taken even a week or two before. But your technical department instead of helping me and making the task easy, they monkeyed around and let me out a day too late. The result of this was I had to miss the steamer which I ought to have taken and I have to waste money all the time (one full month). For a week or ten days I was detained in Berlin. But after quarrelling I got free from them because I was freezing to death for I had no warm clothes.[18]

In this way the Rebel began with a complaint about the department that sponsored his trip. Throughout the journey, he criticised the lack of support – financial and otherwise – that he received from official Communist sources. In each situation he survived because of the goodwill of local activists: people he already knew:

> The very morning I arrived at Bombay I got contact with the Dr and of course I waited for some more contact and almost from morning six o'clock to twelve at night I was wandering on foot for shelter, for I thought that our people who had established there for so many years would get shelter for me in some safe place. But my hope was in vain. At last I had to get into a certain unsafe damn hotel and after some days I again had to trace my old friend Misra and of course he welcomed me as ever before and meantime arranged through Dr to meet the secretariat to give the report in connection with the decision of RILU [Red International of Labour Unions (Profintern)] congress and other suggestions and advice given by you and my future plan to settle in South India as we decided at the centre.[19]

The Rebel's disappointment lay in what he described as the failure of the Comintern to provide him with sure contacts, safe houses and support wherever the CPI sent him. But he still had faith in the power of the centre, here represented by Comrade Mazooth, to whom the letter was addressed. His aim in writing was to exploit the connection with Mazooth in order to reveal these failings in the larger political organisation.

The Comintern as mediator

The main thrust of the Rebel's letter was a complaint about an American who caused dissension within the party in Bombay. The American, alternately referred to as 'man from across the sea', or 'our foreign comrade' or the representative of the Communist International, was trying to identify which members of the local Bombay group were working effectively and which were squandering funds.[20] But, from the Rebel's point of view, he closed off all communication among party workers, limiting the scope of party work:

> Here a comrade who is supposed to be the representative of the C. I. [Communist International] who should force them to go to other industrial centres to organise and develop the work did the contrary. Even when they raised some topic about us he always told them that there was nothing to do with us or to write to us.[20]

But the bad experience did not turn Rebel away from the international movement. His plan was to enlist support in Moscow, put all the 'facts' before the Comintern, and seek a resolution to the problem:

> At last after deep thinking and also by discussing with a few confidential comrades here, we felt that it was our bounded duty to put before the Comintern all the mischief and objectively anti-revolutionary [actions] of our American friend and our people and let you decide for yourself.[22]

In as much as the tone of the Rebel's letter was plaintive or even whining, it revealed a major weakness among some members of the CPI. Being caught up in their roles as followers in a large bureaucratic organisation suppressed their initiative. Modifying many scholars' claims that Indian CPI activists more directly addressed real political issues in India, the experience of this rebel and others shows that in the late 1920s the CPI was weakened by internal wrangling. Also, it relied on an urban base in unions in Bombay and Madras. This left the issue of peasant mobilisation to other Indian parties, but also – at a theoretical level – to the observers and researchers of the Communist International. The draft thesis on the agrarian question was a good example of this.

For the Rebel, the question still was his place in an international movement. With this in mind, he described his attempts towards accommodation with that movement, even with the 'mischief-maker' whom he compared to Mussolini.[23]

> The very same people who sabotaged us and our work here now after the departure of the Communist Mussolini who wanted to establish his absolutism began to change in their attitude and the very letters written and sent to me as personal confessions and flattering me (which I have herewith enclosed) and with the help of the present comrade you will be able to know clearly and distinctly all the guilty acts.Why should these people who kept their mouths shut all these days should write to me suddenly. This shows in what check the 'unknown friend' kept them in relation with us.[23]

The Rebel portrayed the extent of the damage from the foreign agent in terms of squandered funds, time wasted, and the danger of exposing fellow comrades. These were charges that the Comintern would take seriously:

> After his leaving the shores of Bombay finally the Sector decided and sanctioned the money for the passage to the Madras Comrade but still the RILU man probably being instigated and poisoned by the 'foreign Comrade' made some more delay and wasted his time.
>
> Not only did he prepare for his deportation by his foolishness and untactful movements but he also exposed the RILU to the police and as the result of his foolishness the RILU watched strictly which may result in their deportation in the near future. So you can imagine what an enormous money and time is wasted on account of this comrade who instead of accelerating the progress only did the harm and obstruction to the useful work. And also made it much more difficult for any other comrade to come and settle to work in Bombay and perhaps in the whole of India.[25]

Finally, Rebel gave his conclusion: 'Therefore I am of opinion that this American comrade should be handed over to the control commission to take disciplinary measures against him. If necessary you can get more material from Bombay in connection with him.'[26]

More material did come from Ranadive, the leader of the CPI, and Misra concurring with the Rebel's position. Misra went on to request that Mazooth himself come to India to evaluate the situation. Mazooth was acceptable because he was Indian. As the Rebel put it:

> you know that the organisation was in India and the educating of workers and peasants in India only Indians can do. Even if the Comintern sends out five hundred people it will not help anything to India except to steamship companies, Railway companies and hotels and so forth.[27]

The Rebel's message was to rely on Indian skills and Indian contacts like himself: 'Unless there is someone here through whom these comrades can work, it is in vain.'[28]

These examples demonstrate that relations between Indian Communist activists and the Comintern involved a complex mixture of accommodation and competition, support and rivalry. And these were achieved in heavily mediated communication that required safe couriers and translators and, since much of this took place in code, decipherers. Many Indian Communists – the comrade from Peshwar among them – saw themselves as strong partners in the relationship. They expected support from Moscow and to be able to direct the proposals of the Comintern as they applied to India. Yet their tendency to speak out individually encouraged the impression that the CPI was disunited and disorganised.

Comintern agents and CPGB representatives who visited India confirmed that impression, in part by exacerbating the divisions that existed. As a result, the assertiveness of individual Indian Communists seeking Comintern counsel fulfilled the prophetic impression that they were a haphazard bunch.

This issue of impressions dovetails with the debate in Indian scholarship as discussed in Limaye's *Socialist-Communist Interaction* over the Soviet domination of Communist politics in India.[29] A central question has been whether or not Comintern policy was merely an extension of Soviet foreign policy crafted by Stalin. Palme Dutt's *India Today*, which compared India's experience under British imperialism unfavourably to Central Asia's experience under the Soviet Union, provides an example of the intertwining of those issues.[30] Of course, Soviet foreign policy was influential to Comintern propositions. However, the independence, which Indian Communists intermittently displayed, mitigated that tendency.

Advice from the colonies

The Communists in Bombay sent explicit instructions and copious suggestions to the Comintern about how revolutionary actions should develop in India. Not only did they ignore some Comintern dictates, such as the abolition of the Workers' and Peasants' Party, but they also described what they thought should be the ideal structure for the Indian Communist movement:

> 1 I propose that in each province if not in each chief industrial city, at least ten to fifteen students should be sent to be trained
> 2 Their method of sending and technical arrangement and so forth have to be made in Madras
> 3 If any foreign comrades want any longer to settle in India they should take the place in Madras Presidency and settle here because this is the only safety place
> 4 That we should have our illegal press in which our central organ of the party should be printed illegally this also I think should be done in Madras because here we have our own comrades to compose, print etc. and this will save a good lot of money which now goes to the Bourgeois press.
> 5 Also that these Bombay comrades should be compelled to send developed comrades from Bombay as many as possible to various other industrial centres in India to create party groups and link them up illegally to the whole India organisation and in case if no one is competent I myself take charge of this task to move around all over India stopping for ten or fifteen days in each centre to create party group and connect them up with each other for united action, if I can get necessary means for travelling.[31]

This view reveals a south Indian and industrial bias. It does not dismiss the Communist International, but rather shows it as a source for education and support.

However, another Indian Communist suggested to the Indian Commission that:

> a thorough propaganda should be entered up in Indian language. I know that comrades responsible in Comintern for Indian work just now are against such notions. Certain comrades in the Lenin Course have openly denounced such as unnecessary and claim that this be the opinion of the 'leaders' here in Moscow. I strongly denounce all such actions as REACTIONARY and against the interest of the Indian Proletariat and the Indian Revolution. These comrades should from necessary be fought ruthlessly. Indian Agitation and Propaganda has to be organised in four Indian vernaculars, to begin with Urdu and Gujarati. It must necessarily be conducted in Bengali; Tamil, and Gurmukhi. In the last language there is given a journal 'KIRTI' published by the members of the Hindustan Gadar party, the revolutionary peasants organisation of the Punjab and Sikh emigrants in America.[32]

The plea for vernacular publications underscored an acceptance of the capacity of Indians, beyond the intellectual English-educated classes, to join and participate in the Communist movement. These suggestions also show that links to peasant organisations were fundamental to Indian Communists.

What these various communications with Moscow illustrate is that Indian

Communists were taking charge of their movement even when they could not agree among themselves on how the movement should be run. Clearly, there were Communists in India who focused their efforts on labour unions rather than the peasantry, but agrarian movements provided an enormous opportunity to generate mass support. Nevertheless, Indian Communists did not represent a well-organised and well-disciplined party. In fact, their correspondence emphasises their disunity.

Conclusion

Correspondence between India and the Comintern from 1928 to 1932 shows that misunderstandings and disagreements did not stem from lack of communication. Not only was the Comintern informed about what was going on in India and able to produce some insightful reports, but perhaps it knew too much. Nevertheless, communication did not fit the often touted vertical/hierarchical model of directives sent from Moscow to obedient India followers. Furthermore, when Indian Communists were arrested in 1928 as part of the Meerut Conspiracy Case, many of the most talented leaders, with the closest connections to Moscow, were taken away from the movement. What remained were groups of competing activists and organisations vying for legitimacy from both the Comintern and from Indian constituents.

Practices adopted by Indian Communists that constituted a CPI culture contributed to the image fostered in the Comintern that Indian Communists needed to be managed and organised. For example, the stress on underground activity – encouraged by the repression of the British government of India – hindered the fledgling CPI. The mystique of aliases and safe houses that 'Rebel Against Sabotage' embodied, while necessary at some level, also became an ingrained and exciting part of Communist culture. So while Indian Communists were divided by ideology, language and region, the nature of Communist culture and the CPI's use of the Comintern as mediator, exacerbated its appearance as a weak organisation.

The Comintern, of course, was also not monolithic. The ECCI did reflect the reports of the Eastern Commission and the Indian Commission, but those reports and conclusions often represented compromises of very divergent opinions. And the CPGB did not always act in accordance with those recommendations as far as their contact with Indians was concerned.

Therefore, in large part these conflicting ideas about communism in India weakened Indian Communists *vis-à-vis* the growing peasant movement. The multiple voices of Indian Communists on all political issues, but especially on peasants, contributed to the conflict rather than dispelling it.

While Communist rhetoric – and the extent and distribution of the work of Palme Dutt illustrates this best – played a prominent role among peasant organisers in India, peasants were largely ignored by the official CPI. Rather than dismissing all of the Comintern as agents of the Soviet Union or of being blinded by an imperialist CPGB, records of the Communist International show, at times, a remarkable sensitivity to the issues of Indian peasants. But in the critical period beginning in 1930 when peasant organisations were poised for political power, that sensitivity did not translate into action.

Notes

1 Kulanand Vaidik, 'Inqilab', Oral Narrative, Darbhanga, March 1984. Song from the peasant movement in Bihar. Vaidik described it as a marching song used in rallies.

2 Not until 1940 did the local Communists displace the Congress socialists as leaders of the peasant movement and then it happened largely because the socialists were in jail for opposing Indian participation as troops of the empire during World War II. The CPI on the other hand supported the war in which the British and the Soviets were allies.

3 In 1996, due to the important efforts of Purobi Roy and Sobhanlal Datta Gupta, copies of some records from the Russian Centre for the Study and Preservation of Contemporary Historical Documents (RC) have now been brought to the Asiatic Society of Bengal in Calcutta. This will permit wider examination by Indian scholars and further advance our understanding of the role of the Comintern in the Indian Communist movement.

4 For the most comprehensive study of M. N. Roy see Samaren Roy, *The Twice-Born Heretic: M. N. Roy and the Comintern* (Calcutta, 1986).

5 G. Adhikari, 'Preface', in *Documents of the History of the Communist Party of India: Volume One* (Delhi, 1991), p. viii.

6 Madhu Limaye, *Socialist Communist Interaction in India* (New Delhi, 1991), p. 17. He describes the relationship as 'increasingly submissive, with free discussion and dissent being equated to treason'. This is partially true, but as the following report from 'Rebel Against Sabotage' shows, dissent continued.

7 Letter from Stalin to Molotov and Bukharin, 9 July 1927, as quoted in L. T. Lih, O. V. Naumov and O. V. Khlevniuk (eds), *Stalin's Letters to Molotov* (New Haven, Conn., 1995), p. 141.

8 RC 495/42/5, 'Concrete suggestions as to the Communist's immediate task in India', signature illegible, 1928.

9 Sobhanlal Dutta Gupta made this point in 1980, referring to simplistic interpretations of the relationship between Indian Communists and the nationalist movement. Nevertheless, recent scholarship has continued in that trend. See Gupta, *Comintern, India, and the Colonial Question* (Calcutta, 1980), p. 3.

10 Shashi Joshi, *Struggle for Hegemony in India Vol 1: The Colonial State, the Left and the Nationalist Movement* (New Delhi,1994), introduction.

11 RC 495/42/5, 'Some Suggestions for the Indian Commission', 1930.

12 *Ibid.*

13 RC 495/42/5, All-Empire Communist Party of Communist Party of Great Britain.

14 In fact, several members of the CPGB in India worked with the WPP as well.

15 RC 495/19/91, Comrade from Peshwar, Report, 1928.

16 RC 495/19/91.

17 RC 495/19/91, Rebel Against Sabotage to Comrade Mazooth, March 1932.

18 *Ibid.*

19 *Ibid.*
20 One American reported to have come to India to reorganise the Communist Party was Henry Lynd. Lynd arrived in December 1929 and was able to stay until September 1930 when he was caught and deported. He may be the 'man from across the sea'. See G. D. Overstreet and M. Windmiller, *Communism in India* (Berkeley, Calif., 1960), p. 149 and Gupta, *Comintern, India, and the Colonial Question*, pp.190–2.
21 RC 495/19/91, Rebel to Mazooth.
22 *Ibid.*
23 *Ibid.*
24 *Ibid.*
25 *Ibid.*
26 *Ibid.*
27 *Ibid.*
28 *Ibid.*
29 Limaye, *Socialist Communist Interaction in India*, pp. 34–69.
30 R. Palme Dutt, *India Today* (Bombay, 1947), pp. 60–9.
31 RC 495/19/91, Rebel to Mazooth.
32 RC 495/42/5, 'Concrete suggestions as to the Communist's immediate task in India', signature illegible, 1929.

18

The Comintern and the Japanese Communist Party

Sandra Wilson

The connection with the Comintern looms large in all the standard histories of the pre-war Japanese Communist Party (JCP) and in the memoirs written by Japanese revolutionaries and former revolutionaries. It is a striking emphasis when compared to the relative absence of sustained reference to the Comintern in accounts of some European Communist parties. The autobiography of Harry Pollitt, General Secretary of the Communist Party of Great Britain, for example, stands in stark contrast to accounts of the JCP by its leaders, in its concentration on the British labour movement and lack of emphasis on the Comintern despite a great enthusiasm for the Russian model of communism.[1] The consensus among writers on pre-war Japanese communism is that the JCP was 'an obedient subsidiary' of the Comintern;[2] one researcher maintains that the degree of 'blind obedience' shown by the JCP to the Comintern was unusual among national Communist parties.[3]

Some such claims are attributable to the Cold War, when writers sought to damn both Japanese Communists and the Soviet Union by stressing sinister connections. Others stem from an apparent sense of inferiority on the part of some Japanese scholars concerning the depth and extent of Japanese activism, and of Japanese absorption of left-wing thought, prior to the formation of the party in 1922. The implication is that the JCP obeyed the Comintern implicitly because, at least in the initial period, it had no independent theorists or experienced activists of its own and thus was dependent upon outside leadership. A third factor underlying the claim that relations with the Comintern were dominant in the JCP can be found in the attempt to explain the apparent failure of communism in pre-war Japan: Japanese scholars with a broadly leftist perspective, as well as former revolutionaries writing their memoirs, stressed that the movement had failed to develop indigenous roots and had always remained alien.[4] One exception to this overall trend is provided by some Japanese Communists writing immediately after Japan's defeat in the Second World War. The prominent Communist Nosaka Sanzo, for example, claimed that the JCP and the Comintern had never been on close terms.[5] The explanation for this stance, however, undoubtedly lies in a complicated game between the JCP and the American occupiers of Japan, in which the newly legal JCP attempted, disingenuously but perhaps with some brief success, to convince the Americans that the party had no substantial connections, past or present, with Moscow.[6]

It is undeniable, despite Nosaka's statement to the contrary, that the JCP and the Comintern were indeed closely connected from the party's founding until its virtual destruction in 1932–33. However, the stereotype of the weak party, doomed to failure as it sought to do Moscow's bidding under very unfavourable circumstances, hardly does justice to the complexity of the relationship between the centre of international communism and its distant Japanese 'branch'. This chapter seeks to establish three main points about that relationship: first, that Comintern support was probably essential to a party operating in the sort of conditions that Japanese Communists had to deal with; second, that the Comintern exercised great authority over the JCP, but that there were important limitations to that authority; and, third, that the Comintern's insistence on Japan's backwardness despite a clear acknowledgement of the threat of Japanese imperialism contributed directly to the party's effective demise by the end of 1933.

The JCP was less focused on its relationship with the Comintern in the first five years after the party's founding than it later became, for reasons associated with the composition of the party itself; with the Soviet Union's changing perception of the role of Japan in the world revolution; and with the increasing manipulation of the Comintern by Stalin and his followers after 1928, which affected all national Communist parties.

The group of Japanese Communists was more heterogeneous in the beginning of the party's existence, containing experienced Socialist activists with considerable personal prestige within the movement, as well as younger Marxists. The older group in particular did not always follow Comintern instructions, consistently seeking to tailor them to local conditions or to ignore them altogether. In 1924, in fact, several of them successfully pushed for the party to disband, and Comintern instructions to re-establish the party were disregarded until late 1926. In February 1928, however, the leaders of this older group were expelled from the party after forming a new faction which disagreed with the Comintern line on Japan and in some cases repudiated Comintern authority on principle. Thereafter, the core of the party, by definition, was committed to Comintern guidance. It contained few or no 'old Socialists' and a number of individuals who had been trained in the Soviet Union. Overall, it was more homogeneous in outlook and more inclined to follow Comintern directives.

Furthermore, from about 1927 onwards the Comintern's concern with the threat posed by Japanese imperialism to both the Soviet state and the Chinese Revolution stimulated several major pronouncements on revolutionary activity in Japan. Japanese Communists were thus called upon with greater frequency to respond to Comintern views of their national situation, and to demonstrate their loyalty by obedience to a series of directives. On the other hand, those directives were sometimes confusing and contradictory, especially after 1928 with Stalin's use of Comintern policy to 'define and defeat' his opponents.[7] Japanese Communists were far from the power struggles that wracked the Comintern in the 1920s, and, according to one party member's memoirs, were not particularly interested in, for example, the confrontation between Stalin and Trotsky.[8] Nevertheless, the JCP, like other national parties, was directly affected by such struggles. The 1927 Comintern theses on Japan, for instance, were contradicted and overturned in 1931 partly because their author, Bukharin, was now out of favour in Moscow and needed to be thoroughly discredited.

Certainly the Comintern was crucial to the very emergence of the JCP in the early 1920s. As Swearingen and Langer pointed out in 1952, the party's formation was 'a direct result of the Comintern's success in selecting, radicalising, and reorienting a portion of the Japanese "social movement" '.[9] A Korean envoy from the Comintern visited Japan in 1920, after previous indirect attempts by the Comintern to establish contact with Japanese leftists had failed.[10] Several Socialists, including the well-known figures Sakai Toshihiko and Yamakawa Hitoshi, were invited to attend a conference of 'Far Eastern Socialists' in Shanghai that year. Sakai and Yamakawa politely declined; according to Yamakawa's later recollection, they had been wary because they did not know the intermediary, and because it was unclear to them what the Comintern was.[11] Osugi Sakae, a leading anarchist theoretician who did go to Shanghai, believed that the main reason for Sakai and Yamakawa's caution was 'the fear we all felt at that time'.[12] Only ten years previously, several hundred Socialists and Anarchists had been arrested in connection with an alleged plot to assassinate the Meiji emperor. In 1911, twelve of them were executed. Thus was the 'winter period' of Japanese socialism ushered in; the effect of the high treason case on the older generation of Socialists is not to be underestimated.

Osugi Sakae went to Shanghai in 1920 and made contact with the Comintern, returning with the considerable sum of 2,000 yen and a promise of more funds. However, his connection with the Comintern did not last long, as he showed no sign of willingness to convert from anarchism to communism. In 1921 Kondo Eizo also received money from Comintern representatives in Shanghai for Communist activities in Japan – this time 6,500 yen. Two Japanese from the USA attended the Third World Congress of the Comintern in Moscow in mid-1921 and a small group of Japanese delegates, representing no particular organisation but again including at least two Anarchists, travelled through Shanghai to Irkutsk for the preliminary conference of the Far Eastern People's Congress in November of that year. They continued on to the Congress itself, held in Moscow in January 1922, and were joined by a number of other Japanese, some of whom had come from the USA. Katayama Sen, who arrived from Mexico, was given the title of honorary chairman of the conference along with Lenin, Trotsky, Zinoviev and Stalin.Two delegates returned to Japan from the conference with instructions to form a Communist party.[13]

Eight people gathered secretly in Takase Kiyoshi's house in Tokyo to form the JCP in July 1922. It was an illegal organisation then, and remained so until 1945. Two delegates from the party travelled to Moscow to report the party's foundation to the Fourth Comintern Congress of November 1922 and request affiliation. They appear to have grossly inflated the JCP's membership, telling the Congress that the party had 250 members, with another 800 waiting to be approved, even though party membership rarely exceeded 50 in its early years.[14] A committee to draw up a draft platform for the JCP was formed in Moscow in June–July 1922, around the time that similar committees were working on other countries. Something of the importance placed on Japan at this early stage can be gauged from the fact that the most prominent member of the Japan committee was Bukharin.

The Comintern had been and continued to be a Eurocentric organisation.[15] However, after the collapse of the Spartakist uprising in 1919 in Germany, hitherto the Bolsheviks' main hope for a second revolution which would lend support to the Soviet Union, Lenin and others perceived a potential role for the colonial and semi-colonial societies of the non-European world: revolutionary activity in such countries would stimulate nationalism, which in turn would disrupt the movement of resources to the industrialised societies of the West and hence endanger their survival as capitalist systems. In other words, revolution in the West could be stimulated by revolution in the East – or at least by outbreaks of nationalism, since Lenin for one did not believe that socialist revolutions really would take place in countries like China and India.[16]

Japan, however, presented a special case, and one about which the Comintern showed an ambivalence which was to have direct consequences for the JCP. It was Asian but industrially developed, not colonised and, indeed, considered an imperialist threat to the Soviet Union. In short, it was an anomaly.[17] Its status as an advanced country had particular ramifications for the Comintern's attitude to Japanese nationalism: while nationalism in China was regarded as a healthy development because of China's 'backward' economy and semi-colonial status, no such legitimacy was conferred on Japanese nationalism, since nationalism in an advanced capitalist country was regarded as bourgeois and counter-revolutionary.[18]

On the other hand, the agricultural sector in Japan was considerably less developed than the urban sector, and Japan retained an imperial system which the Comintern always seemed to regard in a more sinister light than, say, the British monarchy. Japan could therefore be considered 'backward' as well as 'advanced', and the tension between the two notions was not resolved in Comintern pronouncements on Japan. As the German Communist August Thalheimer suggested in 1922, countries could be divided into categories depending on such factors as their state of capitalist development; and the

'Japanese type', which appeared to contain only Japan, was one in which 'capitalism is developed, but some absolutism still remains'.[19] Similarly, in the 1922 draft platform of the JCP, written in the Soviet Union, the emperor is presented less as a supreme political figure and more as the biggest of the 'semi-feudal big landlords', in a manner reminiscent, as Germaine A. Hoston points out, of Marx's description of the Asiatic despot.[20]

At the same time, both the power of Japanese imperialism and the fact that Japan had the largest industrial proletariat in Asia made the country seem a good candidate for revolution. As E. H. Carr has remarked, from the Soviet point of view, 'Japan was both the Britain and the Germany of the Far East',[21] and as such it loomed larger than China did in Moscow in the early 1920s. Zinoviev, Chairman of the Comintern, showed his interest in Japan when he declared in 1922 that 'what faces us [in Japan] . . . is a new, revolutionary proletariat which is as yet untainted by international opportunism', and that 'the Japanese proletariat holds in its hands the key to the solution of the Far Eastern question'. In short, as he had remarked the previous year, 'we must secure a foothold in Japan'.[22] Georgii Ivanovich Safarov, head of the Comintern's Eastern Department in 1921–22, maintained that as 'the best organised and strongest force' in Eastern countries, the Japanese proletariat would strike 'the first decisive blow against foreign and predatory imperialism and imperialist coercion'.[23] Stalin, too, told a Japanese journalist as late as mid-1925 that 'an alliance between the Japanese and Soviet peoples would mark a decisive moment in the task of liberating the East'. By 1927, however, it was China which was presented as the potential leader of the Asian revolutions. Japan's main role was now as a potential obstacle.[24]

In June 1923, meanwhile, most JCP leaders who were not already in exile were arrested. Of the fifty or so party members apprehended, twenty-nine were prosecuted under the Public Peace Police Law. Yamakawa and two others were acquitted; the others received sentences ranging from eight to ten months.[25] Less than three months after the arrests came another disastrous attack on Japanese leftists. A massive earthquake hit the Tokyo and Yokohama area, killing about 100,000 people. In the ensuing chaos thousands of Korean residents of the affected areas were killed in a kind of pogrom. In addition, the military police took the opportunity to round up a number of known leftists. In one police station nine Socialists were murdered. In another, Osugi Sakae, his activist wife Ito Noe and her young nephew were strangled. Military police attempted unsuccessfully to remove other Socialists from gaol to kill them.

In these circumstances, and in view of the Yamamoto cabinet's announcement in October 1923 that it would support universal male suffrage, JCP leaders decided in 1924 to disband the party, arguing that the time was not yet ripe for it to exist. Only Arahata Kanson opposed the decision; everyone else was 'relieved'.[26] Thus ended what is generally known as the 'First JCP'.[27] Japanese Communists repeatedly petitioned the Comintern to recognise the disbandment, but the Comintern refused, instead issuing instructions to re-establish the party. Meanwhile, a tough new law aimed at Communists, the Peace Preservation Law, was under discussion in the Diet, and Nanba Daisuke, a young man who said his strong belief in communism had forced him to act, was sentenced to death for an unsuccessful attempt to assassinate the Prince Regent.[28] Nevertheless, the party was re-formed in December 1926. In the interim an informal Bureau had remained in contact with the Comintern. Those who had voted to disband the party had not been idle but had concentrated their efforts on the labour movement, eventually forming a Communist-dominated organisation of considerable strength.[29]

Comintern support was almost certainly crucial to the 'Second JCP' of the late 1920s. Formal membership of the party was tiny and the Japanese state took every opportunity to persecute known and suspected Communists. In this context the Comintern did at least two essential things: it provided considerable funds to the JCP and it provided a base outside Japan. In all probability the party would not have survived even until the early 1930s without this support – unless it had been a very different sort of party, able to appeal to a broader constituency, less exclusive and perhaps willing to present itself as compatible with Japanese nationalism. So long as the JCP followed the Comintern line, however, it is unlikely that it could have survived without practical Comintern support.

Party membership never exceeded 1,000 at best, and most estimates are considerably lower.[30] On the other hand, the JCP always had a much larger group of sympathisers than members. The circulation of one of the party's organs, the legal *Musansha shinbun* (*Proletarian Newspaper*), for example, was about 20,000 per week.[31] The government certainly seemed convinced of the importance of Communist sympathisers: a 1928 amendment to the 1925 Peace Preservation Law not only provided for the death penalty for leaders and organisers of groups aiming to 'change the national polity [*kokutai*]', but also allowed for non-members to be charged with 'furthering the aims' of an illegal organisation.[32]

The harsh penalties which could be used against Communists are indicative of the paranoia produced by the JCP within the pre-war ruling class, especially after 1928. The chief direct tactic developed by the state from 1928 onwards was the mass arrest, a very elaborate strategy involving months of planning in which an attempt would be made to arrest every known leftist throughout the country at the same time on the same day. Obviously this required a high level of surveillance as well as the cultivation of spies within the party and the extraction of detailed confessions from those already in custody. Mass arrests were carried out in March 1928 and April 1929, and in 1932 and 1933. On 15 March 1928 more than 1,500 people were arrested, and more than 500 were ultimately charged. Arrests continued after 15 March; the total for 1928 was about 3,400. Some suspects were tortured. On 16 April 1929 there were about 700 arrests, with a total of 4,000 for that year.[33] Considering that party membership was less than 1,000, the authorities were casting their net very widely indeed. With these sorts of tactics the JCP's underground organisation was virtually destroyed by late 1932. Arrested Communists were not usually killed – 1923 was an exception – but all Communists and many sympathisers were very effectively harassed. After 1935 no leaders remained out of gaol except those in exile.

As was noted above, Comintern funds were forthcoming even before the foundation of the JCP. Comintern money provided the overwhelming majority of JCP funds. It was used for regular publications, leaflets, election expenses in 1928 and 1930 when Communists stood as candidates, to establish party headquarters and leaders' 'hideouts' and as salaries for JCP leaders. The money usually came in US dollars and would then be changed at a bank by a party sympathiser. Funds kept arriving until perhaps mid-1931, when the Comintern's representative in Shanghai, Noulens, was arrested and contact between the JCP and the Comintern was temporarily lost. From sources such as party members' memoirs and police reports, it seems that an envoy normally did the round trip every month between the Far Eastern Bureau in Shanghai and the JCP, bringing 2,000 yen each time, or approximately $US 1,000, to the JCP for running expenses.[34] Estimates of JCP expenditure vary, however, and Tachibana Takashi maintains on the basis of the same type of sources that in a typical month as much as 30,000 yen of Comintern money was spent, including expenditure on publications, salaries and so on.[35] By contrast, in March 1929 5 or 6 yen was raised through membership fees and 10 yen through the sale of the party's official newspaper and related pamphlets.[36]

After Noulens's arrest the party relied on money from sympathisers, who were recruited quite successfully. At the peak, in the summer of 1932, according to the party member in charge of fund-raising, there were several thousand sympathisers contributing a total of 20–30,000 yen per month,[37] though official reports suggest that the monthly total was more usually 5,000 yen or less.[38] Sympathisers, however, were also coming under close police attention and desperate measures to raise funds were soon deemed necessary, including opening a dancehall in Tokyo and executing an armed bank robbery in October 1932 which netted 30,000 yen but resulted in the arrest of the robbers, much negative publicity for the party and the severe disillusionment of at least one party leader.[39]

Leaders apparently received 60 yen per month in salary apart from their expenses. This was a generous amount: as Tachibana points out, the starting salary of a graduate of Tokyo Imperial University was about 55 yen per month, while the starting pay for a male worker in a large factory was about 1 yen and 30 sen per day and for a female worker about 80 sen.[40] Each election candidate received 300 yen for expenses; in 1928, the JCP received $US 10,000 from Jacob Janson, the Comintern representative in Shanghai, for election expenses.[41]

Possibly the most important use to which Comintern money was put was publication of the party's newspapers. In a context in which it was very difficult actually to meet, the papers provided a vital means of communication with both members and sympathisers. *Proletarian Newspaper*, the legal paper, appeared fortnightly from September 1925, weekly from January 1926, and later six times a month and even daily, ceasing publication under a court order in August 1929. The party's official organ, *Sekki Akahata* (*Red Flag*), began in February 1928 as a fortnightly publication. Its circulation increased to 600 in March 1929, though there were breaks in publication. From April 1932 it was published six times a month. Several regional newspapers were also published, and *Dai-ni musansha shinbun* (*Second Proletarian Newspaper*), with a circulation of about 10,000, was founded to succeed *Proletarian Newspaper*. It was no simple matter to maintain publication of the newspapers, considering censorship and police raids on printing premises, but 239 issues of *Proletarian Newspaper* were published despite suppression, and the circulation of *Red Flag* increased to 7,000 in 1932.[42]

Apart from providing funds, the Comintern's other major practical role was in training party workers and simply keeping them out of the hands of the Japanese police for a time. During the 1920s there were usually Japanese students at the Communist University of the Workers of the East (KUTV) and elsewhere. Between 1923 and 1926, for example, some forty-three young Japanese Communists first travelled to Shanghai, where they made contact with a Soviet representative, then were smuggled aboard Russian freighters bound for Vladivostok, from where they continued to Moscow on the Trans-Siberian Railway to begin studying for periods of two to three years at KUTV. Most of them returned to party work in Japan. The fact that Japanese Communists had a base in the Soviet Union made it possible for the party continually to be 'restocked' after the waves of arrests. So, for instance, at least fifteen or twenty students at KUTV were sent back to reconstruct the party in Japan after the 1928 mass arrests.[43] On the other hand, they too were mostly apprehended within two or three months of their return, and Tachibana claims that returned students from KUTV had a reputation with both the Thought Police and party leaders for being quick to divulge party secrets under pressure.[44]

After the arrests of April 1929, responsibility for reconstructing the party fell on Tanaka Seigen and Sano Hiroshi. Sano, a nephew of party luminary Sano Manabu, had been a student at the Lenin Institute in Moscow and had worked in Comintern Headquarters after graduating. He returned to Japan in January 1929, having attended the Fifth World Congress of the Communist Youth International (CYI) the previous summer. Sano was arrested in April 1930 and Tanaka in July; in November Kazama Jokichi was sent back to Japan by the Comintern to rebuild and lead the party after five years at KUTV and working for the Comintern. Traffic to and from Moscow was severely curtailed from the early 1930s. Beckmann and Okubo find no evidence that any Communists went from Japan to Moscow after 1932. Only a few KUTV trainees returned to Japan in 1934 and 1935, with another in 1936.[45]

The Comintern undoubtedly exercised great authority over the JCP. One party member, for example, likened the various Comintern theses on Japan to 'divine messages' which demanded and received unconditional obedience.[46] It would not be fair, however, to assume, as Cold War writers, in particular, tended to do, that Japanese Communists were mere automatons. Until the early 1930s at least, there remained a group prepared in almost all situations to attempt to follow Comintern instructions. However, in a sense this means no more than to say that the official party at any given time consisted of that group of Communists prepared to obey the Comintern. Others left or were expelled, and a range of Marxists continued to be active outside the JCP.

The party's original 1922 platform contained the items the Comintern wanted, even though founding members disagreed on the vital issue of whether or not to call for the overthrow of the imperial house. Bukharin himself had apparently inserted the call to abolish the imperial system into the draft platform.[47] Japanese Communists knew that this put them at great risk of arrest, and, in the period before the Peace Preservation Law of 1925, made them subject to much higher penalties than merely forming or belonging to a Communist party would have. In fact, one was liable for the death penalty for publicly advocating the overthrow of the imperial house, but only six to twelve months in gaol for infringing the ban on secret societies.

As we have noted, the various Comintern theses on Japan were confusing and sometimes contradictory; more than once they came as a shock to JCP members. The 1927 Comintern theses on Japan overthrew the manifesto, policies and structure decided on unanimously by a JCP Congress in 1926. Nevertheless, the party accepted Bukharin's 1927 document. Similarly, in 1931, despite initial resistance, it ultimately accepted and tried to implement another Comintern directive, known as the Draft Political Theses, even though the new theses directly contradicted the 1927 set. The 1931 theses, however, were quickly labelled as 'Trotskyist' and abandoned by the Comintern, which issued a new set in 1932 reaffirming the 1927 theses. All were accepted by the JCP, despite the rapid reversals of policy; but, again, it could equally be said that those who did not accept them left or were expelled. Neither does acceptance of the Comintern's directives denote lack of debate or resistance, and there were fundamental points on which significant sections of the JCP contested the Comintern view, as we shall see below. The major departure from the pre-war party, that of Yamakawa's faction, for example, was stimulated by the 1927 theses. The fact that it was so difficult to hold party congresses – despite repeated attempts, none was held between December 1926 and the end of the Second World War – may have increased the dominance of Comintern policy and decreased the likelihood of its modification by Japanese Communists.[48] The preponderance of young, Moscow-trained leaders as the mass arrests from 1928 onwards deprived the party of other leaders probably also increased the likelihood that the Comintern line would be followed within the JCP.

The expulsion of Yamakawa's faction in February 1928 was preceded by a bitter ideological split within the party between Yamakawa and the charismatic Fukumoto Kazuo, and the manner in which this dispute was settled provides another very clear example of the authority of the Comintern. By 1927 most party members had aligned themselves behind Fukumoto, who advocated ideological purity and the formation of a party made up of a minority vanguard of professional revolutionaries. Yamakawa, on the other hand, advocated a united front and the formation of a mass proletarian political party, with a concentration on legal rather than illegal activities. The 1927 theses criticised both sides, particularly Fukumoto, who was now labelled 'Trotskyite'. Yamakawa and Fukumoto were called to Moscow, though Yamakawa did not go. Fukumoto went and was roundly rebuked when he got there. Notwithstanding the fact that he had enjoyed 'the status of a god' in terms of ideological authority within the JCP,[49] Fukumoto immediately submitted to Comintern authority and the dispute ended, at least within the party. Nabeyama Sadachika, a leading Japanese Communist who participated in the Comintern's deliberations on Japan in 1927, attributed the submission of Fukumoto and his erstwhile supporter Tokuda Kyuichi to 'silent authoritarian coercion' from the Comintern;[50] for one historian, the capitulation of the Japanese Communists marks the starting-point for the JCP's loss of autonomy.[51] In December 1927 Yamakawa, who had opposed the establishment of the 'Second JCP', formed a group known as the Labour–Farmer faction (*ronoha*) after a journal the group founded. Following their expulsion from the JCP two months later, *ronoha* members never returned to the party, though they continued to regard themselves as involved in revolutionary struggle. As individuals they remained active critics of the JCP over a number of years, always specifically rejecting the authority of the Comintern.[52]

There are other examples of the JCP's acceptance of Comintern instructions, even when those instructions conflicted with previous practice or were considered to place the party in unnecessary danger. In 1927, for example, the party was instructed to engage in public as well as underground activity, and it did so – for instance, by putting up candidates through a legal party in the general election of February 1928 – despite the higher risk of arrest. Only three months after the JCP's adoption of the 1927 theses and one month after the election came the mass arrests of March 1928 and the near extinction of the party.

There were definite limits, however, to the Comintern's authority and effectiveness in Japan. The most obvious were practical. Moscow was distant and travel arduous, at times dangerous.[53] Contact with the Comintern was not always as close as JCP leaders desired,[54] and at one point, as we have seen, was completely severed. It took some time for Comintern directives to be safely delivered to Japan. The 1931 Draft Political Theses, for example, were memorised by the JCP's new leader, Kazama Jokichi, after the Fifth Profintern Congress in Moscow in August 1930. Kazama did not reach Japan until November 1930, and the theses were published in Japan only in April–June 1931. By this time Safarov, the author of the theses, had already been expelled from the Comintern, and the Comintern was having second thoughts about the content of the theses, which were to be overturned the following year.[55] In his memoirs

Kazama noted the difficulty he experienced in retrieving the complicated theses from his memory on his return to Japan.[56] There was in addition a considerable language barrier between JCP members and Comintern officials. Some returnees from KUTV could function in Russian, but few other JCP leaders knew German, Russian or English, the main languages spoken at the Comintern and also at its Far Eastern Bureau. The Profintern used one Japanese Communist, Kondo Eizo, for propaganda work in the Soviet Union in the mid-1920s despite his poor English: Kondo's Russian audiences apparently could not understand him 'but they cheered when he said "revolution" or "proletariat"'.[57] Conversely, there seems to have been no one at the Far Eastern Bureau of the Comintern at the end of the 1920s who knew Japanese.[58]

An even more basic practical obstacle to the Comintern's authority in Japan was that the JCP simply could not do many of the things it was directed to do. For example, the 1927 theses instructed the JCP to build a mass movement, but this was quite frankly impossible, or soon became so. For one thing, the JCP had very weak links with organised labour. In the second half of the 1920s there were about 300,000 members of industrial unions, but 80 per cent of them belonged to right-wing unions.[59] The party was dominated by intellectuals, and perhaps only 10 per cent of JCP members themselves worked in factories.[60] For another thing, repression, especially from 1928 onwards, made mass action very difficult. The government was particularly shocked by the scale of the arrests of March 1928. One of its responses was to revise the Peace Preservation Law to provide the death penalty for Communist activity; another was greatly to expand the Thought Police. Soon there were more than 2,000 members of the Thought Police nationwide (numbers further increased later), which was three or four times the number of Communist Party members.[61] Not only did this mean more arrests, but more meetings could be broken up and more publications confiscated, making it virtually impossible to build a mass movement. Perhaps the surprising thing is that the Communists remained influential at all. Despite these handicaps, the Comintern in May 1932, when the JCP was near disintegration, again proclaimed that the party must at all costs become 'a genuine mass party, marching confidently to meet the coming revolution'.[62]

A different kind of constraint on Comintern authority over Japan came from the Soviet end. It was not that the Comintern lost authority so much as that it did not always choose to exercise it. Much depended on how important Japan was seen to be at any given time and in what sense. As we have seen, there was an early emphasis on the importance of Japan, demonstrated by the comments of Comintern leaders in the early 1920s and by Bukharin's close involvement with the establishment of the JCP. Stalin, too, sometimes attended meetings of the Comintern's committee on Japan and gave his views; and apart from Bukharin, other prominent Communists also served on the committee. At least part of this early emphasis on Japan concerned the prospects for revolution in that country. By 1927, however, it was evident that revolution was more likely to come to China, and in the 1927 theses Japan appears principally as an imperialist threat to both the Chinese Revolution and the Soviet Union. Thirteen slogans were proposed in the 1927 theses, but domestic affairs did not appear until the fifth ('Dissolution of parliament').

A final caveat on the Comintern's authority in Japan concerns the extent to which the JCP itself, through which Comintern authority was exercised, represented the gamut of Communist activity. Many who were once members of the JCP left or were expelled from the party: apart from Yamakawa's faction, the most notable group defections occurred in 1929 and from 1933 onwards, but there had been earlier departures on ideological grounds by significant individuals such as Akamatsu Katsumaro. Some of them continued to consider themselves as Communists or Marxists, even if the party did not consider them so. While it is noteworthy that, unlike their Chinese counterparts, those Communists who opposed the Comintern did not manage to become the mainstream of the party, it would be misleading to suggest that all revolutionary thought and activity was constrained within the bounds set by the Comintern. Studies such as those by Germaine Hoston and Miriam Silverberg show convincingly that Japanese Marxism was much more than a matter of direction by Moscow, and that Communists were far from isolated in the culture of the 1920s. Japanese Marxists were often original, dynamic and autonomous, as is shown not only by their attempts to adapt Marxism to Japanese conditions, but also by the fact that they were actively interested in much more than the Moscow connection and the proper strategy for the Japanese revolution. Their articles and books were published widely by the capitalist press, and as a result their ideas on a broad variety of subjects thoroughly permeated and achieved high status in the intellectual world.[63] Thus they were very much engaged with their own society. Indeed, the gap between the tiny scale of the formal JCP and the spread of Marxist ideas is one of the most striking features of pre-war Japanese Marxism.

From 1934 onwards there was very little contact between the Comintern and those few Japanese Communists who remained in Japan and out of gaol. Practical difficulties of communication were not the sole reason, because by this time the Soviet Union had established an espionage network in Japan which proved to be very successful and would presumably have been able to act as a channel of communication with Moscow if necessary: the Sorge ring.[64] The inescapable conclusion is rather that the Comintern had lost interest in any possible Japanese revolution, and, in fact, the prospects for such a revolution were extremely dim. The Chinese revolution was more likely and as for Japan, the threat of Japanese imperialism, especially after Japan's invasion of Manchuria in September 1931, made espionage activity more important than encouragement of revolution. In accordance with normal practice, the JCP was not used by Sorge in his espionage activities; indeed, he avoided contact with the Japanese Communist movement. His main Japanese associate, Ozaki Hotsumi, was a Communist by conviction but did not associate with the party.

The Comintern never resolved its original difficulties in categorising Japan, and its ambivalence had fatal consequences for the party. Sometimes the Comintern appeared to endorse the view that Japan was an advanced industrial nation ruled by the bourgeoisie, but more often it insisted that it was a country retaining significant feudal features, notably the imperial system and a backward agricultural sector. The implications for revolutionary strategy were, of course, quite different in each case. Both views alienated a number of Japanese Communists, the first because in shunning Japanese nationalism as counter-revolutionary in an advanced country it seemed to deny the validity of any distinctly Japanese historical experience; and the second because it denigrated Japan's economic and political achievements, placing Japan on a par with pre-revolutionary Russia rather than with the countries of Western Europe. As Hoston indicates, it may have been this latter insult as much as any ideological difference which induced Yamakawa's faction to break with the Comintern line in 1927.[65] The two views could also be conflated – according to the Comintern, Japan was an advanced capitalist society in the urban sphere, while backward and feudal agriculturally – but it was the feudal agrarian base that was reflected in the Japanese state.[66] The Comintern's hard line on Japan by no means stifled discussion within the Communist movement – in some ways, on the contrary, it stimulated discussion – but it did contribute greatly to tensions which eventually destroyed the party just as effectively as external repression did.

The issue which crystallised much of the tension within the JCP and between the JCP and the Comintern was the proper way to evaluate the emperor and the imperial system. It is striking that the Comintern gave such high priority to the emperor, especially in comparison with its attitude towards the British state. A general 'orientalist' attitude at the Comintern may have contributed to the deep suspicion with which the Japanese emperor was always regarded: perhaps an Asian emperor would almost inevitably have been considered a despot. In any event, while Yamakawa's Labour–Farmer faction maintained that the Japanese emperor occupied a very similar position to the British monarch, the Comintern on the whole firmly and explicitly disagreed, and abolition of the imperial system remained prominently on the Communist agenda. By contrast, the monarchy does not appear to have been a major issue for British Communists. In Japan, however, one's attitude to the Emperor in a sense determined whether one could be a member of the JCP or not.

The existence of the Emperor and the 'emperor system' – the Japanese term for the whole system of authoritarian government which derived its legitimacy from the centrality of the emperor – represented both an opportunity and a hindrance for political activists in the 1920s and 1930s. On the whole, it was the right wing which seized on the opportunities and the left which found the Emperor a continuing stumbling block. The right appropriated him as symbol and focus and cited him, mostly without his active acquiescence, as their ultimate authority. For the Communists, the Emperor was a theoretical and tactical problem from 1922 throughout the pre-war years and again after the defeat of Japan in 1945.[67] As Kazama Jokichi wrote, no other slogan tormented the party as much as the call to 'abolish the imperial system'.[68] From the beginning there was a sound tactical argument that adopting the overthrow of the imperial system as a slogan simply invited repression, though it is also arguable that willingness to confront the imperial system was the major factor distinguishing the JCP from other left-wing groups and so constituted a unique attraction. More profoundly, the issue of the emperor was at the heart of the greatest ideological division among pre-war Communists – the debate about whether the Japanese revolution was to be a one-stage or a two-stage revolution – and it was also a central issue in the wave of defections which destroyed the party from 1933 onwards.

The debate over the stages of the Japanese revolution was a long and rich one, lasting roughly from 1927 to 1937. It was stimulated by the various Comintern theses on Japan as well as by developments within Japan,[69] but it certainly exceeded the bounds of Comintern-sanctioned discourse, for, apart from the brief reign of the 1931 political theses,[70] the Comintern more or less consistently adhered to the theory of the two-stage revolution and did not encourage contrary analyses. The debate represents, in other words, a major attempt to adapt Marxism to Japanese conditions.[71] At the heart of the argument about stages lay contending analyses of the present state of the Japanese economy and society. The Comintern and the JCP (together constituting the *kozaha*, or 'Lecture Series' faction, so called after a multi-volume work its scholars produced) argued that Japan was feudal and backward and consequently a bourgeois-democratic revolution must precede the proletarian revolution. The feudal nature of Japan was best revealed in landlord dominance of rural society and in the imperial system. The other side – the *rono* or Labour–Farmer faction which had formed around Yamakawa Hitoshi and been expelled from the JCP early in 1928 – argued that Japan had already undergone significant capitalist development and that the emperor and other feudal features were no more than 'feudal remnants'. Moreover, the emperor was not central to the running of the state but was a mere appendage or ornament to it. Therefore, bourgeois democracy existed, the bourgeoisie was the main enemy and revolution could be achieved in one stage.

The issue of the advisability or otherwise of publicly advocating the overthrow of the imperial system was always critical. As Inumaru Giichi and others point out, the JCP had a dual character in its early years, basically because it represented both the fulfilment of Meiji socialism and the beginning of Japanese Marxism. Socialists from the Meiji period – Sakai Toshihiko, Yamakawa Hitoshi, Arahata Kanson, Yoshikawa Morikuni, Hashiura Tokio – founded the party. The second group had emerged since the First World War and thus had not experienced the trauma of the High Treason Case of 1910–11. Differences between the two groups emerged at, for example, the special meeting convened in 1923 to discuss the JCP's draft platform, when Sakai sought to avoid discussion of the emperor question but younger members like Sano Manabu, Inomata Tsunao, Nosaka Sanzo and Yamamoto Kenzo insisted on discussing it. It was also the second rather than the first group which was enthusiastic about regrouping after the disbandment of the First JCP. There were concomitant differences in style of activism, with Tokuda Kyuichi, for example, strongly advocating public activity by the JCP, at least until the passage of the Peace Preservation Law of 1925, but Sakai and others in the older group opposing public activity.[72]

The various proletarian parties of the second half of the 1920s – that is, non-Communist political parties representing workers – appear to have solved the problem of the emperor by omitting him from their platforms. In this sense too, attitude to the emperor served as a kind of litmus test of Japanese communism; and a united front between the JCP and social democratic parties such as was advocated in the 1927 theses was always a difficult proposition, since the Communists were still enjoined to include 'abolition of the monarchy' among their slogans. Social democratic parties themselves called for abolition of the Privy Council, the House of Peers, the power of the elder statesmen (*genro*) and the Army and Navy General Staffs; advocated independence for Japan's colonies; and even included statements like '[t]he struggle against remnants of feudal society is one of the important duties of the proletarian parties'.[73] They did not, however, call directly for the abolition of the imperial system. Yamakawa's Labour-Farmer faction, of course, also avoided the issue.

Avoidance of the emperor issue was a strategy advocated by some JCP members from the beginning. Not only did Sakai seek to circumvent discussion of it in 1923, but the reference to overthrowing the imperial system was cut out with scissors from the draft platform distributed to participants at the meeting convened to consider the platform.[74] Furthermore, the secretary at that meeting, Takase Kiyoshi, decided privately to omit mention of the discussion from the minutes, as he sympathised with Sakai's extreme unease about the matter. This proved extremely fortuitous, for the minutes were later seized by the police. Takase recorded his relief in his memoirs: 'I rejoiced; I was filled with joy. Starting with Sakai-sensei, I had saved more than twenty comrades from the death penalty.'[75] According to Takase, there was no opposition to the principle of abolishing the imperial system, only opposition to making the aim publicly known. Even Sano Manabu, who had pushed for discussion of the issue, was strongly against publicly advocating it, given the conditions prevailing in Japan at that time.[76]

It appears that there was agreement among party members that while acceptance of the Soviet draft would be reported to Moscow, all reference to abolition of the imperial system would be omitted from materials intended for domestic consumption.[77] Despite the tactical problems encountered by Japanese Communists, and the debate in Japan about the theoretical significance of the emperor, the Comintern continued to insist (except briefly in 1930–31) on the primacy of overthrowing the imperial system, though not without advice to the contrary from Japanese Communists. During the drafting of the Comintern's 1927 theses on Japan, for example, there was a dispute on the subject between Bukharin and Nabeyama Sadachika, but Nabeyama was defeated.[78]

The most dramatic consequence of the Comintern's intransigence concerning the Emperor came in 1933, and it delivered a blow from which the pre-war party never recovered. In June 1933, Nabeyama and another very prominent Communist, Sano Manabu, issued a statement from prison recanting their former beliefs and announcing their conversion to love of country. They still identified themselves as Socialists, but distanced themselves from the communism of the JCP and the Comintern. As Sano wrote in his prison diary, it was necessary 'to open up a unique path to socialism with our own national strength'.[79] Sano and Nabeyama also supported war if it had a progressive significance: the goal should be the achievement of socialism in Japan, Korea, Taiwan, Manchuria and China proper.[80] As Masumi Junnosuke and others have remarked, it was a left-wing version of the old idea of Asian solidarity.[81]

The defection of Sano and Nabeyama came as a great shock to the JCP, but it did not occur in a vacuum. As Hoston has convincingly shown, the 1933 stance had definite antecedents: in the national socialism and apologia for Japanese expansionism developed in the years after the Russian Revolution by Takabatake Motoyuki, Akamatsu Katsumaro and Takahashi Kamekichi, and in the departure from the JCP as early as 1929 of a group of junior members, the 'dissolutionist faction' (*kaitoha*), whose dissatisfactions with the party closely prefigured those of Sano and Nabeyama four years later.[82] The latter group maintained that the party was alienated from the Japanese masses, that it was inappropriate to call for the abolition of the imperial system and that the party should separate from the Comintern.[83]

Sano and Nabeyama, however, had joined with none of these earlier critics of the JCP. Nabeyama said later that despite his dispute with Bukharin over the Emperor in 1927 he had not particularly felt at that time that conditions in Japan were different from elsewhere and should be acknowledged as such; nor did he feel 'nationalistic'. Avoiding the issue of the emperor was simply a matter of tactics.[84] Sano had previously been a vocal critic of the Labour–Farmer faction for its avoidance of the emperor issue. He wrote much later that by the time of his arrest in June 1929 he had come to doubt the wisdom of working with the Comintern, but that he had suppressed his doubts.[85] In any event, he was still propounding internationalism as a defendant at his public trial in 1931.[86] The departure of the dissolutionist faction in 1929 had no profound effect on the party, at least in the immediate sense. By 1933, however, the context was very different.

In September 1931 the Japanese army invaded Manchuria, supported by a great deal of nationalist chauvinism in the mainstream press, if not initially by the cabinet of Wakatsuki Reijiro. The JCP, one of very few groups to speak out publicly against the 'Manchurian Incident', was swimming against a strong tide. Social democratic and labour organisations vacillated in their response but eventually endorsed the army's actions, and more conservative groups gave enthusiastic support to the invasion. The following month, the Comintern's Otto Kuusinen, an associate of the deposed Bukharin, completed the draft of the document which would become known as the 1932 theses on Japan. The 1932 Theses completely overturned Safarov's 1931 Draft Political Theses, which for a brief period had lent support to the theory of one-stage revolution in Japan. Safarov had been denounced as 'Trotskyist' and removed from the Comintern; and Japan's invasion of Manchuria had increased Soviet fears of Japanese imperialism. The 1932 theses did not hesitate to use words like 'barbaric', 'backward' and 'feudalistic' to describe Japanese society,[87] though, perhaps surprisingly, they placed very little emphasis on constructing a broad front to oppose war in China. The imperial system was once more 'the main pillar of political reaction and of all the relics of feudalism' in Japan, as well as 'the backbone of the present dictatorship of the exploiting classes'.[88] The 1932 theses came as a considerable shock to Japanese Communists, a number of whom were in the midst of a long public trial which they were using as a vehicle for vigorous propaganda based on the previous set of Comintern theses.[89]

It is difficult to know whether the 1932 theses had a direct effect in encouraging Japanese Communists to abandon their former beliefs, or if JCP members would have been better able to withstand the pressure to recant had the theses not renewed and strengthened the call to abolish the imperial system. Recantations undoubtedly were encouraged by the jingoistic atmosphere surrounding the army's exploits in Manchuria; by the increased level of police harassment of Communists after the Manchurian Incident and the publication of the 1932 theses; and, for some, by the bank robbery by party members in October 1932, shortly before the end of the public trial. Certainly, the roots of Sano and Nabeyama's joint statement lie in the events of 1932 and even 1931 rather than those of 1933. They had been discussing their change of views between themselves for six months before issuing the statement, and Nabeyama, at least, wrote in his memoirs that it was only after the end, in October 1932, of the sixteen-month public trial in which both had been sentenced to life imprisonment that he had the leisure to think over the events of the previous year. It was then that his views began to change.[90]

The fact that rejection of international communism came this time not from relatively junior party members but from leaders of the stature of Sano and Nabeyama magnified the shock for lower-ranking party members and sympathisers enormously. Nabeyama had been the Japanese representative to the Profintern and had participated in the discussions on Japan in Moscow in 1927. Sano, too, was well trusted by the Comintern. In 1924 he had been given the task of reorganising the party after its dissolution. He had been a member of the Comintern's committee on Germany, a great honour considering the hopes the Comintern continued to hold for Germany in the 1920s,[91] and had been sent to both Berlin and India on Comintern business. In Japan, he had been not only the chairman of the party's Central Committee but its acknowledged theoretical leader from the late 1920s. As editor of the legal *Proletarian Newspaper*, too, Sano had represented the party's public face.[92] Sano and Nabeyama together also represented the two major streams in the party: Sano had been a lecturer at Waseda University, while Nabeyama had been a labour union leader.

In 1933, however, in a statement widely publicised in the press and circulated among imprisoned Communists, Sano and Nabeyama denounced both the Comintern and the JCP. The JCP, they said, had no mass base and was unrealistic in its goals, largely because it had trusted the Comintern instead of the Japanese people.[93] The internationalism professed by the JCP amounted to no more than defence of the particular interests of the Soviet Union and sacrifice of the legitimate interests of Japan. Unlike Yamakawa Hitoshi, who, while rejecting the authority of the Comintern and emphasising the need for each country's Communist party to be autonomous, had continued to believe in the internationalism of the labour movement based on co-operation rather than central direction,[94] Sano and Nabeyama rejected internationalism as such in favour of a sort of populist nationalism (*minzokushugi*).[95]

The Emperor was central to the 1933 joint statement. In 'apostasy' (*tenko*) the issue of allegiance to the emperor – really, the emperor's power symbolically to represent the Japanese people and thus to stand for what was culturally distinctive about a rapidly industrialising nation – came together with the issue of allegiance to an outside, possibly hostile force: the Soviet Union as represented by the Comintern. Sano and Nabeyama rejected both the 1932 theses and their own previous statements in claiming that the imperial system of Japan, unlike tsarism, had never been an exploitive or repressive force. The imperial house, on the contrary, had been 'an expression of national unity'.[96] The form of the revolution in each country would depend on the 'special characteristics' of each country, and in Japan it was not only natural but also possible to carry out a 'one-country socialist revolution' under the imperial family. Directly contradicting the optimistic claim of the 1932 theses that 'patriotism and loyalty to the monarch' among the masses were rapidly fading away and that 'a swing of the masses to the left is taking place',[97] Sano and Nabeyama asserted, probably more realistically, that the Japanese people loved and respected the emperor, and that the slogan 'abolish the imperial system' contravened the wishes of the people and alienated the party from the masses.

As a corollary, Sano and Nabeyama called for separation of the JCP from the Comintern, which 'did not recognise the special characteristics historically accumulated by Japan and other countries', for rejection of the JCP which blindly followed the Comintern and for the establishment of a new political party to build one-country socialism under the imperial house.[98] Though few other Communists took to this latter idea, Sano retained his belief in emperor-centred socialism, writing a book at the end of 1945 which called for a 'people's emperor' to usher in the new democratic Japan in the wake of defeat in the Second World War.[99]

Sano and Nabeyama were of course immediately expelled from the JCP, but, unlike the situation in 1929, a large number of other Communists this time followed their lead and 'recanted' from 1933 onwards. Nervousness spread to other workers' organisations. Several left-wing labour and cultural associations, which had previously supported the party and opposed war, such as the Proletarian Writers' Union and the Proletarian Artists' Union, disbanded within a year. One article written for a labour periodical in October 1933 called for the removal of abolition of the emperor system from the labour organisation's aims, on the grounds that such an aim ignored the 'essence' of trade unions, that it alienated the union from the mass struggle and promoted factionalism and that it was a harmful piece of recklessness that fostered confusion between the JCP and the union.[100] The authorities were delighted with the wave of defections and put much effort into encouraging them. In July 1933, just over a month after the joint statement, 548 Communists either already convicted or awaiting trial under the Peace Preservation Law had formally renounced their party affiliations. By mid-1936, three-quarters of the 438 Communists serving gaol sentences had 'recanted'.[101]

Whether or not the party could have withstood the other pressures to which it was subjected in the pre-war period, it is clear that the Comintern's emphasis on the power of the Japanese monarchy, and more generally its insistence that Japan was 'backward' and had not yet experienced a bourgeois revolution, were major factors in the disintegration of the JCP. The Comintern's attitude resulted in the weakening of an already tiny party by provoking splits as various party members objected that the focus on the imperial system was tactically or ideologically wrong. It also ensured a head-on collision between Japanese Communists and the state-sanctioned view of the Japanese polity as an organic unity centred on the Emperor. In the circumstances of the early 1930s, and particularly after the invasion of Manchuria, this conflict was presented to Japanese Communists in the starkest of forms, and it became impossible to ignore the distance between the Communist view of the world and that apparently shared by the greater part of those for whom Communists struggled.

Meanwhile, the last member of the Central Committee of the JCP, Hakamada Satomi, was arrested in March 1935. Small pockets of Communist activity continued, but there was virtually no contact with the Comintern and no central direction of the party. By this time, in any case, the importance of Japan for the Comintern was represented overwhelmingly not by any JCP member but by the German master spy, Richard Sorge, whose information from Tokyo was to prove vital to the making of Soviet strategy up until his arrest in October 1941.

Notes

I am grateful to Professors Wada Haruki and Kurita Naoki, Dr Barry Carr and Ms Shibuya Iwane for their comments on an early draft of this chapter.

In accordance with Japanese usage, Japanese names are given with the surname first.

1 Harry Pollitt, *Serving My Time: An Apprenticeship to Politics* (London, 1940).

2 R. Swearingen and P. Langer, *Red Flag in Japan: International Communism in Action 1919–1951* (Cambridge, Mass., 1952), p. 43.
3 Tachibana Takashi, *Nihon Kyosanto no kenkyu (1)* (Tokyo, 1983), p. 62.
4 Nabeyama Sadachika is one former Communist who wrote strongly in this vein, emphasising also the dominant authority of the Comintern. See *Watashi wa Kyosanto o suteta* (Tokyo, 1949).
5 Nosaka Sanzo, *Bomei jurokunen* (Tokyo, 1946), p. 69; Wada Haruki, *Rekishi toshite no Nosaka Sanzo* (Tokyo, 1996), pp. 133, 163.
6 Wada, *Nosaka Sanzo*, p. 133. A post-war official history of the JCP does not deny a Moscow connection, but does downplay it: see Central Committee of the Communist Party of Japan, *The Fifty Years of the Communist Party of Japan* (Tokyo, 1973).
7 K. McDermott, 'Stalin and the Comintern during the "Third Period", 1928–33', *European History Quarterly*, 25: 3 (1995), 418.
8 Nabeyama, *Watashi wa Kyosanto o suteta*, p. 111.
9 Swearingen and Langer, *Red Flag*, p. 3.
10 T. E. Durkee, 'The Communist International and Japan, 1919–1932', unpublished Ph.D. Dissertation, Stanford University, 1953, pp. 13–16; Inumaru Giichi, *Daiichiji Kyosantoshi no kenkyu: zoho: Nihon Kyosanto no seiritsu* (Tokyo, 1993), pp. 74–6.
11 Yamakawa Kikue and Sakisaka Itsuro (eds), *Yamakawa Hitoshi jiden: Aru bonjin no kiroku, sono ta* (Tokyo, 1961), p. 389.
12 Osugi Sakae, *Ito Noe senshu, v. 11: Nihon dasshutsuki, Gokuchuki* (Tokyo, 1991), p. 19.
13 *Yamakawa jiden*, pp. 390, 392; Durkee, 'Communist International', pp. 16–20, 26–31.
14 Inumaru, *Daiichiji Kyosantoshi*, pp. 252–3; G. M. Beckmann and Okubo Genji, *The Japanese Communist Party 1922–1945* (Stanford, Calif.,1969), p. 49. See also Masumi Junnosuke, *Nihon seitoshiron*, 5 (Tokyo, 1979), p. 417.
15 See F. Claudin, *The Communist Movement: From Comintern to Cominform, Part One*, trans. Brian Pearce (New York and London, 1975), pp. 244–50; H. Gruber, *Soviet Russia Masters the Comintern: International Communism in the Era of Stalin's Ascendancy* (Garden City, New York, 1974), pp. 243–76.
16 G. A. Hoston, *The State, Identity, and the National Question in China and Japan* (Princeton, 1994), pp. 32, 177–8; Claudin, *Communist Movement, Part One*, pp. 245–6.
17 Historians of the Comintern, too, have tended to perpetuate the confusion about Japan's status by confining their brief references to Japan to sections on the 'colonial and semi-colonial' members of the Comintern.
18 Hoston, *State*, p. 328.
19 Inumaru, *Daiichiji Kyosantoshi*, p. 258.
20 Hoston, *State*, p. 254.
21 E. H. Carr, *The Bolshevik Revolution 1917–1923*, vol. 3 (Harmondsworth, 1966), p. 486.
22 Quoted in Murata Yoichi, 'Kominterun bunken oboegaki (3)', *Rekishigaku kenkyu*, 406 (March 1974), 48; Swearingen and Langer, *Red Flag*, pp. 11–12, 13.
23 'The Interrelation Between the National Revolutionary Movement and the Revolutionary Proletarian Movement' (Safarov's Statement at the Tenth Session of the Congress of the Toilers of the Far East, 27 January 1922), in Xenia Joukoff

Eudin and R. C. North, *Soviet Russia and the East 1920–1927: A Documentary Survey* (Stanford, 1957), p. 229.

24 'Stalin's Interest in the Pan-Asian Movement' (interview), *ibid.*, p. 336.

25 See Nosaka Sanzo, *Fusetsu no ayumi*, 5 (Tokyo, 1981), p. 201.

26 Masumi Junnosuke, *Nihon seijishi 3: Seito no choraku, soryoku sentaisei* (Tokyo, 1988), p. 133; Beckmann and Okubo, *Japanese Communist Party*, p. 76; Durkee, 'Communist International', pp. 51–3.

27 The term 'First JCP' was coined by the judicial authorities during investigations after the mass arrests of March 1928 and April 1929 to distinguish the earlier party from the reconstructed party of 1926 onwards, but it was adopted also by the defendants themselves and has remained commonplace: Inumaru, *Daiichiji Kyosantoshi*, p. 501.

28 On the Nanba case, see R. H. Mitchell, *Thought Control in Prewar Japan* (Ithaca and London, 1976), pp. 51, 53–4.

29 Masumi, *Nihon seijishi 3*, pp. 133–7. See also Stephen S. Large, *Organised Workers and Socialist Politics in Interwar Japan* (Cambridge, 1981), pp. 68–71, 84–100.

30 Beckmann and Okubo, *Japanese Communist Party*, p. 275, give 1,000. Tachibana, *Nihon Kyosanto (1)*, p. 94, gives a peak figure of 600, and Masumi, *Nihon seitoshiron*, 5, p. 385, of 500.

31 Tachibana, *Nihon Kyosanto (1)*, p. 188.

32 See Mitchell, *Thought Control*, pp. 88–90.

33 Tachibana, *Nihon Kyosanto (1)*, pp. 218–19, 315.

34 *Ibid.*, pp. 179, 367–80; Masumi, *Nihon seitoshiron* 5, p. 499. Tachibana (vol. 1, pp. 367–9) suggests that the JCP also lost contact with the Comintern in 1929.

35 Tachibana, *Nihon Kyosanto (1)*, pp. 179–80. One estimate of JCP expenses for April 1929 was 3,850 yen: Kazama Jokichi, *Mosuko to tsunagaru Nihon Kyosanto no rekishi, v. 1*, Tokyo, Tenmansha, 1951, p. 239.

36 Kazama, *Mosuko to tsunagaru*, p. 238.

37 Masumi, *Nihon seitoshiron* 5, pp. 471, 499–500.

38 Quoted in Beckmann and Okubo, *Japanese Communist Party*, p. 236.

39 See Nabeyama, *Watashi wa Kyosanto o suteta*, pp. 149–50.

40 Tachibana, *Nihon Kyosanto (1)*, pp. 179–80.

41 Kazama, *Mosuko to tsunagaru*, p. 205.

42 Beckmann and Okubo, *Japanese Communist Party*, pp. 95–6, 140, 176, 188, 225. *Second Proletarian Newspaper* reached a circulation of 50,000 before being absorbed by *Red Flag* in March 1932. *Red Flag* had been initially established in April 1923, but lapsed. In 1928 it became the first official party organ.

43 Masumi, *Nihon seijishi 3*, p. 139; Masumi, *Nihon seitoshiron* 5, p. 461; Swearingen and Langer, *Red Flag*, pp. 23–4; Durkee, 'Communist International', pp. 127–31.

44 Tachibana, *Nihon Kyosanto (1)*, p. 282.

45 Beckmann and Okubo, *Japanese Communist Party*, pp. 253–4, 261.

46 Miyauchi Isamu, *1930nendai Nihon Kyosanto shishi* (Tokyo, 1976), pp. 85, 117.

47 Inumaru, *Daiichiji Kyosantoshi*, p. 260.

48 Tachibana, *Nihon Kyosanto (1)*, p. 277.

49 Mizuno Aki, *Dan'atsu ni koshite (Okayama-ken shakai undoshi (6)* (Tokyo, 1978), p. 5.

50 Nabeyama, *Watashi wa Kyosanto o suteta*, p. 113.

51 Tachibana, *Nihon Kyosanto (1)*, p. 147.

52 Arahata Kanson gives an account of the beginnings of the *ronoha* and of its theoretical differences from the JCP in *Kanson jiden* (Tokyo, 1961), pp. 483–7. On the differing attitudes of the two groups to the Comintern, see *Yamakawa jiden*, p. 429. For an example of Yamakawa's continuing criticism of the Comintern, see Yamakawa Hitoshi, 'Kyosanto ryokyoto no tenko' (written for *Chuo koron*, July 1933), in Takabatake Michitoshi (ed.), *Yamakawa Hitoshi shu* (Tokyo, 1976), pp. 225–7.

53 See, for example, Nabeyama, *Watashi wa Kyosanto o suteta*, pp. 114ff.

54 See Beckmann and Okubo, *Japanese Communist Party*, p. 196.

55 *Ibid.*, pp. 227, 229; Masumi, *Nihon seitoshiron* 5, p. 468.

56 Kazama Jokichi, *Mosuko Kyosan Daigaku no omoide* (Tokyo, 1949), p. 285.

57 Durkee, 'Communist International', pp. 55–6.

58 Tachibana, *Nihon Kyosanto (1)*, pp 140–1.

59 Masumi, *Nihon seitoshiron* 5, p. 385.

60 Tachibana, *Nihon Kyosanto (1)*, p. 225. On the other hand, the leftist influence was strong within the rural tenant farmers' movement in the same period: see Nishida Yoshiaki, 'Senzen Nihon ni okeru rodo undo, nomin undo no seishitsu', in Tokyo Daigaku shakai kagaku kenkyujo (ed.), *Gendai Nihon shakai 4* (Tokyo, 1991), pp. 263–313.

61 Tachibana, *Nihon Kyosanto (1)*, p. 267. See also E. Tipton, *The Japanese Police State: The Tokko in Interwar Japan* (Sydney, 1990), p. 24.

62 'Theses on the Situation in Japan and the Tasks of the Communist Party, May 1932', in Beckmann and Okubo, *Japanese Communist Party*, p. 336.

63 G. A. Hoston, *Marxism and the Crisis of Development in Prewar Japan* (Princeton, 1986); M. Silverberg, *Changing Song: The Marxist Manifestos of Nakano Shigeharu* (Princeton, 1990), esp. pp. 209–29. See also Masumi, *Nihon seitoshiron* 5, p. 434.

64 On Sorge's ring, see C. Johnson, *An Instance of Treason: Ozaki Hotsumi and the Sorge Spy Ring* (Stanford, 1964).

65 Hoston, *State*, p. 417.

66 *Ibid.*, p. 256.

67 On issues surrounding the Emperor in the JCP in the immediate post-war period, see Wada, *Nosaka*, p. 185.

68 Kazama, *Mosuko to tsunagaru*, p. 103.

69 Hoston, *Marxism*, pp. 55–94.

70 For the text of these theses, see Beckmann and Okubo, *Japanese Communist Party*, pp. 309–31.

71 Hoston, *Marxism*, xiii.

72 Inumaru, *Daiichiji Kyosantoshi*, p. 502.

73 See Yamakawa Hitoshi, 'Musan seito wa ikanaru koryo o motsu beki ka', written in September 1925, in *Yamakawa Hitoshi zenshu, Vol. 6.*

74 Tachibana, *Nihon Kyosanto (1)*, p. 66.

75 Takase Kiyoshi, *Nihon Kyosanto soritsushiwa*, (Tokyo, Aoki shoten, 1978), p. 152.

76 *Ibid.*, p. 140.

77 Nabeyama, *Watashi wa Kyosanto o suteta*, p. 62.

78 Interview with Nabeyama in Ishido Seirin and Gomikawa Junpei, *Shiso to ningen* (Tokyo, 1974), p. 245.

79 Quoted in G. A. Hoston, 'Emperor, nation, and the transformation of Marxism to National Socialism in prewar Japan: the case of Sano Manabu', *Studies in*

Comparative Communism 18: 1 (1985), 43. For an account by Nabeyama of his own state of mind just prior to the joint declaration, see Nabeyama, *Watashi wa Kyosanto o suteta*, pp. 146–53.

80 Sano had supported the principle of 'progressive wars' as early as 1927, but in those days he primarily meant anti-imperialist wars. See Sano Manabu, 'Waga haigaishugisha no teikokushugi sensoron', *Marukusushugi*, 37, (May 1927), 4.

81 *Nihon seijishi 3*, p. 150. On the 'superior socialism' that Sano and Nabeyama wanted to construct in Japan, see also Yamakawa, 'Kyosanto ryokyoto no tenko', pp. 228–9.

82 Hoston, *State*, pp. 328, 334.

83 Shimane Kiyoshi, 'Nihon Kyosanto rodoshaha – Mizuno Shigeo', in Shiso no kagaku kenkyukai (ed.), *Tenko*, vol. 1 (Tokyo, Heibonsha, 1959), pp. 150–63.

84 Interview with Nabeyama, in Ishido and Gomikawa, *Shiso to ningen*, pp. 245, 247, 259.

85 Sano Manabu, 'Gokuchuki', in Nabeyama Sadachika and Sano Manabu, *Tenko jugonen* (Tokyo, 1949), p. 86.

86 Yamabe Kentaro (ed.), *Gendaishi shiryo, vol. 17: shakaishugi undo 2* (Tokyo, 1966), p. 79.

87 Hoston, *Marxism*, pp. 71–4.

88 'Theses on the Situation in Japan and the Tasks of the Communist Party, May 1932', in Beckmann and Okubo, *Japanese Communist Party*, p. 336.

89 See Fukumoto Kazuo, *Kakumei undo razo* (Tokyo, San'ichi shobo, 1962), pp. 142–4; Takabatake Michitoshi, 'Ikkoku shakaishugisha: Sano Manabu, Nabeyama Sadachika', in *Tenko*, p. 173.

90 Nabeyama, *Watashi wa Kyosanto o suteta*, pp. 146, 154.

91 See Claudin, *Communist Movement, Part One*, p. 127.

92 Takabatake, 'Ikkoku shakaishugisha', pp. 170–1.

93 There are extensive quotations from Sano and Nabeyama's joint statement in Beckmann and Okubo, *Japanese Communist Party*, pp. 245–49.

94 *Yamakawa jiden* p. 429.

95 See Yamakawa, 'Kyosanto no ryokyoto no tenko', pp. 226–7.

96 Takabatake, 'Ikkoku shakaishugisha', p. 166.

97 'Theses on the Situation in Japan and the Tasks of the Communist Party, May 1932', in Beckmann and Okubo, *Japanese Communist Party*, pp. 342, 343.

98 Takabatake, 'Ikkoku shakaishugisha', pp. 166–7.

99 Sano Manabu, *Tennosei to shakaishugi* (Tokyo, 1946).

100 'Tennosei haishi, Sobietto kenryoku juritsu o kodo koryo yori sakujo seyo' (October 1933), in Yamabe Kentaro (ed.), *Gendaishi shiryo, vol. 15: shakaishugi undo 2* (Tokyo, 1965), pp. 853–4. Thanks to the censors, this article never reached its intended readership.

101 P. G. Steinhoff, 'Tenko: Ideology and Societal Integration in Pre-War Japan', unpublished Ph.D. Dissertation, Harvard University, 1969, p. 6.

Index